ISFAHAN
AND ITS PALACES

Edinburgh Studies in Islamic Art

Series Editor: Professor Robert Hillenbrand

Titles include:

Isfahan and its Palaces
*Statecraft, Shi'ism and the Architecture of Conviviality in Early
  Modern Iran*
Sussan Babaie

Islamic Chinoiserie: The Art of Mongol Iran
Yuka Kadoi

ISFAHAN AND ITS PALACES

STATECRAFT, SHI'ISM AND THE ARCHITECTURE OF CONVIVIALITY IN EARLY MODERN IRAN

SUSSAN BABAIE

Edinburgh University Press

For my parents Vadjiheh and Ebrahim
For Richard and Jiyan
In memory of my brother Sass

Edinburgh University Press is one of the leading university presses in the UK. We publish academic books and journals in our selected subject areas across the humanities and social sciences, combining cutting-edge scholarship with high editorial and production values to produce academic works of lasting importance. For more information visit our website: edinburghuniversitypress.com

Edinburgh University Press Ltd
The Tun – Holyrood Road
12 (2f) Jackson's Entry
Edinburgh EH8 8PJ

First published in hardback by Edinburgh University Press 2008

Typeset in 10/12 pt Trump Mediaeval by
Servis Filmsetting Ltd, Stockport, Cheshire,
and printed and bound by Printforce

A CIP record for this book is available from the British Library

ISBN 978 0 7486 3375 3 (hardback)
ISBN 978 1 4744 3719 6 (paperback)

Published in association with al-Sabah Collection, Dar al-Athar al-Islamiyyah, Kuwait.

Contents

List of Figures   vi
List of Plates   ix
Series Editor's Foreword   x
Preface and Acknowledgments   xi
Note on the Transliteration System   xiv
Safavid Dynastic Chart   xv
Timeline of Safavid Capital Cities and
   Major Structures   xvi

CHAPTER 1   Introduction: Conviviality, Charismatic
Absolutism, and the Persianization of Shi'ism   1

CHAPTER 2   Peripatetic Kings and Palaces: From Tabriz to
Qazvin in the Sixteenth Century   30

CHAPTER 3   Dwelling in Paradise, or Isfahan "Half the World"   65

CHAPTER 4   "The Abode of Felicitous Rule" or the
Daulatkhane Royal Precinct   113

CHAPTER 5   The Spatial Choreography of Conviviality:
the Palaces of Isfahan   157

CHAPTER 6   Feasting and the Perso-Shi'i Etiquette of Kingship   224

CHAPTER 7   Epilogue: The Fall of Isfahan   267

Bibliography   274
Illustration Acknowledgments   292
Index   294

Figures

1.1 Map of the Muslim empires in the early modern period 3
1.2 Map of Safavid Iran at around 1628 3
2.1 Schematic rendering of the royal precinct in Tabriz when the city was the capital of the Turkmen dynasty of the Aqqoyunlu in the fifteenth century 32
2.2 Qazvin, schematic map (after Szuppe) 48
2.3 Qazvin, schematic reconstruction of the Maydan and the Ali Qapu 49
2.4 Qazvin, the Ali Qapu seen from the Maydan-e Asb 51
2.5 Qazvin, the Ali Qapu, the domed octagonal chamber behind the façade 52
2.6 Qazvin, Chehel Sotun, interior of the ground floor 54
3.1 Isfahan, panoramic view after an engraving from Kaempfer, *Amoenitatum* (1712) chronicling his visit to Isfahan in 1684 65
3.2 Isfahan, a detail from Kaempfer's panorama 67
3.3 Isfahan (Omidvar) 70
3.4 Isfahan, Chahar Bagh Promenade after the engraving that illustrates the chronicle of the Dutch traveler Cornelis de Bruyn's visit to the city in 1704–5 72
3.5 Isfahan, the Allah Verdi Khan Bridge after an engraving for Coste's *Monuments modernes de la Perse* (1867) 73
3.6 Isfahan, map (after Gaube and Wirth) 75
3.7 Isfahan, map focusing on the area south of the old city and the Safavid additions after 1590/1 77
3.8 Isfahan, reconstructed panorama based on a conflation of satellite images, Kaempfer's "*Planographia*" (4.1), and modern maps of the city 79
3.9 Isfahan, Maydan-e Naqsh-e Jahan after an engraving from Kaempfer, *Amoenitatum* (1712) 89
3.10 Isfahan, the Qaysariyye or Royal Bazaar and its *naqqarakhane* (kettledrum house) on the upper galleries flanking the gateway, after an engraving from the *Atlas* volume of Jean Chardin, *Voyages* (1811) 90

4.1 Isfahan, Kaempfer's *"Planographia,"* from an engraving in
his *Amoenitatum* (1712)   114
4.2 Isfahan, reconstruction rendering of the Maydan   115
4.3 Isfahan, Ali Qapu and Tauhidkhane (Omidvar)   119
4.4 Isfahan, Ali Qapu, rear view from the Daulatkhane   131
4.5 Isfahan, Daulatkhane (Royal Precinct)   140
4.6 Isfahan, Ali Qapu, *talar*   145
4.7 Isfahan, Ali Qapu, audience hall   147
5.1 Isfahan, reconstruction rendering of the Talar-e Tavile
(Hall of Stables)   158
5.2 Ground plans of the Safavid *talar* palaces of Isfahan   159
5.3 Isfahan, "A Night Reception at the Talar-e Tavile"   161
5.4 Ground plans of the *hasht-behesht* types of palaces   165
5.5 Isfahan, Ayenekhane Palace (Hall of Mirrors)   167
5.6 Isfahan, Ayenekhane Palace, after an engraving from
Coste, Monuments   168
5.7 Mazandaran, Ashraf, Cheshme Emarat   171
5.8 Kashan, Bagh-e Fin Palace   172
5.9 Kashan, Bagh-e Fin Palace (interior)   173
5.10 Mazandaran, near Ashraf   175
5.11 Mazandaran, Saqqanafar in a village east of Amol   177
5.12 Isfahan, Chehel Sotun (exterior)   187
5.13 Isfahan, Chehel Sotun Palace, after a photograph from
Dieulafoy, *La Perse* (1887)   188
5.14 Isfahan, Chehel Sotun, southeast corner   189
5.15 Isfahan, Chehel Sotun, view from the *talar*   190
5.16 Isfahan, Chehel Sotun audience hall, "Shah Tahmasb"   192
5.17 Isfahan, Chehel Sotun audience hall, "Shah Abbas II"   193
5.18 Isfahan, Hasht Behesht Palace   198
5.19 Isfahan, Hasht Behesht Palace interior, after an
engraving from the *Atlas* volume of Chardin's,
Voyages (1811)   201
5.20 Isfahan, Hasht Behesht Palace, south porch   203
5.21 Isfahan, Khwaju Bridge (1651/2)   208
5.22 Isfahan, Sa'adatabad palace   209
6.1 Istanbul, Topkapı Palace site plan (after Necipoğlu)   227
6.2 Istanbul, Topkapı Palace (after Necipoğlu)   247
6.3 Istanbul, Topkapı Palace, the Council Chamber and the
Tower of Justice   247
6.4 Istanbul, Topkapı Palace, the Gate of Felicity   248
6.5 "The banquet of the Austrian ambassador at the Council
Chamber," from the travels of Hans Ludwig von
Kuefsteins in 1628 (after Teply)   249
6.6 Istanbul, Topkapı Palace, view looking through the Gate
of Felicity toward the doorway and grilled window of the
Chamber of Petitions, the formal audience chamber   250

6.7 Agra, Red Fort, site plan (after Koch)   253
6.8 Delhi, Red Fort, site plan (after Koch)   254
6.9 Agra, Red Fort, Amar Singh Gate and a view of the
       fortifications   254
6.10 Agra, Red Fort, Diwan-i Amm   255
6.11 Agra, Red Fort, Diwan-i Amm, view from the *jharoka*
       throne out to the courtyard   255
6.12 Delhi, Red Fort, Diwan-i Amm   256
6.13 Delhi, Red Fort, Diwan-i Amm, view of the interior
       arcade with its magnificent scalloped arches and
       carved sandstone pillars   256

Plates

BETWEEN PAGES 78 AND 79
1   "Yusuf Gives a Royal Banquet in Honor of his Marriage"
2   "Da'ud Receives a Robe of Honor from Mun'im Khan"
3   Qazvin, Chehel Sotun Palace
4   Isfahan (Omidvar). Looking east, the tree-lined Chahar Bagh Promenade
5   Isfahan (Omidvar). Looking north over the Maydan
6   Isfahan, Shaykh Lotf-Allah Chapel-Mosque
7   Isfahan, Masjed-e Jadid-e Abbasi, Royal Mosque or Imam Mosque
8   Isfahan, Masjed-e Jadid-e Abbasi portal

BETWEEN PAGES 142 AND 143
9   Isfahan. Looking west over the Maydan-e Naqsh-e Jahan (Omidvar)
10 Isfahan, Ali Qapu and Tauhidkhane (Omidvar)
11 Isfahan, Ali Qapu, exploded perspective renderings
12 Isfahan, Ali Qapu Palace-Gateway
13 Isfahan, Ali Qapu. The "Music Room"
14 Isfahan, Chehel Sotun
15 Isfahan, Chehel Sotun. Looking from the southeastern corner
16 Isfahan, Chehel Sotun. The *talar*

BETWEEN PAGES 238 AND 239
17 Isfahan, Chehel Sotun. The audience hall
18 Isfahan, Chehel Sotun audience hall. Detail of Shah Tahmasb mural
19 Isfahan, Chehel Sotun audience hall. Detail of Shah Abbas the Great mural
20 Isfahan, Chehel Sotun audience hall. Detail from lower right-hand side of Shah Abbas mural
21 Isfahan, Hasht Behesht Palace (1669)
22 Isfahan, Hasht Behesht Palace. View of the interior of the north porch
23 Isfahan, Hasht Behesht Palace. Pylon and *muqarnas* covered lantern
24 "Shah Jahan Honors the Religious Orthodoxy"

Series Editor's Foreword

'Edinburgh Studies in Islamic Art' is a new venture that offers readers easy access to the most up-to-date research across the whole range of Islamic art. Building on the long and distinguished tradition of Edinburgh University Press in publishing books on the Islamic world, it is intended to be a forum for studies that, while closely focused, will also open wide horizons. Books in the series will, for example, concentrate in an accessible way on the art of a single century, dynasty or geographical area; on the meaning of works of art; on a given medium in a restricted time-frame; or on analyses of key works in their wider contexts. A balance will be maintained as far as possible between successive titles, so that various parts of the Islamic world and various media and approaches are represented.

Books in the series are academic monographs of intellectual distinction that mark a significant advance in the field. While they are naturally aimed at an advanced and graduate academic audience, a complementary target readership is the world-wide community of specialists in Islamic art – professionals who work in universities, research institutes, auction houses and museums – as well as that elusive character, the interested general reader.

Professor Robert Hillenbrand

Preface and Acknowledgments

Iran has a cultural attitude all its own. It is Persian, but not as a matter of ethnicity. And it is predominantly Muslim, but with an entirely different experience of Islam than its brethren in faith. For all its seeming marginality in the world today, this is a place painfully alert to the world; it is where new cultural schemes are born in the wake of unimaginable human calamities, where world religions are hatched, and where people have always found a way to make convivial and compelling lives. This book is my attempt to understand precisely such an Iran through the lens of a particularly pregnant moment in its history.

Those who know Isfahan know it to be one of the most glorious cities ever built. But many have never even heard of it. In the early modern age of travel, trade and diplomacy, it was known to be unrivaled in the elegance of its public spaces, its park-like avenues, magnificent mosques and madrasas, bazaars and palaces. Some of that luster has been clouded by the encroachment of commercialization and tourism; and a great deal has been demolished to make room for modern roads, plumbing, apartment towers, and now possibly a subway system. Still, "walking in the city" as de Certeau would have us do, yields glimpses of those everyday experiences that the architectonics of urban space must have activated in the denizens of the Safavid city. Isfahan is more than a Safavid city but it is its Safavid history, with its dramas in architecture and in rituals of conviviality, that I could not shake off.

Slow gestation of this book has allowed me to explore new ways of thinking about Isfahan and about its urban spaces, architecture, and rhythms of life. I started with the palaces but have been roaming the Safavid city, peeling away at the houses, at the city's "artistic" café culture, at the echoes of its forms and functions in other urban centers in Iran, or elsewhere. I return to the architectural and urban expressions of authority, despite the general disdain for empires, because the experience of Isfahan is so closely braided with the building of the city as the embodiment of the first and only empire that was Persian and Imami Shi'i. Compelled by their self-proclaimed link with the family of the Prophet Mohammad, and a mandate to uphold justice, the Safavids, in enunciating their particular form of kingship, incorporated ritual performances of conviviality into the daily life of the city. Feasting was paramount among the ceremonials of the Safavids and for those rituals I noticed they built special buildings. Those palaces are truly extraordinary and those convivial gatherings most exceptional when we call to mind how the early modern surge in imperial absolutism usually came with aloofness, god-like transcendence and the forbidding distances created inside and around palaces. To get an intimation of the uniquely Perso-Shiʻi kingship model that the Safavids fostered and for which they built a capital city and many palaces, I learned a great deal from the ways in which the social anthropology of space and of art have allowed for imagining the conceptual and historical clusters of action, activation, and actors. At the end of this venture, I have learned how much more there is to do. And I am certain the history of Isfahan and its palaces can be recast in more ways than this book does.

For the making of this book, many institutions and people have come to my assistance. I wish to express my deepest gratitude for the generous support of the Soudavar Foundation of Geneva toward the publication costs of this book. The subvention funds from the Department of the History of Art, University of Michigan, are deeply appreciated. More importantly, I have been very fortunate for my colleagues there and for my years at Michigan. Margaret Cool Root and Megan Holmes have been incomparably generous with their time, their insightful advice, and their friendship. I thank them for making this a better book and me a better person. To Leela Wood, a thank you is just not enough. The entire final production of this book, including making my images look their best, would have been impossible without her cheerful and generous assistance. Megan Holmes (Ann Arbor), Massumeh Farhad (Washington, DC), Martin Powers (Ann Arbor) and SinhaRaja Tammita-Delgoda (Colombo, Sri Lanka) read the manuscript or parts thereof at different stages of writing; for their extremely helpful comments, I am grateful. In its earlier stages of development, I benefitted from conversations with Kathryn Babayan. Two brilliant young architects, John Comazzi (University of Minnesota) and Sam Zeller (Chicago), helped me make the visual evocations of the lost architectural forms and spaces of Isfahan so much more persuasive than I could have ever imagined. Rob Haug's cheerful assistance and map-making skills are also gratefully acknowledged. A decade ago, Nima Massumi helped me capture the best images of the palaces I have ever produced; I thank him for that. With deft editorial touch, Diane Mark-Walker, Kerry Boeye, and Peg Lourie have made this a better read. I thank them for so gently making me sharpen my pen. I greatly benefitted from the advice of the two anonymous manuscript readers; I thank them for their intellectual generosity.

Heartfelt gratitude goes to the many colleagues, friends, and relatives in Iran who helped me get to books and archives, to buildings and neighborhoods, and to nearly every Safavid site in Iran; I could not have done any of the research, and this book, without the bounty of their support. I want to acknowledge the debt I owe Dr Lotf-Allah Honarfar, whose monumental work on the historical edifices of Isfahan remains the most useful book on the city. But this note of gratitude is also for the walks and talks we did about Isfahan. To my Safavid historian colleague Nozhat Ahmadi (Isfahan), I owe thanks for being my boon companion in my most recent field trips to Isfahan and its environs. My cousins Mehran Davachi and Mandana Iraj made sure I got to cities and villages where the Safavids left their footprints. I owe much gratitude to the late Dr Bagher Ayatollahzade Shirazi, who as the head of the research division of the Iranian Cultural Heritage Organization during my earlier field trips made access to difficult-to-access buildings and parts of buildings possible. Safavids knew it best; access is everything!

My parents never doubted this venture and never ceased to support me. I am so fortunate to have them share in the joy of witnessing its fruition in this book. And none of this would have been possible without Richard Harmon's moral and intellectual support of my work. He and Jiyan are my "half the world," the other half is Isfahan, of course!

Note on the Transliteration System

I have deliberately minimized the usual transliteration acrobatics. Preference is given to Persian pronunciation of words and names – *Ketabkhane* instead of *Kitabkhana*, or *Daulat* instead of *Dawlat* – for which the *Cambridge History of Iran* has been adopted, with some modifications. Anglicized names and terms remain unchanged except when the Arabicized version has predominated and where the referent also has a proper Persian home; so *ayvan* instead of *iwan*, or *Nauruz* instead of *Nawruz*. Such terms as have entered English-language dictionaries as sultan and harem are utilized when speaking generally; but not when it is part of a proper name, such as Shah Soltan Hossayn. I have not used diacritical marks unless the proper pronunciation of the term bears significantly on the discussion. City names in common usage, such as Isfahan, remain unchanged unless in the Persian title of a book, such as Esfahan. As much as I have tried, I am certain there are inconsistencies, maybe even egregious ones, for which I beg the reader's indulgence.

Safavid Dynastic Chart

Shaykh Safi al-Din (d. 1334), founder of the
Safaviyye Sufi Order

Shaykh Junayd (d. 1460)
Haydar (d. 1488), father of Isma'il

ISMA'IL I (1501–1524)

TAHMASB I (1524–1576)

ISMA'IL II (1576–1577)

MOHAMMAD KHODABANDE (1578–1587)

ABBAS I (1587–1629)

SAFI I (1629–1642)

ABBAS II (1642–1666)

SAFI II (SOLAYMAN) (1666–1694)

SOLTAN HOSSAYN (1694–1722)

Afghan Invasion and the Fall of Isfahan

TAMASB II (1722–1732)
ABBAS III (1732–1736)

Timeline of Safavid Capital Cities and Major Structures

TABRIZ (1501–1555/6)

Shah Isma'il (1501–1524)
Ancestral shrine in Ardabil; Dar al-Hadith (Reading Hall for the *Hadith*)
Governors of Isfahan, Mausoleum of Harun-e Velayat (1513) and Masjed-e Ali (1522)
Hunting lodge-palace in Khoy
Shah Tahmasb (1524–1576)
Additions to Ardabil Shrine 1534–1540s; courtyard façade of the Dar al-Huffaz and the tomb chambers, the Jannat Sara (c. 1540), Dar al-Hadith (?)
Beginning construction at Qazvin, 1544/5

QAZVIN (1555/6–1598)

Shah Tahmasb (1524–1576)
Refurbishment of the Maydan-e Asb (hippodrome)
Addition of Ali Qapu Gateway between the Maydan and the royal precinct
Sa'adatabad palace precinct (Daulatkhane) with gardens and pavilions
The Chehel Sotun Palace, completed c. 1555/6

ISFAHAN (1598–1722)

Shah Abbas I (1587–1629)

1590/1, commencement of construction in Isfahan, Maydan-e Naqsh-e Jahan, the Qaysariyye, the Ali Qapu as a two-story gateway into the royal gardens

c. 1596, beginning of construction of the Chahar Bagh Promenade and the Hezar Jarib royal pleasance

1598, official transfer of the capital to Isfahan

c. 1598, Ganj Ali Khan complex for governor of Kerman

c. 1602, modification of the Maydan periphery

1602/3–1618/19, Shaykh Lotf-Allah Chapel-Mosque

1602/3–1615, Ali Qapu raised to five-story tower as a Palace-Gateway

1602–1607, Allah Verdi Khan Bridge

1611/12–1638, Masjed-e Jadid-e Abbasi (Royal Mosque)

1611, founding of cities of Farahabad and Ashraf (Cheshme Emarat, Abbasabad) in Mazandaran

Shah Safi I (1629–1642)

1630s, Talar-e Tavile and Ayenekhane Palaces

Shah Abbas II (1642–1666)

1644, *talar* addition to the Ali Qapu Palace-Gateway

1647–50s, the Chehel Sotun Palace

1651/2, Khwaju (Hasanabad) Bridge

1650s, Sa'adatabad royal pleasance on the banks of Zayande River

1657/8, Ju'i (Rivulet) Bridge

1659/60, Chahar Bagh-e Khwaju

Shah Solayman (1666–1694)

1669, Hasht Behesht Palace

Soltan Hossayn (1694–1722)

1710/11, Soltani (Chahar Bagh or Madar-e Shah) Madrasa

1711, commencement of the Farahabad royal pleasance

Neither is there aught which does not celebrate His praise.

Qur'an 17: 44

Introduction: Conviviality, Charismatic Absolutism, and the Persianization of Shi'ism

"The King undertakes dispensing justice and building."[1]
"Eat together and not separately, for the blessings are associated with the company."[2]

AT A TYPICAL banquet held in the latter half of the seventeenth century at the semi-open, pillared reception hall (*talar*) of the Chehel Sotun Palace in Isfahan, several hundred guests enjoyed a multi-course meal accompanied by sherbets and wine as they delighted in the music, dance, and other entertainment (Figures 5.13, 5.1 and Plate 19). Presiding over the feast was the Safavid (1501–1722) shah, who sat in the semi-vaulted ayvan recess from which the ever-expanding spaces of the talar accommodated the hierarchical seating of the guests. Slender wooden columns, covered in faceted mirrors, colorfully painted and gilded, delineated a tripartite space and gave the ceremony its social order. Sumptuous textiles and carpets covered every surface where richly clad guests and hosts sat on cushions and mingled as food and drinks were served in gorgeous dishes and utensils of painted porcelain, glazed ceramic, carved aromatic woods, engraved jade, inlaid metal, and blown glass.

To the initiated, such feasting, with its luxurious accoutrements and opulent rituals, epitomized the obligations that bonded the ruler and the ruled and constituted an indispensable element in the performance of kingship. Yet, no other palace like the Chehel Sotun, with its front occupied by an entirely open and light-filled pillared hall, had ever been built, be it in Iran or elsewhere in the Islamicate world, where architectural forms and spaces may be said to have instantiated the ceremonial structure of such royal banquets: seating arrangements, hierarchical order of access and remove, choreographed command of the field of vision. Indeed, the architectural accommodation of feasting and of proximity to the king in Safavid Isfahan, and the king's personal engagement as the host – moderating the rhythms of the banquet by signaling when the musicians should play or when and to whom wine should be served – represented a markedly idiosyncratic practice of absolute rule in the early modern age. The established paradigms of contemporary absolutist and expansionist empires in the Islamicate world – the Ottomans and the Mughals, rivals of the Safavids – as well as in the realms of Christiandom so privileged transcendent seclusion and aloofness that they precluded the need for specialized architecture for convivial gatherings in the company of the king.

The Safavid distinction lies precisely in its deliberate subversion of those paradigms. Its dynastic legitimacy pivoted both on the charisma of an alleged genealogical descent from the Prophet Mohammad through Imam Ali, and on the display of royal splendor (*farr*), a critical concept in the ancient Persian ideology of kingship to which all who came to rule the Persianate world laid claim. The implementation of absolute rule in this uniquely Perso-Shi'i imperial ideology necessitated an affective form of kingship with an effective architectural and urban accommodation of its performance. Moreover, the Safavid conception of a charismatic form of authority nurtured the making of enunciative strategies that peaked in the dramatic synergies cast across the urban spaces, architectural form of the palaces, and the ceremonial practices of conviviality when Isfahan served as the capital from 1598 until the fall of the Safavids in 1722. Tracing the many ways in which social action and meaning intersected with spatial and visual representations of power in Safavid Iran motivates this study of the palaces and the city of Isfahan.

Just as the Safavid political agenda took shape through time, so will this study also consider the paradigmatic shifts in architecture, urban space, and royal rituals through changing relationships between politics and culture in the Safavids' earlier, sixteenth-century capital cities of Tabriz and Qazvin. Investigating this development of Safavid enunciations of kingship through architecture, furthermore, requires that these practices be disentangled from the universalizing palatine paradigms of Islamicate architecture. Ceremony and architecture are considered here in their mutually supportive role in the creation of this singularly Perso-Shi'i ethos of absolute rule.

The Safavid beginnings

The impulse to spotlight the particularities of the Safavid practice is historically motivated by the fact that the sixteenth and seventeenth centuries mark a crucial turning point when the Safavid dynasty created, at the crossroads between Asia and Europe, the first Imami Shi'i empire in the history of Islam (Figures 1.1 and 1.2). The dynasty was founded by Isma'il (1501–24), whose personal lineage anchored the peculiar Safavid synthesis of imperial ideologies. Shah Isma'il had royal blood. His mother was the daughter of Sultan Uzun Hasan (1453–78), the chief of the Turkmen tribal federation of the Aqqoyunlu (1378–1508) whose realms included western Iran, eastern Anatolia, northern Iraq, Azerbaijan, and Armenia. His father was a nephew of the sultan. Not exceptionally for royal progeny in the

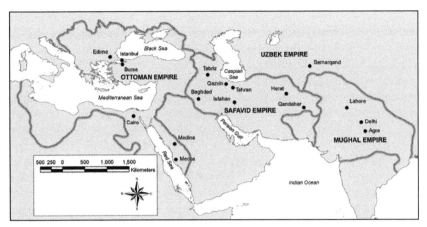

Figure 1.1 *Map of the Muslim empires in the early modern period approximating the dominions of the Ottomans, the Safavids, the Mughals, and the Uzbeks toward the end of the reign of the Safavid Shah Abbas the Great (1587–1629).*

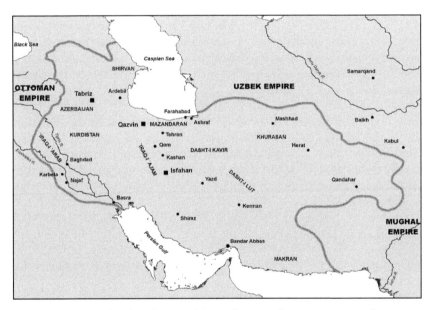

Figure 1.2 *Map of Safavid Iran at around 1628 when it was at its largest span and included much of today's Iraq, the Caucasus, and Afghanistan.*

Persianate world, he was of mixed ethnicity: Turkmen, Persian, and Greek.[3] Isma'il's claim to the throne found legitimacy on account of the *farr* or *khvarnah* that drew from the pre-Islamic concept of Persian kingship and conferred upon him, as upon all those Islamic rulers who held sway over parts or all of greater Iran, the aura of royal splendor and its associated divine right to be king.[4]

More importantly, he had a hallowed ancestry through his paternal side, reaching back to the great Sufi master Shaykh Safi al-Din and the Safaviyye mystical order. The Safaviyye claim of a blood link through Safi al-Din and traceable to the Seventh Shi'i Imam Musa al-Kazim (d. 799) enabled Isma'il to legitimize his place as a regent ruling in the absence of the Twelfth Imam. Imami, or Twelver, Shi'ism, made the state religion by Isma'il, is founded on the belief, first, that Imam Ali, the Prophet Mohammad's son-in-law and cousin, and the descendants of Fatima and Ali (the *Ahl al-bayt*, "the People of the [Prophet's] Household") were His only legitimate successors and, second, that the historical caliphs accepted by Sunni Muslims were usurpers of this familial blood right.[5] Thus, in the ideology prevalent among his followers, Isma'il possessed the qualities of *ensan-e kamel* (the perfect man) invested with the mandate to carry forth the ideals of Persianate kingship and Shi'i Islam. With the rise of the Safavids came the first truly expansive imperial reach of Imami beliefs and, as it turned out, the only polity of Shi'ism to last into modern times.[6]

A few other Shi'i dynasties had ruled parts of the vast Islamicate world in the course of its pre-modern history, but either they were not Twelver (or Imami) or else they remained tied to the system of authority that was associated with the caliphate and that dominated much of the Islamicate world in its early history. Between the death of the Prophet Mohammad in 632 and the rise to power of the Umayyads (661–750), the first Muslim dynasty, strife over succession raged among the followers of the Prophet and split the community into the two major groups that remain dominant today. The Sunnis, who won a majority, followed the *sunna* or tradition based on the assumption of the historical succession of rule first by the four closest companions of Him (Abu Bakr, Omar, Othman, and Ali, collectively known as the Rashidun Caliphs) and then by the Umayyad and Abbasid (750–1258) dynasties. The Shi'is rejected the historical occurrence of caliphal rule and instead adhered to the faith that Imam Ali was the Prophet's choice for succession, hence their designation as *shi'a*, a shortened form of the Arabic phrase "the faction of Ali."

With the tenth-century weakening of the office of the caliph in Abbasid Baghdad, increasingly powerful and autonomous polities in the provinces of the imperium claimed political and military authority. Among those new forces were at least two followers of Shi'ism. The Buyids (932–1055), themselves of Iranian stock, appropriated the crown of temporal rule through a confederate system under the tutelage of the spiritual authority of the Abbasid caliph in Baghdad. The Fatimids (909–1171) of Egypt and Tunisia went further, by declaring themselves as the rival, and rightful, caliphs on the basis of their claim to legitimacy as Isma'ilis, a sect of Shi'ism that traced its lineage through the Prophet's daughter Fatima down to the Sixth Imam, Ja'far al-Sadeq (737–65).[7] Notwithstanding these short-lived and limited flowerings of its political authority, Shi'ism remained the creed of a minority and indeed subject to the imperial suzerainty of Sunni caliphs and sultans through the fifteenth century.

The historical marginalization of political Shi'ism in the Islamicate world should not, however, lead us to isolate it from considerations of how Muslim ideologies of kingship developed in the first place. Indeed, caliphal authority in its orthodox and classical conceptualization embraced both the spiritual and the temporal leadership roles inherited from the Prophet Mohammad. As Aziz al-Azmeh has shown, Muslim kingship emerged from a complex interweaving of this new Qur'anic culture with the traditions and practices of late antiquity in the Middle East and the Mediterranean region that fell under the sway of Islam and that included in its vast geography an unprecedented diversity – pagan, Judeo-Christian, Zoroastrian, and other renditions of kingship that spanned from Rome to Byzantium to Sasanian Persia, and beyond.[8] In the abstract, the divine mandate that defined the Prophet's role as the politico-religious leader of the *umma* or Muslim community was also intermixed with notions of the sacralization of the king that were adapted from Byzantine and Sasanian ideologies. Legitimacy in Muslim kingship was, moreover, profoundly indebted to the non-negotiable, albeit variously interpreted, principle of justice that is at the core of the Qur'an; maintenance of justice was a prerequisite of Muslim rule.[9] The Safavid conceptualization of absolute rule couched this fundamental feature of Islam in the doctrinal framework of Twelver Shi'ism, thus laying claim to the universal authority of the Prophet while localizing this claim through the intricately intertwined features of classical Muslim and ancient Persian features of kingship.

Just as importantly, the Safavids shared with the Sunni empires in the Persianate world the Turco-Mongol heritage that derived from the medieval Turkic incursions from Central Asia and from the Mongol invasions of the thirteenth century. The royal ideologies of those predominantly Sunni polities to which the Safavids became heir (the fifteenth-century Timurid and Aqqoyunlu empires) and with whom they were contemporaries (the Ottomans and the Mughals) merged symbols and practices of the centralized and absolutist caliphal paradigms of classical Islam with the confederate political structures and doctrines prevalent among the Turkic and Mongol peoples. Following especially the model established by Genghis Khan and his successors in the Persianate world, imperial authority among those Turco-Mongol rulers issued from the collective energies and aspirations of the participating tribes. In the age of centralization and absolutism that took hold in the sixteenth and seventeenth centuries in the Persianate realms, this common heritage of the Turco-Mongol past and its confederate ceremonials of power, which were rendered visible in gigantic gatherings on the move and in tents, were variously interpreted by the Safavids of Iran, the Ottomans of Turkey, and the Mughals of India.

The need for personal engagement in the conduct of sovereignty in the Turco-Mongol tribal polities required peripatetic life habits and gave priority to tentage over permanent palaces and spontaneity of ceremonial enunciations of kingship. But absolute rule in the centralized empires of the sixteenth and seventeenth centuries hinged on the empowerment of social elites loyal exclusively to the seat of kingship, and on the permanence and centrality of that seat of authority, the palace complex in an imperial capital city. The Ottomans flavored their Turco-Mongol heritage with the absorption into the ruling elite of the conquered and converted Christians and with the adoption of Byzantine practices, especially after the conquest of Constantinople in 1453, when a new fortified palace was built and the ceremonies of kingship were codified into rigid processionals and rare appearances of the sultan. The Mughal cultural synthesis included a vast array of religious notions and kingship practices, notably those of their majority Hindu subjects. There, the maintenance of sovereignty required the incorporation of non-Muslim elites into the imperial household at the same time that it necessitated constant warfare. The seat of rule for the Mughals was multiplied in fortified palaces at major cities of the realm, and its authority was made palpable through the daily ceremonial appearances and disappearances of the emperor.

The Safavids, too, incorporated non-Muslim subjects, this time Christians from the Caucasus, as a converted military and administrative slave elite, a subject to which we will turn later in this book. As in the Ottoman case, the formation of the slave elite in the Safavid world facilitated the political restructuring of the royal household away from the tribal confederacies of the earlier periods and toward absolute rule in a centralized polity. In contrast to their rivals on the east and the west, however, the Christian Caucasus was marginal to the initial conquests of the Safavids, whose rule was spread across entirely Muslim territories. Hence, the articulation of legitimacy and authority in the Safavid realms did not pose the same challenges as those that required the incorporation of non-Muslim notions and practices of kingship in the Ottoman and Mughal spheres. Rather, the notional divergences in kingship models were between the long-established Sunni paradigms of kingship readjusted to the Turco-Mongol confederate practices, on the one hand, and the need to transform those models to a Twelver Shiʿi mode of kingship in an arena that had to take account of rooted Iranian cultural norms. The Safavid alternative thus forged a wholly different paradigm, one that redefined the notion of legitimate descent in a Persianized Shiʿi framework. In this way, their imperial legitimacy rested on twin claims of descent both from the "terrestrial" lineage of Persianate kings ancient and recent and from the "celestial" lineage that began with Imam Ali and continued through the family of the Prophet Mohammad.

More specifically, the Safavid dynastic sovereignty and temporal authority depended on the assumption of the prerogatives and responsibilities of the absent Twelfth Imam, who had disappeared in 931 and was (and still is) considered to be the promised Mahdi or Messiah of Shi'i Islam.[10] The processes of conceptualization and consolidation of this enterprise of kingship took several turns, including a transition from an esoteric, mystically oriented rendition of Twelver Shi'ism in the first half of the sixteenth century to a less exaggerated, more normative practice integrated into the institutions of imperial authority. And while awaiting the return of the Mahdi, the Safavid shahs' position had to be negotiated by the politico-cultural crafting, through the discharge of justice, generosity, and righteousness, of a terrestrial vision of the promised kingdom, a mirror-image, if still imperfect, of the celestial paradise made palpable here on earth. Isfahan and its palaces became the embodiment of this promised city of paradise.

A prerequisite of this particular ideology of kingship, this book further suggests, was the seamless integration of two opposing ideas of humility and absolutism for which the architecture of the palaces and urban design of the city of Isfahan served as the stage set. The specialized ceremonial palaces developed along with the building of Isfahan as the new capital city made access and proximity to the king, and the ritual expression of "openness," their determining and distinctive architectural features. At the same time, the spatial and architectural experience of the palaces and the city had to be moderated by the representation of the conceptual distance that the authority of absolute rule in a vast and centralized empire would entail.

It was through the kinetic and visual experience of space and the mediated rituals, especially of feasting, at Isfahan that kings and the urban elite, architects, designers and builders, and denizens of the Safavid world partook in repeated performances and representations of this uniquely Perso-Shi'i conception of kingship. In order to better grasp these architectural and ritual enunciations of imperial power, this book probes the intricate elements of the palaces – the plans, elevations, decorations, landscaping, and formal and functional relationship to urban spaces – for what they yield of the Safavid architectural and ritual paradigm of kingship and its social practices. The contrast between the apparent transparency and accessibility of the palace complex in Isfahan and the fortified and restricted palatial complexes of the Ottomans and Mughals, not to mention the French and the Spanish, for example, sharpens the contours of the distinctive Safavid expression of the early modern centralized absolutism. To state the obvious, all kings sponsored the

building of magnificent palaces for the stage-managed opulence of
the rituals of kingship. However, in this early modern milieu the
king was accorded so sacred a status that he had to recede behind
veils of separation, both physical and conceptual. Given the prevalent impulse to differentiate between the quasi-divine ruler and his
utterly ordinary subjects, the Safavid development of the architecture of conviviality in Isfahan, with its articulation of the rituals of
proximity to the shah as the host of imperial feasts, strikes a paradoxical note.

While other scholars have expertly analyzed the Safavid contribu-
tion to the political ideology of Twelver Shi'ism and its impact on
modern state formation in the Middle East and especially Iran, little
attention has been devoted to the conceptual and structural interde-
pendency of these politico-religious impulses and their visual cultural valences. My goal is to elucidate the urban context, the
architectural conveyor, and the ceremonial conduct that made
Isfahan so extraordinary a city for the grounding of political authority in Twelver Shi'ism and that made the Safavids so vital an empire
within the competitive arena of commerce and politics of the early
modern period.

This particular approach to Isfahan, empire building, and social
life not only requires a wide range of discursive material but also has
to contend with some inherent shortcomings. Archival information
on the architects of specific buildings, designers of urban spaces and
functions, or circumstances of patronage in this period of Iranian
history is scarce. For the palaces, such data are entirely absent. As
discussed later in the book, this great loss of archival material is in
large part due to the disbanding of the chancellery and discarding of
its documents after the Afghan occupation in the 1720s. Persian
chronicles and European travel accounts, the most commonly utilized sources on Safavid Iran, also yield the official court perspective
and the colorfully prejudicial but helpfully detailed observations of
the outsiders.

A word should be said about the European sources, which are relatively numerous and often complemented with the only visual approx-
imations we have of many of the destroyed buildings and ensembles.
Their greatest focus in both graphic and textual representations is on
Isfahan, a fact that points to the intensified level of diplomatic and
commercial interaction between the increasingly confident European
expansionist project and the securely centered Safavid Empire at the
opening of the seventeenth century. Nevertheless, merchant travelers
and unofficial ambassadors, such as the Venetians who flocked to the
court of the Aqqoyunlu in Tabriz during the last quarter of the fifteenth
century, provide us with a descriptive window onto pre-Safavid Tabriz
and help us imagine the earliest urban and palatial models that the
Safavids inherited and appropriated. In the nearly complete absence of
physical remains of Aqqoyunlu and Safavid Tabriz, these descriptions

and other European ones from the sixteenth century are extremely important complements to the scant Persian references to the buildings and the city spaces. Chapter 2 will utilize such descriptions extensively in order to suggest reconstructions of the first two capital cities, Tabriz and Qazvin, and especially of their respective palace ensembles, while at the same time acknowledging that much in the European textual representations might be conjectural, imagined, or indeed clouded by the distance between the time of the visit and the writing of the travel account. Would it have been possible, for instance, for a European to have had access to the private zones of life at the palaces, as in the Venetian merchant accounts of the harem in the palace precinct in Tabriz? Later visitors such as Jean Chardin report how access to the harem was given by their "insider" contacts or else made possible when the harem was absent, as perhaps during a summer retreat.

Notwithstanding questions about "probabilities" and "truths" in the discursive and visual vestiges of travel, such European representations reflect the complexities of the cultural matrix from which they are generated and not necessarily that of those observed.[11] As has been noted, the European audience of these narratives was given access through established visual and literary topoi to "fugitive traces of a moral critique" that was both Eurocentric and Christian.[12] Indeed, the self-reflective utility of such knowledge as is gained through the texts and images of travel and encounter is exemplified in a case study of the frontispieces made for the published copies of the travel account of Adam Olearius, the secretary of the 1637 embassy from the Duke of Holstein to the court of Shah Abbas the Great (1587–1629).[13] Olearius' mapping of Safavid Iran in this instance demonstrates how deeply the representations of the other were rooted in the discourse of difference that helped shape a European identity. Given their cultural charge, then, their utility needs to be carefully considered in light of extant material and local Persian sources, and must ultimately be seen not as reportage but as constructs of an inescapably exoticized other that the Safavid world must have presented to European visitors.

Other pieces of evidence on social life may be culled from unexpected places: cookbooks, treatises on religious law, manuals of good conduct, biographies of poets, and the like.[14] These tend to provide evocative glimpses of the shared mental worlds and cultural practices that cluster around notions of generosity, loyalty, legitimacy, etiquette, and in general social codes of behavior and discharge of expectations. The following chapters place them against one another and against other evidence – the visual/architectural, the epigraphic, the poetic, and some incidental discursive sources on the city.

The interpretive strategy of this book builds on the premise that the Safavid "script" for kingship found its affirmations in the rhythms of daily life of the court and the city and in the repeated performances of royal rituals for the conduct of which special urban spaces and architectural forms were devised.[15] In turn, the palaces and urban spaces of Isfahan relate to notions of power through the social and political dynamics that animate them. Feasting is paramount among those animating cultural elements in the field of interpretation that help explain the basis and representation of power. It has been viewed in the past as a relic of Turco-Mongol tribal habits, inherited by the three principal later empires in the Islamicate world but discarded by all except the Safavids, who presumably retained nomadic habits and tribal forms of kingship. Rethinking the evidence of history – embodied in palace architecture, urban spaces, and the extant visual and discursive material – suggests a profoundly strategic role for the architectural accommodation of the rituals of conviviality in constructing the politico-cultural fabric of the Perso-Shi'i empire of the Safavids.

Ceremonial conviviality in Isfahan

Close reading of the royal practice of feasting and its comparison to such practices elsewhere will come in Chapter 6, but its conceptual centrality to this study of palaces and cities requires a preamble here. The point to emphasize is that the convivial gatherings of the Safavid court were motivated by changing social and political dynamics of the empire and not relics of ceremonies of the past. At their pinnacle as the imperial rendition and institutional representation of the political culture of the Safavids, rituals of feasting developed in lockstep with the architectural disposition of the palaces, which led to the increasing refinement and sophistication of both when Isfahan became the capital city. A European description, briefly summarized at the opening of the book, characterizes such feasts by recalling one at the Palace of Chehel Sotun with its multipillared open hall where hundreds of guests were feasted after the building's construction in the middle of the seventeenth century (Figures 5.16, 5.17 and Plate 19).

Such convivial gatherings were not conducted for pleasure alone.[16] Nor were they held because the Safavids had an especially generous temperament or were compelled to share the fruits of kingship. All rulers needed to communicate, reinforce, and legitimate their right to govern and also articulate the relationship between themselves and their people, to enunciate kingship. These spectacles used food to conduct politics through feasting ceremonies where the shah hosted hundreds of people, in the company of his court and government officials, all seated according to a prescribed hierarchical order of proximity or distance from the king. The event was enlivened with music and dancing, and all feasted not just on fruits, sweets, stews, rice dishes, and wine, but on what they represented as the emblems of the Safavid outpouring of largesse and hospitality.

In seventeenth-century Isfahan, feasting became paramount among other courtly ceremonies, suggesting that it served to facilitate the merging of the reinvented ancient Persian traditions of kingship with the more recently configured Twelver Shiʿi notions of royal authority. The two strands of cultural and political ideology had already melded into the concept of *fotovvat* or chivalric humaneness that was at the core of the early Safavid mystical articulation of legitimacy and its anchoring of justice. These newly synthesized socio-political symbols were orchestrated into repeated performances at the core of the Safavid imperium. Transmuted and aggrandized, feasting ceremonials both contributed to the formulation of Safavid kingship and helped to reveal the underlying contours of its political institutions and ideologies of dominance and deference. It is in their particularized forms that these rituals of conviviality and the palaces in Isfahan help us interpret Safavid notions of kingship.

This is not to attribute a Shiʿi or Sunni "essence," an inherent doctrinal characteristic, to building forms and spatial organization. Rather, it is to urge a close reading of the city, its architecture, and its related ceremonial functions. In that respect, for example, the particularities of the ceremonial palaces in Isfahan with their open-pillared halls help us see how feasting the multitudes in the presence of kings, sharing food and conviviality with the kings, and displaying extravagant generosity and accessibility for the gaze of the ruled conspired as strategies for proclaiming authority and legitimacy unlike any practiced by the contemporaries of the Safavids. While later in this book Safavid feasting rituals will be compared with those of their contemporaries, here it should be emphasized that in no other environment of absolutist rule in the early modern age did kings actually preside at opulently choreographed and populated feasts in which they acted as the host: controlling the rhythms of eating, drinking, and entertaining; giving with their own hands a morsel of food or a cup of wine to signal hierarchies of favor; conversing and joking with their guests.

To preside at the table of bounty and conviviality was considered a prerequisite of kingship in the medieval Islamicate world, just as it was in Europe.[17] In a world that was feudal in its power structure, royal authority depended on mutual largesse and loyalty. With the centralization of empires under absolutist polities in the sixteenth and seventeenth centuries, these feasting practices began to morph into rituals that expressed increasing distance and aloofness. It is at just this historical juncture, however, that the Safavids developed the divergent Perso-Shiʿi conception of kingship, giving rise to the singular manner in which their urban palatial architecture accommodated the socio-political rituals of elaborate feasting in public whenever there were diplomatic delegations and royal visitors seeking audience, as well as during important Persian seasonal festivals such as Nauruz (the Persian New Year at the spring equinox) and Mehregan (the first day of autumn).

Royal remoteness and accessibility

Scholarship has focused on interpreting this especially public and convivial cultural production of the Safavid court in light of both unchanging tribal practices of rule, in which kingship is a shared office, and a
nomadic pattern in which the king has to be mobile and accessible.
Casting the ideological armature of Safavid authority in the belief mold
of Perso-Shi'ism demands a rethinking of the relationship between
architectural and urban forms and ceremonial enunciations of power.
In the symbiosis of the two strands of legitimacy, in which the shah was
at once the *saheb qiran* (the Lord of the Felicitous Conjunction, the
Muslim idea of the master of the world) and the *shahanshah* (the
Persian king of kings), he was vested with the authority to command
on behalf of the Prophet and on account of *farr* or royal splendor. Thus
the Safavid shah occupied a station as sacred and exalted as those of the
Ottoman sultan analogized as "a pearl in the oyster," the Mughal
emperor as the "Sun of Righteousness," or the French "Sun King." In
an apparent paradox, however, Shah Abbas the Great (1587–1629), also
known as Abbas I, who founded Isfahan as the Safavid capital and
whose centralizing administrative and military strategies restored
Safavid stability, referred to himself as "the dog at the threshold of Ali
[the first Shi'i Imam]" and reportedly considered the ability to mingle
with the denizens of Isfahan to be a privilege of kingship.

Absolutism, legitimacy, and authority in early modern conceptualizations of empire tended to rest on a foundation of separation and
remoteness; like the Divine, the king was to be above and beyond
the mundane, the earthly, the palpable, and the accessible. But he
was also in charge of one of God's myriad kingdoms on earth. After
the dissolution of the caliphate (with its universal authority challenged by competing claims of the Umayyads of Spain, the Fatimids
of Egypt, and the Buyids in western Iran), the separation in orthodox Sunni Islam between the temporal and the spiritual stations of
authority was accentuated. This, in turn, mandated enunciations of
kingship that would affirm this mediated relationship between the
sacred and the mundane. Safavid shahs were entitled to rule precisely because their absolute rule derived from the indivisibility of
the notions of spiritual and temporal authority in Twelver Shi'ism,
a resource for legitimization of kingship at variance with that of
Sunnism. This suggests that Safavid absolutism had to be practiced
differently for its authority to remain viable. It is in this context
that feasting and other rituals of hospitality and conviviality and
their sites of performance – the palaces and urban spaces – began to
communicate a charismatic practice of absolutism where access to
the king and his personal engagement, even if illusory, were paramount.

The Twelver Shi'ism of the Safavids was enforced as the religion of
the state at the founding of the dynasty and the accession of Shah

Ismaʻil in 1501, but it did not solidify as a normative practice until the end of the sixteenth century, when Shah Abbas the Great completed the century-long process of institutionalizing its doctrines and its administrative structure. Shiʻism as practiced by the brotherhood of the Safaviyye, whose adherents helped install Ismaʻil as the shah, was predicated on the mystical relationship of the *morid* to his *morshed*, the disciple to the master. This master-disciple relationship reverberated upwards, with the master himself being the disciple of Imam Ali, and in turn, serving as the spiritual intercessor on the mystic's path to union with the Divine. In such a *selsele* (genealogical) arrangement, the role of the master could be fulfilled by almost any descendant of the Imams (*seyyed*) who possessed the exceptional purity, sanctity, and power to intercede on behalf of the devotees or was perceived to possess such charisma. The devotion of the Qezelbash followers of Shah Ismaʻil and the Safaviyye Order was maintained through ecstatic dances, trancelike recitations, fearless charges into battle, and a general disregard for the legalistic aspects of religious practices that characterized this early phase of Safavid mystical Shiʻism. In this religious framework the learned doctors or *ulama* held, at best, a tenuous position of influence. With the structure of spiritual authority so loosely conceived – as it was in mystical orders such as that of the Safaviyye – power could be usurped, a vulnerability that was exposed several times during the sixteenth and even seventeenth centuries in Safavid Iran.[18]

A charismatic form of absolutism developed from these esoteric and exaggerated mystical beliefs and practices of the devotees of Shah Ismaʻil and the Safavid family. It ended with the extreme piety and orthodoxy of Shah Soltan Hossayn (1694–1722). By the latter half of the seventeenth century, as discussed later in this book, the institutionalization of Twelver Shiʻism had invested the clerical establishment with such omnipotence that Shah Soltan Hossayn's exercise of power depended on the support of the office of the Shaykh al-Islam (chief theologian of the city) – a formula akin to codependent kingship. Redefining the relationship between the temporal and the spiritual leadership of the Shiʻi community, the *ulama* had begun to "recover" the space that had been occupied by the Safavid shah for nearly two centuries. With the gradual obscuring of the role of the Safavid shah as the deputy of the Imam, proximity to the shah could be replaced by the mediation of the *ulama*.

Isfahan and the Safavid political mandate

As with other expansionist imperial regimes in the early modern period, the characteristic structures and procedures of Safavid Iran developed gradually. Several key structural elements of these imperial enterprises, with variations according to cultural specificities, may be enumerated: a fixed capital city; a more permanently stationed court;

a reformed household in which a new privileged society composed of courtiers, concubines, and *gholam*s or slave elite assumed critical positions and where loyalty and dependence centered upon the king; a centralized socio-economic structure of production, distribution, and consumption; a wide network of international trade and diplomacy; and a palace ensemble and city environment whose spatial and functional interrelations represented the centralizing structures of authority. Just as the construction of the empire was a gradual project, so was the crystallization of the shape, location, and function of an imperial capital city. The elasticity of borders, caused by the constant expanding and contracting of the imperial territories, and the internal transformations of the polity could necessitate change in the location of the imperial capital. Among the great early modern empires, the Ottomans designated Istanbul (Constantinople) as the capital after Edirne and Bursa, the Mughals shifted among cities for decades until Delhi assumed ascendancy, and the Hapsburgs moved their capital to Madrid only after a centralizing agenda had developed firm roots and Charles V abdicated the throne in favor of his son Philip. Isfahan, the third and final capital of the Safavids, fits precisely this pattern of empire building.

In the Safavid imperial trajectory, the sixteenth century witnessed the prominence of two capital cities: Tabriz (1501–1555/6) and Qazvin (1555/6–1598). The interplay between the formation and consolidation of the nascent empire and the development of royal precincts and urban strategies for the ceremonial representations of kingship in those earlier capital cities will be addressed in Chapter 2. Considering these first capitals serves to underscore the Safavid deployment of urban and palatine strategies as integral elements in the making of the empire; it also serves as a historical background to the conception of Isfahan as a new kind of capital city, one that was deliberately configured to express the centering of a new kind of empire based on Twelver Shi'ism.

Isfahan and its astonishing architectural and ceremonial enunciations of these changing paradigms of Safavid authority (Figures 3.1, 3.3, 3.8 and Plate 4) absorb the rest of the book. Chapter 3 is devoted to the elucidation of the historical landscape of Isfahan – its Safavid urban design and political and religious underpinnings. As the capital in the seventeenth century, it was conceived and designed to represent in its fullness the Perso-Shi'i definition of the city of paradise, an earthly representation of the celestial Paradise. Isfahan signified the long-awaited triumph, in abeyance since the assassination of Ali in 660, of Twelver or Imami Shi'ism. It concretized the dream of a *ka'ba* (the point of adoration) for the Twelver Shi'is, who considered themselves the lovers of the Fourteen Infallibles, the *Ahl al-bayt* – that is, the Prophet Mohammad, His daughter Fatima, His son-in-law Ali, and their eleven male descendants. In so doing, Isfahan arose as the counterbalance in the Islamicate world to the Sunni domination, through Ottoman Istanbul, of the holy site of Ka'ba in Mecca.[19] In this new *ka'ba* (*ka'be-ye sani*, the second Ka'ba), the urban spaces and palaces and the ceremonials of kingship facilitated the goals of the Imami Shi'i Empire of the Safavids.[20]

Essentialist stereotypes

Granted, politico-religious mandates do not translate into forms, but they do generate architectural and spatial solutions to functional and symbolic imperatives. Moreover, and while we do not seek to define forms as Shi'i or Sunni, we must ask after the strategies that make clear the ideological framework of those representational acts. How might the palaces of this place and period be classified into a Persian and Safavid subtype, much as an Italian *palazzo* may be Tuscan and Medici Renaissance, or a French *palais* may be Bourbon and Baroque? Just as a generalized rubric such as the "European palace" does not sufficiently characterize all palaces in Europe, an "Islamic palace" does not suffice for an understanding of the Safavid palaces. Especially given the striking parallel changes in Safavid political structure and its palatial architecture, it is necessary to cast a net of historical and cultural specificities over buildings and over what lies within and without them and what takes place inside and outside their architectural spaces.

Histories of art and architecture have generally failed to recognize the cultural multiplicity and regional specificities of the ideological and architectural representations of the early modern age in much of the Islamicate world. In its histories of art and architecture, the geographies and chronicles of diverse cultural landscapes collapse into monolithic categories such as "Islamic" or "Persian" cities and palaces.[21] Without careful, nuanced periodization or cultural differentiation, the terms *palace* and *Persian*, for example, may invoke unchanging and vaguely familiar images of the ancient Persian city of Persepolis or of generically enchanting gardens and royal pavilions. They do not, as they should, conjure up such palaces as the Ali Qapu, the Chehel Sotun, the Hasht Behesht, or the Hezar Jarib, all of which, together with the city of Isfahan, earned legendary fame through stories told by the traveling communities of merchants, ambassadors, scholars, and adventurers as well as through the luxury goods that spread across the trading worlds of the seventeenth and eighteenth centuries (Figures 4.2, 5.9, 3.2, Plates 12 and 14).

Under the rubric of "Islamic" architecture, copious scholarly ink has been spilled on the history and typology of royal gardens and palaces. Some of this scholarship remains colored by an essentialist language that implies all palaces from the Islamicate world represent variations on a timeless "Islamist" artistic and architectural mandate. Accordingly, and without concern for historical specificities, one can readily describe the general outline of any Islamic palace in a few phrases: a fortified assemblage of pavilions, loggias, apartments, courtyards, gardens, and water elements such as pools and channels; the entire ensemble is segregated by gender into a ceremonial male world and a private female one (the harem); and the whole is sensuously and extravagantly appointed, regardless of the social functions and meanings of individual buildings or spaces. The example of Isfahan's palace complex challenges such totalizing understandings of Islamicate palaces.

The four palatine paradigms

More recent scholarship looks closely at the local histories of Islamicate palaces and takes issue with old stereotypes regarding kingship and architecture.[22] With the emergence of more historically probing studies and a greater sense of the categories and typologies of palaces within their respective cultural frameworks, it has even been possible to collate the interdependence of architecture and power with the articulation of paradigms of Islamicate palaces.[23] Schematic as the four paradigms may appear, they represent a useful point of reference for our question here of how, and whether, Safavid palaces fit, or diverge from, such models.

From the early period of Islam (the seventh and eighth centuries), and notwithstanding regional specificities, two models of palace design emerge.[24] The earliest experiments in Islam of building for kings developed in urban centers and publicly proclaimed the indissolubility and codependency of religion and politics.[25] Here, the juxtaposition of the congregational mosque and the palace facilitated the expression of a fundamental aspect of the Islamic notion of polity in which kingship is conceived as an extension of the Prophet's role vis-à-vis the *umma* (Muslim community): religious and temporal leadership were inseparable aspects of the same office.[26] This was the case in the major cities of rule in the seventh and eighth centuries during the Umayyad (661–750) and early Abbasid (750–1258) periods, of which Damascus and Baghdad are the best known.[27]

The second, more complex type of palace ensemble emerged from a major shift in the manner in which kingship was conceptualized by the Abbasids, who reappropriated, through the lens of Islam, the ancient Near Eastern and the Byzantine models of sacred absolutism. Starting with the Abbasid dynasty in Baghdad and Samarra, and their rival caliphates of the Umayyads of Spain (756–1031) in Madinat al-Zahra, and of the Fatimids of Egypt (909–1171) in Cairo, they built palaces that represented in their structure and use the shift to imperial and absolutist rule.[28] In each instance, moreover, rituals such as imperial processions or audiences with the caliph, veiled and enthroned, reinforced the remote sanctity of the ruler. These were practices that departed significantly from the unpretentious, accessible, and egalitarian style of leadership advocated and exemplified by the Prophet. Instead, the caliphal posture of aloofness and distance, inspired by similar practices in ancient Near Eastern and Byzantine traditions, aspired to strike awe among the populace and to appeal to other universal notions of sacral kingship.

Abbasid Samarra was a sprawling ensemble of palaces that, together with its attendant buildings, was laid out on the scale of a city and set safely away from Baghdad, the famed Round City known as Madinat al-Salaam (the City of Peace), and that became over-crowded and rife with social unrest and danger only a decade or two after its founding in 762. Madinat al-Zahra, inspired by Samarra, also grew in an extra-urban landscape not far from the capital at Cordova. The Fatimid palace ensemble in Cairo also derived from the Abbasid model, but, unlike Samarra, its massive size and location on the edge of the old Fustat reconfigured the shape of the city in the tenth century.[29]

In all three of these examples, the vastness of the palaces, their remoteness, and their imposing character, made palpable through vertical walls that blocked views and the horizontal distances that needed to be traversed, signified the relationship, both conceptual and practical, between the ruler and the ruled. Furthermore, the formal and spatial relationships of the structures and spaces within the built environment – gates, courtyards, domed audience chambers and halls, and ayvans (iwans; vaulted porches) – gave shape to the sequential experience of liminal spaces and ceremonial procedures of access and remove. The famous description of the Byzantine embassy sent to Baghdad in 917 vividly shows how the architectural setting itself allowed the caliph to communicate to the people his inviolable holiness and to display his might and magnificence.[30]

The political authority of the caliphal powers, which had already begun to weaken by the tenth century, dissolved in the eleventh century when the dynasties of the Spanish Umayyads and the Fatimids collapsed and when the Abbasids were stripped of their power by regional military opposition. At this point, a third palatine paradigm emerged: the citadel-palace positioned within a city and designed to convey a powerful twin message of distance and access. Such citadel-palaces were heavily fortified and made to appear even more daunting by being built either on an elevated spot or as a cluster of structures inside the fortifications that evoked an awesome sense of scale and distance. The Mamluk Citadel in Cairo and the Nasrid Alhambra in Granada are the best-known examples of this type.[31]

From late in the tenth century until the mid-thirteenth-century Mongol invasions, the Islamicate world was fragmented into domin-ions, many of which were headed by warrior clans of distinct ethnic composition with not a trace of the universal claims to author-ity so characteristic of earlier periods: Kurdish Ayyubids (1171–1249) and Circassian Mamluks (1250–1517) in Egypt and the eastern Mediterranean; Arab and Berber dynasties in Spain and western

regions of North Africa (eleventh–thirteenth centuries); Persian
Samanids (819–1005) and Buyids (932–1055) in Iraq, Iran and Central
Asia; and Turkic Ghaznavid (977–1187), Ghurid (1163–1215), and
Seljuq (eleventh–thirteenth centuries) dynasties in Greater Iran,
Northern India, Iraq, and Anatolia. The degree to which each regional
power defined and executed its political and hegemonic ambitions
varied according to its landscape of operation. The Mediterranean
coastal region faced the Crusader kingdoms and the Christian
Reconquista; those rising from the Persianate world aimed for greater
domination by expanding their frontiers (India and Anatolia) and by
seizing from the Abbasid caliphate the authority to rule as sultanates.

The separation between the sacred religious role of the caliph and
the profane political role of the sultans has been credited for this third
paradigm in palatine traditions of the Islamicate world.[32] Moreover,
the decidedly military composition of the ruling elite in various parts
of the Islamicate world at this juncture has been considered to have
influenced the preference for the fortified citadel-palace. It is important to emphasize that, despite shared political and cultural practices,
the representation of kingship followed a different line of development in the western Islamicate world than it did in the Persianate
cultural sphere. Nevertheless, the imperial city of Baghdad, until its
conquest in 1258 by the Mongol hordes, remained alive in both
popular and royal imagination as a cultural center to emulate across
much of the Islamicate world.

The crises in caliphal status, however, created a cultural space into
which entered alternate modes of practicing and representing kingship. This is especially true in the tenth and eleventh centuries in the
eastern Islamicate world, where the vacuum stimulated the rede-
ployment of the Persianate ethos of kingship, preserved and revivi-
fied through such literary monuments as the *Shahname* (Book of
Kings), with an urgency and potency unseen since the advent of
Islam.[33] The *Shahname*, composed of some seventy thousand cou-
plets culled from written and oral histories by the poet Firdausi (d. c.
1020–5), recounted the epic story of Persian kingship from its legendary founding up to the advent of Islam and the beginning of Arab
domination. For nearly every man who ascended the throne in the
greater Iranian world since the thirteenth century, regardless of
ethnic and cultural differences, a lavishly produced copy of the
Shahname, which often had paintings as well as illuminations,
served as a literary-historical foundation for the construction of his
royal genealogy.[34] This remarkably enduring relevance of the
Shahname to the construction of royal legitimacy was the impulse
behind the production of the copy made for Shah Tahmasb (1524–76),
the son of Shah Isma'il, during the 1520s and 1530s, arguably the
greatest illustrated Persian manuscript ever made.[35]

This schema of Islamicate palatine paradigms should not, however, be interpreted as an indication of unvarying architectural for-

mulas within each category. For example, the palaces of the Persian-ized Turkic Ghaznavids, as in Lashkari Bazar in Afghanistan, or of the Great Seljuqs in Isfahan diverge significantly from the citadel-palace typology; the Ghaznavid palaces tended toward the Abbasid Samarran prototypes; while the Great Seljuqs of Iran preferred extra-urban garden pavilions to the citadel-palaces of their Anatolian kin.[36] In other words, and as should be expected, the "palatine paradigm" needs to allow for regional variations and ideological, religious, and cultural meanings pertinent to a given place and time.

The Mongol invasions of the early thirteenth century were devas-tating and life altering. Greater Iran and Iraq, the main targets of Mongol attacks in western Asia, were severely depopulated, the agri-cultural infrastructure was decimated, cities were plundered, and libraries were burned down. In their wake Mongol overlords, now the Ilkhanid (1256–1335) kings, established new practices and articulated the nature of their role to the masses in new ways. The fourth of the palace paradigms expresses this reinvented enunciation of kingship, one that emphasized decentralization and a nomadic lifestyle.[37] Elements of the fourth paradigm were already in place in the pre-Mongol era among Turkic tribes of Central Asia; nomadic habits of shifting centers of rule, peripatetic courts, and tentage as royal archi-tecture had entered the established practices of the Middle East. In the decentralized mode of governance of these Turkic tribes, the old and established cities in Afghanistan, Iran, Iraq, and Turkey were further enhanced with new religious and civic foundations to serve as their sultanic cultural and political centers. Nowhere, however, did they confine their courts and households to an urban ensemble of palaces. Instead, extra-urban retreats and favorite oases and meadows were appropriated as palaces through the erection of tents for the res-idential and ceremonial needs of the court. In this context, the capital was wherever the itinerant sultan and the royal household chose to settle temporarily.

With the Mongol sack of Baghdad in 1258, which resulted in the slaughter of the inhabitants and the destruction of the Abbasids – the last caliph, according to Mongol tradition, was killed by being wrapped in a lavish palace carpet and trampled to a pulp by horses – the trajectories of Persianate Muslim kingship and its enunciations in architecture, art, and ceremonial were permanently separated from those followed by western Islamicate dominions. Genghis Khan's conquests between 1209 and 1227 spread across much of the eastern and central parts of Asia. By 1241, his sons and grandsons had expanded this greatest of all contiguous land empires to cover nearly all of Asia and as far into Europe as Hungary. In the process, the dis-ruption between the eastern and western zones of the Islamicate world left a deep cultural "gash" of separation.

The Ilkhanids, who followed the Mongol Hülegu's conquests in greater Iran, constituted the principal west Asian branch of the

Mongol empire. There were three others: one ruled by Kubilai Khan in the East (the Yuan Dynasty), another in Central Asia (the Chaghatay Khanate), and finally the "Golden Horde" in Russia. Of these four branches the Ilkhanids came closest to adopting the cultural norms of their new subjects. Yet even after conversion to Islam, the Ilkhanids summoned legitimacy through descent from Genghis Khan, whose given title the "Khan of All Between the Oceans" acknowledged his ambitious plans for the conquest of all of Asia. Like their "brothers in rule," the Great Khans of China, whom we know as the Yuan dynasty (1279–1368) and to whose seat the Mongol branch in western Asia were *il khans* or the subordinate khans, the Ilkhanids, too, had to anchor their authority to the structures of kingship that could be locally legitimized. Thus the Ilkhanid acquisition of Islamic and Persianate modes of authority brought about the convergence of traditions as diverse as that of the Mongol codes of law known as the *yasas*, the Islamic *shari'a* laws, and the etiquette and lineage of ancient Persianate kingship.

After the capture of Baghdad, the Mongol successor states no longer needed to seek legitimacy from the Abbasid caliphs, who were reduced to puppet kings under the protection of the Mamluk sultans of Egypt. The post-Mongol Muslim rulers were, more importantly, also inclined to find a balance between dynastic tradition (*'urf*) and Islamic law (*shari'a*).[38] Yet the influence of the caliphate did not entirely cease to operate, for it formed the structural foundation of temporal authority in orthodox Sunnism. In fact, the heir-successor to al-Musta'sim, the murdered Abbasid caliph, found refuge in Mamluk Cairo, whence the caliph continued to exert his religious influence and performed his duties with regard to the holy sites in Mecca and Medina. The Ottoman conquest of Cairo (the seat-in-exile of the caliph) and of the holy cities of Islam early in the sixteenth century produced the crucial linkage for their claim to absolute authority in their dominions. In contrast, the Mongol intervention completely loosed the Persianate world to the east from caliphal fetters, although it was still largely Sunni as well.

Mongol overlords were scarcely the first foreigners to have self-consciously recovered and appropriated the cultural trappings of Persianate kingship for the purposes of legitimizing their place in the pantheon of ancient kings. Neither were they the last of the Turco-Mongol conquerors and rulers of this part of the Islamicate world. In the fifteenth-century Turkmen Aqqoyunlu (in western Iran) and Turkic-Tatar Timurid (eastern Iran and Central Asia) realms, the entire region found a hegemonic cultural language of kingship that was Persianized and Turco-Mongol, but that was reinterpreted differently by each of the three principal empires that dominated the period from the sixteenth to the eighteenth century.[39]

Tabriz of the Aqqoyunlu, and Samarqand and Herat of the Timurids in the fifteenth century supplanted the multiple centers of culture and politics so characteristic of the earlier medieval period and prefigured in their imperial institutions and procedures the capital cities of the early modern empires of the Ottomans, the Safavids, and the Mughals. Like the Ilkhanids, the Aqqoyunlu and Timurid rulers patronized cities without committing themselves to their walled confines. They, too, were closely tied to the religious, cultural, and intellectual institutions of such urban centers as Tabriz, Samarqand, Herat, and Shiraz, where they founded madrasas (theological colleges), *khanaqahs* (hostel-retreats for Sufis), observatories, mosques, and shrines. They also patronized the urban industries that served as their royal *karkhane*, workshops that supplied artistic goods such as textiles and carpets, manuscripts, and fine metal vessels for the consumption of their highly refined courtly milieus. Yet when the Aqqoyunlu or the Timurids were not on the move for warfare, hunting, or pasturage, they still preferred to reside outside the city walls (Plate 2). The permanent architecture of Timurid palaces, for example, consisted mainly of an enclosed garden with, ordinarily, a pavilion (Plate 1).[40] Tents supplemented the sheltered space in the gardens. Otherwise, wherever and whenever needed (as in massive wedding or circumcision ceremonies during Timur's own lifetime), royal tent cities were pitched and walled to resemble a proper Islamicate palace ensemble.[41]

The Ottomans, the Safavids, and the Mughals were heirs to this fifteenth-century Turco-Mongol cultural discourse but established empires more centralized than those of their forebears. From the Timurid and Aqqoyunlu synthesis of traditions emerge the palaces of Istanbul, Isfahan, Agra, Delhi, and Lahore. But in each case, the semantics of power and its symbolic representations in architecture and art differed in accordance with the specific cultural representations of kingship.

The "four paradigms" is a useful tool for organizing the cultural practices and patterns that informed architectural, ideological, and social operations of kingship in the Islamicate world. Certain aspects of the conceptualizations of dominion transcended regional specificities in their general outlines. Allusions to and evocations of divine kingship in the traditions of the ancient Near East, for example, were universal. But even such universals had to be locally meaningful: the Mediterranean-focused Romano-Byzantine past, for instance, may have served the Seljuqs of Anatolia (1077–1307) or the Ottomans well, but it had little to offer to the Great Seljuqs of Iran (1038–1194) or the Safavids. One must be similarly alert to oversimplified and essentialized categorizations such as "tribalism" and "nomadic" practices of kingship.[42] This latter point is especially important when considering the palatine tradition of the Safavids.

To reconsider the relationship between Safavid practices in the Isfahan phase and the Turco-Mongol heritage of the Persianate world does not negate the significance, so central to scholarship, of Timur's grandiose vision of world domination as a model for the centralizing and absolutist Safavid, Mughal, and Ottoman empires. The successor states drew upon the Timurid discourse of power and its palatine tradition as they developed their own early modern permutations of imperial authority. Nevertheless, and notwithstanding the significant precedent set by the Turkmen Aqqoyunlu for the Safavids (to be further discussed in Chapter 2), broad similarities between the feasting practices of the Timurids and the Safavids have led to the historically inaccurate and critically misleading assumption that an unwavering continuum of medieval and nomadic principles and practices of kingship extended through the two dynasties. Scholarship on the Safavids in general, and on their ceremonials and palaces in particular, reflects this calcified and entrenched view. Accordingly, little consideration has been given to the changing political and cultural circumstances that informed the early sixteenth-century Safavid capital of Tabriz in contrast to those relevant to seventeenth-century Isfahan. In fact, one has to strain to put the Isfahan palaces of the Safavids into the model of the four paradigms: if Islamicate palaces were to be grouped into "four distinctive palatine paradigms," the Safavid palaces in Isfahan fit the mold only in their very general outlines.[43]

They present distinctive forms that suited a charismatic implementation of royal absolutism, one that was chiseled to suit Perso-Shiʿi expectations regarding legitimacy. The uniqueness of the Safavid synthesis and its invention of new palatine forms in Isfahan undermine the "universal" application of the four categories of paradigm outlined above. Still, this study affirms and extends the underlying premise of the "four palace paradigm" in its hypothesis that palace architecture synchronizes with the prevailing structure of political power.

Safavid palaces of the Ali Qapu (Lofty Gate), the Chehel Sotun (Forty Columns), the Talar-e Tavile (Hall of Stables) and the Ayenekhane (Hall of Mirrors), all in Isfahan – the first two still standing, the latter two no longer extant – represent a radical departure from the architectural solutions adopted by their predecessors or their contemporaries (Figures 5.1, 5.5, Plates 12 and 14). They display utterly novel configurations of space, form, function, and decoration. Yet, these palaces have often been presented in earlier research merely as slightly more opulent variations on the fifteenth-century Timurid royal precincts. Ironically, the Timurid royal ensembles are known to us only through Persian chronicles, while the Persian sources that would pertain to the Safavid palaces in Isfahan have often been neglected in scholarship. Adopting a prismatic approach that gives equal attention to texts (chronicles, epigraphy, and panegyrics among other

discursive sources) authored by both Persians and Europeans, as well
as to the extant visual evidence, reveals the uniqueness of the Safavid
palaces and yields a textured tapestry of significations.

Building upon the political, cultural, and urbanization parameters
that contributed to the renewal of Isfahan as the Safavid capital
(Chapter 3), Chapters 4 and 5 delve deep into the royal ensemble,
unfolding the relationship between city spaces and the palace
precinct and then the palaces inside and outside the precinct.
Moving in and out of the royal domains, both urban and extra-urban,
and through individual buildings and their sites, these chapters elucidate the architectural history of the whole and its constituent parts
in historically situated stages. Accordingly, the utter singularity of
the Ali Qapu Palace-Gateway and its complex building history and
functional transmutations will require multiple visits, so to speak,
over the course of Chapters 3 through 5. In the end, this book suggests that Isfahan, its palaces, and their permanent and impermanent contents embodied a new constellation of representations and
functions, access to which depended on glimpses, even if at times
fleeting, of the cultural matrix of the Perso-Shiʿi ethos of kingship.
The ceremonial practices and symbolic renditions of these novel
structures of power offer us windows onto the Safavid world and its
social life in relation to its imperial constructs. Ceremonial, a staple
ingredient of every manifestation of kingship, has long been ignored
or misrepresented in Safavid studies. In recovering this cultural
matrix it becomes clear that the smallest details pertaining to the
palaces – even the dinnerware and dress, or draping strategies and
decorative schemes, or the mere offering of a morsel of food by the
royal person – were essential ingredients particular to the consciously crafted Safavid vision of power. Buildings like the Chehel
Sotun Palace, where the feast in the first paragraph took place, signal
this ideologically motivated intentionality of the ceremonial procedures in Isfahan.

The following chapters proceed from the cities and the palaces in
the sixteenth century, to the urban renewal of Isfahan as the Safavid
capital, to the architecture of the palaces in Isfahan, and conclude
with the feasting rituals. Through the mediation of architecture and
urban space, they discuss the myriad ways in which the Safavid etiquette of kingship evolved and was represented over the span of the
sixteenth and seventeenth centuries.

Notes

1. Mahmud b. Hedayat-Allah Afushte Natanzi, *Noqavat al-asar fi zekr al-akhyar*, ed. Ehsan Eshraqi, 2 vols (Tehran: Bongah-e tarjome va nashr-e ketab, 1366/1987), 376 and translated in Robert McChesney, "Four Sources on Shah Abbas's Building of Isfahan," *Muqarnas* 5 (1988): 106.

2. This *hadith* (saying attributed to the Prophet Mohammad) is invoked in a chapter devoted to the social etiquette of eating and drinking by Vaʿez Kashefi, *Fotovvatname-ye soltani*, edited by Mohammad Jaʿfar Mahjub (Tehran: Bonyad-e Farhang-e Iran, 1350/1971), 233; this book of chivalric conduct and the quote will be further discussed in Chapter 6. Kashefi's source seems to be the *Sunan* of ibn Majah (d. 886), one of the six major collections of the *hadith*, which is generally viewed favorably by Shiʿis and with suspicion by Sunnis. For ibn Majah and the *hadith* traditions, see John Burton, *An Introduction to the Hadith* (Edinburgh: Edinburgh University Press, 1994, reprinted 2001), esp. 159–62.

3. John Woods, *The Aqquyunlu: Clan, Confederation, Empire*, rev. and expanded edn (Salt Lake City: University of Utah Press, 1999), 107. Ismaiʿl's maternal grandmother, Despina, was a daughter of the Byzantine John IV of Trebizond.

4. Kingship in the Islamic era (from the seventh century onwards) appealed to this concept of *farr* or *khvarnah* regardless of the ethnicity or lineage of the ruling elite. The subject is most recently and expertly analyzed by Abolala Soudavar in, *The Aura of Kings: Legitimacy and Divine Sanction in Iranian Kingship* (Costa Mesa, CA: Mazda Publishers, 2003), esp. 1–39.

5. Loyalty to Imam Ali was not exclusive to the Imami or Twelver Shiʿism. Several important studies have recently considered the history of Shiʿism in Iran and especially its transmutations under the Safavids: Said Amir Arjomand, *The Shadow of God and the Hidden Imam: Religion, Political Order, and Societal Change in Shiʾite Iran from the Beginning to 1890* (Chicago: University of Chicago Press, 1984), esp. 105–211; Kathryn Babayan, "The Waning of the Qizilbâsh: The Spiritual and the Temporal in Seventeenth Century Iran" (PhD dissertation, Princeton University, 1993) and her *Mystics, Monarchs and Messiahs: Cultural Landscapes of Early Modern Iran* (Cambridge, MA: Harvard Middle Eastern Monographs, 2003); Rula Jurdi Abisaab, *Converting Persia: Religion and Power in the Safavid Empire* (London: I. B. Tauris, 2004). On the doctored evidence and constructed Imami lineage of the Safavids, see especially Ahmad Kasravi, *Shaykh Safi va tabarash* (Tehran: Jar, 2536/1976).

6. Vali Nasr, *The Shia Revival: How Conflicts within Islam Will Shape the Future* (New York; London: W. W. Norton, 2006), considers the current dilemmas presented by Shiʿism, especially the Twelver branch, that has long dominated Iran and has been emboldened by the awakening of its Iraqi component.

7. For the seminal study of Shiʿism in Iran, see Amir Arjomand, *The Shadow of God*; for the Buyids, see Roy P. Mottahedeh, *Loyalty and Leadership in an Early Islamic Society* (Princeton: Princeton University Press, 1980); for the Fatimids, see Michael Brett, *The Rise of the Fatimids: the World of the Mediterranean and the Middle East in the Fourth Century of the Hijra, Tenth Century CE* (Leiden: Brill, 2001) and Heinz Halm *The Empire of the Mahdi: the Rise of the Fatimids*, trans. Michael Bonner (Leiden: Brill, 1996).

8. Aziz Al-Azmeh, *Muslim Kingship: Power and the Sacred in Muslim, Christian and Pagan Polities* (London; New York: I. B. Tauris, 1997), offers the most sophisticated theoretical framing of notions of kingship in Islam but his analysis is almost entirely concerned with the Sunni and

caliphal articulations of power and authority with only the slightest of references to the Safavid "difference," see pp. 190–3.

9. The literature on Islam and its mandate for justice is voluminous. For an introduction, see Jonathan Porter Berkey, *The formation of Islam: Religion and Society in the Near East, 600–1800* (Cambridge; New York: Cambridge University Press, 2003). A most accessible, concise, and compelling consideration of the theme of justice, contained in the earliest of the Quranic revelations, is offered by Michael Sells, *Approaching the Qurʾán: The Early Revelations* (Ashland, OR: White Cloud Press, 1999).

10. Babayan's *Mystics, Monarchs and Messiahs* admirably explicates this messianic frame of reference.

11. European constructs of the "other" especially as pertaining to Iran, are a subject of considerable interest, not least because it is so rarely dealt with; but it remains beyond the scope of this book. Nevertheless, I found the following studies especially helpful in formulating a scholarly view in dealing with the European travel accounts and their accompanying visuals: Peter Mason, *Infelicities: Representations of the Exotic* (Baltimore; London: Johns Hopkins University Press, 1998); Ivo Kamps and Jyotsna G. Singh, eds, *Travel Knowledge: European "Discoveries" in the Early Modern Period* (New York: Palgrave, 2001); Stuart B. Schwartz, ed., *Implicit Understandings: Observing, Reporting, and Reflecting on the Encounter Between Europeans and Other Peoples in the Early Modern Era* (Cambridge: Cambridge University Press, 1994); Richard G. Cole, "Sixteenth-Century Travel Books as a Source of European Attitudes toward Non-White and Non-Western Culture," *Proceedings of the American Philosophical Society* 116, No. 1 (15 February 1972): 59–67; Marcus Milwright, "So Despicable a Vessel: Representations of Tamerlane in Printed Books of the Sixteenth and Seventeenth Centuries," *Muqarnas* 23 (2006): 317–44; Rhoads Murphey, "Review: Bigots or Informed Observors? A Periodization of Pre-Colonial English and European Writing on the Middle East," *Journal of the American Oriental Society* 110, No. 2 (April–June 1990): 291–303; and the classic study by Mary B. Campbell, *The Witness and the Other World: Exotic European Travel Writing, 400–1600* (Ithaca; London: Cornell University Press, 1988).

12. A fascinating study of the transformations in travel writing is by Paul Zumthor, "The Medieval Travel Narratives," *New Literary History* 25, No. 4, 25th Anniversary Issue (Part 2) (Autumn 1994): 809–24, esp. 816–19.

13. Elio Brancaforte, *Visions of Persia: Mapping the Travels of Adam Olearius* (Cambridge, MA; London: Harvard University Department of Comparative Literature, 2003).

14. A body of fragmentary "literature" is preserved in collections, *majmu ʿas*, in Iranian libraries which contain descriptions or references to buildings and cities. I have been unable to consult these directly. Nevertheless, there seem to be corresponding references to most of the relevant material in official histories to which I have had access. For an introduction to the subject, see Iraj Afshar, "Maktūb and Majmūʿa: Essential Sources for Safavid Research," in *Society and Culture in the Early Modern Middle East: Studies on Iran in the Safavid Period*, ed. Andrew J. Newman (Leiden; Boston: Brill, 2003), 51–61.

15. Interconnected performances of politics and architecture have been studied by, among others, Gülru Necipoğlu, *Architecture, Ceremonial*

and Power: The Topkapi Palace in the Fifteenth and Sixteenth Centuries (Cambridge, MA: MIT Press, 1991), and Alice Jarrard, *Architecture as Performance in Seventeenth-Century Europe: Court Ritual in Modena, Rome, and Paris* (Cambridge: Cambridge University Press, 2003).

16. A great deal has been written on court society and its practices but the rituals of feasting and their architectural corollaries are rarely addressed. For a few seminal studies on strategies of kingship and ceremonials, see Norbert Elias, *The Court Society*, trans. Edmund Jephcott (Oxford: Blackwell, 1983); Al-Azmeh, *Muslim Kingship*; D. Cannadine and S. Price, eds, *Rituals of Royalty: Power and Ceremonial in Traditional Societies* (New York; London: Cambridge University Press, 1987), especially Cannadine, "Divine Rites of Kings," 1–19. J. R. Mulryne and Elizabeth Goldring, eds, *Court Festivals of the European Renaissance: Art, Politics and Performance* (Aldershot; Burlington, VT: Ashgate, 2002) covers a wide range of material comparable to the subject of this book.

17. For general considerations of the symbolic-political significance of feasting, see the classic study by Elias, *The Court Society*. More recently, Roy Strong, *Feast: A History of Grand Eating* (London: Jonathan Cape, 2002) offers a richly-documented, popular and eminently readable account of feasting.

18. For the popular and messianic revolts by the followers of the Sufi or mystical Qezelbash and Noqtavi communities, see Babayan, *Mystics, Monarchs and Messiahs*, esp. 57–117.

19. The Ottoman dominion over the holy sites came about after their conquest of Egypt (1517) and all that Mamluk sultans had inherited from the Abbasid line of caliphs who had sought and received refuge in Cairo after the Mongol invasion and sack of Baghdad in 1258.

20. The epigraphic program of the Masjed-e Jadid-e Abbasi on the south side of the Maydan or public square of Isfahan (begun in 1611) positions the mosque and Isfahan in a metaphorical connection with the holy sites of Islam. The analogy with Ka'ba is found in the poetic inscriptions that decorate a pair of silver doors installed on the orders of Shah Safi in 1636; Lotf-Allah Honarfar, *Ganjine-ye asar-e tarikhi-ye Esfahan* (Isfahan: Ketabforushi-e Saqafi, 1344/1965–6), 433–4.

21. Moreover, these essentializing designations are rooted in pre-modern historical terms. So, for example, in art-historical survey books covering world art, the Islamicate world is routinely sandwiched between chapters devoted to the medieval period. No matter how "modern" the sixteenth-century architectural practices of the Ottoman world or the architect Sinan's buildings may have been, their discussion tends to remain confined to the historical narratives before and around the time of Chartres Cathedral. For a few especially egregious considerations of the arts from the Islamicate world, see Helen Gardner, *Gardner's Art Through the Ages*, 10th edn (Fort Worth: Harcourt Brace, 1996) and Marilyn Stokstad, *Art History* (New York: Abrams, 1995). For a thought-provoking analysis of the Eurocentric perspective on the narratives of art history and its plotting of time and space, see Robert S. Nelson, "The Map of Art History," *The Art Bulletin* 79, no. 1 (March 1997): 28–40. A similarly vexing problem arises from the field of colonial and post-colonial studies whereby scholarly attention pours onto those states and regions that were subjected to Euro-American

colonization. Since the advent of modernity may also accompany, even if implicitly, such colonizing enterprises, those falling outside its ambit have remained largely confined to scholarly obscurity of this sort as well.

22. For a few pertinent examples of the revisionist approach, see Oleg Grabar, *The Alhambra* (Cambridge, MA: Harvard University Press, 1978); Necipoğlu, *Architecture, Ceremonial and Power*, Gülru Necipoğlu, ed., *Ars Orientalis* 23 (1993); Ebba Koch, "The Mughal Waterfront Garden," in *Gardens in the Time of the Great Muslim Empires: Theory and Design*, ed. Attilio Petruccioli (Leiden; New York: Brill, 1997), 140–60; Nasser O. Rabbat, *The Citadel of Cairo: A New Interpretation of Royal Mamluk Architecture* (Leiden; New York: Brill, 1995); D. Fairchild Ruggles, *Gardens, Landscape, and Vision in the Palaces of Islamic Spain* (University Park, PA: Pennsylvania State University Press, 2000); Scott Redford, *Landscape and the State in Medieval Anatolia: Seljuk Gardens and Pavilions of Alanya, Turkey* (Oxford: Archaeopress, 2000).

23. Three earlier paradigms were charted by Jere L. Bacharach, "Administrative Complexes, Palaces, and Citadels: Changes in the Loci of Medieval Muslim Rule," in *The Ottoman City and Its Parts: Urban Structure and Social Order*, ed. Irene A. Bierman, Rifa'at A. Abou-El-Haj, and Donald Preziosi (New Rochelle, NY: A. D. Caratzas, 1991), 111–28. A fourth paradigm was added by Gülru Necipoğlu, "An Outline of Shifting Paradigms in the Palatial Architecture of the Pre-Modern Islamic World," *Ars Orientalis* 23 (1993): 3–24.

24. Bacharach, "Administrative Complexes, Palaces, and Citadels," 111–28; Necipoğlu, "An Outline of Shifting Paradigms," 5–12.

25. This is notwithstanding the problematic cases of the Umayyad princely residences of the first quarter of the eighth century, of which all extant structures are located far from urban centers. See, for example, Oleg Grabar, "Umayyad Palaces Reconsidered," *Ars Orientalis* 23 (1993): 93–108.

26. Priscilla Soucek, "Solomon's Throne/Solomon's Bath: Model or Metaphor," *Ars Orientalis* 23 (1993): 109–34.

27. For Damascus, see Finbarr Barry Flood, *The Great Mosque of Damascus; Studies on the Making of an Umayyad Visual Culture* (Leiden and Boston: Brill, 2001); for Baghdad, see J. Lassner, "The Caliph's Personal Domain: The City Plan of Baghdad Re-Examined," in *The Islamic City*, ed. A. H. Hourani and S. M. Stern (Oxford: Cassirer; Philadelphia: University of Pennsylvania Press, 1970), among others.

28. On Madinat al-Zahra, see Ruggles, *Gardens, Landscape, and Vision*; on Fatimid palaces, see Paula Sanders, *Ritual, Politics, and the City in Fatimid Cairo* (Saratoga Springs, NY: State University of New York Press, 1994).

29. The Fatimids were Isma'ili Shi'is whose rituals, however, were to emulate and challenge the Abbasid model.

30. The descriptions of the ambassadors' long journey through rooms, halls, gardens, and passageways are recounted and analyzed in Hugh Kennedy, *When Baghdad Ruled the Muslim World: the Rise and Fall of Islam's Greatest Dynasty* (Cambridge, MA: Da Capo Press, 2005), 152–6.

31. Rabbat, *The Citadel of Cairo*; Grabar, *The Alhambra*.

32. Bacharach, "Administrative Complexes, Palaces, and Citadels."

33. For an important, recent consideration of the significance of the *Shahname* to the Persianate ethos, see Babayan, *Mystics, Monarchs and Messiahs*, xxix–xxx, among other places.

34. Robert Hillenbrand, ed., *Shahnama: The Visual Language of the Persian Book of Kings* (Edinburgh: Edinburgh University Press, 2004). On the Great Mongol *Shahname*, the first monumental and illustrated copy to have survived, see Oleg Grabar and Sheila Blair, *Epic Images and Contemporary History: The Illustrations of the Great Mongol Shahnama* (Chicago: University of Chicago Press, 1980).

35. The great Safavid *Shahname* was produced at the *ketabkhane* (scriptorium-atelier) in Safavid Tabriz. Before its dismantling and dispersion, it was published in a facsimile: Martin Dickson and Stuart Cary Welch, eds, *The Houghton Shahname*, 2 vols (Cambridge, MA: Harvard University Press, 1981). Ironically, little serious scholarship has emerged since this publication set the groundwork. We do not know, for example, how the iconography of the paintings may relate to the Safavid promotion of Twelver Shi'ism. See, however, Robert Hillenbrand, "The Iconography of the *Shāh-nāma-yi Shāhī*," in *Safavid Persia: The History and Politics of an Islamic Society*, ed. Charles Melville (London; New York: I. B. Tauris, 1996): 53–78.

36. Redford, *Landscape and the State*.

37. The fourth paradigm is added by Necipoğlu, "An Outline of Shifting Paradigms," 3–24. Publications on the Mongols are voluminous; see, for example, David Morgan, *The Mongols* (Oxford; New York: Blackwell, 1986) and Jack Weatherford, *Genghis Khan and the Making of the Modern World* (New York: Crown, 2004).

38. Necipoğlu, "An Outline of Shifting Paradigms," 15.

39. Little has been written on the Aqqoyunlu as a cultural zone. See, however, Woods, *The Aqqoyunlu*. For the greater attention to the Timurids, on the other hand, see the following: Thomas W. Lentz and Glenn D. Lowry, *Timur and the Princely Vision: Persian Art and Culture in the Fifteenth Century* (Los Angeles: Los Angeles County Museum of Art, 1989); Lisa Golombek and Donald Wilber, *The Timurid Architecture of Iran and Turan* (Princeton, NJ: Princeton University Press, 1988); Lisa Golombek and Maria Subtelny, eds, *Timurid Art and Culture: Iran and Central Asia in the Fifteenth Century* (Leiden; New York: Brill, 1992); and *The Cambridge History of Iran: Vol. 6, The Timurid and Safavid Periods*, ed. Peter Jackson (Cambridge: Cambridge University Press, 1986).

40. Golombek and Wilber, *Timurid Architecture of Iran and Turan*; Bernard O'Kane, *Timurid Architecture in Khurasan* (Costa Mesa, CA: Mazda Publishers in association with Undena Publications, 1987).

41. Ruy González de Clavijo, *Embassy to Tamerlane, 1403–1406*, trans. Guy Le Strange (New York and London: Harper and Brothers, 1928) on the ceremonies and tents; Peter A. Andrews, *Felt Tents and Pavilions: The Nomadic Tradition and its Interaction with Princely Tentage* (London: Melisende, 1999) on tent architecture.

42. Necipoğlu has articulated, for example, the Umayyad tribalism in contrast to Abbasid absolutism and sedentary practices of rule; Necipoğlu, "An Outline of Shifting Paradigms," 6. Similarly and more problematically, she has given voice to a long-held scholarly view that Safavids continued the tribal modes of behavior and conduct of kingship that were established by the Turco-Mongol rulers of the

Persianate world in the medieval period; Gülru Necipoğlu, "Framing the Gaze in Ottoman, Safavid, and Mughal Palaces," *Ars Orientalis* 23 (1993): 303–42; and Necipoğlu, *Architecture, Ceremonial and Power*, 242–58.

43. While our emphasis remains on the ceremonial palaces, it should be noted that several hunting lodges of the Safavid period have survived. Notwithstanding a few very useful articles in which the buildings are inventoried and measured, they await scholarly consideration; see Wolfram Kleiss, "Schlösser und Herrensitze auf dem Lande aus Safavidischer und Qadjarischer Zeit," *Archaeologische Mitteilungen aus Iran* 20 (1987): 346–68.

CHAPTER TWO

Peripatetic Kings and Palaces: From Tabriz to Qazvin in the Sixteenth Century

BEFORE ISFAHAN TOOK center stage in Safavid history, the dynasty's founding and early history were bound to the two political capital cities of Tabriz and Qazvin and their religious pendant, Ardabil, the ancestral and spiritual home of the family and its mystical order of Safaviyye. The urban and palatine landscapes of these cities suggest the tentative early stages of an architecture of power that pivots on the conceptual urgency of centering the empire, its implementation of absolute rule, and its ceremonial representations of the form of Persian kingship that build upon the doctrinal foundations of Twelver Shi'ism. The degree to which the earlier patterns and practices of royal ritual and ideology intersect with or contribute to the formation of the Safavid paradigm will be central to this consideration of Tabriz, Qazvin and, more tangentially, Ardabil. Feasting and other procedures of royal conviviality formed an important component of this nascent ideology of Perso-Shi'i kingship but, as this chapter will argue, palace architecture and urban design in the earlier Safavid capitals remained largely aloof to the practical representations and accommodations of that uniquely Safavid posture of imperial authority which would emerge in Isfahan. This chapter, then, bridges the pre- and early- Safavid past to its Isfahan future. It also aims to expose the centrality of the urban projects, especially at Qazvin, in the making of a centralized and absolutist empire of Twelver Shi'ism. The architectural ebbs and flows, so to speak, of that enterprise suggest a more complex picture than scholarship has accorded the early history of the Safavids.

The Tabriz of Shah Isma'il had already been at the crossroads of politics and commerce for centuries and been described by many European travelers. Very little survives from its fifteenth-century history, however, and nothing of its palaces, making the European descriptions all the more crucial for a recovery of Safavid Tabriz and its royal ensemble. Of these, Domenico Romano's represents an especially important starting point: "I do not think I ought to omit to mention a beautiful palace which the great Sultan Assambei had built; and though there are many large and beautiful palaces in the city built by the kings, his predecessors, yet this, without comparison, far excels them all."[1] The palace that so excelled all others was the famous (now lost) Hasht Behesht, or Astibisti, as Romano says it was called in the Persian language. Until recently known only as an anonymous Venetian merchant, Romano visited Tabriz around 1510 and was impressed by the thriving and well-developed city that the founder of the Safavid dynasty, Shah Isma'il I (r. 1501–24), had seized from the Aqqoyunlu clans. Construction of the Hasht Behesht had been begun by the Aqqoyunlu Sultan Uzun Hasan (1453–78), Romano's Sultan Assambei or Hasan Beg, and completed by his son and successor Yaqub (1478–90).

As Romano describes the Hasht Behesht Palace at Tabriz – and as its name, the Eight Paradises, suggests – the edifice was an octagonal structure with a nine-fold plan featuring eight rooms that rotated around a central domed space, hence a *hasht behesht* (Figures 2.1 and 5.4, Plate 1). Romano notes that Uzun Hasan's Hasht Behesht was two stories tall and had a domed room at the center occupying the entire height of the building. A single staircase reached the second floor, "the dome, the rooms and anterooms," according to Romano, whose admiration for the sight is effusive: "This building, on the ground floor, has four entrances, with many more apartments, all enameled and gilt in various ways, and so beautiful that I can hardly find words to express it."[2] The palace was raised on a terrace or "mastabé." The single main entrance could be reached through a flight of stairs, and the whole was placed at the center of what is clearly described as a *chahar bagh* or four-quadrant garden. The garden, famed as Eshratabad (Garden of Joy), was described as "an earthly paradise inhabited by mortal men."[3] Romano carefully records the decorative use of water at the Hasht Behesht, noting that paths made out of marble led to the platform with a "channel of a streamlet paved and skillfully worked out in marble." He adds, "This streamlet is four fingers broad and four deep, and flows all around in the form of a vine or snake. It rises at one part, flows round, and at the same place again the water is conducted away elsewhere."

The landscaping and waterworks in this palace included colorful glazed tiles ("plastered in different colours, and . . . conspicuous far off like a mirror") and gutters or spouts that spurted water out of huge dragon heads at the corners of the platform. Romano says that the spouts were "of bronze and so large that they would do for a cannon, and so well made as to be taken for live dragons." Similarly impressive were the interior murals, where battles, the reception of embassies, and hunting exploits – presumably all depicting episodes from Uzun Hasan's life – were rendered with such skill that the figures appeared to Romano "like real living human beings." Such descriptions of "realistic" representations of motifs and figural themes are of great interest to scholars. The account is especially important, however, for its evocation of the architecture of the Palace

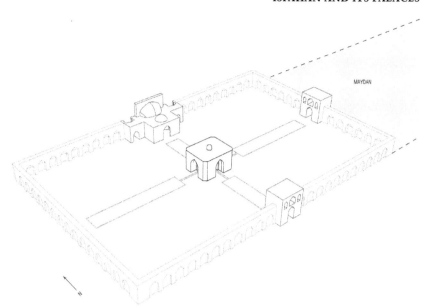

Figure 2.1 *Schematic rendering of the royal precinct in Tabriz when the city was the capital of the Turkmen dynasty of the Aqqoyunlu in the fifteenth century.*

Shah Isma'il (1501–24), the founder of the Safavids, made the city his capital (1501 until 1555/6) and took over the Aqqoyunlu royal precinct, the Daulatkhane. Known as Eshratabad (the Abode of Joy), the walled precinct was laid out as a *chahar bagh* (four-quadrant garden) with its most famous feature, the Hasht Behesht Palace, at its center. This rendering only approximates and alludes to parts of the ensemble gleaned from fifteenth- and sixteenth-century European and Persian descriptions. The precinct was located outside the city proper and had three main entrances: the gate on the north side consisted of a number of structures for the visitors to the court; the one on the eastern flank faced a public square or maydan and served as a gateway for the court to attend parades, equestrian games and other such spectacles; the third was reserved for the harem, whose quarters were located just inside it.

of Hasht Behesht, which embodies the quintessence of Persianate palaces since at least the post-Mongol period.

Another Hasht Behesht Palace was built some two hundred years later in Safavid Isfahan under the patronage of Shah Solayman (1666–94) (Figure 5.18). That later palace, which will be discussed in Chapter 5, reverts to the most common typology of palace designs in Persianate architecture and reinterprets its principal features, the nine-fold plan (or cross-in-square) and the garden setting. During the two centuries between the construction of these two famous Hasht Behesht palaces – one in Tabriz, the other in Isfahan – a host of palaces, funerary buildings, and other structures arose that appropriated and refined the *hasht-behesht* plan and its synergistic conceptualization of architecture, landscape, and waterworks. A Hasht

Behesht garden in Agra is attributed to the emperor Babur (1526–30), the founder of the Mughal dynasty in India, although there is no indication that this garden also had a *hasht-behesht* type pavilion.[4] Emperor Akbar's Todar Mal at Fatehpur Sikri and Sher Mandal in Delhi's "Old Fort," both datable to the mid- to late sixteenth century, represent the currency of this Timurid building type in India.[5] Numerous pavilions are recorded to have been based on the *hasht-behesht* plan and distributed throughout greater Iran, Central Asia, and India.[6] The fruits of these experiments are seen in such spectacular seventeenth-century monuments as the Taj Mahal in Agra and the Hasht Behesht Palace in Isfahan.

For our purposes, fifteenth-century Timurid and Aqqoyunlu palaces and their urban and extra-urban environments mark a key transitional period for understanding the Safavid approach in sixteenth-century Qazvin, and especially in Isfahan. When, in the middle of the sixteenth century, Shah Tahmasb, the second Safavid ruler, adopted Qazvin as his capital, new construction, especially at the royal precinct, drew from but also transformed those pasts. The palace ensembles of the fifteenth-century Timurids and the Aqqoyunlu clarify how the relationship of the ruler and the ruled was architecturally delineated in cities, especially with regard to the distance of the principal palaces from urban centers. The imperial landscape of Isfahan in the second century of Safavid rule, including its functionally and architecturally distinctive palaces, can be traced to this time of great change. The era straddles, on one side, the fifteenth-century Turco-Mongol and Sunni-Sufi notions of kingship and its related architecture and ceremonials, and on the other, the Perso-Shi'i concepts of kingship. The latter evolved out of religious and ethnic tensions between the Sunni orthodoxy's dominance in the Persianate world and the emergent Twelver Shi'ism of the Safavid state, and also between the long-established and sedentary Persian (Tajik) bureaucratic class and nobility and the newly empowered tribal confederacies of the Turkmen aristocracy of the Qezelbash (Red Heads) with whose support the Safavid family rose to imperial dominance.

The capital city at Tabriz

Contrary to the normative practices of the late medieval period, Shah Isma'il maintained Tabriz, the capital of his foes, as his center of rule.[7] Such continuity, despite the violent termination of one dynasty at the sword of the other, calls into question most expectations of Islamicate kingship practices. A closer examination of this rather aberrant choice by Shah Isma'il and his followers reveals the peculiarities of the Safavid ascent and the urban-palatine representations of the transition from the old Sunni-Sufi, Turco-Mongol form of kingship to the new Shi'i-Sufi Perso-Turkic dispensation.

For the Safavid family (*dudman*) and their Qezelbash allies, Tabriz represented a geographical and psychological nexus of authority, power, and legitimacy. Shah Isma'il's family lineage and early life were tightly entwined with that of the Aqqoyunlu aristocracy. Through his mother, Halime Begi Agha (or Alamshah Khatun), he was a grandson of the Aqqoyunlu Soltan Uzun Hasan, while his father, Haydar b. Junayd Safavi, was a nephew of Uzun Hasan.[8] The reign of Uzun Hasan had already initiated the transformation from a clan-based polity (confederation of Turkmen tribal chiefs) to a Perso-Islamic agrarian empire that aimed to refashion the relationship between the shah and the subject populations of sedentary peoples. Shah Isma'il was heir to these changing circumstances. In addition to his inside track at the court of the Aqqoyunlu in Tabriz, Isma'il had also inherited the leadership of the Safaviyye Order from his father.

It was from Ardabil, the city east of Tabriz where an important ancestral Safavid shrine and the home of the Safaviyye Sufi Order were located, that Isma'il and his Qezelbash followers burst onto the political scene in western Iran and eastern Anatolia (Figure 1.2). The paternal shrine of Shaykh Safi al-Din had become the locus of growing militancy and millenarianism in the aftermath of the 1488 murder of Isma'il's father at the behest of the Aqqoyunlu Soltan Yaqub and his allied clans.[9] Forces in Ardabil gathered momentum around the Sufi concept of the *ensan-e kamel*, the Perfect Man – and the Safaviyye brotherhood and its Sufi Qezelbash community of devotees and disciples found its embodiment in the youthful Isma'il. Extremist Shi'i beliefs, centered on notions of sacral kingship and the theophany of the shah, opened the way for understanding the shah as the representative of the Imams, especially the Hidden Imam. In the context of the mystical master-disciple relationship, the Safavid shah's devotion to the Imam represented the ideal model for that of the Qezelbash disciples to the shah. In turn, the aspirations of the Qezelbash for spiritual and political ascendancy were linked to the station of Isma'il as shah, who also was believed by the Safaviyye Order to possess the charisma of their supreme master, Shaykh Safi-al-Din.

The conflict between the Aqqoyunlu Yaqub and his short-lived successors, on the one hand, and the Safaviyye brotherhood (among other rival groups), on the other, resulted in the strengthening of the political and popular power of the Safaviyye dissenters, the elevation of Isma'il to the throne in 1501, and the eventual installation of the Safavid Imami-Shi'i dispensation. As John Woods has argued, the Isma'il-Qezelbash mandate was to purge the realms of "Aqqoyunlu transgressions against God and His representatives – the house of Ali b. Abi Talib and the family of Shaykh Safi al-Din Ishaq."[10] The convergent agendas also included restoring the paramount authority of the spiritual and temporal powers associated with the family of the

Prophet, especially through Imam Ali and his successors, as well as the structural and spiritual order of the Safaviyye brotherhood. These goals were welded together as the two-pronged, legitimizing sword of justice. Shah Isma'il's rise to power was followed by the en masse extermination of the Aqqoyunlu aristocracy and support system. The shah and his confederates, furthermore, did not hesitate to exact personal vengeance against those who, along with Soltan Yaqub, were involved in the campaign against Haydar, Isma'il's father; their remains were exhumed and incinerated, while all the pregnant princesses were slaughtered.

Shah Isma'il's appropriation of the city of Tabriz as the capital of his new dynasty runs counter to the more common practice of shedding the fetters of the defeated past in favor of a new beginning; this is especially glaring given the conflicted circumstances. Even more striking was his willingness to stage royal ceremonies in the urban-palatine ensemble of his grandfather Uzun Hasan and his foe Yaqub. Still, according to Woods, the continuity achieved by situating the locus of power in Tabriz and its palaces may well have been understood as a dynastic continuity, probably in the time of Isma'il as much as in the later Safavid official view.[11] Shah Tahmasb's historian Qazi Ahmad-e Qomi noted that "That eminence [Shah Isma'il] was [from] the eldest son of Sultan Junayd and the nephew [sister's son] of Hasan Padishah [Uzun Hasan]; and because of these two considerations, the luster of sovereignty and guidance radiated from his august brow." Again, as Woods has interpreted it, this should be taken to stand for "the union of the spiritual authority of the Safavid order and the worldly domination of the Aqqoyunlu Empire."[12]

The maydan-palace ensemble in Tabriz

Tabriz possessed a *qal'e*, a fortified citadel on the hillsides east of the city. A single palace stood on the site when Shah Isma'il came to power, but, as Romano says, it was uninhabited and presumably not habitable.[13] Given the common aversion in the Persianate practice to reusing the palaces of deposed rulers, Isma'il's appropriation of the Hasht Behesht Palace expresses a strong link between the past and present in this early Safavid discourse (Plate 1).[14] Uzun Hasan's Hasht Behesht was located in the Eshratabad Gardens and served as the Daulatkhane in Tabriz.[15] This ensemble comprised the residential and administrative heart of the household and court. It appears that the Hasht Behesht was somewhat separated from Tabriz by one of the two rivers that ran through the city.[16] According to Romano, "The palace is built in the centre of a large and beautiful garden, close to the city, with only a stream dividing them to the north."[17] In addition, and quite significantly, Tabriz was "like Venice" in Romano's assessment – it was without walls, although the city relied on the fortifications provided by the surrounding mountains and hills for its protection.[18]

The Hasht Behesht Palace, the central feature of the entire ensemble, was located on a terrace and was, according to some sources, where Uzun Hasan and his successors held audiences when in residence in the city. Romano's description indicates that the Hasht Behesht served as a ceremonial edifice, while another building in its vicinity became the living quarters (harem): "About a bowshot from the palace [the Hasht Behesht] there is a harem of one storey, so large that a thousand women might conveniently live there in different rooms." The harem apartments seem to have been built as a single edifice – a fact deduced from Romano's statement that

> Among the rooms is a large one like a hall, with the walls all adorned with gold and plaster, looking like emerald and many other colours. The ceiling of this harem is ornamented with gold and ultramarine. From this hall there are many chambers on every side, with all the doors superbly decorated with gold and blue, and many signs and letters made of mother of pearl, in beautiful patterns.

As with the adjacent ceremonial Hasht Behesht and many such textually known pavilions, water was incorporated into the building: "through the centre of this hall flows a stream of pure water, a cubit in breadth and as much deep."

Here, it is worth introducing a cautionary note. As discussed in Chapter 1, the European lens is not only tinted by the very fact that it was an outsider's perspective of an utterly different cultural world; it is also often mired in exaggerated claims of privileged access. No European could have toured the harem, for example, when the harem was in residence. Nevertheless, it was possible for them either to have seen the places inside the complex while the court was away or else to have been given descriptions by harem eunuchs; both procedures were recorded by later travelers such as Jean Chardin. Moreover, our reliance on descriptive sources, necessitated by the total loss of archaeological evidence, renders any reconstruction largely conjectural and at times quite confusing.[19] For example, was this Daulatkhane the same as the one noted during the 1540 visit by the Venetian Cypriot Michele Membré in his *Relazione* (letters) to the Signory, the Venetian government?[20] Membré's words, "they were *rebuilding* the house of Shah Tahmasb," and features of his description indicate that this was the same Eshratabad that Isma'il had inherited from his Aqqoyunlu predecessors with, perhaps, some new buildings added since 1510.[21] Such an ensemble, indeed nearly a hundred years old by the time of Shah Tahmasb, may have needed some updating and refreshing, but as far as can be ascertained, Tahmasb did not build a whole new palace ensemble in Tabriz.

Instead, at about this same time or soon after, he concentrated on building a new capital city in Qazvin and its royal abode, to which we will turn later in this chapter.

Similarly vexing are references to a recreational pool or lake at the court in Tabriz and to Isma'il's boating excursions on a massive pool when he was a young boy living at the court in Tabriz, as well as after he became the shah. Shah Tahmasb was also said to have gone boating in the same body of water.[22] In Romano's 1510 description, the pool is clearly located in the courtyard of the unfinished, colossal fourteenth-century Mosque of Ali Shah. In Membré's 1540 description, what appears to be this same pool is obliquely and circuitously linked with the palace of Shah Tahmasb. The conflation of these two references has led some scholars to suggest that the Mosque of Ali Shah and the palace were so adjoined as to allow the court to use the pool for leisure activities.[23] Romano's description, however, leaves little doubt that the two were quite separate, although one may also conclude that a public square (maydan) formed the urban space of separation between the two. At any rate, since the unfinished mosque did not serve as a mosque, its pool, and especially the little stone-pillared kiosk in its midst, could also have offered a place for courtly flirtations in the outdoors.

Michele Membré's 1540 description of the interior of the garden-palace ensemble records a painfully confusing sequence of chambers, halls, courtyards, gardens, rivulets, and varying functions. Whatever additions may have been made since Romano's visit in 1510, one can clearly deduce from the two accounts that the Hasht Behesht and the harem buildings were the principal royal structures within the walled garden precinct.[24] The other edifices appear to have been associated with the three gates of the precinct and were used for ceremonies and to regulate traffic in and out of the royal domain.

The precinct gates marked the termini of the axial alleys that subdivided the royal precinct into a *chahar bagh*, a four-quadrant garden: all four alleys led to the Hasht Behesht Palace (Figure 2.1). The south gate had an ayvan (a pointed-arch frame containing a vaulted space), as Romano's description "arched with bricks" indicates. Romano says that it was not very large, but beyond this relatively modest entrance gate was located a "gallery, a bowshot in length and six paces broad, which from one end to the other has seats of the finest marble, with a kind of railing with a design, as an ornament in relief of plaster, of various colours, quite a wonder to behold from the excellence of the workmanship." This was a long and narrow pillared hall, with "columns of fine marble," a row of marble seats at its back and an equally long pool in front that was "always full of water . . . In it there are always four or five couple of swans; around it there are rose trees and jessamines, and a smooth road leading direct to the royal palace." From Romano's description, it appears that this delightfully open gallery with its scenic setting was probably intended for private royal use, much like a "summer-house" that he says was attached to the harem apartments, where "the queen and her maidens" stay "to do needlework, according to their custom."

Whereas the south gate appears to have been a harem gate, the one on the north side consisted of a complex of buildings and courtyards that served public functions. According to Romano, here was a "certain place like a cloister, paved with brick, with seats of marble round it. This place is so large that it will hold three hundred horses, as the lords who came to the court used to dismount here when Assambei was reigning." This passage suggests that the lords had dismounted in this forecourt only during the reign of Uzun Hasan and that the practice had lapsed by Shah Isma'il's time even though the Safavid shah occupied this same ensemble during his sojourns in Tabriz. Having gathered at this forecourt of the royal precinct at Tabriz, those summoned for audiences or business at the Hasht Behesht would pass through a magnificently decorated gateway that was, according to Romano's enthusiastic description,

> an arch fifteen yards high and four yards wide, beautifully worked in plaster from top to bottom. The door is made of marble, in one square carved piece . . . The rest of the marble is cut into designs, and when it is exposed to the rays of the sun it shines so brilliantly on both sides, that it appears like crystal, since the marbles found in Persia do not resemble ours, but are much finer; they are not opaque, but are more a species of crystal.[25]

Beyond this "lordly door" was the "fine paved road" that led to the Hasht Behesht.

The third entranceway into the Aqqoyunlu royal precinct in Tabriz, still in use during the Safavid period, was on the east side and, Romano tells us, faced "an immense maidan or piazza." The gate that led from the Eshratabad gardens to the maydan was surmounted by "a large edifice with many rooms, and a covered hall looking over the garden." On the maydan side was "an arched gallery," into which "Assambei used to retire with many lords whenever a feast was made on this maidan, and frequently when ambassadors came they used to put them up here, as it was a fine place and had many apartments." Romano's description also notes that "This door is further than the others from the royal palace, with a splendid view of the maidan, on which are the mosque and the hospital" he had mentioned earlier. No other feature of the maydan is recorded except that "a wall only" spanned the gap between the mosque and the hospital.[26]

Membré adds to this description that the maydan was "very neat and level and large; and in the middle of the said square there is a tall pole, which is of wood, with a gilded apple on the top," a reference to a popular equestrian game played in Safavid times.[27] Curiously, he says that there were three mosques on this maydan: two, side by side, on the north side, which had presumably survived from earlier times, and a third mosque that he claims was under construction in 1540 on the orders of Shah Tahmasb. Such an unlikely configuration – nowhere do we find three mosques located so close to one another in a comparable sort of public space – must be attributed to Membré's failing memory, since he gives only a few words to this entire maydan ensemble.[28] Notwithstanding the utter confusion over the number, scale, and date of mosque(s) structures in this location, the maydan in Tabriz was most likely an assortment of buildings erected by Uzun Hasan, Soltan Yaqub, Shah Isma'il, and Shah Tahmasb in successive campaigns of construction and refurbishment prior to the destruction wrought during Ottoman attacks and occupations.

This maydan and its adjoining Daulatkhane precinct represent what must be considered a conventional formula in Persianate urban planning. Similar juxtapositions informed, for example, Seljuq Isfahan, as well as the maydan-palace ensembles of Safavid Qazvin and Isfahan, discussed in greater detail in the next chapter. It suffices here to note that the maydan in Tabriz – like all those that preceded the Maydan-e Naqsh-e Jahan (Image of the World Square), the principal imperial urban center in Safavid Isfahan – intimates urban enunciations of kingship in ways that become emphatically delineated and performed only in the Isfahan phase of Safavid rule. Some of the potentialities of the ceremonials of kingship in the Safavid period are already exploited in Uzun Hasan's maydan-daulatkhane juxtaposition. The "arched gallery" at the eastern gate onto the maydan in Tabriz, for example, afforded "a splendid view" of the maydan, and there the shah would entertain his honored guests when feasts were held at the maydan. Other aspects, such as the way this ceremonial space marked the threshold between the public and private zones of royal display and discourse, also proved important for the later Isfahan developments. Although Romano's reference, written decades after Uzun Hasan's reign, has the character of hearsay, it preserves at least the memory of such ceremonials of access and visibility. In the following century, the confederate form of kingship implied in Romano's account is re-formed into the absolutist polity of the Safavids, whose imperial practices of proximity and distance assume radically different ceremonial, spatial, and architectural characteristics.

In the Tabriz of Uzun Hasan, Shah Isma'il, and Shah Tahmasb, the Hasht Behesht appears to have constituted the sole formal ceremonial palace in the entire urban ensemble. Otherwise, and presumably for larger gatherings, the maydan and the gardens provided additional spaces of ceremony. For a festival in February 1540, according to Membré, for example, "in the square where he [Shah Tahmasb] is with his court, they place pavilions in rows."[29] These tented pavilions, decorated with carpets and textiles, served as gathering places for the guests, courtiers, and of course the shah himself. His special royal tent included a throne, "a seat of gilded wood, covered with

velvet." We shall return to this festival and its feasting ritual in the
final chapter. For now, however, it is worth noting that such festivities – in this case, probably related to *id al-fitr*, which marks the end
of the month of fasting – were brought out into the public domain of
the maydan, where "the people of the land and the soldiers, an infinite number, stand all around by the walls [of the maydan] and in the
streets." The Hasht Behesht Palace in the Daulatkhane of Tabriz
could not possibly have accommodated the required display of hospitality, generosity, and valor of the magnitude described by Membré
with its multitudes of people, from among both courtly circles and
the citizenry, lining the maydan periphery and cheering the equestrian games and performances in which the shah would take part as
well.[30]

Topographies of rule

Aloofness from the urban display of palatine grandeur is part of a pervasive Turco-Mongol pastoralist practice in which the idea of a
capital city was predicated on mobility – the center of rule was wherever the ruler resided. The Turkic and Mongol overlords of the
Persianate world, whose far-reaching dominions had been gained and
had to be maintained through warfare, relied on the nomadic practices of their Inner and Central Asian roots. The combination of a pas-
toral way of life and the needs of warfare required constant
movement of the court and government from city to city and
between geographical regions. Such patterns of movement must also
be considered in light of the seasonal mobility whereby the whole
clan would seek cooler or warmer climes in summer or winter.

In the fourteenth century, for example, Tabriz was one among
several Ilkhanid "capitals"; Maraghe and Soltaniyye were the other
cities of rule, and the ancient site of Takht-e Solayman served as a
summer palace. The Turkmen clans that ruled western Iran and
eastern Anatolia during the fifteenth century continued to move
about as well, despite the centrality of Tabriz to their particular confederate configuration of rule.[31]

The fifteenth-century Timurid imperial household assumed similar
peripatetic practices: Samarqand and the nearby Shahrisabz, Herat,
and Shiraz each served as the capital at different times. Timur's
Samarqand had its rival capital at the old city of Kesh, which lay close
to the village where Timur had been born. Kesh was renamed
Shahrisabz (The Green City) by Timur, who lavished resources on a
monumental building campaign to turn this into a second imperial
capital nine leagues to the south of the ancient Samarqand on the Silk
Road. Babur wrote that "Temür Beg, who was born and raised in Kish,
endeavored to make it his capital and had superb buildings constructed there."[32] His famous Aq Saray (The White Palace), the gigantic royal garden-palace in Kesh, was still incomplete when the city

was visited in 1404 by Ruy Gonzalez de Clavijo, the chamberlain of King Henry III of Castile and one of the Spanish ambassadors dispatched to forge anti-Ottoman alliances with their powerful common foe, the Turks.[33] Clavijo received an audience in Samarqand, too, where he describes the ceremonies that took place at "a great orchard, with a palace therein, where Timur was in residence, and this . . . lay some distance without the city."[34] Many of the imperial ceremonial affairs of Timur were conducted either in garden pavilions and tents that ringed Samarqand or at the encampment set up wherever the great conqueror took rest: both may be exemplified by depictions from Safavid and Mughal manuscripts of the fifteenth and sixteenth centuries (Plates 1 and 2).

To the ruling elite in all these instances, the socio-political importance of the city was secondary to that of the royal encampment, which could assume the scale of a city with all its associated amenities. Whether in traditional resting and grazing spots well beyond cities, in the vicinity of urban centers, or at the frontier regions for the conduct of war, it was the encampment that enunciated through its grandeur – the size and number of tents as well as the costly materials with which they were built – the spatial, architectural, and ceremonial dimensions of kingship (Plate 2).[35]

This elasticity of the concept of a capital city is evident in the Turco-Mongol habits of seasonal moves between the cold and warm climates and between verdant and arid lands, a practice known in Turkic terms as *yaylaq* and *qeshlaq*, summer and winter encampments or quarters.[36] As a place for a restorative time of retreat, the yaylaq was, and remains, associated with greenery, cool air, and extra-urban and countryside locales. Yaylaq was where summer months were spent in temperate weather and green meadows far away from the urban heat and its nearby parched lands. Any permanent architectural accommodations at a yaylaq consisted of open and airy pavilions that took advantage of the mild climate and cooling breezes in gardens, atop mountains, and beside lakes. This notion of retreat was the aristocratic by-product of a purely pragmatic need and reflected the waning of pastoralism rather than its enduring relevance. Yaylaqs were in fact the lush grazing fields of the uplands to which nomadic tribes hastened when hot weather dried out the meadows in the lowlands. In contrast to yaylaq, the qeshlaq was associated with the warmer lowlands for wintering and could be linked to the encampments in the vicinity of cities. Shah Isma'il's successive qeshlaqs in Tabriz, Herat (at the Bagh-e Eram), Qom, and Isfahan, recorded by the historian Amir Mahmud ibn Khwand Amir, exemplify the link between winter residence and urban centers.[37] In most instances, the shah stayed at encampments outside the city or tented pavilions within gardens on the outskirts of the city for the duration of the sojourn while he engaged in hunting.

The dual practice of yaylaq and qeshlaq reflected the military and economic necessity of mobility, not a romanticized desire for freedom from the stifling confines of urban life, as nomadic ways of being have so often been portrayed. Neither Timur nor Uzun Hasan, or any of their cultural progeny, lived the bare-essentials-on-horseback nomadic life that cinematic and literary portrayals have led us to believe in. They set up empires and lived imperial lives of worldly sophistication that drew from urban institutions – guilds and workshops, madrasas and mosques, bazaars and caravanserais. Timur famously took as war booty artists, craftsmen, and architects from every city he conquered and transferred them to Samarqand to form his imperial workshops. Yet, in keeping with the Turco-Mongol traditions of confederate rule and its reciprocal obligations, the chief (the Islamicate emir and sultan and the Persianate shah) roamed his territories, mustered armies from potential allies, subjugated the rebellious, and persuaded the doubtful. In other words, the conduct of kingship necessitated the king's presence, often with sword in hand. The regeneration of nomadic Turkic domination, through Timur's conquests, and its associated clan wars and ways of life in the fifteenth century renewed cultural tensions with the Perso-Islamic urban world. How, then, did this yaylaq-qeshlaq formula accommodate the urban-architectural needs of the increasingly sedentary polities of the early modern period?

The bipartite city of rule

In the yaylaq-qeshlaq Persianate practice neither the garden and its palace or pavilion nor the encampment serves the same function vis-à-vis the city as does the Italian villa or the *munya* (agricultural estate) of Islamic Spain.[38] The Italian villa is counterpoised by the city palazzo; the munya by the urban citadel-palace. In these examples, the centrality of the urban seat of authority remains implicit in the dialogic relationship between the intra-mural palace and the extra-mural agricultural estate and retreat. In contrast, urban expressions of kingship among the Turco-Mongol tribal confederacies in the thirteenth to fifteenth centuries represent a bipartite phenomenon of rule. At "capital" cities in this period, intra-mural life was enhanced monumentally with the royal patronage of mosques, madrasas, *khanqahs* (dervish hostels), mausoleums, caravanserais, hospitals, soup kitchens, workshops, and bazaars. Yet the princely abode of felicity, the *daulatkhane* or the imperial residence-cum-administrative center, remained outside the urban confines.

Timurid gardens that ringed the cities of rule – Samarqand or Herat, for example – were the principal royal residences and not some out-of-town retreat subsumed to an urban palace precinct.[39] Timur's Aq Saray at Shahrisabz was an enclosure with a series of enormous buildings and open spaces.[40] The descriptions by the Spanish ambassador Clavijo convey the immensity of the complex, which comprised a monumental entrance gateway with chambers and galleries for special guards and waiting guests (the remains of which are the only parts extant), a huge courtyard with arcades around its periphery, a second formal gateway beyond which stood a large audience chamber with numerous attendant rooms, apartments and banqueting hall for the harem, and a vast orchard and garden beyond. Clavijo's account further makes note of the magnificence of the blue and gold tilework. Even so, as grand as the Aq Saray was, and notwithstanding its distance from Samarqand, where most ceremonial events were held, the architectural and decorative features of this palace could scarcely compete with the enormity and luxury of the tentage at royal encampments of Timur in the vicinity of Samarqand.

Shahrisabz, in any event, was the royal city complementing Samarqand, the urban center of rule. The relationship between the two was comparable to that between Samarra and Baghdad. In 836, the Abbasids abandoned the imperial capital of Baghdad, which was designed according to an ideal plan but was disastrous in practical terms – it had been conceived as a nimbus, with the palace–mosque–government ensemble at the center of a round, walled city.[41] In place of what proved to be a problematic capital city erected on the scale of a palace, Samarra was built as a palace on the scale of a city, many kilometers away from the subject populations of the capital. The Samarran model informed many other palaces, from the Spanish Umayyad Madinat al-Zahra to the Ottoman Topkapı.[42] Yet, rarely did the schizophrenia of the Abbasid paradigm, with its segregation of the popular and the palatine cities, find any echoes in the subsequent history of Islam.

The bipartite city of rule in the Turco-Mongol tradition was not intended to establish twin cities for the subjects and the masters. Rather, the Central Asiatic nomadic habits of yaylaq–qeshlaq fused with the sedentary urban life of the Persianate world to create an urban–royal paradigm in which the extra-mural gardens and their permanent features – the pools, water channels, landscaping, and small pavilions and kiosks – were supplemented with elaborate tent architecture. As an admixture of nature–culture or wilderness–cultivation, these tented and mobile royal abodes, be they pitched in gardens near or within cities of rule or in meadows away from urban settlements, dominated the landscape of kingship in the Islamic world from Istanbul to Samarqand. The yaylaq–qeshlaq dynamic was variously adopted and adapted, to suit the discourse of kingship, by Ottoman sultans, Safavid shahs, and Mughal emperors in their respective dominions. Such politico-social transformations crystallized in the form of an urban-centered absolutism during the sixteenth and seventeenth centuries.

Scholars generally agree on the preceding characterization of palatine paradigms. What remains to be reconsidered – and, indeed, revised – is the assumption of the primacy of Timurid practices and their architectural and urban model. The scholarly "classicization" of the fifteenth-century Persianate cultural hybrid of the Timurids has imposed a perspective in which everything that came in their wake is inevitably found to owe its forms to the generative cultural powers of the Timurid period. In such a scheme, which has been vigorously applied to the Safavid world because of its shared cultural sphere of operation, everything post-Timurid is a mere variation on the Timurid.

The Aqqoyunlu alternative

As already noted, the fifteenth century also witnessed the rise and fledgling control of Turkmen clan confederacies in the western and northwestern territories of the Persianate world. The mobility and peripatetic lifestyle of the Turkmen dynasties of the Qaraqoyunlu (Black Sheep; 1380–1468) and the Aqqoyunlu (White Sheep; 1378–1508) required Timurid-style flexibility regarding the concept of a capital city and encampment practices. Cities such as Tabriz, which embodied a seemingly firm idea of a capital city in the time of Uzun Hasan, could just as well be abandoned at will.

The Aqqoyunlu Soltan Yaqub, for example, virtually deserted his capital, Tabriz, after an incident in 1486 that led to a popular revolt in the city.[43] A Turkmen soldier had murdered a wealthy Armenian merchant for refusing to convert to Islam. In punishment, the soldier was beheaded, and Yaqub's men delivered the head to the Armenians, who took vengeance by kicking it around in the streets of their quarter. This propelled the Muslim community, and especially the religious class, who were led by the Naqshbandi Dervish Qasem, to seek permission from the sultan to bury the soldier. The funeral turned into a protest march in front of the palace precinct and resulted in the arrest and murder of the popular Dervish Qasem at the hands of Soltan Yaqub and his courtiers. The Muslim population of Tabriz reacted with an explosive uprising against the sultan; the revolt was brutally put down by Yaqub, who unleashed his soldiers to plunder the city. As Woods suggests, the animosity between the Aqqoyunlu court and the urban religious communities may have contributed to the abandonment of Tabriz and the royal residence, including the Hasht Behesht Palace, which Yaqub had only recently completed.

Nevertheless, it was the Aqqoyunlu Tabriz, especially as conceived by Uzun Hasan, that offered to the youthful Shah Isma'il a particularly relevant urban-palatine solution, a more accessible and politically better-situated alternative in affirming his own succession and legitimacy than the one suggested by the Timurids. Indeed, after Isma'il took Tabriz as his capital, he made few urban-architectural interventions of his own. The Hasht Behesht Palace, which served as Isma'il's Daulatkhane, remained largely unchanged as well. Shah

Isma'il's reign, characterized by its continual state of war – wars of conquest (such as in the Khorasan region in northeastern Iran and Central Asia) as much as wars of conflict (against the Ottomans in the west and the Uzbeks in the east, for example) – yielded very little in the way of monumental architectural representations.[44] His adoption of the Tabriz-Ardabil nexus of power suggests something of the predicament of an imperial world in the making, just as it may very well reflect the complex nature of the Safavid agenda, which was both a continuation and a radical reform of the Aqqoyunlu Empire.

The urban ensemble of a maydan–daulatkhane in Tabriz prefigures those conceived by Shah Tahmasb's urban designers in Qazvin and Shah Abbas the Great's in Isfahan. In all these instances, the emphasis is on the link between the "abode of felicitous rule," or the royal enclosure of residence–governance, and urban life by the use of such public spaces as an equestrian maydan (a hippodrome) for martial practices and public entertainment. In Tabriz, such a maydan was enclosed by a simple wall dotted with what appear to have been three important monuments: the massive gate into the palace precinct on its west side and, within this same circumference, "a fine mosque . . . built with a rich and useful hospital attached." Nothing similar to the purposeful architectural-functional dialogue across the space of the maydan that we shall see at Isfahan, however, is implied by the Tabriz ensemble. Isma'il, moreover, seems to have built little in Tabriz that would have altered the Aqqoyunlu royal precinct or maydan.

What is obvious, yet worth highlighting here, is that Shah Isma'il's reign was driven by forces and sources different from those of his Timurid or Aqqoyunlu predecessors. Isma'il founded a new dynastic rule on the basis of decades spent roaming across vast territories for the sake of conquering and consolidation of his dominion. This is not the same as having a nomadic habit or simply preferring a peripatetic existence. Despite Isma'il's constant movements, the Safavid royal household mastered some fundamental aspects of its patronage obligations within the realm of Persianate cultural practices related to the production of courtly arts.[45] The Safavid court refurbished the famed royal *ketabkhane* of Tabriz – itself a repository of masterworks and knowledge of generations of artists who had produced some of the greatest examples of Persian painting since the Ilkhanid times early in the fourteenth century.[46] To the already stellar roster of the Tabriz atelier, which included such names as Soltan Mohammad, Shah Isma'il and Shah Tahmasb added master painters such as Behzad, whose work had revolutionized the Timurid style of painting at the *ketabkhane* in Herat. From this early Safavid enterprise a brilliantly distinctive style coalesced out of the Turkmen (Tabriz) and Timurid (Herat) styles; its choicest fruit was the spectacularly illustrated and illuminated copy of the *Shahname* datable to the 1520s–30s and known as the *Shahname* of Shah Tahmasb.[47]

In both its circumstances of production and its iconographic program, this *Shahname* manuscript provides compelling evidence of the gradual crystallization of the notion of a capital city in the Safavid ideology of rule. The blending of the ateliers of the defeated dynasties was complemented by a carefully choreographed scheme in which depictions of the stories of the legendary and historical Persian kings and their perennial battles with enemies and evildoers from beyond the borders of Iran stood in for the role the Safavid shahs assumed in restoring the ancient glories of Iran in the face of mighty antagonists such as the Ottomans and Uzbeks at its peripheries.[48] As Timur had done in Samarqand, Isma'il brought to Tabriz the masters of all the arts and crafts from his conquered lands. The impact of the encounter between these cultural and visual worlds is beyond the present discussion. The point here is that the centralized production of firmly established Persianate icons of imperial authority such as the *Shahname* was welded together with the centralization of rule – even if as yet only in potential – in the context of a capital city.

Adopting Tabriz as the Safavid capital, however, did not preclude the desire, or need, to construct an alternative, even competitive, royal abode. Isma'il set out to revive the ruined city at Khoy, an area on the northwestern frontiers where troops were traditionally mustered. He raised, among other buildings, "a large palace . . . which in the Persian tongue is called Douler Chana, signifying," as Romano says, the "pleasant abode."[49] Here he had built a walled garden-palace, which is described by Romano as a single-vaulted pavilion at the center of a garden. Isma'il also had erected, "before the gate which looks west," three round turrets that were fashioned out "of the horns of Namphroni stags, and it is considered that there are none like them in the world." The allusion to a *hasht-behesht* type of building (a single-vaulted pavilion at the center of the garden) for what is in essence a hunting lodge in Khoy reinforces an impression of the malleability in function of the domed octagonal pavilion in the history of Persianate palatine architecture. We shall revisit, at length, the typology of *hasht behesht* in Chapter 5 of this book. For now we stress the fact that Isma'il chose this militarily significant spot and emphasized its richness in game, thus highlighting the significance of war and the hunt, the two key, ancient concepts of Persianate kingship. Prowess in war as much as in hunting undergirds the iconography of this palace-city and complements, in its earliest stages, the emergence of the new polity and religious dispensation of the Safavids.

Such fluidity in the configuration of power and authority vis-à-vis notions of center-periphery, or capital and empire, continued to inform early Safavid polity, although it gradually incorporated the centralization policies of Shah Tahmasb and especially Shah Abbas the Great in the middle of the sixteenth and early in the seventeenth centuries, respectively. As we shall see in the following chapter on Isfahan, throughout the Safavid period the transference of the capital cities – from Tabriz to Qazvin to Isfahan – was indivisibly intertwined with transformations in polity and the implementation of political, economic, and social reforms.

Envisioning a new beginning at Qazvin

Tabriz remained the capital until 1555/6 (965 AH), when Shah Tahmasb (1524–76) officially left the city of rule he had inherited from his father for Qazvin, a city farther "inland" from contested Safavid–Ottoman borders on the northwestern frontiers of Safavid Iran (Figures 1.1 and 1.2).[50] An old city in a region of sizeable military, urban, and agricultural significance, Qazvin was refashioned as the new capital city.[51] Unlike Tabriz, which had been converted into the center of the new Safavid order with little architectural intervention, Qazvin was subject to considerable deliberate planning. About a decade prior to the transfer of the capital, the construction of a freshly conceived Daulatkhane was set into motion (Figures 2.2 and 2.3). This Daulatkhane and its adjacent public square were designed to articulate, in urban-architectural and functional–ceremonial terms, the prerequisites and prerogatives of a *maqqarr-e saltanat* (seat of sovereignty). The transfer of the capital also marked the conclusion, at least for a while, of the Safavid-Ottoman hostilities, as agreed in the Treaty of Amasya in 1554/5.

The court's official move to Qazvin and the signing of the peace treaty with the Ottomans coincided with another momentous decision. This was Shah Tahmasb's 1556 "Edict of Sincere Repentance," the formal decree of renunciation (*taube*) of "undisciplined passions," that included dancing, music, wine, sodomy, and the magical pleasures of painting.[52] Tahmasb's "Sincere Repentance," recounted in his *Tazkere* (*Memoirs*) as a self-portrait of piety, stood in sharp opposition to the esoteric and mystical practices of his father, Shah Isma'il, and the latter's Qezelbash devotees and supporters. Instead, it reaffirmed the primacy of the *shari'a* or religious law as sanctioned by the Imami community of the *ulama* and the *mujtaheds* (jurisconsults).[53] As will be the case in Isfahan as well, the city of Qazvin was conceptualized on the premise that such spiritual cleansing precipitated a new politico-religious beginning.

The link between the transfer of the capital to Qazvin and Shah Tahmasb's act of renunciation and renewal had, in fact, been forged once before. The other instance of this confluence of piety and politics took place in 1544/5, when a similar renunciation of pleasures seems to have inspired Shah Tahmasb's withdrawal of energetic patronage and maintenance of his magnificent *ketabkhane* (royal workshop–library).[54] The shah was a painter and calligrapher himself and should be counted among the most avid and discerning patrons in

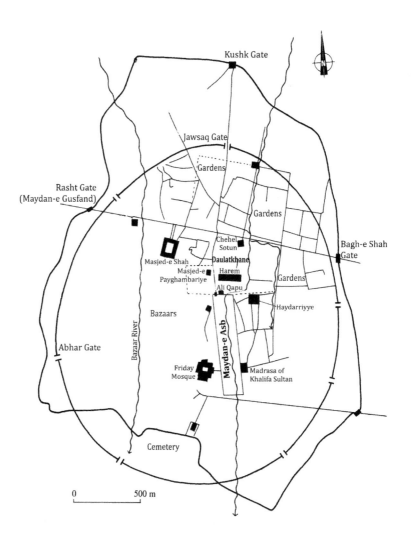

Figure 2.2 *Qazvin, schematic map (after Szuppe).*

The map marks the main features of the urban development of Qazvin
when it became the Safavid capital under Shah Tahmasb from 1555/6 until
1598. The Maydan-e Asb (hippodrome) was originally outside the medieval
city. The placement of the Safavid walled royal precinct (Daulatkhane)
north of the long and narrow public square reoriented the urban focus. The
Ali Qapu (Lofty Gate; Figures 2.3 and 2.4) provided access to the
Daulatkhane, of which only the Chehel Sotun (Plate 3 and Figure 2.6)
palace has survived. A curious fact of the sixteenth-century Safavid capitals
of Tabriz and Qazvin was the absence of imperial patronage for
congregational mosques because of the Shi'i theological debate over the
permissibility of Friday prayer during the absence of the Twelfth Imam.
The Masjed-e Shah (Royal Mosque) in this plan is of nineteenth-century
date.

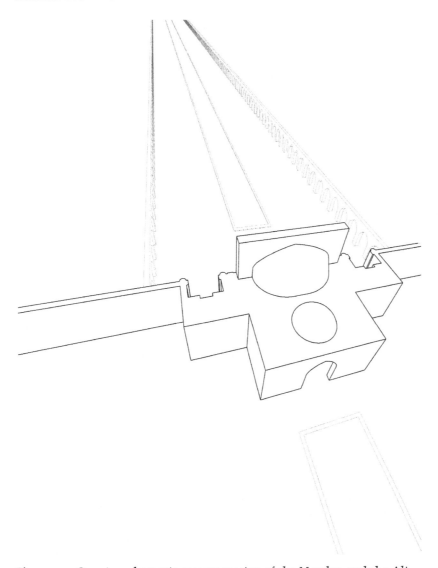

Figure 2.3 *Qazvin, schematic reconstruction of the Maydan and the Ali Qapu.*

In Safavid Qazvin, the Ali Qapu was the principal gateway through which most of the traffic to and from the court passed. Unlike the seventeenth-century Ali Qapu in Isfahan (Plate 12), it did not have any formally appointed space from which the court could view the equestrian games and martial parades at the Maydan.

the history of the Persianate production of the arts of the book. Paradoxically, the dampening of Tahmasb's enthusiasm for the works produced by the *ketabkhane* jump-started, it seems, the flourishing of other centers of production, among which the competitive market-based ateliers in Shiraz are the most noteworthy.[55] With the transfer of the capital to Qazvin, the luster of the court workshop was regained somewhat because of the need for the execution of wall paintings for some of the pavilions in the newly constructed palace precinct (Figure 2.6).[56] Nevertheless, there should be no doubt that the latter part of the sixteenth century witnessed the decentralization of the production of the arts of the book in Safavid Iran and the dispersal of the great masters in their search for more lucrative environments.[57]

It was also in 1544/5 that the urban conversion of Qazvin into the capital city had begun to take shape with the purchase of a vast stretch of land north of the walled city (Figure 2.2).[58] On the order of Shah Tahmasb, they

> called on the skilled engineers and artful builders of [Safavid] dominions [who] designed a square garden named Bagh-e Sa'adat and in the midst of that garden, [he] designed excellent buildings and lofty talars (pillared kiosks) and ayvans (vaulted porches) and pools. And the door of its gateway is built exceedingly tall and beautiful . . . The width of the garden is geometrically subdivided into square zones [with pathways] and triangular and hexagonal lawns. He made a large ('azim) stream to run through the middle of its street and planted plane and white poplar trees along its borders.[59]

This ensemble of buildings and gardens, composed as a rectangular space of about 651 by 672 meters, became known interchangeably as the Daulatkhane and the Bagh-e Sa'adatabad (Garden of Felicity).

Abdi Beg-e Shirazi, the poet and Safavid bureaucrat, was entrusted with the task of composing a descriptive encomiastic poem on the Qazvin palace precinct, a five-part poem known as *Jannat-e 'adn* (Garden of Eden).[60] Such Edenic associations were part of the crystallization of the vision of a new capital city from the outset. The 1544/5 decision to begin construction in Qazvin converged with the pietistic turn on the part of Tahmasb himself. Together, they signaled the ascendancy in Safavid polity of the legalistic Imami Shi'ism and occasioned Tahmasb's first attempt to break from the esoteric Sufi practices associated with his messiah-king father and Isma'il's Qezelbash cohorts in rule.

The palace precinct was located north of the medieval city to facilitate access to water, a scarce commodity in Qazvin. It was drawn through an extensive *qanat* system (the subterranean canals) from the mountains to the north.[61] Describing an area farther north of the Sa'adatabad precinct, Qazi Ahmad Qomi, the historian of Shah Tahmasb, indicates that the gardens in this area were taken over for the mansions of the newly transferred high society of the Safavid court and government and that these garden-mansions amounted to a city known as Ja'farabad.[62]

Whether these references may be taken as evidence of extra-mural development of the royal domain remains in doubt.[63] Abdi Beg

Shirazi's remarkable poetic description of the palace precinct in Qazvin suggests that the new structures were placed outside the old walls: "Next to Qazvin, the king of kings designed [*fekande tarh*] a city [*shahri*] with hundreds of beauties and ornamentation."[64] Given Abdi Beg's designation of Ja'farabad as a royal city next to Qazvin, it is possible to surmise, as later observers also noted, that the walls of Qazvin were in a state of disrepair. In addition, and as Szuppe has suggested, they may have been in bad enough shape by the time of the construction to allow for the integration of the new city into the old without having to consider the Daulatkhane as an extra-mural development. Nevertheless, as in Tabriz, the royal enclosure was tangential to the city proper, and a maydan or public square mediated the distance between the two.

In Qazvin, the public square was known as the Maydan-e Asb-e Shahi (the Royal Hippodrome) (Figures 2.2, 2.3 and 2.4).[65] A long, narrow rectangle of about 420 by 150 meters, this maydan was an open space that stretched south of the Sa'adatabad–Daulatkhane into the old city. As such, the Maydan-e Asb created the other focal point of the new capital city. Here, the maydan and the palace were conjoined to create a space that orchestrated both the representation and

Figure 2.4 *Qazvin, the Ali Qapu seen from the Maydan-e Asb.*

Forming a typical Persianate façade, its *pishtaq* is composed of a framed, tall ayvan (vaulted opening) flanked by smaller, superimposed niches. A doorway leads into a lofty domed chamber (Figure 2.5) with smaller rooms on either side; another one on the north side of the building opens to the Daulatkhane.

the enactment of Safavid imperial authority.[66] The Saʿadatabad
garden-palace ensemble served as the residence of the royal household and as the seat of rule. While the grandeur of the palace remained
hidden from the public eye, the performance of the prerogatives of
kingship – military parades, executions, equestrian sports, festivals,
and receptions of large ambassadorial retinues – was brought out into
the public arena of the Maydan-e Asb. The Ali Qapu gateway, a façade
composition in the familiar *pishtaq* formula of a tall ayvan opening
framed and flanked by shorter replicas of that basic form, led into the
palace precinct through a vaulted internal octagon (Figure 2.5).
Situated on the south end of the palace and the north side of the
maydan, the Qazvin Ali Qapu marked the liminal space between the
inner sanctum of the palace and the public theater of the maydan
(Figures 2.3 and 2.4). Commercial amenities such as markets and caravanserai occupied the outlying areas of the maydan.

Little is known about the architectural articulation of the periphery of the maydan. Nor is there any evidence for mosques or other

Figure 2.5 *Qazvin, the Ali Qapu, the domed octagonal chamber behind
the façade.*

The alternating of glazed and unglazed bricks and the elegance of the
radiating pattern that accentuates the loftiness of the dome give us a rare
glimpse of sixteenth-century Safavid architectural trends. The murals on
the lower walls are characteristic of sixteenth-century decorative
techniques in which floral patterns and epigraphic cartouches are subtly
raised in stucco and painted in colors. The tiled perforated window may
belong to early seventeenth-century restorations of the Ali Qapu.

major imperial foundations along its sides. The Seljuq Great Mosque of Qazvin stood at a distance from the southwestern side of the maydan, with no other mosque anywhere in the vicinity of the maydan itself, a subject to which we shall turn shortly (Figure 2.2). Nevertheless, the Maydan-e Asb and the Saʿadatabad palace together represent a significant departure from the preceding urban models. The strict geometric regularity of the maydan space itself, its alignment on the same axis with the palace precinct, and the marking of the spatial and symbolic relationship between the two loci of Safavid authority with the imperial insignia of the Ali Qapu gateway – all of these architectural and urban features of the Qazvin campaign, and the very shift in the geography of the imperial center, must be considered as key elements of the Safavid discourse of power as much in Qazvin as, we shall argue, in its heightened form in the Isfahan of Shah Abbas the Great.

The boundaries and layout of the Saʿadatabad royal precinct, like those of the maydan area, can only be traced from literary sources. Abdi Beg Shirazi's *Rauzat al-safat* and *Dauhat al-azhar*, two of the five versified descriptions of the palace area, are the most important documents on Saʿadatabad.[67] Saʿadatabad was a vast walled park separated into four quadrants by two intersecting avenues. Modeled on the classic form of the Persianate *chahar bagh* (the four-quadrant garden), the entire area was subdivided, by water channels and alleys, into numerous gardens. Some of these gardens and their buildings were used for the royal residence, the harem, or ceremonial and governmental functions. Others were given to the princes and courtiers to develop as their own garden-residences.

The two most important edifices in the palace ensemble were the *divankhane* (the chancellery or government office) and what is now known as the Chehel Sotun, a ceremonial hall (Figure 2.2 and Plate 3). As its governmental function would require, the *divankhane* stood in a garden just behind the Ali Qapu gate and near the harem.[68] The Chehel Sotun, the only building from the vast ensemble to have survived, was placed at the crossing of the two main avenues in the precinct.[69] According to both Persian and European chronicles, the Chehel Sotun was the palace where audiences and banquets took place and where the more private ceremonial functions of the court were held. Although it has been repeatedly altered in subsequent ages – its ring of heavy piers on the ground floor and the pillared balcony on the upper story are later additions – the building was clearly based on the familiar *hasht-behesht* model, a modified octagon with alternating arched openings and piers on the lower level (Figure 5.4).

According to Abdi Beg, wall paintings depicting literary themes and courtly rituals of entertainment graced the interior niches (Figure 2.6).[70] The decorative scheme must have been influential, because Abdi Beg's descriptions, and most likely pavilions such as the

Figure 2.6 *Qazvin, Chehel Sotun, interior of the ground floor.*

The interior configuration of such *hasht-behesht* types of pavilion ordinarily includes a central pool and a sequence of openings into small chambers that provide a cool respite for royal gatherings. Its damaged murals are of different dates: the raised and painted floral and vegetal patterns are probably contemporary with the building (1550s); the large figural compositions seem to have been added in the middle of the seventeenth century.

Chehel Sotun, seem to have inspired an entire generation of artists who portrayed the buildings and their murals in book paintings.[71] It is conceivable that both the architectural and the decorative schemes at Tahmasb's palace also inspired princely and elite mansions in Qazvin and elsewhere. While no such houses have survived, the pictorial evidence from the latter half of the sixteenth century is indication of their widespread popularity (Plate 1).

Like the entire maydan-palace configuration, the Chehel Sotun and its garden setting may be viewed as a transition between the Timurid *chahar-bagh* pavilions and the vastly enlarged and differently configured palaces in Safavid Isfahan. In its scale and its centralized distribution of spaces, the Qazvin Chehel Sotun is closer to Timurid pavilions in the princely gardens of Herat and Samarqand than to the palaces in seventeenth-century Isfahan, whose generously proportioned spaces were aligned along a central axis as a series of open pillared and enclosed halls.[72] But in its location at the crossing of the two main axes of the entire precinct, Tahmasb's Chehel Sotun denotes the emergence of a different understanding of the architectural representation of authority. In the Turco-Mongol steppe tradition, the palace consisted mostly of movable tents pitched according to a hierarchical order. The famed garden pavilions of the Timurids served not as the central ceremonial space but as a subsidiary unit to the more sumptuous and larger tents. In Qazvin, the Chehel Sotun was not just another pavilion in a *chahar bagh*. Rather, it occupied the physical center of the imperial precinct; it stood as the symbolic eye of the monarch, the keystone of the imperial structure that Tahmasb had so painstakingly refashioned. As the architectural representation of the nexus of power, the Chehel Sotun at Qazvin prefigures, on a smaller scale, the importance of the theme of centering in the palatine architecture of Isfahan.

The absent Imam and the congregational mosque

Given the interlace of architecture, urban space, and the Perso-Shi'i discourse of Safavid kingship, the manner of the accommodation of the public display of religious duties, especially congregational prayer, poses a particularly thorny issue in the sixteenth century. The Qazvin phase in Safavid polity displays marks of stress in the spiritual crises and socio-political tensions that it witnessed and denotes movement in its consolidation of the gains and furtherance of the influence of the Twelver Shi'i variant of kingship.

The absence of royal patronage for a major congregational mosque, be it in the capital cities of Tabriz and Qazvin or any other city in Safavid Iran, presents one of the most potent indicators of this transitional state of Safavid authority in the sixteenth century.[73] Neither Shah Isma'il nor Shah Tahmasb (or his successors until the ascent of Shah Abbas in 1588) had built a major congregational mosque in the first two capital cities or in any other Safavid city. Such mosques, built throughout the history of Islam, tended to be spacious enough to accommodate a large portion of the male population of a city at the Friday noontime prayer, the only obligatory prayer to require the presence of the congregation, hence its designation as the *Masjed-e Jom'e* or Friday Mosque. Moreover, the Friday noon prayer was ordinarily followed by a *khotbe* (sermon) delivered by an Islamic cleric (*imam jom'e*) who was appointed by the shah to this office of religious authority in the city. Notwithstanding the various ways the post and its practices were shaped throughout history, the Friday noon prayer and sermon affirmed the sovereignty of the ruling household, king, shah, emir, or sultan in whose name and under whose banners of justice the community had formed and to whom it gave its allegiance. It may at first seem surprising, then, that the first Safavid shahs did not build congregational mosques, given the immense benefits of this form of patronage for the promotion and normalization of Shi'ism.

The conversion from the dominant paradigm of Sunni orthodoxy to the emergent Twelver Shi'i legalism and its *shari'a*-based rationalist practices in the early Safavid period posed daunting problems of legitimacy.[74] In Twelver Shi'ism – especially given its expectation of the return from Occultation of the Twelfth Imam (the Mahdi or Messiah) – the imperial aspirations of the Safavids required theological acrobatics and complex webs of legitimization. The Safavids manufactured a genealogical and spiritual link to the first Shi'i Imam Ali and the family of the Prophet. Soon after the early phases of conquest, they set out to subjugate the esoteric Shi'i-Sufi beliefs and practices of their Qezelbash devotees in favor of the normative Shi'i legalism of the professional clerical class. Finally, they imported scholars from Jabal 'Amil (in southern Lebanon) to help articulate and disseminate the new dispensation.[75]

In the absence of the awaited Mahdi, Safavid authority pivoted on rule in the name of the family of the Prophet and on the maintenance of justice. Discussion about the permissibility of Friday prayer in this period of Occultation dominated legal-religious debate in the sixteenth century. It began with the pronouncement by the notable religious scholar Al-Muhaqqiq al-Karaki in 1511 that Friday congregational prayer was not obligatory until the return of the Mahdi. The period of debate concluded early in the seventeenth century, in the reign of Shah Abbas the Great, whose patronage of such famous scholars as Shaykh Lotf-Allah and Shaykh Baha'i helped lift the constraints. We shall delve more deeply into the significance of this debate in relation to the building of a congregational mosque when we turn to Isfahan. For now suffice it to say that the absence of a theological resolution to this question left the Safavid shahs in the sixteenth century bereft of the benefit of marking kingship with all the architectural icons of that tripartite enunciation of imperial authority – the interlinked spaces of the palace, the mosque, and the bazaar – that had been the normative Islamicate practice.

Preparing for Isfahan

This chapter has aimed to delineate the significance of the geographical shifts in the choice of capital cities and their associated and particularly Safavid urban-spatial forms and palatine-architectural configurations. The preceding discussions of architecture, planning, and political geography are more than a background against which Isfahan will be cast. They constitute, I argue, the essential components of the formation of the new Safavid polity.

As will also be seen in Isfahan, the centering on Qazvin was ideologically driven. We know, for example, that even before the new buildings at the Daulatkhane were ready for occupancy, the court had already moved to Qazvin by the middle of the century, choosing to reside at the old palace precinct (about which little is known) while awaiting the completion of the new. Such haste may be explained by the Ottoman threat, which imposed precarious conditions on life in Tabriz. Alternatively, and perhaps more importantly, the transfer of the capital was coordinated, and accordingly narrated, as a self-consciously staged paradigm shift. As noted earlier, several events took place in 1554/5 – the transfer of the seat of rule, the signing of the Treaty of Amasya, and the issuance of the Edict of Sincere Repentance. The official significance given to these events reveals the symbolic value placed on them as cleansing processes that preceded the narrative of the birth of a new era. The freshly conceived seat of rule in a newly refurbished capital city (the Daulatkhane and Qazvin) was sufficiently distant, in both space and time, from the beleaguered Tabriz to obscure the troublesome memories of the repeated losses of the former capital to the invading Ottoman armies and of the monumentally demoralizing defeat of Shah Isma'il and his Qezelbash armies at the hands of the Ottomans in the battle of Chaldiran in 1514.[76]

The peace treaty had sealed the potentialities of this new beginning and the opportunity to repackage the components of the empire in light of the shifts in the religious structure of the polity. In fact, the transfer of the capital is also interwoven with the beginning of a structural transformation in the Safavid household. Slave soldiers, recruited, sent in tribute, or taken by force, from among Georgian and Circassian youth, were incorporated into a new military corps that helped relieve the shah of the burden of having to share the practical military basis of his authority with the Qezelbash elite.[77]

In urban terms, Shah Tahmasb propelled the refashioning of the Twelver-Shi'i form of kingship through the building, literally, of the two foci of authority and legitimacy at Qazvin and at Ardabil, with his vast constructions at the Shrine of Shaykh Safi al-Din in the latter. As legitimacy was still deeply rooted in his ancestral lineage at this stage, Shah Tahmasb's political capital of Qazvin must have necessitated the pendant of Ardabil to make the Safavid spiritual authority whole.

By the late sixteenth century, the consolidation of Safavid polity as a centralized and absolutist enterprise was on the verge of full realization through other fundamental reforms that were set in motion by Shah Abbas the Great.[78] Like Qazvin, Isfahan was conceived in the wake of several "cleansing" procedures. The *gholam* system of slave armies, initiated by Tahmasb, assumed new powers and contours under the tutelage of Shah Abbas. In place of the *iqta'* system of Turco-Mongol practice in which land was granted to the Qezelbash chiefs in return for their loyalty and military and economic support of the Safavid household, the new elite were paid directly out of a royal treasury that had been centralized and enriched by the rapid conversion of the state lands (*mamalek*) into a royal demesne (*khasse*). Equally important in the larger shift away from earlier structures of rule, Abbas eliminated his own Qezelbash *lale* or tutor, Morshed Qoli Khan Ostajlu, who had used Abbas as a pawn in the First Civil War, which began with the death of Shah Tahmasb in 1576 and was concluded by Shah Abbas in 1590.[79] This was an act of great symbolic import insofar as it broke the conceptual umbilical cord to the Qezelbash confederacies that held together the legitimacy of the throne and that constituted the power that propelled its engine of authority.[80]

Several facets of the choice of Isfahan as the capital have been advanced and will be discussed in the next chapter. Here, another parallel should be drawn between Qazvin and Isfahan, which relates to another peace treaty. In 1590, less than three years into his reign, Shah Abbas the Great had to concede Tabriz to Ottoman occupation under the Treaty of Qostantaniyya (Constantinople).[81] The decision was calculated, it seems, to free him from troubling border conflicts on the northwestern frontiers, where he relinquished all territories to the Ottomans. Instead, he embarked on a strategy to recapture the northeastern areas from the Uzbeks, whose incursions into Khorasan had threatened that economically and spiritually rich province. (The Shrine at Mashhad served as the holiest site of pilgrimage outside Iraq for Twelver Shi'is.) Tabriz was recaptured in 1602, but just as this first capital, the site of the emergence of Safavid polity and the center of rule for the founder of the dynasty, was being handed over to the enemy in 1590, a new vista was opening onto the city of Isfahan. The construction of Isfahan as the seat of rule began in 1590/1.

Notes

1. The chronicle appears in the collection of Venetian travelers' narratives, *A Narrative of Italian Travels in Persia, in the 15th and 16th Centuries,*

trans. and ed. Charles Grey, works issued by the Hakluyt Society 49 pt. 2 (New York: B. Franklin, 1960), 173–8. It is published together with Josafa Barbaro and Ambrogio Contarini, *Travels to Tana and Persia*, trans. William Thomas and S. A. Roy, ed. Lord Stanley of Alderley, works issued by the Hakluyt Society 49 pt. 1 (New York: B. Franklin, 1964). The anonymous merchant has been identified by Jean Aubin as Domenico Romano; see his "Chroniques persanes et relations italiennes: Notes sur les sources narratives du regne de Šâh Ismâ'il Ier," *Studia Iranica* 24 (1995), 247–59.

2. *A Narrative of Italian Travels in Persia*, 174.

3. From the travel account of the Flemish Joos van Ghisele, quoted in Woods, *The Aqqoyunlu*, 137.

4. Babur's Hasht Behesht in Agra is mentioned in his memoirs; see Zahiruddin Muhammad Babur, *Baburnama: The Memoirs of Babur, Prince and Emperor*, trans. Wheeler Thackston (Washington, DC: New York; Oxford: Freer Gallery of Art and Oxford University Press, 1996), 369, 392, 408, 418 and 444. For an art-historical consideration of this garden and its pre-Indian past in Babur's history, see Catherine B. Asher, *Architecture of Mughal India*, The New Cambridge History of India I: 4 (Reprint edition, New Delhi: Cambridge University Press, 1995), 19–24. For an analysis of the Hasht Behesht, considered as the primordial Agra *chahar bagh* (four-quadrant), see Ebba Koch, "The Mughal Waterfront Garden," 140–60, esp. 140 and fn. 5.

5. Ebba Koch, *Mughal Architecture: An Outline of its History and Development (1526–1858)* (Munich: Prestel, 1991), 46 and fig. 23 for Todar Mal and 38–42 for Sher Mandal. For the Fatehpur Sikri palace-city, see Michael Brand and Glenn D. Lowry, *Akbar's India: Art from the Mughal City of Victory* (New York: The Asia Society Gallery, 1985), esp. 35–54.

6. Golombek and Wilber, *The Timurid Architecture of Iran and Turan*, 174–80; Lisa Golombek, "From Tamerlane to the Taj Mahal," in *Islamic Art and Architecture in Honor of Katharina Otto-Dorn*, ed. Abbas Daneshvari (Malibu, CA: Undena Publications, 1981), 43–50.

7. This is not to say that appropriation of the capital city of the fallen dynasty was uncommon, as the case of Constantinople demonstrates. Rather, the point here is to underscore the normative practice in Islamicate and Persianate worlds, where the abandonment of the old capital city was considered a more potent indicator of defeat than the appropriation of that city.

8. Woods, *The Aqquyunlu*, 107. Woods' work is not only the most comprehensive and cogent work on the non-Timurid, fifteenth-century history of Iran but also an excellent exposé of the complex social, cultural, political, and economic transformations from the Turco-Mongol Chingizid (Genghiz Khanid) polity to an Iranian-Islamic mode that sets the stage for the Safavid ascendancy and its revolutions; see especially pp. 1–23 and 125–38.

9. See Kishwar Rizvi, "Transformations in Early Safavid Architecture: The Shrine of Shaykh Safi al-din Ishaq Ardabili in Iran (1501–1629)" (PhD diss., Massachusetts Institute of Technology, 2000) and Rizvi, "'Its Mortar Mixed with the Sweetness of Life:' Architecture and Ceremonial at the Shrine of Safi al-Din Ishaq Ardabili during the Reign of Shah Tahmasb I," *The Muslim World* 90, no. 3/4 (Fall 2000): 323–51.

10. Woods, *The Aqqoyunlu*, 167–72 for the succession period and Isma'il-Qezelbash extermination of the Aqqoyunlu and their confederacy of clans; Woods' analysis informs the following passages.

11. Woods, *The Aqqoyunlu*, 168–9.

12. Qazi Ahmad Qomi, *Kholasat al-tavarikh*, ed. Ehsan Eshraqi, 2 vols (Mu'assase-ye Entesharat va Chap-e Daneshgah, 1359/1980), 36 and adapted from the quotation in Woods, *The Aqqoyunlu*, 168; my translation is slightly different, but the gist remains the same.

13. *A Narrative of Italian Travels in Persia*, 169–70.

14. For an overview of Isma'il's buildings, see Sussan Babaie, "Building on the Past: The Shaping of Safavid Architecture, 1501–76," in *Hunt for Paradise: Court Arts of Safavid Iran, 1501–1576*, ed. Jon Thompson and Sheila Canby (New York and Milan: Asia Society, Museo Poldi Pezzoli and Skira Editore, 2003): 26–47, esp. 27–37.

15. Woods, *The Aqqoyunlu*, 125–38 and fn. 53 for further references.

16. Descriptions of Aqqoyunlu and early-Safavid Tabriz are not always in agreement about the location and constituent features of the royal–public arenas of encounter in the city. The following picture is a composite of the sources and relies heavily on the European descriptions, especially that given by Domenico Romano, whose visit to Tabriz in 1510 fits in between the Aqqoyunlu demise and the Safavid consolidation and predates the Ottoman destructions and interventions of the post-Isma'il period.

17. *A Narrative of Italian Travels in Persia*, 173.

18. *A Narrative of Italian Travels in Persia*, 166–7.

19. The following is based on descriptions by Romano in *A Narrative of Italian Travels in Persia*, 173–8; Josafa Barbaro, whose account is contemporary to Uzun Hasan, *Travels to Tana and Persia*, 51–60; Michele Membré, *Mission to the Lord Sophy of Persia (1539–1542)*, trans. A. H. Morton (London: School of Oriental and African Studies, University of London, 1993), 29–30.

20. Membré, *Mission to the Lord Sophy*, vii–xxviii for Membré's mission and biography, and 29–31 for the palace.

21. Emphasis on "rebuilding" is mine.

22. *A Narrative of Italian Travels in Persia*, 168; Membré, *Mission to the Lord Sophy*, 30–1.

23. Morton makes this link in his footnotes to the passage by Membré, *Mission to the Lord Sophy*, fn. 1 in both pages 30 and 31.

24. Membré, *Mission to the Lord Sophy*, 29–31.

25. *A Narrative of Italian Travels in Persia*, 176–7.

26. The above quotations are from *A Narrative of Italian Travels in Persia*, 177.

27. Membré, *Mission to the Lord Sophy*, 29.

28. For another reading of Membré's description, not too different from the one offered here, see Sheila R. Canby, *The Golden Age of Persian Art: 1501–1722* (New York: Abrams, 2000), 46–7.

29. Membré, *Mission to the Lord Sophy*, 32.

30. The example of Tabriz in the fifteenth and sixteenth centuries has its corollary in Timurid Samarqand and Herat, where a similar elasticity in the ceremonial primacy of the urban royal enclosure may be found, that is, if indeed royal precincts within urban confines were in vogue at all.

31. Before Uzun Hasan moved the capital to Tabriz, the Aqqoyunlu center was at Aleppo, indicating the broader Anatolian-Syrian beginnings of the

Turkmen clans that came to rule western Iran and eastern Anatolia as an integrated dominion in the latter half of the fifteenth century; for their early history, see Woods, *The Aqqoyunlu*, 59, esp. 41.

32. Babur, *Baburnama*, 87.
33. On Kesh/Shahrisabz and Aq Saray Palace, see Clavijo, *Embassy to Tamerlane*, 206–10; Golombek and Wilber, *Timurid Architecture of Iran and Turan*, 271–5. On Timur's defeat of the Ottoman Beyazid and the European hope for an ally on the east, see Beatrice Forbes Manz, *The Rise and Rule of Tamerlane* (Cambridge: Cambridge University Press, 1989), 73ff.
34. Clavijo, *Embassy to Tamerlane*, 218.
35. On tents and tentage, see Andrews, *Felt Tents and Pavilions*.
36. C. E. Bosworth, "Yaylak (t., originally yaylagh)," *Encyclopaedia of Islam* (Brill Online, 2007).
37. Khwand Amir, *Zayl-e tarikh-e habib al-siyyar*, 66–75.
38. Scholarship on the architectural history of the Italian villas is too vast for this note; for a general study with bibliographic references see Guaita Ovidio, *Italian Villas* (New York: Abbeville Press, 2003). A case study of city palazzo versus country villa is Francesco Gianazzo di Pomparato, *Famiglie e Palazzi: dalle Campagne Piemontesi a Torino Capitale Barocca* (Turin: Gribaudo Paravia, 1997). For the *munya*, see Ruggles, *Gardens, Landscape, and Vision*, 35–7.
39. For Timurid gardens and pavilions, see Terry Allen, *Timurid Herat*, Beihefte zum Tübinger Atlas des Vorderen Orients, Reihe B, Nr. 56 (Wiesbaden: Reichert, 1983); Terry Allen, *A Catalogue of Toponyms and Monuments of Timurid Herat* (Cambridge, MA: Aga Khan Program for Islamic Architecture at Harvard University and the Massachusetts Institute of Technology, 1981); Golombek and Wilber, *Timurid Architecture of Iran and Turan*, 174–86; Lisa Golombek, "The Gardens of Timur: New Perspectives," *Muqarnas* 12 (1995): 137–47; Bernard O'Kane, "From Tents to Pavilions: Royal Mobility and Persian Palace Design," *Ars Orientalis*, 23 (1993): 249–68; Maria Subtelny, "Agriculture and the Timurid Chahārbāgh: The Evidence from a Medieval Persian Agricultural Manual," in *Gardens in the Time of the Great Muslim Empires: Theory and Design*, ed. Attilio Petruccioli (Leiden: Brill, 1997), 110–28.
40. Clavijo, *Embassy to Tamerlane*, 207–10.
41. On Baghdad and Samarra, see J. Lassner, *The Topography of Baghdad in the Early Middle Ages* (Detroit: Wayne State University, 1970); Lassner, "The Caliph's Personal Domain"; J. M. Rogers, "Samarra: A Study in Medieval Town-Planning," in *The Islamic City: A Colloquium*, ed. Albert Hourani and S. M. Stern (Philadelphia: University of Pennsylvania Press, 1970), 119–55; Alastair Northedge, "An Interpretation of the Palace of the Caliph at Samarra," *Ars Orientalis* 23 (1993): 143–70; Kennedy, *When Baghdad Ruled the Muslim World*, esp. 130–59.
42. On the Samarran reverberations, see Ruggles, *Gardens, Landscape, and Vision*, 86–109 and Necipoğlu, *Architecture, Ceremonial and Power*.
43. Woods, *The Aqqoyunlu*, 141.
44. For the ramifications of such transitional stages of conquest in the patronage of art and architecture, see Babaie, "Building on the Past," 27 and 44–6.
45. The exhibition, "Hunt for Paradise: Court Arts of Safavid Iran, 1501–1576," and its catalogue have recently considered the richly varied

and technically superior production of functional arts, including textiles, metalwork, and illuminated and illustrated manuscripts, in the early decades of Safavid rule; Jon Thompson and Sheila Canby, eds, *Hunt for Paradise: Court Arts of Safavid Iran, 1501–1576* (New York and Milan: Asia Society, Museo Poldi Pezzoli and Skira Editore, 2003), esp. 27–37.

46. For the coalescence of styles and the workings of the *ketabkhane* in Tabriz, see Sheila Canby, "Safavid Painting," in *Hunt for Paradise: Court Arts of Safavid Iran, 1501–1576*, edited by Jon Thompson and Sheila Canby (New York and Milan: Asia Society, Museo Poldi Pezzoli and Skira Editore, 2003), 72–133; Mariana Shreve Simpson, "The Making of Manuscripts and the Workings of the Kitab-khana in Safavid Iran," in *The Artist's Workshop, Studies in the History of Art*, ed. P. M. Lukehart, Center for Advanced Study in the Visual Arts, Symposium Papers 22 (Washington, DC: National Gallery of Art, 1993), 105–21.

47. For the *Shahname* of Shah Tahmasb, see Dickson and Welch, *The Houghton Shahnamah*.

48. Hillenbrand, "The Iconography of the *Shāh-nāma-yi Shāhī*."

49. *A Narrative of Italian Travels in Persia*, 165.

50. M. Mazzaoui, "From Tabriz to Qazvin to Isfahan: three phases of Safavid history," *Zeitschrift der Deutschen Morgenlaendischen Gesellschaft* (1977): 514–22.

51. Little has been written outside the Persian language on the history of the city of Qazvin in general, while most of these works have been inspired by the following: Seyyed Mohammad Ali Golriz, *Minu dar ya bab al-jannat-e Qazvin* (Tehran: Tehran University Press, 1337/1958).

52. Babayan, *Mystics, Monarchs, and Messiahs*, 319 and 308–25, where she also places the significance of the edict in the context of Tahmasb's dreams and his reconstruction of a personal narrative through his memoir, *Tazkere*.

53. The relationship between Qazvin and Isfahan in light of the conversion of Isfahan into the political and religious capital of the Safavids will be discussed in Chapter 3.

54. Canby, "Safavid Painting," 122–3, surveys the dwindling manuscript production during the later years of Tahmasb's patronage and the link between his increased superstitious religiosity and the production of an idiosyncratic manuscript known as the *Falname* or *Book of Divination*, which will be the subject of an exhibition in 2009, to be organized by Massumeh Farhad at the Freer Gallery of Art and Arthur M. Sackler Gallery, the Smithsonian Institution, Washington, DC.

55. Lâle Uluç has shown that luxury manuscripts made in the second half of the sixteenth century in Shiraz workshops were produced by blending a speculative market-based economy with a semi-secured source of patronage supplied by a steady demand for such manuscripts by the contemporary Ottoman elite; see her "Selling to the Court: Late Sixteenth-Century Manuscript Production in Shiraz," *Muqarnas* 17 (2000): 73–96 and her *Turkman Governors, Shiraz Artisans and Ottoman Collectors: Sixteenth-Century Shiraz Manuscripts* (Istanbul: İş Bankası yayınları, 2007).

56. Ehsan Echraqi, "Description contemporaine des peintures murales disparues des palais de Šâh Tahmâsp á Qazvin," in *Art et société dans le monde Iranien*, ed. Chahryar Adle (Paris: Editions Recherche sur le civilisation, 1982), 117–26.

57. Mughal India was among those more lucrative environments; see, for example, Priscilla P. Soucek, "Persian Artists in Mughal India: Influences

and Transformations," *Muqarnas* 4 (1987): 166–81, and Abolala Soudavar, "Between the Safavids and the Mughals: Art and Artists in Transition," *Iran* 37 (1999): 49–66.

58. The massive loss of evidence and the very preliminary stage of archaeological investigations at this moment in Safavid Qazvin and especially the palace precinct make it difficult to advance much further than what has already been done in an excellent article by Maria Szuppe, "Palais et Jardin: Le Complexe Royal des Premiers Safavides à Qazvin, Milieu XVI – Debut XVII Siècles," in *Sites et monuments disparus d'apres les temoignages de voyageurs*, ed. R. Gyselen, *Res Orientales* 8 (Bures-sur-Yvette: Groupe pour l'Etude de la Civilisation du Moyen-Orient, 1996), 143–77. See also such important works as Ehsan Echraqi, "Shahr-e Qazvin," in *Nazari ejmali be shahr-neshini va shahr-sazi dar Iran*, ed. M. Y. Kiyani (Tehran: Ministry of Ershad-e Eslami Publications, 1365/1986), 320–36 and Mahbubeh Amir Ghiyasvand, "Bagh-e Sa'adatabad va kakhha-ye Safaviyan dar Qazvin," in *Majjale-ye Bastan-Shenasi va Tarikh* no. 1 (Fall/Winter 1367/1988): 28–41, among others. The following discussion of Qazvin's royal ensemble depends on those articles. I would also like to acknowledge the help I have received from Ms. Afsaneh Ardabili at the Qazvin offices of the Iranian Cultural Heritage Organization.

59. Qomi, *Kholasat al-tavarikh*, 312–13.

60. For an excellent literary-cultural analysis of the 4,100-verse-long poem, see Paul Losensky, "The Palace of Praise and the Melons of Time: Descriptive Patterns in 'Abdi Bayk Sirazi's *Garden of Eden*," *Eurasian Studies* II, no. 1 (2003): 1–29. In the absence of most other evidence, this description is extremely helpful in imagining the precinct. It would be a mistake, however, to read the poem as a "realistic" description of the site when it fittingly belongs to a literary scheme of poetic commentary.

61. For the problem of irrigation and water shortages in Qazvin, see Szuppe, "Palais et Jardins," 147–50.

62. Qomi, *Kholasat al-tavarikh*, 399.

63. See also Szuppe, "Palais et Jardins," 150–2.

64. The description is titled *Dauhat al-azhar* and constitutes the second *masnavi* (a multiple-rhyme form of poetry) of Abdi Beg Shirazi's five-part poem which is collectively known as *Jannat-e 'Adn*; see Khwaje Zayn al-Abedin Ali Abdi Beg Navidi Shirazi, *Jannat al-asmar/Zinat al-awraq/Sahifat al-Ekhlas*, ed. Abolfazl H. O. Rahimof (Moscow: Academy of Sciences of the Soviet Socialist Azarbaijan, 1979); translation of the passage, on p. 26, is mine.

65. For a summary of the sources and a good analysis of this feature of Qazvin, see Szuppe, "Palais et Jardins," 171–5.

66. The remainder of this sub-section in the chapter is adapted from my essay "Building on the Past," 42–3.

67. The most cogent analysis of the Safavid sources on the palace, including the poem, is found in Szuppe, "Palais et Jardin," especially 156–70.

68. The close relationship between the harem and the *divankhane*, also seen in Isfahan, needs further study once preliminary archaeological findings have been made available.

69. Canby, *The Golden Age*, 69; Szuppe, "Palais et Jardin," 161–3.

70. The few badly damaged wall paintings on the upper story of the Chehel Sotun are generally considered to be of the same date as the building. Their thematic and stylistic correspondence with mid-sixteenth-century paintings and the descriptions by Abdi Beg Shirazi seem to

confirm their authenticity. For the murals, see Echraqi, "Description contemporaine des peintures murales."

71. Pictorial conventions notwithstanding, such pavilions and decorative schemes may be found in manuscript paintings, especially those produced in Shiraz; for a few examples, see Babaie, "Building on the Past," figs 2.1 and 2.18, pp. 26 and 45 and Uluç, "Selling to the Court," figs 14 and 15.

72. For descriptions of the Timurid pavilions, see Golombek and Wilber, *The Timurid Architecture of Iran and Turan*, vol. 1, 174–83.

73. This issue has been considered in Babaie, "Building on the Past," 44–6.

74. The religious debates on this issue have been addressed by several scholars; see especially Devin J. Stewart, "Notes on the Migration of 'Amili Scholars to Safavid Iran," *Journal of Near Eastern Studies* 55, no. 1 (1996): 81–103, esp. 98–9 and Stewart, "The First Shaykh al-Islam of the Safavid Capital Qazvin," *Journal of the American Oriental Society* 116, no. 3 (1996): 387–405. I owe a special thanks to Devin Stewart for his kind help in my earlier consideration of this question in "Building on the Past." Reference to and acknowledgment of his work was accidentally omitted in that publication.

75. Abisaab, *Converting Persia*, emphasizes the role of the clergy from Lebanon. For more on this transformation, the role of Isfahan as a capital of Twelver Shi'ism, and scholarship on the subject, see Chapter 3 in this book.

76. On Chaldiran and its devastating impact on the early Safavid morale, see Hans R. Roemer, "The Safavid Period," in *The Cambridge History of Iran:* Vol. 6, *The Timurid and Safavid Periods*, ed. Peter Jackson (Cambridge: Cambridge University Press, 1986), 189–350, esp. 224–6.

77. For recent considerations of the slave question in Safavid Iran, see Hirotake Maeda, "The Ghulams of Safavid Dynasty: The Case of Georgian Origin," *Toyo Gakuho* 81 (1999): 1–32; and Sussan Babaie, Kathryn Babayan, Ina Baghdiantz-McCabe and Massumeh Farhad, *Slaves of the Shah: New Elites of Safavid Iran* (London; New York: I. B. Tauris, 2004), Chapters 1 and 2.

78. See the following among a rich field of research: Roger Savory, "The Safavid Administrative System," in *The Cambridge History of Iran:* Vol. 6, *The Timurid and Safavid Periods*, ed. Peter Jackson (Cambridge: Cambridge University Press, 1986), 351–72; A. Banani, "Reflections on the Social and Economic Structure of Safavid Persia at Its Zenith," *Iranian Studies* 11 (1978): 83–116.

79. On the civil war that followed Tahmasb's death, the Qezelbash cabals and the alliances between Safavid princely contenders and their Qezelbash backers and handlers, see Babayan, "The Waning of the Qizilbâsh."

80. Babayan, *Mystics, Monarch, and Messiahs*, 357–61, for Abbas' "reforms" and the link between the elimination of the Qezelbash and the artisan groups who resisted the shah's centralization project.

81. On the Treaty of Constantinople, or Istanbul, and its harsh conditions, see Roemer, "The Safavid Period," 266–7.

CHAPTER THREE

Dwelling in Paradise, or Isfahan "Half the World"

THE RHETORICAL CLAIM *esfahan nesf-e jahan* (Isfahan, Half the World), repeated to every local or foreign visitor by the modern-day denizens of Isfahan, is often dismissed for its post-modern hyperbolic nostalgia (Figure 3.1). It is, in fact, such a deeply held conviction that it actually found its way into seventeenth-century literature when the city was architecturally refashioned into a self-conscious paradise.[1]

The tangled architectural and spatial relationships of urban and palatine Safavid Isfahan, on the one hand, and their intertwined cere-monial functions, on the other, make it impossible to represent an architectural history of the Isfahan palaces without first considering their metropolitan host. It is, then, as a preamble to the consideration of the palaces that this chapter delves into Isfahan's urban and cultural history. Moreover, since neither the urban scheme nor the palatial complex came about in a single construction campaign, my aim in this chapter is to elucidate the continuity and change within the urban-architectural practices of pre- and early-Safavid eras. Accordingly, the following discussion will focus on the most significant cultural forces that contributed to the city's development as a capital. One of those

Figure 3.1 *Isfahan, panoramic view after an engraving from Kaempfer, Amoenitatum (1712) chronicling his visit to Isfahan in 1684.*

This impossibly elevated view looks south toward the Soffe Mountains, to evoke the grandeur of the city when it served as the Safavid capital from its official transfer in 1598 through the dynasty's fall in 1722.

forces, the history of Shi'ism in Isfahan, serves to bridge the gap in our understanding between Isfahan as a "secular" political capital of the Safavids, as it has been cast in the past, and its place as the first and only capital of a centralized imperial regime of Twelver Shi'ism in the history of pre-modern Islam.

In the year 1006 AH (1597/98 CE), Isfahan officially became the new capital city of the Safavid dominion (Figure 3.7).[2] At the order of Shah Abbas the Great, several civic and royal construction projects had already begun and some existing buildings had been prepared for the transfer. The new construction was anchored on a great public square and a boulevard (Figures 3.3, 3.8, Plates 4 and 5). The Maydan-e Naqsh-e Jahan, the Image of the World Square, measures about 83,000 square meters, second only to Tiananmen Square in Beijing in area, or seven times the size of Piazza di San Marco in Venice. As the Englishman Thomas Herbert noted, "The Maydan is without doubt as spacious, as pleasant and aromatic a market as any in the universe. It is a thousand paces from North to South, and from East to West above two hundred, resembling our Exchange, or the Place-Royal in Paris, but six times larger" (Figure 3.9).[3] The Chahar Bagh avenue, a 4-kilometer-long, verdant public promenade, served principally as an arterial link between the older northwestern neighborhoods of the city and its new residential quarters, developed north and south of the Zayande River and between the palaces located inside and outside the city (Figures 3.4 and 3.5).

Each urban space served as the pivot around or along which the life of the reconstituted capital unfolded. Marketplaces, coffee shops, and other places of daily retreat surrounded the Maydan. A royal bazaar entranceway, the Qaysariyye, on the north side of the square, facilitated large-scale trade at the same time that it conducted traffic from the Maydan to the medieval city center near the Seljuq congregational mosque (Figure 3.10). A multifunctional palace called the Ali Qapu on the western side and the royal chapel-mosque of Shaykh Lotf-Allah across from it on the eastern side of the Maydan located these architectural icons of imperial power on the flanks of the public square (Plate 9) The great congregational mosque, Masjed-e Jadid-e Abbasi, on the southern side served to redirect the rhythms of daily worship through the Maydan (Plate 7). Public leisure space was conceived on a park-like scheme along the Chahar Bagh Promenade. Here, a sequence of gardens, each with its own monumental balconied gateway, delineated the avenue's length, while stately trees along the promenade cast their shadows over a canal at the center, where water was conducted through ornamental pools toward the river (Figure 3.4). The Chahar Bagh continued south of the river and over the new Allah Verdi Khan Bridge (popularly known as the Si-o se Pol or Thirty-three-span Bridge), which brought traffic to the Armenian enclave of New Julfa and to the mansions of the new Safavid elite while also facilitating access to the country retreat of the Hezar Jarib palace-garden (Figures 3.5 and 3.2).

Figure 3.2 *Isfahan, a detail from Kaempfer's panorama.*

The panorama highlights the location of the country retreat of Hezar Jarib (Thousand Acres) on the foot of the Soffe Mountains. Constructed by Shah Abbas the Great, it was part of the initial urban renewal project begun in 1590/1 that turned Isfahan into the Safavid capital after 1598. Hezar Jarib was a terraced garden located at the end of the public promenade of Chahar Bagh, which crossed over the Zayande River to link the center of Safavid Isfahan to its new urban and suburban developments.

Chahar bagh, a Persian garden type of considerable historical significance for Islamicate societies, comprises a four-quadrant subdivision of a lot, usually enclosed, in which all the arts of the garden – horticulture, agriculture, aquaculture, and architecture – are synthesized to create an artful contrivance of nature.[4] In Isfahan, the Chahar Bagh Promenade intersects with the Zayande River to create a *chahar bagh* on the macro level of the city, dividing it into quadrants and in effect transposing the garden's paradisiacal associations onto Isfahan, the city of paradise.

Isfahan, the city of rule

In between the two foci of the city – the Maydan and the Chahar Bagh – spread the royal precinct with palaces, leisure pavilions, residential quarters, administrative buildings, stables, kitchens, and royal workshops amid gardens, ornamental lakes, and pools (Figure 4.1 and Plate 9). The Daulatkhane was an assemblage of royal spaces and functions clustered separately into inner and outer zones corresponding in turn to restricted and semi-restricted arenas of private and public life

(Figure 3.7). The palace precinct occupied the physical center of the new imperial capital city and communicated with its urban environs through an assortment of gates and partitioning strategies. In accord with the Islamic practices that invariably subdivide the palace (and private homes, in general), the palace in Isfahan, too, was an ensemble of buildings and gardens composed of two interrelated sections: the *andarun* (within) and the *birun* (without).

This Daulatkhane, however, was not intended to be viewed from the outside as a single, massive building, be it of the fortified variety like the Mughal Red Forts and the Ottoman Topkapı, or of the externally unified building type, such as the European palaces of the Louvre and the Escorial (Figures 6.1, 6.7 and 6.9). Instead, and quite unexpectedly for pre-modern city-palace architecture, the Isfahan Daulatkhane assumed a different urban "façade" on each of its publicly exposed stretches (Figure 4.1, Plates 5 and 9). On its eastern flank, from the grounds of the Maydan-e Naqsh-e Jahan, the sprawling palace precinct was summed up, principally, in two gateways: one was the impressive five-story tower of the Ali Qapu Palace, which served as a ceremonial stage and a gateway into the judicial and civic or public functions of the precinct's accessible zone of birun (without); the other was the Harem Gate, consisting of a recessed, double-story gate that led to a tunnel of additional gates and eventually to the harem, the andarun zone (Figure 4.2).[5] Otherwise, the pedestrian in the Maydan experienced the palace "wall" vicariously through the two-story arcade and the inner row of shops – cabinetmakers, saddlers, cotton combers, makers of leather shoes, coffeehouses, to name a few – that served as both the western periphery of the Maydan and the eastern boundary of the royal precinct.

The other chief side of the Daulatkhane, its western side, was delineated by the great public promenade of Chahar Bagh, where double-story gates with balconies faced one another overlooking the avenue (Figure 3.4). All these gates led inside to gardens. Those that were on the side of the palace led to some of the major garden pavilions inside the Daulatkhane (such as the Hasht Behesht Palace); they were restricted to the inner sanctum of the royal household. Those gates across from the palace side of the promenade were, on the other hand, accessible for public use.

The north side of the Daulatkhane was comprised of administrative buildings of the Daftarkhane (royal chancellery) and its associated ensemble of public buildings, arteries and smaller squares (Chahar Hauz and Maydan-e Nau), and the tree-lined wall of a major ceremonial palace, the Chehel Sotun (Figures 3.8, 4.1, 4.5 and Plate 9). Here, too, a multiplicity of functions and architectural-urban forms and spaces were merged in order to demarcate the "façade" of the palace ensemble without resorting to walls and fortifications. On the southern side, where the harem section of the Daulatkhane and its related gardens and pavilions were located, the boundaries of what had been walled gardens in the first half of the seventeenth century developed by the early eighteenth century into shared walls between the royal precinct and a market-madrasa-caravanserai complex that was built by the last Safavid king, Shah Soltan Hossayn (Plate 4).[6]

The Safavid Daulatkhane did not hide behind impenetrable façades; nor was its outer face designed to be perceived as a single massive building. In both respects, it claimed a place outside the traditions of Islamicate palaces, especially those located in an urban context. The Alhambra in Granada; the Citadel of Cairo; the Mughal Red Forts in Agra, Delhi, and Lahore; the Ottoman Topkapı; and palaces in Madrid, Paris, and Beijing, for that matter, all harness the architectural language of seclusion and security. The Daulatkhane of Isfahan, however, eschews fortifications, towers, and moats in favor of a subtle architectural articulation of accessibility and transparency.

The Safavids, like their contemporaries and predecessors, had to painstakingly institute measures to legitimize and protect their dominion, both conceptually and practically. Isfahan in the early modern age was as much a site of political contention and jockeying for power as Delhi, Istanbul, and Paris during this same period. The Safavid shahs also made the same claims to sanctity and divine right of kingship as did their contemporary Mughal emperors, Ottoman sultans, and French and Spanish kings. The Safavid claim, however, was anchored on the promise of the Mahdi (the Twelfth Imam), whose charisma lent legitimacy to rule provided that it was based on justice and accessibility.[7] Messianic claims were not unique in this early modern age; the Mughal emperors Akbar and Jahangir, in particular, deployed a multiplicity of means – theological, political, and cultural, including paintings and buildings – to construct an ideological link between temporal authority and spiritual legitimacy of kingship. Yet, and as will be discussed later in detail, the merger of an Imami-Shi'i structure of legitimacy and an Iranian discourse of kingship mandated an emphatically accessible and charismatic conduct of sovereign power within the urban context.

Persuasion, through the repeated and compelling performance of deputyship on behalf of the Awaited Imam, was fundamental to the Safavid Perso-Shi'i etiquette of kingship. It was also persuasion, and not prevention, that gave Isfahan its particular imperial flavor; spatial boundaries between the sacred arena of the palace and the profane domain of the city were artfully blurred. Instead of confronting pedestrians with a monolithic and opaque wall of separation, the Safavid palace insinuated its way into the public's field of vision through a multiplicity of angles and functions. The architectural and urban solutions reached in Isfahan were unique. The shopping arcades, garden gates, administrative buildings, and tree-lined gardens that masquerade as walls and mediate the restricted access and veiled gaze of the public into the palace are not found anywhere else on this same magnified scale in the early modern period.

Safavid Isfahan

With a series of momentous architectural interventions beginning in 1590/1 (998/9 AH), and in anticipation of the official transfer of the capital in 1598, Safavid Isfahan grew for over a century to occupy a pivotal place in the history of urbanism in the Persianate world and to become known as one of the greatest metropolitan centers of the early modern age. The span from 1590/1 through 1722 represents Isfahan's "metrographic" apogee, the high point in the topography of urbanism in Islamic Iran (Figures 3.3 and 3.7).

Figure 3.3 *Isfahan (Omidvar).*
Looking south over the Maydan-e Naqsh-e Jahan (Image of the World Square) and toward the mountains, the principal features of the Safavid city are: the royal bazaar on the north side of the Maydan (bottom of the picture); the Ali Qapu Palace-Gateway on the west side of the Maydan (right side); the Shaykh Lotf-Allah Chapel-Mosque on the east side (left side); the Masjed-e Jadid-e Abbasi or Royal Mosque on the south side of the Maydan. The Daulatkhane or palace precinct is the leafy area that extends beyond the western periphery of the Maydan. The Zayande River is visible in the distance.

The urban scheme did not, of course, arise overnight; nor was it the result of afterthoughts, as has been suggested, that emerged as a consequence of the resistance by bazaar grandees to refurbishments aimed at the old city center and the subsequent and forced change of plans.[8] Such concerted, even radical, reconstitution of the city as was commenced by Shah Abbas the Great and largely completed by his immediate successors, Shah Safi (1629–42) and Shah Abbas II (1642–66), in the period between 1590/1 and the early 1660s had no precedent in Isfahan since the building programs of the eleventh- and twelfth-century Seljuqs. Even then, at the height of its international fame in that vast medieval Islamicate world, Isfahan developed over an extended period of time, in gradual steps, and not according to a master plan and in the course of a mere few decades.[9]

Cities mature organically, and solutions to urban needs more often than not give rise to new problems. Cycles of construction and destruction, regeneration and decline have unexpected effects on how a city grows. Isfahan in the seventeenth century, at its zenith as a metropolis, was not immune to such vicissitudes of nature, culture, and politics, all of which could require adjusting to shifts in emphasis or social practice. For example, the crystallization of Safavid urban ceremonials contributed to the transformation of the functions and form of the Ali Qapu from a two-story gateway into the palace precinct built in the 1590/1 campaign, to the five-story multifunctional palace-gateway erected during the first fifteen years of the seventeenth century, to the addition in front of the massive tower in 1644 (Figure 4.2, Plates 10, 11 and 12). Such adjustments should not detract from our grasp of the underlying Safavid agenda, which was accomplished in a rapid succession of building campaigns and provides compelling evidence that Isfahan's urban and architectural fabric did not merely evolve on an ad hoc basis as needs or desires arose. The "addendum" theory, dominant in modern scholarship, will be supplanted here with one that favors seeing in Safavid Isfahan a rigorous conceptualization of a capital city and its constituent parts as a perfect mirror of the ideal *shari'a*-based, Perso-Shi'i imperial order.

The medieval roots of Safavid Isfahan

What was Isfahan like when the building campaign of Shah Abbas I began? Medieval Isfahan, like most sizable cities in the Persianate world, was centered on a cluster of public buildings and a maydan (Figure 3.6). Here, the nodal point was the Maydan-e Kohne, or the Old Maydan, which included the Great Mosque of Isfahan (until Safavid times, the city's oldest and most venerated congregational mosque) as well as the Seljuq marketplace and possibly its administrative center. Neither the shape of the Maydan-e Kohne nor the exact relationship between the public space and its attendant

Figure 3.4 *Isfahan, Chahar Bagh Promenade after the engraving that illustrates the chronicle of the Dutch traveler Cornelis de Bruyn's visit to the city in 1704–5.*

Seen at its south end, where it reaches the Hezar Jarib retreat, the avenue was over 4 kilometers long and represented an extraordinary example of the synthesis of an urban artery with a public space of leisure. Both the promenade and some of its adjacent gardens were intended for leisurely strolls and picnics. A water channel with ornamental pools ran along its center while stately trees along its sides alternated with lofty gateways that opened onto mansions and gardens of the elite.

buildings is known. Medieval sources do not speak of a contiguous space with geometrically regularized boundaries. In other words, this Old Maydan was not "designed" as a square, a rectangle, or a circle with buildings formally positioned to give shape to its periphery and its open space, although as a social arena it must have played a significant role in regulating life among the mosque, the marketplace, and the administrative edifices in its general vicinity.[10]

A wall comprising several gates encircled the city in such a way that the Maydan-e Kohne fell approximately at its center.[11] Between the urban center and the peripheral walls lay the residential quarters, or *mahalles*, that subdivided the city into self-contained urban collectivities, each with its own neighborhood mosque and public

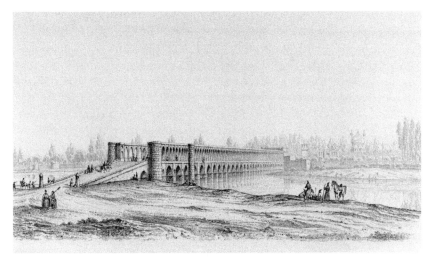

Figure 3.5 *Isfahan, the Allah Verdi Khan Bridge after an engraving for Coste's* Monuments modernes de la Perse *(1867)*.

The bridge carries the Chahar Bagh Promenade across the Zayande River. Completed in 1607, the bridge takes its name from the converted Armenian commander-in-chief of Shah Abbas the Great who was placed in charge of its construction. It is popularly known as the Si-o Se Pol, the Thirty-three-span Bridge, for the rhythmic march of its elegant arches, which could be closed to serve as a dam regulating the flow of water.

amenities, as was the norm in cities throughout the Islamic world. Some of these old neighborhoods can still be traced by following their winding streets and alleyways and the intersecting of the neighborhood's major arteries.[12]

In addition to the Maydan-e Kohne and the Great Mosque, the other notable legacy of Seljuq Isfahan was its famed gardens, which seem to have developed outside the city boundaries.[13] Historical precedents for royal garden developments in Isfahan reach back to at least Buyid times (932–1062). This was the period when Isfahan had become an important political counterweight to Abbasid Baghdad in the political fashioning of temporal versus caliphal religious dominion.[14] According to the late tenth-century Arab geographer Ibn Hawqal, palaces and mansions lined the banks of the Zayande River, and lush gardens covered the Marbanan (Marbayn) area west of the city walls. In every case, royal and elite retreats were located at a considerable distance from the walled city.[15]

During the twelve years that Isfahan was the center of rule for the Seljuq Tughrul (1051–63), and despite stiff popular resistance by Isfahanis, the city burgeoned with not only mosques, madrasas, marketplaces, and houses, but also extra-urban royal retreats.[16] The Persian traveler Naser Khosrau, who visited Isfahan in 1052 (444 AH), described it as "a city located on a flat plain and with a delightful climate." Furthermore, he says: "The city has a high, strong wall with gates, embrasures, and battlements all around. Inside the city are courses for running water, fine tall buildings, and a beautiful and large Friday mosque."[17] Al-Mafarokhi's *Mahasen Esfahan* (The Advantages of Isfahan) lauds the beauty of the Seljuq gardens, especially the four famous gardens that may have formed a *chahar bagh*.[18] Although the *chahar-bagh* garden type was not new or unique to Seljuq Isfahan, this aspect of the history of Isfahan possibly gave rise to a rhetorical reference to an especially venerable slice of Isfahan's past; the later Safavid Chahar Bagh was an act of mimesis parallel perhaps to the relationship of the old and new Maydans. Nevertheless, the Seljuq royal gardens, too, stood well outside the city walls on what appears to have been the southeastern side in an area not far from the city gate associated with the citadel. Both Alp Arsalan and Malik Shah spent their early years (*vali 'ahdi*) in Isfahan, and Malik Shah finally moved his center of rule from Ray to Isfahan.

The medieval walled city was equipped with a securely fortified citadel, the Qal'e Tabarrok, located in the southeastern part of Isfahan and dating, in its original construction, to the Buyid reign in the tenth century (Figure 3.6).[19] Qal'e Tabarrok was in a quarter of the city where the subterranean waterbed was at its highest level, thus making it possible to dig a proper moat.[20] As was customary in most Islamic cities – and indeed nearly all medieval cities – and regardless of residential or leisure accommodations for kings, the ruling elite could always count on the safety of a well-guarded and fortified haven within the walled city.[21] Some of the outer walls and towers of the citadel were still standing late in the nineteenth century, but our present-day picture of the structure depends mainly on Jean Chardin's observations during his two sojourns in Isfahan in the 1660s and the 1670s.[22] The earthenware outer shell of the Qal'e consisted of white-washed, high, thick, and crenellated walls marked at regular intervals with round watchtowers. With 370 houses, an arsenal with its own maydan for martial practices, a mosque, a *hammam* (bathhouse), a dungeon and a commander's residence, the Qal'e functioned in seventeenth-century Safavid times primarily as the quarters for most of the cavalrymen of the royal household, who in turn provided the most stringent security for the royal treasury and the arsenal.

Regardless of its changing functions over the centuries, the Qal'e Tabarrok was principally a defensive stronghold and as such served generations of kings, conquerors, and rebels in their quest for safety from local or external threats. In Safavid times, and especially the seventeenth century, the Qal'e was utilized as a place of refuge by Farhad Beg, the rebellious governor of Isfahan before Shah Abbas the Great transferred the capital, and was prepared for Shah Soltan Hossayn in the time leading up to the Afghan invasion.[23] It did not, however, serve as a residential or ceremonial space in the Safavid period (if at all in any other time), when ceremonies of kingship demanded different kinds of access and display.

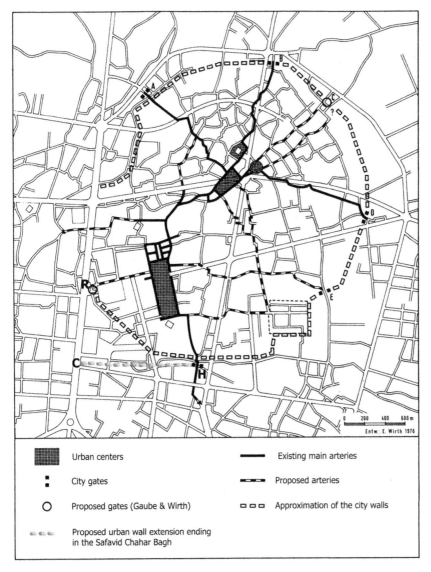

Figure 3.6 *Isfahan, map (after Gaube and Wirth).*

The main urban features and the location of the walls in the seventeenth century are superimposed onto a modern map. The general outlines of the medieval Maydan-e Kohne and its adjacent Friday Mosque are marked at the center of the circular walls, with the pre-Safavid citadel, Qal'e Tabarrok, as a square outlined on the lower right side. The shift to the southwest in Safavid times is indicated by the location of the vast, rectangular Maydan-e Naqsh-e Jahan and the Chahar Bagh Promenade toward the lower left of the old city. 'R' marks the Daulat Gate, one of the two principal formal gates into the Safavid city; 'H' marks the Hasanabad Gate leading out of the city toward Shiraz. 'C' in this map is at the end of a proposed urban wall that served, as this book suggests, as a gateway onto the Chahar Bagh from the southwestern corner of the harem.

The Safavid city grew to encompass an area that medieval Isfahan had left undeveloped. This was the land on the west and southwestern side, where an existing maydan and an adjacent garden provided the space to accommodate the new urban plan (Figures 3.6 and 3.7). Several scholars have debated the urban-architectural parameters of this area of the city in relation to the walls, gates, and the old Isfahan center.[24] It is now quite clear that the nineteenth-century walls of the city, recorded by the French architects Pascal Coste and Eugene Flandin, surround a much larger area than those enclosing the seventeenth-century city.[25] What remains unresolved, with significant bearing upon this discussion, is the question of the gates and walls in this same southwesterly location of the old city, where the new maydan and palace precinct were constructed.

Before the 1590/1 construction project by Shah Abbas the Great, this garden and maydan would have been positioned to the west of the principal north–south artery of the walled city (Figure 3.6). As the German scholars Heinz Gaube and Eugen Wirth have shown, this was the main trade route that linked, through markets, the Old Maydan to the southernmost Hasanabad Gate en route to the city of Shiraz. Chardin described this route as an almost uninterrupted bazaar running the length of the city.[26] We will return shortly to the significance of this arterial orientation of the old city. Suffice it to note that while the axes of the old north-south artery and the new Maydan of the seventeenth century ran parallel, the orientation of the Maydan, with its southeasterly tilt, necessitated an adjustment to accommodate the direction of the *qibla* for the two mosques on the Maydan (Figure 3.7, Plates 6 and 7). Thus, in order for the mosques to properly face Mecca – which lay southwest of Isfahan – they had to be positioned on an axis that was skewed in relation to the axis of the Maydan.

Here, however, attention should be focused on the fact that the position of the gates (and therefore of the walls) in the area of this maydan-bagh remains obscure in the sources and hypothetical, at best, in modern scholarship.[27] In turn, the assumption that walls connected hypothetical gates (between gates R and H in Figure 3.6) has made it difficult to discern how the function of the "residual" maydan-bagh relates to the master plan of Shah Abbas the Great.

Records from the early sixteenth century show that Shah Isma'il made several visits to Isfahan, where he lodged at the garden known as Bagh-e Naqsh-e Jahan.[28] These notes provide the earliest clear evidence of the presence and function of an older maydan-bagh in this area. The garden's adjoining maydan, not having yet assumed a definitive shape or its name from the garden, as it had by Shah Abbas's time, served as a hippodrome (*maydan-e asb*) for mustering troops in anticipation of war campaigns, for equestrian sports such as polo, and for public executions.[29] In the summer of 1504, for example, after a fierce battle with Mohammad Karre, the rebellious governor

Figure 3.7 *Isfahan, map focusing on the area south of the old city and the Safavid additions after 1590/1, adapted from a modern city map in combination with Kaempfer's "Planographia" (4.1).*

1) Maydan-e Naqsh-e Jahan; 2) Qaysariyye or Royal Bazaar; 3) Ali Qapu Palace-Gateway; 4) Shaykh Lotf-Allah Chapel-Mosque; 5) Masjed-e Jadid-e Abbasi or Royal Mosque; 6) Tauhidkhane Sufi shrine and public refuge; 7) Talar-e Tavile Palace; 8) Chehel Sotun Palace; 9) Hasht Behesht Palace; 10) Chahar Bagh Promenade; 11) Madrese-ye Soltani or Chahar Bagh; 12) Ayenekhane Palace; 13) Allah Verdi Khan Bridge; 14) Khwaju Bridge; 15) Ju'i Bridge. The gray areas to the left of the Maydan demarcate the Daulatkhane or royal precinct: the darker side approximates the *birun* (public zone), the lighter side the *andarun* (harem zone).

of Abarqu, Shah Isma'il ordered the body of his defeated foe to be burned here.[30]

While it still remains open to speculation whether the walls of the city had stretched, by the sixteenth century, to embrace the south-western zone, it is certain that this area was on the periphery of the city and was scarcely populated or occupied. Some evidence, although not secure since it significantly postdates the actual events, points to the presence of gardens at an even earlier time, when Timurid or Turkmen (Aqqoyunlu or Qaraqoyunlu) overlords constructed a pavilion in this same area in the fifteenth century.[31] Together with the record of visits by Shah Isma'il, there is reason to believe that the garden did indeed serve as a royal residence for some time in Isfahan. This maydan-bagh on the southwestern side of the Old City left an available and useful royal space for Shah Abbas's planners to conceptualize the nucleus of the Safavid capital, with the Maydan and Bagh-e Naqsh-e Jahan, the imperial, paradisiacal "Image of the World," grafted onto the remains of the earlier maydan and bagh.

The wall–gate debate

The wall–gate debate in modern scholarship needs further probing because it reveals the significance of Shah Abbas's master plan and its mediatory role in propelling the city into a "modern" urban age. A comparison between the location of the walls and gates before the transfer of the capital and afterwards during the seventeenth century represents the underlying ideological trappings of a charismatic form of authority that pretended to need no fortifications to protect it. The new proposal for the location of the walls and gates in the Safavid city presented below is based on Chardin's descriptions, that mine of information upon which much knowledge of the seventeenth-century city has depended. The walls of the city have invariably been drawn with the Hasanabad Gate (H in Figure 3.6) linked to the Daulat Gate (R in Figure 3.6), cutting right through the palace precinct with no consideration of how the urban, extra-urban, and royal spaces intersect.[32] There is of course no doubt about the location of the two principal city gates of Hasanabad and Daulat. Yet several aspects of architectural developments in the area between them undermine the validity of the neat lines drawn by modern scholarship.

It is certain that the Hasanabad Gate mediated the final stretch of a prominent bazaar artery inside the city and the commencement of a major trade route to the south. The history of the Daulat Gate (Gate of Felicity or Royal Gate) is less certain. Regardless of whether this same gate or one in its vicinity had predated the Safavids, it was the seventeenth-century reconstitution of the urban contours – its perimeters and its layout – that brought the Daulat Gate to functional and formal prominence among all the major gates of the city.[33] Here

Plate **1** *"Yusuf Gives a Royal Banquet in Honor of his Marriage"*
from a Haft Awrang *(Seven Thrones) by Jami (d. 1492); probably Masshad,*
Khurasan, Iran, Safavid dynasty, 1556–1565; opaque watercolor, ink and
gold on paper; 34.2 × 23.2 cm (13⁷/₁₆ × 9¹/₈ in).

The Haft Awrang was a royal manuscript commissioned by prince Ebrahim
Mirza, the son-in-law of the Safavid Shah Tahmasb (1524–76). The artist
casts the classical story in the guise of a contemporary royal banquet. The
event takes place on the terrace of a pavilion under sumptuously decorated
textile canopies that are fastened to the corners of the building and upheld
with poles. The extraordinary pictorial device of overlaying intensely
patterned planes and shifting angles invites the viewer to imagine a royal
garden setting with an octagonal pavilion, like the Hasht Behesht in Tabriz,
where tents and canopies supplemented the limited space of the building,
a characteristic of the Persianate palatine traditions of the fifteenth and
sixteenth centuries.

Plate **2** *"Da ud Receives a Robe of Honor from Mun im Khan." An illustration from an unidentified Dictionary; attributed to Hiranand; India, Mughal dynasty, reign of Emperor Akbar, ca. 1604; album page; color and gold on paper; 23.8 × 12.3 cm (9³/₈ × 4¹³/₁₆ in).*

The defeated Afghan was made to submit to Mughal sovereignty by donning the robe of honor that Mun im Khan, Emperor Akbar's commander-in-chief, had offered him. The khal at ceremony, widely practiced throughout the history of Islam, takes place in front of an imperial tent, so marked because of its domed shape. The placement of the royal tent ensemble outside the walled capital city in this painting exemplifies a Turco-Mongol practice in which imperial encampments served as complementary sites to capital cities. In the Ottoman and Safavid worlds, however, the urban palace complex – in Istanbul and Isfahan – became fixed as the capital of the empire in the sixteenth and seventeenth centuries, respectively.

Plate 3 *Qazvin, Chehel Sotun Palace.*

The building is popularly known as the Chehel Sotun (forty columns) because of its pillared porches, even though they are of an undetermined, later date. The "core" building (1550s) is the earliest surviving example of a two-story, octagonal type of pavilion known as the hasht-behesht (eight paradises), so named because of its internal subdivision of space into eight chambers circling a central, often domed unit (Figure 5.4 A). It was one of the principal structures in the public administrative zone of the Safavid royal precinct.

Plate 4 *Isfahan (Omidvar).*

Looking east, the tree-lined Chahar Bagh Promenade runs from the lower
right side of the picture to the left. This was the public thoroughfare that
demarcated the western boundary of the royal precinct, here visible in
its general outlines as a vast, green area between the Chahar Bagh in the
foreground and the Maydan in the distance. The blue-tiled domed building
in the lower right-hand side of the picture is the early eighteenth-century
Safavid Madrese-ye Soltani or Chahar Bagh.

Plate 5 *Isfahan (Omidvar)*.

Looking north over the Maydan and its principal buildings, with a glimpse of the Daulatkhane on the left side.

Plate **6** *Isfahan, Shaykh Lotf-Allah Chapel-Mosque (1602–29), seen from the Ali Qapu across the Maydan.*

The entranceway recedes behind the exterior façade of the row of shops that constitute the periphery of the Maydan. The composition of an ayvan with flanking blind arches and the overall tiled surface sheathing (restored) are typical of seventeenth-century Safavid architecture. The gently tapered, golden-yellow dome is askew relative to the longitudinal axis of the Maydan so that the mihrab, the prayer niche inside the domed chamber, is properly oriented toward Mecca.

Plate **7** *Isfahan, Masjed-e Jadid-e Abbasi, Royal Mosque or Imam Mosque (1611–38).*

The architects ingeniously resolved the mismatched axis of the Maydan and the orientation toward Mecca by creating the cascading effect of a massive domed prayer chamber behind and to the side of a tall entrance gateway. The paired minarets rising above the main pishtaq façade further facilitate the visual transition.

Plate **8** *Isfahan, Masjed-e Jadid-e Abbasi portal.*

Recessed and made to appear as if arms opened out to embrace the worshippers, this impressive gateway represents the characteristic Safavid architectural penchant for theatricality. The tall pishtaq façade, with its lofty ayvan and elegant minarets, is entirely sheathed in haft rangi (seven-color) tile panels.

began the Chahar Bagh, the promenade that provided the city's inhabitants a place for leisurely outings, for picnics, and for watching the meandering of people alongside channels (*juy*) of running water under shaded trees (Figures 3.7 and 3.8). Furthermore, the gate was one of the two "official" entry points to the city, and hence also one of the two sites of the ceremonials of *esteqbal*, the welcoming rituals that often started miles outside the city, if not – depending on the status of the guest – at the borders of the Safavid dominion, and concluded in Isfahan at the Maydan and the Ali Qapu Palace.[34]

Past the proper gate and at the official beginning of the boulevard, Shah Abbas had built a magnificent pavilion known as Jahan Nama (Reflection of the World) (Figures 3.8 and 4.1).[35] This building provided the necessary cover for occasional spontaneous visits of women, who could enter through a passageway from the harem area of the palace precinct and watch people from behind the extravagantly grilled windows on the Chahar Bagh façade of the pavilion. The pavilion marked the site of the most ceremonial gate of the city, and crowning the promenade, with two of its faces closed to the curious eyes of outsiders, the building established the symbolic presence of the veiled but vigilant royal gaze. In this regard, the Jahan Nama may be considered an auxiliary to the Ali Qapu on the Maydan, a subject to which we will return.

What would a city wall have done to this configuration of a pavilion, boulevard, and adjacent gardens? As noted earlier, gardens acted as a buffer zone mediating the space separating the Chahar Bagh from the western side of the Daulatkhane. These were the gardens whose exterior balconied gateways, echoed by similar ones across the way, shaped the flanks of the boulevard. Their interior garden spaces

Figure 3.8 *Isfahan, reconstructed panorama based on a conflation of satellite images, Kaempfer's "Planographia" (4.1), and modern maps of the city.*

The cube-like building at the start of the Chahar Bagh Promenade, on the lower right side, is the Jahan Nama (Reflection of the World), a Safavid pavilion reserved for the harem that was accessed through a covered alley inside the harem zone.

remained inaccessible to all but the harem, whose quarters were adjacent to this part of the city (Figures 3.4 and 4.1). The German observer Engelbert Kaempfer's so-called bird's-eye view and its accompanying legend identify this feature of the Daulatkhane (marked "u") as an "Enclosed route, one of the walls of the old city."[36] An old wall of the city apparently had been transformed, at least by the time of Kaempfer's 1680s visit, into a protected internal road in the palace precinct. This covered alley gave the shahs a way to roam between the inner palace (the andarun) and parts of the outer palace (the birun) without being detected (Figure 3.7). It also gave women of the harem direct and safe access to the gardens on the western side of the precinct, to the Jahan Nama palace, and to the Chahar Bagh. The location of the harem at the foot of the enclosed route, confirmed by Chardin in the 1670s as well as Kaempfer, does not indicate that the harem was in the shadow of the old city walls. Placing the apartments of the royal women and children in such close proximity to the walls would have been an utterly unreasonable solution for such a consciously gendered society. Rather, it signals the recovery of the old walls for new uses.

With the appropriation of this southwesterly part of the city for the development of the Safavid capital, the old wall that linked the Hasanabad and Daulat Gates would seem to have been reutilized as an internal wall subdividing the palace precinct into zones that were defined by the degree of access men and women could have exercised and the measured opening and closing of the diaphragm of public and private exposure. In other words, the old city wall was turned into a functioning internal route within the palace precinct.

An alternative, and contrary, reading of the "covered route/old wall" feature suggests that the wall was converted to the covered route after the construction of the Hasht Behesht Palace in 1669. Both Chardin and Kaempfer visited, and prepared their descriptions and images, after the construction of the Hasht Behesht, which was built by Shah Solayman (1666–94) as a semi-private palace in Bagh-e Bolbol, the Garden of the Nightingale, one of the most famous gardens in the Daulatkhane (Figures 3.7, 4.1 and 5.18). Such a scenario ignores, however, the fact that Bagh-e Bolbol, as a garden and before the addition of a palace, was already incorporated into the Chahar Bagh scheme during the early seventeenth-century development of the promenade, as evidenced by several Persian sources.[37]

Chardin's observations

The Persian chronicles provide only brief descriptions, but they can be supplemented with the detailed observations of the Chahar Bagh made in the 1660s and 1670s by the French traveler Jean Chardin. An overlooked piece of information given by Chardin helps to clarify the position of the palace precinct in relation to the walls. It also resolves the problem of drawing walls through the Daulatkhane, a subject completely ignored in urban histories of Isfahan.[38] Counting from the Jahan Nama–Daulat Gate side, Chardin recorded a succession of seven ornamental pools with waterfalls and fountains, culminating in the river and the Allah Verdi Khan Bridge (Figure 3.5). The first, a small quadrangular pool, was in front of the Jahan Nama pavilion. It was followed by a much larger quadrangular pool that was graced with a pentagonal seat in the middle and protected by a banister. The even larger third ornamental pool, shaped as an octagon, stood in front of the garden gate that led into the two gardens of Bagh-e Takht and Bagh-e Bolbol. The latter was associated with the harem from the beginning of the construction project and became even more prominent, as noted earlier, when the palace of Hasht Behesht was added in 1669.

The fourth pool is the key for understanding the shifts in the urban boundaries of the palace precinct. It was relatively small and was situated so as to provide for a waterfall. Most importantly, two large gates were positioned on either side of it, presumably at a distance and opening onto the Chahar Bagh Promenade. One of the gates, luxuriantly decorated with a gilded mural, opened onto the suburb, as Chardin puts it. This was the Abbasabad, one of the new enclaves with a massive housing project built, starting in 1611, on the orders of Shah Abbas to accommodate a relatively large community from Tabriz that was displaced as a result of Safavid–Ottoman wars in northwestern Iran.[39] The other similarly grand gate across the Chahar Bagh opened onto the palace precinct (C in Figure 3.6). As Chardin's description makes clear, this too was a proper gate on the scale of a city gate and not one of the garden gateways that lined the Chahar Bagh.

Chardin describes three more pools before reaching the river and the Allah Verdi Khan Bridge, which places the two city-scale gates near the fourth pool, somewhere in the vicinity of where Shah Soltan Hossayn's Royal Madrasa (Madrese-ye Soltani) came to stand early in the eighteenth century (Plate 4). If this were the southwesterly limit of the Daulatkhane until the eighteenth century, it is possible that the city walls, however they may have retained their shape and function, were extended from the Hasanabad Gate to this gate on the Chahar Bagh. Such a scenario eliminates the burden of having to explain the positioning of the harem in the royal precinct at the foot of the city walls or the bisecting of the precinct by the wall. It also fits the general picture of construction both in the palace precinct and the Chahar Bagh, about which more will be said in the next chapter.

This gate into the Daulatkhane was indeed located far from the main residential, ceremonial, and administrative zones of the precinct. Its principal role was to allow members of the royal household to exit the gardens on the southwestern corner of the precinct at a junction closer to the river; to enjoy leisurely strolls in the

Chahar Bagh, along the riverfront, across the bridge and along the Chahar Bagh extension south of the river; and to reach the country residence of Hezar Jarib at the end of the avenue (Figure 3.2).

A city without walls

That enclosing the city with walls was less than desirable, even inadvisable, in Safavid Isfahan is clearly indicated by the fact that of all the building works commenced by Shah Abbas and continued by his successors over the span of the seventeenth century, not a single stretch of any defensive wall was freshly built, nor were any of the old ones repaired.[40] A clear indication of the degree to which Safavid Isfahan developed irrespective of its old walls is embedded in Chardin's observation that the old walls were poorly maintained and that they were so overtaken by the growth of houses and gardens as to be scarcely visible.[41] For a city in the plains, like Isfahan, with no major natural defenses available save for the river, the absence of walls signals the degree to which the Safavid ethos was built upon the bedrock of the Perso-Shi'i charisma of the kings and the assertion of the divinely safeguarded authority of the shahs.[42] Isfahan as the capital city was to knit through its urban features the image of this particular form of legitimacy and authority. Its palaces do exactly the same. Just as the city remained brazenly unwalled, so did the palace precinct, where the fortifications, watchtowers, and moats of earlier and contemporary palatine architecture gave way to ostentatious and deceptive displays of transparency. An integrated urban design, in which the two pivotal spaces, the Maydan and the Chahar Bagh, were at once public and royal, accessible and restricted, demanded transcending the walled limitations of the Old City.

The master plan of Safavid Isfahan

The Safavid capital city issued, I argue, from a master plan of imperial intentions rather than from a haphazard congeries of social needs and urban ideas. The conceptually and spatially integrated Maydan–Chahar Bagh scheme of Isfahan has no equal either in the Islamicate and Persianate worlds of the past or in the contemporary world of the early modern age. Its architectural and urban particularities speak to the regal mode of operation that the Safavid household had devised, refined, and mastered. To be a king and a proponent of Shi'ism required the construction of a new cultural matrix, self-consciously embodied in the layout and architecture of Isfahan, where distinctions were drawn between the Perso-Shi'i contours and textures of authority and those upheld by the rival and neighboring Sunni variants of caliphal-inspired kingship.[43]

The Seljuq legacy of Sunni Isfahan, although venerated for its grandeur, presented an inadequate urban landscape for setting up a hegemonic Shi'i "house." This was not just a matter of potential religious differences. The recycling of mosques and madrasas, a common practice almost everywhere else, did not suffice in an age when Isfahan took center stage in promulgating normative practices of Twelver Shi'ism, a point to be discussed further in this chapter. Moreover, Shah Abbas the Great's initial attempt simply to refurbish the old maydan, Maydan-e Kohne, met with resistance from prominent local families in the bazaar, a landowning and mercantile class of Iranian notables suspicious of the shah's monopolizing schemes already under way.[44]

Instead, Shah Abbas had the Old City cleaned up and refreshed, but as the evidence suggests, neither the space nor the history of the old city center could accommodate the symbols of the new dynasty. In sharp contrast to past practices of conquerors and newly crowned kings, Shah Abbas the Great left no official imprint of his reign on the venerated Great Mosque of Isfahan, a point that has eluded scholars.[45] There were, in fact, no monumental additions to the Old City – no new major mosques, madrasas, caravanserais, towers, palaces, or government buildings. Instead, all of the architectural and urban energy of Safavid Isfahan was concentrated on the freshly developed zones of the city.

A new history of Isfahan's construction

The particular sequence in which various buildings were constructed in the Maydan and the Chahar Bagh – the two major urban arenas that formed the physical environment of the new capital – has led scholars in the past to assume that Shah Abbas's building campaign initially was not coordinated with his decision to transfer the capital. Understanding the growth of Safavid Isfahan as a series of random architectural-urban events, however, leaves little room for a nuanced consideration of intentionality and agency other than the supposedly universal urge afflicting kings to build for self-glorification, preservation of one's memory, political gain, and, perhaps, as a genuine gesture of benevolence toward the ruled. Facile as this picture may be, it has long dominated scholarship on the building works of Isfahan. It is time now to place the urban and architectural scheme in the context of the unique Safavid discourse of kingship that determined it.

To correct the narrative, it is necessary to revisit the building history of Safavid Isfahan, paying special attention to the initial phases of its transformation into a capital city. The point of departure for all discussion on Safavid Isfahan has been the date of the earliest construction, now securely fixed by Robert McChesney at 1590/1.[46] The main projects that converted medieval Isfahan into the new capital city of Shah Abbas the Great concluded in 1611, when building of the Royal Mosque started at the south end of the Maydan

(Figure 3.7 and Plate 7).[47] Within these two decades construction
began on all the key elements of Shah Abbas's new capital: the
Maydan-e Naqsh-e Jahan cluster with its perimeter shopping area,
the royal bazaar of Qaysariyye, the Palace of Ali Qapu, the royal
chapel-mosque of Shaykh Lotf-Allah, and the congregational Royal
Mosque (Figures 4.2, 3.10 and Plate 6). During this period, construction also began on the Chahar Bagh Promenade, with its two termini
marked by a gate-pavilion at the northern (city) end and by the royal
country pleasance at the Hezar Jarib Gardens at the southernmost
end (Figures 3.8, 3.4 and 3.2). Private and public gardens as well as
pools and gates delineated the intervening length of the promenade,
the Allah Verdi Khan Bridge linked the two sides across the Zayande
River, and the new satellite cities of Abbasabad and New Julfa on the
north and south sides of the river housed the displaced Tabrizis and
Armenians, respectively (Figure 3.5).

These buildings, however, did not come about in a convenient
sequence that meets the oft-expected synchronization of actions and
intentions or hinges architectural and spatial representations on a
historically situated metanarrative. The messy nature of building,
not to mention of planning a city, precludes the possibility of such a
linear engineering of history. When construction takes place on such
a vast scale in the course of a mere two decades, as in Isfahan, the fact
that, for example, the Maydan was built in two stages (one of which
preceded the official transfer of the capital) should not automatically
be taken to mean that the city developed in a haphazard fashion or
that it constituted an urban refurbishing unrelated to the transformation of the city's political status.

As mentioned above, those who accepted the notion of the random
sequence of construction generated the theory that the first buildings, begun in 1590/1, had resulted from a reaction to the resistance
by local notable families to Shah Abbas's plans to renovate the place
of their businesses in the old bazaar.[48] In place of the Old Maydan,
where scholars have contended he would have wanted to modernize
the city, Shah Abbas shifted his attention to the available lands of the
old Maydan-e Asb and Bagh-e Naqsh-e Jahan. There he began to build
in earnest with the construction of the Qaysariyye Bazaar, the level-
ing of the Maydan, and the marking of its perimeter with the walls of
a single-story arcade before a row of shops that could be whitewashed
and decorated with murals, as they were in 1595.[49]

These initial works of 1590/1 were then followed, according to
most scholars, with a series of projects that purportedly issued from
mostly unrelated impulses to beautify, to aggrandize through competitive architecture the position of the Safavids relative to their
rivals, or simply to respond to the demands of growth. Thus, it has
been argued, the Chahar Bagh Promenade project followed in 1596, a
date provided by Monajjem, one of Shah Abbas's historians.[50] The
building history of the Chahar Bagh may be further fleshed out by the

writings of Eskandar Beg Monshi, the principal historian of Shah Abbas the Great.[51] Starting from its two termini, at the time of the official transfer in 1598, the promenade was developed in stages. Ground was first broken at the Daulat Gate, the northernmost end of the avenue, and the Hezar Jarib royal pleasance, its southernmost end on the slopes of the Soffe Mountain (Figures 3.6 and 3.7). Construction on flanking gardens, canals, and ornamental pools and fountains of the promenade must have continued for several years, until at least 1607, when the Allah Verdi Khan Bridge connecting the two stretches of the avenue over the river was finished.[52]

As the Chahar Bagh project was approaching completion, the modification of the Maydan-e Naqsh-e Jahan and a series of new projects began in 1602.[53] The investigations of Eugenio Galdieri have provided irrefutable archaeological evidence of this second phase of building at the Maydan.[54] The work included alterations to the Maydan profile and the addition of buildings. The new second row of shops opening onto the Maydan advanced its sides into the space of the Maydan and thus diminished its area (by about 3,743 square meters) to its final measurement of about 83,000 square meters. Moreover, the construction of a second story of rooms raised the profile of the peripheral "walls" while at the same time monumentalizing the entire composition and investing it with the rhythmic beat of closed and open spaces on the intersecting horizontal and vertical axes of the Maydan façades.

The Shaykh Lotf-Allah Mosque and the Ali Qapu Palace

It is generally accepted that two new monumental buildings, the Shaykh Lotf-Allah Mosque and the Ali Qapu Palace, were also added, one after the other, at the time when the modifications to the Maydan were carried out (Figure 3.7, Plates 5 and 6). Neither archaeological nor textual evidence, however, supports this sequence of construction, which has become calcified in scholarship. Elsewhere, I have refined the construction history of these structures.[55] Here, a reiteration of the basic data will clarify the integrity of the entire Maydan scheme.

Galdieri's archaeological evidence of phased construction at the Ali Qapu synchronizes, in the first two of its five phases, with the two stages of construction of the Maydan itself.[56] McChesney's redating of the two Maydan construction campaigns to 1590/1 and 1602 also allows us to redate the initial Ali Qapu, a monumental two-story gateway at the threshold between the Maydan and the palace precinct, to the very first building campaign in Isfahan in 1590/1, when the city was being prepared to serve as the capital. The second phase of construction at Ali Qapu coincided with the modifications of the Maydan in 1602. At this time an additional two-story unit, primarily for ceremonial purposes, was raised above the original building. The

Shaykh Lotf-Allah Mosque, the private royal chapel across from the
Ali Qapu, was begun afterwards, in the 1602–3 campaign. More will
be said about the Ali Qapu's architectural and functional evolution.
Here it is worth emphasizing, however, that the Maydan project – in
its two phases with its bazaar component, the entrance gate to the
royal residential gardens, and the chapel-mosque – were all conceived
as part and parcel of the same reform campaign that guided the spatial
reorganization of the empire, on both the macro level of the Safavid
domains and the micro level of the capital city of Isfahan.

The Royal Mosque

The addition to the south side of the Maydan, begun in 1611, of the
great congregational mosque, the Masjed-e-Jadid-e Abbasi or Royal
Mosque, when all other monumental features of the Maydan-e
Naqsh-e Jahan were already in place, is far from a sign of a change of
heart on the part of Shah Abbas the Great, as has been suggested
(Figure 3.7, Plates 5, 7 and 8). Rather, the reasons for raising such a
congregational mosque must have been rooted in the very initial
plans for the refashioning of Isfahan as the capital. Two related issues
clarify this point. One is that, despite the deep-seated popular vener-
ation of the Seljuq Friday mosque, the Great Mosque of Isfahan, Shah
Abbas did not extend his patronage to anything substantive in that
building – no refurbishments, no mounting of decrees (*farman*), no
epigraphic grafting of his name. In short, the shah felt no urge to do
as all his predecessors since the eighth century had done and leave his
mark on the old mosque. Instead, his city was to be a new center not
only of imperial ambitions but, more pointedly, of Shi'i imperial
ambitions.

For Shah Abbas, a new congregational mosque was a prerequisite
of kingship. Moreover, this late sixteenth-, early seventeenth-century
period in Safavid history witnessed the definitive conclusion of a long
debate over the permissibility of Friday prayer (the congregational
noon prayer) during the Occultation of the Twelfth Imam, the Mahdi
or Messiah. While awaiting the return of the Mahdi, Shi'i theocracy
and the Safavid household had wrestled for a century with the place
of temporal kings in the Shi'i scheme of authority.[57] In fact, so entan-
gled were the Safavids in the debate as to leave them both vulnerable
to accusations of apostasy by their Sunni Ottoman foes and without
rightful claim to the privilege of founding imperial congregational
mosques.[58] The Masjed-e Jadid-e Abbasi in the Maydan of Isfahan was
the very first congregational mosque to have been built by a Safavid
shah, an unambiguous and very public gesture of confidence in the
shari'a-sanctioned resolution of the thorny issue of kingship and its
legitimacy.[59] Financed jointly by the shah and Mohebb Ali Beg Lale,
the tutor of the *gholam* pages and himself a member of the *gholam*
household elite, the building accomplished several goals at once.

Cast in the light of Safavid–Ottoman rivalry, it may be postulated that the building of such an imperial congregational mosque was intended to address the century-long Ottoman insinuations of Safavid illegitimacy as Muslim rulers. Equally significant is the local Safavid audience for whom the ascendancy of Twelver Shi'ism was crystallized in this mosque and its marking of the resolution of the debate over the legitimacy of the Friday prayer.

Shah Abbas the Great may have begun this mosque after his initial building campaign partly because the land on the southern side of the Maydan was not entirely open and available. Houses or property of individuals ranging from government officials and courtiers to a poor old woman had stood in the area where the mosque was to be built.[60] The procurement of the land, according to the sources, was complicated by property laws and the desire not to break ground in an unlawful or coerced manner for this politically critical congregational mosque. Furthermore, while other buildings were under way, construction on the Royal Mosque may have also been postponed to a time when the shah had secured the borders of his realm, especially those beleaguered by Ottoman incursions and threats. Such a moment of victory came in 1611, when Tabriz was retaken for the last time from the Ottomans, and after the signing of a lasting peace treaty on the contested northwestern frontiers in 1612.[61]

The inception of the mosque coincided with a number of key construction campaigns in centers of the Safavid domain that commenced between 1611 and 1613 and were completed in the next two decades.[62] Besides the Royal Mosque at the Maydan in Isfahan (completed in 1637 by Shah Safi), the royal cities of Ashraf and Farahabad in the Mazandaran region by the Caspian Sea were founded (Figure 1.2). Significantly, the other congregational mosque of the Safavid period was constructed during this campaign in Farahabad, the royal center in Mazandaran to which Shah Abbas the Great retreated frequently and of which he was especially fond, since he traced his matrilineal heritage to Mazandaran. This cluster of building campaigns is politically significant because it demonstrates the two-pronged Safavid conquest: along the perimeter of Safavid territory, military action had secured borders after a century of devastating defeats and losses on the northwestern frontiers; on the domestic front, the early Safavid heterodoxy of its Qezelbash-driven messianic and mystical practice of Shi'ism was displaced by an orthodoxy of Twelver Shi'i imperial structure promulgated and preserved by an increasingly powerful clerical class. These profoundly transformative restructurings of Safavid polity included the gradual but decisive replacement of the Turkmen Qezelbash power base in the Safavid court and government administration with the slaves of the household (gholams), who were mostly of Caucasian (Armenian and Georgian) and Iranian origin.[63]

The transfer of the capital in 1590/91

Here we may profitably revisit the still-debated motivations for
moving the capital for the second time at the end of the sixteenth
century (Figures 1.1 and 1.2).[64] The transfer of the capital to Isfahan
may not have issued so much from a need for security, for better trade
and diplomatic routes, or for a temperate climate – the most compelling reasons for the decision, according to much scholarship.
Rather, it seems to have been propelled by the urgency of halting the
long-standing political and religious problems from spiraling out of
control. The enduring strength of confederate tendencies represented
by the Qezelbash made the decisive break from the past all the more
necessary for the preservation of Safavid pre-eminence. In this regard,
Isfahan was a clean slate upon which Shah Abbas the Great could
erect a new paradigm of authority. There was a desperate need to
refresh and secure the political structure. A precedent for this relo-
cation to Isfahan, or reallocation of the center, may be found in Shah
Tahmasb's attempt to transform the religious-political order by
moving the capital to Qazvin, as discussed in Chapter 2. Large areas
of the imperial dominion were still very much wedded to their old
Sunni practices and beliefs. So alive were they, in fact, that even the
Safavid Shah Isma'il II (1576–8) would attempt to reinstitute the
sunna (the orthodoxy), albeit for more complex reasons.[65]

Internecine wars, court intrigue, and the political jockeying of the
Qezelbash, with the Safavid blood princes serving as their pawns had
severely undermined the authority and efficacy of the royal household. More importantly, with Qezelbash military power still considerable, the group's extremist Sufi practices (*qolovv*) reinforced its
opposition to the normative Imami doctrine that Safavid shahs, especially Tahmasb, had so painstakingly tried to instill in Safavid
society. This was a task that had pitched the royal household
against powerful forces both internal (the majority Sunni population)
and external (the rival neighbors – the Uzbeks, Mughals, and
Ottomans – were all Sunni empires). The foundations of religious
reform were laid through several initiatives, such as the creation of
patronized religious offices of the *shaykh al-Islam* (jurist–consult)
and the *sadr* (the chief cleric in charge of religious law) within the
administrative structure of Safavid polity, and through the importation of prominent Shi'i scholars from Jabal 'Amil (in present-day Syria
and southern Lebanon) to compose, teach, and propagate the practice
of Twelver or Imami Shi'ism. Safavid shahs had deployed various
means – direct and indirect, charismatic and coercive – to speed the
process of conversion in Iran, and they had anchored their authority
and legitimacy on the establishment of Twelver Shi'ism.

Qazvin had failed to serve as a secure platform from which to
launch all these efforts, a fact that became dramatically obvious after
the death of Tahmasb and the outbreak of the Second Civil War

in 1576. A succession of weak and ineffectual kings, whose very existence as shahs depended on the balance of power between the harem and the Qezelbash aristocracy, assumed the throne in Qazvin. There was, then, an urgent need to establish anew the basis for spiritual and temporal authority that constituted the Safavid claim to legitimacy. This necessitated the creation of a new capital, a new seat of rule and of religious authority. Its spiritual foundation relied on the vested interests of the clerical class, which was patronized by the shah and embraced by the household through bonds of marriage.[66] Its politico-administrative implementation relied on the unwavering loyalty of the *gholams*, the slave elite that was bonded to the Safavid household and given positions of power previously held by the Qezelbash. Isfahan was not just a pleasant, abundant, and strategic site. It was fertile ground in which to plant the seeds of the new order. And the planting of the seeds of a new order is what earned Shah Abbas I the title of "the Great" in history.

Of the new construction projects in Isfahan, the Maydan-e Naqsh-e Jahan proclaimed itself unambiguously as the heart of both the capital and the empire (Figures 3.3, 3.7, 3.8 and 3.9). Its massive scale and the orderly disposition of its forms and functions would conjure up metaphorically the reconstituted and securely anchored structure

Figure 3.9 *Isfahan, Maydan-e Naqsh-e Jahan after an engraving from Kaempfer,* Amoenitatum *(1712).*
Notwithstanding the pictorial contraction of the Maydan into a square (instead of a rectangle), this image evokes something of quotidian life in the Maydan: daily market stalls set up in front of the royal bazaar entrance; shows of wrestlers, animal battles, etc., taking place in the lower right-hand corner; the line-up of cannons (captured from the Portuguese at Hormuz) in front of the Ali Qapu Palace and the Harem Gate on the far side; a pair of polo goal posts in front of the Royal Mosque on the Maydan's south side.

Figure 3.10 *Isfahan, the Qaysariyye or Royal Bazaar and its* naqqarakhane *(kettledrum house) on the upper galleries flanking the gateway, after an engraving from the* Atlas *volume of Jean Chardin,* Voyages *(1811).*

of Safavid polity. The Qaysariyye (Royal) Bazaar at the north end of the Maydan facilitated the flow of economic and social activities between the older Seljuq and newly built Safavid parts of the city (Figuer 3.10). Its royal association, notwithstanding its very designation as such and its grand scale and function as a cloth market (a purview of trade, especially in the age of the royal monopoly on the silk trade), was reinforced in the public eye, and ear, as it were, by the placement of the *naqqarakhane* or the kettledrum house on the second floor of its principal façade.[67] In cities of rule, it was the *naqqarekhane* that regulated, with its martial music, the quotidian rhythms of life, such as the morning and evening calls to open and close gates (such as the bazaar gates), as well as the announcement of public festivals, parades, and appearances of the king.

Directly across from this grand symbol of royal beneficence and commercial health rose the minarets and domes of the magnificent congregational Friday mosque, famed in its time as the Masjed-e Jadid-e Abbasi, the New Abbasi Mosque (known popularly as the Masjed-e Shah or Royal Mosque), the symbol of Imami Shi'i triumph.[68] On either side of the Maydan, two royal monuments, the Ali Qapu Palace and the Shaykh Lotf-Allah Mosque, juxtaposed worldly authority and the otherworldly legitimacy of that authority across the width of the public square.

Isfahan, the rival "capital" of Shi'ism

A local history of Shi'ism in Isfahan is yet to be written. The Safavid episode of that narrative reveals much about the motivations and ties that led the city's political power structure – along with its cohort in the Shiʻi hierocracy – to convert Isfahan into the new capital city.[69] The choice of Isfahan, a stronghold of extremist Sunnism in centuries past, as the new center of Shiʻi learning enabled it to compete with the traditional centers of Qom and Mashhad. Could this opportunity to begin afresh the (re)composition of a normative *shariʻa*-based Twelver Shiʻism, with vestigial Sufi tendencies from the sixteenth century, be the impetus behind the choice of Isfahan as the capital? Sufism, stripped of its earlier exaggerated practices, survived in its intellectualized and gnostic philosophical variants into the first half of the seventeenth century. More importantly, a fertile environment emerged that allowed the normative, and eventually dogmatic, practices of Imami Shiʻism to rise to prominence.

Isfahan was located at a safer distance from the beleaguered Safavid–Ottoman frontiers than Qazvin, the Safavid capital in the latter half of the sixteenth century. Following the Second Civil War and the uncertainties of the years that led into and began Shah Abbas's reign, his reconstitution of the imperial household as well as the balancing of both internal and external forces seems to have necessitated a change in the matrices of power from those that had failed the shah's predecessors.[70] Isfahan's geographical location at the center of the recently secured Safavid domains lent symbolic cachet to the choice of the new capital city. Other motivating factors for relocating the capital to Isfahan included its centrality vis-à-vis the principal trade routes – north–south roads linked the Caspian Sea to the Persian Gulf, while numerous east-west arteries connected with internal and international networks. The coincidence of the military and administrative functions of these routes should be considered as another, perhaps equally compelling, motivating factor. Indeed, in the hyperbolic language of official history, as conveyed by Eskandar Beg Monshi, the principal historian of Shah Abbas, it was the ideal location and climate of Isfahan that anchored its political significance: "Having gone there often, the special qualities of that paradisiacal city, the suitability of its location, and the waters of Zayande River as well as the Kawthar [Paradise]-like channels which branch off the aforementioned river and flow in every direction, [all of these things] lodged in the resplendent heart [of the shah]."[71] Nevertheless, scholars have tended to think of the choice of Isfahan more in terms of retreat from the limitations and threats posed by Qazvin's location than in terms of the advantages of a new site for the confluence of dynastic ambitions and religious expediencies.

Certainly, Isfahan does not stand out as the most obvious choice for the launching of a new center of Shiʻi learning. Najaf and Karbala in Arab Iraq (as against Persian Iraq, as it was known until the framing of the modern nation-state) and Mashhad and Qom in Iran were major magnets of Shiʻi devotion and learning. Each figured prominently in the Shiʻi collective memory and was invested with the holy remains of Shi'i personages – Imam Ali, Imam Hossayn and his family, Imam Reza, and the latter's sister, Fatima Ma'sume. So sacred were these sites that none had ever served, or could presumably ever come to serve, as the political nerve center of a temporal power.[72] Tabriz, the first Safavid capital and one of the principal urban centers for Turco-Mongol rulers of Iran since the Mongol Ilkhanid dynasty had risen to prominence (694/1295–756/1355), is not known to have provided particularly fertile soil for seeds of religious learning to grow, although mystical extremism, especially of the Qezelbash variety, had developed roots in this region since the fourteenth-century rise of Shaykh Safi, Shaykh Haydar, and their followers in Ardabil. Qazvin, despite its political centrality in the second half of the sixteenth century and its important role in launching the teachings of the imported Shi'i scholars, seems to have been eclipsed in its development of home-grown religious aspirations by such cities as Qom and Kashan.[73]

Isfahan had over the centuries adhered to its Sunni convictions with gusto.[74] Unlike its rival city of Qom, where Shi'ism had taken firm root from the early centuries of Islam in Iran, Isfahan remained resistant for the most part, with only traces of Shi'i sympathy during, for example, the reign of the Shi'i Iranian Buyids (932–1055), who assumed the reins of political sovereignty from the caliph in Baghdad.[75]

In between this earlier marginalization of Shi'ism in the city and its rise under the Safavids lies a significant period of Shi'i activities in Isfahan. Sometime in the third century of the Islamic calendar (ninth century CE), a large number of *seyyeds* (descendants of the Prophet Mohammad) must have immigrated to Isfahan, since there are several Imamzades (tombs for the descendants of the Imams) dating from that century built in the city; among them the Imamzade Ebrahim is the best known.[76] These Imamzades, together with some important Shi'i treatises and compilations of stories of the Imams that were written in ninth-century Isfahan, have prompted the Iranian historian Rasul Jafarian to claim that several Shi'i scholars must have arrived in Isfahan during that period, some of whom were, evidently, the disciples of Imam Hadi (Ali al-Hadi, the Tenth Twelver Imam 835–68) and Imam Sadeq (Ja'far al-Sadiq, the Sixth Twelver Imam 737–65).[77] This evidence has led Jafarian to assert that Isfahan was something of a new center of Shi'i scholarship in the ninth century.[78] By the tenth century, the oft-ferocious Sunnism of Isfahanis had been diluted by the increase in numbers of both the Imami and Zaydi Shi'is (whose political theory permitted the leadership of the community to more than one follower of Imam Ali).[79] This trend was further reinforced by the impact of those Sunni Muslims who were devotees or friends of the family of the Prophet.

Shi'i scholarship seems to have survived in Isfahan even during the twelfth and thirteenth centuries, when the rival Sunni Hanafi and Shafi'i factions became prominent in the city's life, alongside the royal-institutional support of such Seljuq (1036–1194) grandees as

Khwaje Nezam al-Molk, the founder of the Nezamiyye Madrasa system in Isfahan and Baghdad as well as other theological colleges in medieval urban centers.[80] Given the inflammatory relations between the Hanafi and Shafi'i clans of Isfahan – an enmity so intense that the Shafi'i leadership betrayed the city during the Mongol siege of 638 AH (1240/1 CE), thereby causing the massacre of both clans and much of the city's population – Shi'ism may have benefited from an anti-Sunni backlash, a popular revulsion.

Growing support for Shi'ism in Isfahan

During the ensuing Ilkhanid reign (1256–1335), the Shi'i cause was helped enormously by the Jovayni family's rise to administrative prominence. The Jovaynis ruled on behalf of the Ilkhans in Baghdad, and their patronage injected new energy for expansion into the Shi'i community. Both Ata Malek and Shams al-Din Jovayni had Shi'i tendencies. Shams al-Din appointed his son Baha al-Din Jovayni, reputedly a Twelver Shi'i believer, to the governorship of Isfahan. He in turn lent his support to Emad al-Din Tabari, a jurist and speculative theologian and one of the key figures in the spread of Shi'ism in Isfahan.[81] In Tabari's *Manaqeb al-taherayn* (Glorious Deeds of the Pure Ones, completed in 1274–5), the author relates that in his time and thanks to Jovayni patronage and Baha al-Din's support, Shi'is of Isfahan had begun for the first time in centuries to follow openly and express their devotion to the precepts set by the Twelve Imams and the family of the Prophet. The very fact that Emad al-Din Tabari was invited by the governor to engage in debates with Sunnis in Isfahan, and that he wrote most of his treatise on Twelver Shi'ism in Isfahan, indicates that its popular practice had flourished there in the thirteenth century.

Perhaps even more important is the fact that Tabari wrote his *Tohfat al-abrar*, an instructional book expounding the principles and doctrinal practices of Twelver Shi'ism, in clear and accessible Persian. In an environment where Arabic predominated linguistically in religious scholarship, this choice of Persian signals the growing popularization of Shi'ism, a trend that picked up momentum after the Safavids declared Shi'ism the religion of the realms.[82] Already in the late thirteenth and early fourteenth centuries, then, Isfahan had begun to play a notable role in popularizing and Persianizing the creed of the Prophet's family.

This Shi'i ascendancy, however, did not translate into mass conversion; nor did it mean that Shi'is did not suffer from their minority status and challenges to their doctrine. It is recorded, for example, that during the month of Muharram, when Twelver Shi'is, in particular, engage in an intense period of ritual mourning to commemorate the martyrdom of Imam Hossayn and his family, the Sunni residents of Isfahan denigrated their beliefs by assuming a celebratory attitude, donning new clothes, grooming their appearance, and dancing and congratulating one another in public – all behaviors associated with religious *'ids* or festivals.[83]

Royal support for Shi'ism may have also begun to materialize in more concrete terms when the Mongol-Ilkhanid ruler of Iran Öljeitu (known also by his Islamic name of Soltan Mohammad Khodabande) converted from Sunni Islam to Shi'ism in 1309/10.[84] He ordered the minting of new coins that bore the names of the Imams and decreed that the *khotbe* (Friday noon prayer sermon) include their names, while at the same time excluding those of the four historical caliphs, whose legitimacy Sunnis upheld. This was indeed a clear and recognizable subversion of what had been customary among the Sunni Muslim majority throughout the historical and geographical span of Islam. Such newfound energy did not, however, meet with an entirely enthusiastic reception. Popular resistance erupted in Qazvin and Isfahan, and Soltan Mohammad Khodabande in 1310/11 had to dispatch armies to Isfahan to extinguish the fire that was fanned there by Maulana Nezam al-Din Abu Eshaq, the fanatical Sunni doctor. Abu Eshaq was arrested and brought to the shah, but to no avail, since Soltan Mohammad Khodabande died in this same period.[85]

Nevertheless, as Twelver Shi'ism gained stability in some of its principal theological doctrines in Ilkhanid Iran, Isfahan, too, must have seen a consolidated and enlarged Shi'i presence in aristocratic circles, if not also in the populace at large.[86] Among the clear signs of this interface between the popular and the royal is the famed mihrab of Öljeitu at the Great Mosque of Isfahan.[87] This monumental and magnificently carved stucco mihrab was added in the month of Safar in 710 AH (June 1310) soon after Soltan Mohammad Khodabande's conversion to Shi'ism. Its epigraphic program is unusual in that it makes no use of the Qur'an; it is also noteworthy for its Shi'i invocation of the names of the family of the Prophet (the *ahl al-bayt*) and its use of the phrase "There is no God but God, Mohammad is His Prophet, Ali His deputy."[88]

By the second half of the fourteenth century, there must have been enough Shi'is in Isfahan to have formed a neighborhood of their own; the Muslim traveler Ibn Battuta (d. 1368/9) seems to indicate having seen just such an enclave. Further evidence of a relatively peaceful coexistence of Sunni and Shi'i populations of Isfahan may be gauged from other epigraphic markings in the buildings and additions dated to the fourteenth and fifteenth centuries at the Madrasa Imami, also known as the Madrasa of Baba Qasem, the Imamzade Isma'il, and the so-called Ayvan of Omar (on the eastern side of the courtyard) in the Great Mosque of Isfahan. In all these buildings the epigraphic Shi'i invocations occur in an otherwise Sunni context of patronage or popular consumption.[89] As Jafarian has noted, this tolerance toward Shi'ism in Isfahan may also be found both in the coins minted in the fourteenth century and in the appearance of what he calls a tendency toward Twelver Imamate Sunnism expressed in the epigraphic hybridity of fifteenth-century monuments in Isfahan.[90] In the hindsight of history, by the advent of the Safavids in the sixteenth century, Isfahan had been "softened" enough to embrace Shah Isma'il's creed of Imamate authority and to abstain from any form of overt resistance to the imposition of his sovereignty.

Safavid sponsorship of Shi'ism

The Safavid sponsorship of Shi'ism as a state religion, not just of a minority community but of the imperial domains, began at the very foundation of the dynasty in Tabriz and proceeded throughout the sixteenth century. In practical terms, it depended upon the importation of noted Shi'i scholars from Jabal 'Amil and their integration into the ecclesiastic hierarchy.[91] The Shi'ification project was accomplished with mixed success during the first century of Safavid rule. One of the greatest obstacles to the claims of Safavid shahs to the ideal of Imamate authority was the fact that the Shi'i jurists of the realm could not agree on the legitimacy and permissibility of the Friday prayer (salat al-Jum'a). The Shi'i practice in which congregational Friday prayer was to be shunned in the absence of the Imam had exposed the early Safavids to Sunni accusations – by Ottoman and Uzbek rivals, in particular – of apostasy and insinuations of illegitimacy. Shahs Isma'il and Tahmasb and their immediate successors were keenly aware of the political significance of the restoration of the Friday prayer for the legitimization of Safavid sovereign authority. It was largely to that end that the Safavids were eager to employ the Shi'i scholars of Jabal 'Amil, whose juridical philosophy was sympathetic to the imperial designs of the Safavids. Their legal opinion simultaneously gave legitimacy to the political foundation of Safavid rule and helped to establish the clerical assumption of Imamate authority.

Nevertheless, the resolution of the Friday prayer controversy was hampered by the complex intersecting interests and agendas of various social groups – the royal household, the Qezelbash aristocracy, the Persian nobility, the urban merchants and artisans, and the lower strata of Safavid society – together with the diverse ethnicities and doctrinal tendencies of religious forces that ranged from extremist Sufism and folk Shi'ism, to rationalist Shi'ism and Sunnism, all in full play during the tumultuous sixteenth century.[92] Uncertainty about the practice of Friday prayer and its accompanying sermon, which allowed the religious jurist publicly to affirm the authority of the king, left Safavid shahs in the awkward position of having failed to commission a single congregational mosque in any of their cities of rule during the sixteenth century.[93] With the transfer of the capital to Isfahan and greater centralization of Safavid polity, Shah Abbas I reinvigorated the Safavid patronage of the 'Amili scholars by inviting some of the most influential members of that theological school to assume positions of religious leadership in his new capital city. Lotf-Allah al-Maysi (d. 1622/3), better known as Shaykh Lotf-Allah, Mir Damad (d. 1631/2), the philosopher and court jurist, and Shaykh Baha'i (d. 1621), the famous Gnostic philosopher, mathematician, and Shi'i scholar, were among the 'Amili theologians who had forged unprecedented close ties with Shah Abbas I and who were appointed to the position of the Shaykh al-Islam of the new capital.[94] The profound influence of the philosophical and legal opinions of these Shi'i scholars on the articulation of the urban scheme of Isfahan, and especially on the launching of the first imperial congregational mosque of the Safavids, remains woefully under studied. Both Shaykh Lotf-Allah and Shaykh Baha'i were instrumental in advancing Shi'i juridical arguments that legitimized, and even made incumbent upon the faithful, the performance of congregational Friday prayer during the period of Occultation of the Mahdi, thus paving the way for the resumption of the building of congregational mosques in Safavid Iran.

Shaykh Lotf-Allah, religious leader of Isfahan

Shaykh Lotf-Allah had grown up and trained in Mashhad in the shadow of the shrine of Imam Reza before seeking refuge in Qazvin to escape the fate that befell the denizens of Herat when, in 1588/9, the Uzbeks captured Herat and massacred its Shi'i population.[95] The Shi'i scholar was given a lectureship at the court of Shah Abbas the Great in Qazvin and soon after was sent to assume the state-sponsored religious leadership of Isfahan. As a consequence of his royal patronage, Shaykh Lotf-Allah was included in the royal household, which paid his salary and teaching expenses from the royal treasury, and his daughter was given into the royal harem and married to Shah Abbas the Great. His unwavering loyalty to the shah, his promulgation of the Safavid dynasty's descent from Imam Ali's holy lineage, and his extension of juridical support to the Safavid claim to rightful temporal authority on behalf of the Mahdi (Messiah) rendered Shaykh Lotf-Allah the most significant Safavid ally among the clerical class. Thus he upheld the opinion that the performance of the Friday prayer was unconditionally required of every Shi'i, a position at odds with that of nearly every other cleric in Safavid Iran.[96]

The 1602–3 building campaign at the Maydan-e Naqsh-e Jahan included the commencement on its eastern flank of the exquisitely proportioned, single-chamber, single-domed royal chapel-mosque that was probably constructed by Shah Abbas for Shaykh Lotf-Allah and that was associated with his madrasa, where he had resided since his dispatch on royal orders to teach in Isfahan (Plate 6). Recent scholarship, especially by Abisaab, has confirmed that this chapel-mosque was intended for Shaykh Lotf-Allah from the outset and has thus concluded a debate that had arisen from the fact that contemporary

sources do not link him to the chapel-mosque.[97] Contrary to Abisaab's
and Blake's assertions, however, the Mosque of Shaykh Lotf-Allah was
not intended as the new congregational mosque of the city. Such an
assumption ignores the complete architectural incongruity of the
Shaykh Lotf-Allah Mosque as a congregational edifice, especially
given that a new congregational mosque would need to accommodate
large masses of the residents of Isfahan, who would have been diverted
from the medieval Masjed-e Jom'e, the Great Mosque. The task of
building such a congregational mosque, undoubtedly integral to the
entire Maydan project, began in 1611 at the time when Shah Abbas
the Great also embarked on the building of another major congregational mosque, this one in his Mazandaran city of Farahabad.[98]

Instead, the Shaykh Lotf-Allah Mosque exemplified a singularly
creative refashioning of the *maqsura* feature of congregational
mosques associated with the patronage of Sunni kings. The maqsura
constituted an especially sanctified zone at or in the vicinity of the
mihrab occupied by the ruler when he attended Friday prayer.[99] The
exclusivity of the maqsura ordinarily received heightened architectural attention – domes aggrandized the rarity of the spot, and inventive methods of construction and decoration were employed to sheath
the space in a splendor worthy of royal presence. In Isfahan the Shaykh
Lotf-Allah Mosque represents just such an idea, but here wrought on
the scale of a free-standing building rather than a domed chamber or
a fenced-off area. Its graceful dome is held aloft through a system of
supports, not seen before, that merge the four walls of the prayer
chamber into massive corner pendentives. The ring of intricately
grilled windows mediates the pendentive zone and the dome and
allows for shafts of light to appear as though mysteriously upholding
the dome. The sheathing of the entire interior in tilework of predominantly turquoise blue creates an awesome visual impact, heightened
by the placement of a sunburst pattern in golden yellow in the inner
dome. The Shaykh Lotf-Allah Mosque is a jewel-box of a building, not
unlike the maqsura at the Great Mosque of Cordova and the maqsura-
like edifice of the North Dome at the Great Mosque of Isfahan.[100]

The dialogic relationship between the patronized cleric Shaykh
Lotf-Allah and the Shi'i shah is embodied architecturally and functionally across the width of the Maydan, where the Shaykh Lotf-
Allah Mosque and the Ali Qapu Palace face each other (Plate 5).
Regardless of whether the shah had intended the chapel-mosque to
serve as a base for his father-in-law and principal juridical voice,
Shaykh Lotf-Allah, the very royal associations of this small house of
worship enunciate its intended function as an emblem of the piety
and legitimacy of the Safavid household. The chapel-mosque and the
palace create one symbolic–spatial axis of the Maydan. The other,
with which they intersect, links the royal bazaar of Qaysariyye with
the congregational mosque, Masjed-e Jadid-e Abbasi. Together they
constitute the connective tissue of the socio-political, economic, and

religious foundations of the empire in the physical structure of the Maydan-e Naqsh-e Jahan.

The complex enterprise of Shiʿification and normalization of the political practice of Perso-Shiʿi kingship required the forging of alliances among various social collectivities – the clerical class, the Sufi orders, the Qezelbash military and administrative aristocracy, the old landed nobility, and the prominent merchant families. One case of such negotiated identities, albeit violently settled, is that of the Noqtavi millenarian movement in the sixteenth century.[101] Their mystic version of Islam attracted followers among the urban artisan and merchant classes as well as the Qezelbash members of Safavid society. Claiming legitimacy on behalf of the expected Mahdi (Messiah), the Noqtavi clash with the state-sponsored rationalist practice of Twelver Shiʿism reached its zenith during the Second Civil War (1576–90) and was finally and vehemently suppressed by Shah Abbas I. Despite such expressions of resistance and revolt, Shah Abbas managed to consolidate Safavid power and authority through means, brutal at times, couched in the guise of the charisma of Imam Ali and the Imami-inspired articulation of kingship.[102] His order to gouge out the eyes of his sons and grandsons, potential contenders for the Safavid throne who were thus made impotent for the post, and the systematic annihilation of the Noqtavi leaders – one was hung by the throat from a camel saddle and paraded in Qazvin, while another "was hit with the sword into the halves of justice by the blessed hand itself" (an allusion no doubt to Solomonic justice) – were measures taken to consolidate power and the normative practice of Twelver Shiʿism, even though not all were sanctioned by the *ulama*.[103] Shiʿi scholars, such as Shaykh Lotf-Allah and Shaykh Bahaʾi, lent their support and provided the necessary veil of legitimacy to the political design.

Shaykh Bahaʾi, chief theologian of the capital

Shaykh Bahaʾi, the Shiʿi jurist, scholar, and Gnostic philosopher, was the most important and instrumental member of the clergy during the formative period of rule from Isfahan. His mastery of mathematics, geometry, and astronomy, among other sciences, is recorded in numerous treatises. To him is attributed the calculation of the correct direction of *qibla* (the point to which Muslims turn for prayer) for the Royal Mosque, the Masjed-e Jadid-e Abbasi in Isfahan.[104] He was deeply engaged in the design of the extensive epigraphic program whose inscription bands graced the main portal, the ayvan frames, and the domes and minarets of the Royal Mosque.[105] He also drafted the *waqf* deed (endowment) for this mosque of which the shah and the *gholam* Mohebb Ali Beg Lale were the principal endowers.[106]

Shaykh Bahaʾi was originally appointed in 1576 by Soltan Mohammad Khodabande as the Shaykh al-Islam (chief jurist consult) of Isfahan.[107] Despite his family's close ties with the court, he remained largely aloof from the political intrigues and crises that afflicted the Safavids during the last years of Isma'il II and Khodabande and the beginning years of the reign of Shah Abbas I, having gone as far as to leave his post for a long journey to the holy cities of Islam and the Ottoman lands. In 1600, Shah Abbas appointed him again to the post of Shaykh al-Islam of Isfahan.[108] Besides assuming the role of chief theologian of the new capital, Shaykh Baha'i also served as the principal voice of juridical counsel to the shah.

Among Shaykh Baha'i's prolific output is the famous *Jame'-e Abbasi*, which expounds on the *shari'a* bases of religious practice, especially pertinent to the Safavid household in Isfahan. The treatise, commissioned by Shah Abbas and written in Persian, made accessible to the court the principles of Imami faith; as such it contributed significantly to the court-sponsored process of the Persianization of Shi'ism. We will return to the relevance of Shaykh Baha'i's treatise to the palaces and court ceremonials, but for now it suffices to emphasize the significance of this manual of "political ethics" in regulating and codifying the conduct of the household in accordance with the *shari'a*.[109] Shaykh Baha'i's juridical arguments on the necessity of the resumption of Friday prayer (also vigorously supported by Shaykh Lotf-Allah), his deep involvement with the entire campaign of the first congregational mosque of the Safavids at the south end of the Maydan, and his Persian manual for the correct *shari'a*-based Imami Shi'i conduct of the restructured Safavid household in its new imperial capital city – these all were among the multifarious strategies of Shi'ification and Persianization that characterize the imperial designs Shah Abbas I carried out in alliance with Shaykh Baha'i, Shaykh Lotf-Allah, and other members of the clerical elite. It is in light of the intentionalities of urban design and their synergies with the institutionalization of the Perso-Shi'i ethos of kingship that Isfahan should be read as the city of paradise, the Safavid reiteration on earth of the Promised Paradise.

Isfahan: the politics of space

Although Isfahan was already well developed and quite prominent on the map of the medieval cities of Asia, the early modern Safavid refashioning of the city as the capital was not shaped by the same gradual integration of the new urban elements into the old fabric of the city as were, for example, Istanbul, Madrid, Paris, and London. Safavid urban development was largely a matter of annexing medieval Isfahan to an entirely new city consisting of a freshly conceived assemblage of forms, functions, and meanings and absorbing and accommodating the city's established resources, both human and material. Whereas in Istanbul or Paris the new, centralized imperial skin was grafted onto the old through the strategic positioning of monumental structures and the establishment of spatial or ceremonial linkages between the old and new functions and symbols, in Isfahan the integrity of the old city was left intact, while an entirely new city was partnered with it internally through the grand bazaar artery (Figure 3.6). Externally, the new Safavid city became the filter through which trade and diplomatic missions had to pass if they were to reach the marketplaces, caravanserais, mosques, and other points of interest in the old city.

Equally significant is the fact that the architectural interests of the court followed and were integrated into the urban development of Isfahan rather than preceding it. In the case of Madrid or Agra, for example, in contrast to Safavid Isfahan, urban renewal issued, rather unsystematically, from the transfer of the court and the construction of a permanent imperial seat.[110] While a similar imperial imprint characterizes nearly all these early modern reconstituted capital cities, Isfahan represents an exceptional urban solution to the problem of how to adapt an old city to emergent political ideologies.

In nearly all the large imperial polities of the early modern period, the conversion of the capital city involved a political transition toward centralization and absolutism and began with either the addition of a new palace ensemble or a substantial intervention in the royal precincts built by past rulers. Irrespective of the scale and nature of the conversion, architecture represented the relationship between the seat of authority, the palace, and the city. Urban public spaces for political, social, and commercial exchange and encounter – maydans/ squares/piazzas, marketplaces, avenues, civic centers, and parks, commemorative monuments, palaces and houses of governance and of worship – articulated these relationships. Moreover, the link between architecture and political ideology was narrated differently in each city of rule and depended on the degree to which destruction, reconstruction, and new construction were possible or permissible in each context.

In Madrid, for example, Philip II (r. 1556–98) had substantially remodeled the old (Islamic) palace of Alcazar when the city was chosen as his capital in 1561.[111] The medieval city was too small to house the influx of courtiers and officials, and expansion was directed outward to the east of the city. While the Alcazar remained the main seat of the court in Madrid in the 1630s, Philip's grandson, Philip IV, added the Buen Retiro, a massive ensemble that began as a cluster of royal apartments adjacent to the monastery of San Jerónimo. This, as Brown and Elliott point out, "permanently changed the face of the capital."[112] In contrast to these additive constructions, in Isfahan the new palace precinct was embraced within and synchronized with a completely new urban scheme.

The Red Fort at Agra, too, developed over a long period of time, beginning with Emperor Akbar's fortified royal residence from 1564, which was expanded architecturally and enhanced ceremonially by successive Mughal emperors, reaching its apogee under Shah Jahan's exacting scheme of bilateral symmetry as an indicator of imperial iconography (Figures 6.7 and 6.9).[113] But in all its transformations, the Agra Red Fort remained, "urbanistically" speaking, aloof from the larger city.[114] In Istanbul, the famed Constantinople of Byzantium loomed large in the minds of the Ottoman conquerors (led by Mehmet Fatih in 1453) (Figure 6.1).[115] A new palace, Yeni Saray (better known as the Topkapı), was placed in the same spot on the Third Hill where the ruined old Byzantine palace had stood.[116] Other symbols of Constantinople's past, such as the magnificent Byzantine church of Hagia Sophia and the ancient Romano-Byzantine urban center at the Hippodrome, were converted and adapted to new uses for the Ottoman capital city. In Paris, the gargantuan Louvre Palace was the result of centuries of architectural responses to changes in politics and taste.[117] Here again, the palace was set amid medieval city spaces with little intervention in the urban fabric that surrounded it. As with the Louvre in Paris, the Buen Retiro in Madrid also remained aloof from the medieval urban squalor in the midst of which it was placed. The Isfahani definition of imperial space stretched, on the other hand, well beyond the palace to the royal residential quarters and their associated public amenities (neighborhood maydans and bazaars).

These conceptualizations of the capital city in the early modern age of centralized empires articulate the urban and spatial relationships between various social groups and the seat of rule. The Hapsburg nobility built mansions in the vicinity of the court after Philip II transferred the capital from Toledo to Madrid in 1561.[118] Similarly, the French nobility's *hôtels* were clustered around the Place des Vosges in Paris (constructed under Henri IV, 1605–12). This was a public square with such a degree of geometric precision – expressed in its ground plan and the elevation of the arcade and residences that delineate its periphery – that the clash of differing urban layouts becomes acutely tangible in the contrast between this seventeenth-century public space and the rhythm of winding narrow streets of its medieval neighborhood. In both cases – Madrid and Paris – such socially motivated architectural gestures as mansions seek proximity, both literally and figuratively, to the nexus of power. In both, however, the separation in urban terms is made visible by the fact that these upscale residential quarters remain independent from the plan of the imperial capital of which the palace is the central focus.

In Isfahan, the urban and palatine schemes issued forth as correlatives of a single, hegemonic conceptual and political agenda. Freshly conceived, on an unprecedented scale, the city of Isfahan grew according to a design wholly different from its medieval predecessor but still closely tied in to its urban roots. And in this grand scheme, the proximity of a city dweller to the royal household pivoted on the quotidian and perambulatory experience of the capital city in the way the urban design anticipated the social positioning of the noble owners of the mansions in the city.

There is nothing extraordinary about seeking proximity to the king and the abode of power and authority, although strategies may vary and lived experience is bound to alter the initial designs. The Ottoman solution consisted of two types of residences. One was the urban mansion (*saray*), often located in the city but at a remove from the very secluded and formidably fortified palace of Topkapı in the old city. From the sixteenth century onwards, when the centralization of Ottoman rule had reached its maturity, the elite also chose to build their elegant *yalis* (villas with balconies and porches facing the waterfront) along the Bosporus at a considerable distance from the Topkapı, while at the same time consciously imitating the design of royal retreats in the hanging gardens of the palace on the shores of the Golden Horn.[119]

The Mughal urban mansions, *haveli*, of the same general period are largely lost and nearly impossible to assess.[120] Among the few details known is the location of the garden-mansions in Agra, where they stood side by side along the Yamuna River on the bank opposite the Red Fort and the Taj Mahal.[121] This configuration, too, separates the elite from the sort of urban engagement that we find in the city of Isfahan and its planned residential quarters. It is precisely the staged relationship between the grandees and the shahs in Isfahan's mansions, palaces, and public urban spaces that enunciates the tight-knit structure of Safavid polity and its urban representations.[122]

In a city without walls, as the new Isfahan had for all practical purposes become, the implied center–periphery rapport permeated all aspects of urban and imperial design. Imaginary circles of significance radiated out from the inner core of the Maydan and the Daulatkhane to embrace the totality of the Safavid dominion in a hierarchically and iconographically ordered system of urban spaces. In this reading of the city, the Maydan components delineated, embraced, and protected the "core matter" that was represented by the deliberate positioning of the symbols of religion (the two mosques) and commerce (the bazaar). The public square also facilitated, in the liminal space of the Ali Qapu Palace, the enunciation of imperial authority. The Daulatkhane palace ensemble represented, in its Islamicate palatine tradition of formal and functional plentitude, imperial prerogatives and responsibilities that are distinctively Islamic and Perso-Shi'i.

Democratized spaces of leisure at the Maydan and the Chahar Bagh Promenade brought the denizens of the capital into public zones of urban life. The multifunctionality of similar urban spaces as marketplaces and parade arenas, found in both the Islamicate and Christian worlds in this period, did not necessarily translate into urban dedication to leisure time. While, in fact, the very notion of leisure time will need to be better situated in this historical context, it is worth emphasizing that Safavid Isfahan's design was premised on accessibility to the general citizenry of its principal urban arenas of entertainment. As such, it indeed represents a distinctive accommodation of public leisure among early modern capital cities.

Housing arrangements of various social groups – from the merchant families of the Abbasabad quarter to the Armenian Julfan suburb, to *gholam* residences along the Chahar Bagh – inscribed the new capital with radiating rings of social and imperial bonds and obligations. These planned housing projects found, in the suburban palace of Hezar Jarib (also known as Abbasabad for its patron Shah Abbas I), their imperial correlative on the outermost circle (Figures 3.1, 3.2 and 3.8). In other words, Isfahan in its visual and spatial representations of the center-periphery enunciates the structure of Safavid polity and its political, religious, social, and cultural dominion over these Perso-Shi'i realms of Iran. The Isfahan of Abbas I and his immediate successors served as a slate upon which were mapped the inner workings of the relationship between the reformatted imperial structure of power and the society of Safavid Iran. This braiding of the new and the old, the center and the periphery, in the rituals and etiquette of kingship, will be explored in the next chapter as we turn to the palaces in Isfahan.

Here, it is worth reiterating the very premise of my argument in this chapter. Safavid Isfahan, in its deliberate distribution of urban functions and their associated spatial and architectural articulations, represents a methodical rendering of a planned city. As the new capital city of a polity that was, moreover, constitutive of the promised justice embedded in the order of a Twelver Shi'i kingship, Isfahan of the Safavids made use of tangible allusions to paradise by deploying the metanarrative of a *chahar-bagh* garden in its master plan. Its emphasis on the harmony of parts and their metaphorically interlinked meanings grafts onto the terrestrial site an imagined representation of the paradisiacal realm and makes this realm legible to the city dweller.

Notes

1. Eskandar Beg Monshi, *Tarikh-e alam ara-ye Abbasi*, ed. Iraj Afshar, 2 vols (Tehran: Entesharat-e Amir Kabir, 1350/1971), 544; the exact origin of this phrase needs further probing.
2. Ibid.
3. Thomas Herbert, *Travels in Persia 1627–1629*, abridged edn ed. W. Foster (London: G. Routledge and Sons, Ltd, 1928), 127.
4. Masashi Haneda, "Maydan et Bagh. Reflexion à propos de l'urbanisme du Šah 'Abbas," in *Documents et Archives Provenant de L'Asie Centrale: Actes du colloque franco-japonais, Kyoto* (Kyoto International Conference Hall et Univ. Ryukoku, 4–8 octobre 1988), ed. Akira Haneda (Kyoto: Association Franco-Japonaise des Études Orientales, 1990), 87–99; M.

Bazin, "Bāg ii., Garden, general overview," *Encyclopaedia Iranica*, Vol. 3 (1989): 393–5; David Stronach, "Čahārbāg," *Encyclopaedia Iranica*, Vol. 4 (1990): 624–5; Sussan Babaie, "Paradise Contained: Nature and Culture in Persian Gardens," *The Studio Potter* 25, no. 2 (June 1997): 10–13.

5. On the gates that served the palace, see Chapter 4 below.

6. Honarfar, *Ganjine*, 685–722.

7. For further discussions of these intertwined issues of Twelver or Imami Shi'ism and kingship, see Amir Arjomand, *The Shadow of God*, and Babayan, *Mystics, Monarchs and Messiahs*.

8. Haneda, "Maydan et Bagh," 88–91, supports the "afterthought" argument on the basis, mainly, of the divergent axes of the Maydan and the orientation of the Qibla (direction of prayer for the orientation of the mosques on the Maydan periphery); McChesney, "Four Sources," 117–18, bases his "afterthought" conclusion on Shah Abbas' aborted effort to clean up the Old Maydan and its bazaars as a reason for the development of the new Maydan area.

9. Shafaqi, *Joghrafiya-ye tarikhi-ye Isfahan*, 262–72.

10. Arab and Persian historians and travelers are discussed in Hossein Kamaly, "Politics, Economy and Culture in Isfahan, 540–1040" (PhD dissertation, Columbia University, 2004).

11. For the early development of Isfahan, the seminal article by Lisa Golombek, "Urban Patterns in pre-Safavid Isfahan," *Iranian Studies* 7, no. 3 (1974): 18–44, remains the principal work of scholarship. For the development of the walls of the medieval city, also see Heinz Gaube and Eugene Wirth, *Der Bazar von Isfahan* (Weisbaden: Ludwig Reichert Verlag, 1978), fig. 14, p. 42; and Heinz Gaube, *Iranian Cities* (New York: New York University Press, 1978), 65–82.

12. For the neighborhoods, see Shafaqi, *Joghrafiya-ye tarikhi-ye Isfahan*, 375–400. The footprint of one such urban pattern can be traced around a seventeenth-century house in the neighborhood west of the Great Mosque of Isfahan between the Jammale and Darb-e Qasr quarters; a study of the houses and residential neighborhoods of Isfahan will be the subject of my next book.

13. For references to these gardens and palaces, see Honarfar, *Ganjine*, 56–8.

14. For the Buyids, see Mottahedeh, *Loyalty and Leadership*.

15. Ibn Hawqal, *Surat al-arz*, 367 AH/977–78 CE, as quoted in Shafaqi, *Joghrafiya-ye tarikhi-ye Isfahan*, 268–70.

16. Oleg Grabar, "The Visual Arts, 1050–1350," in *Cambridge History of Iran*: Vol. 5 *the Seljuq and Mongol Periods*, ed. J. A. Boyle (Cambridge: Cambridge University Press, 1968), 626–48, for an overview of Seljuq architectural and artistic production and the problem of studying this period. Essays in the volume edited by Robert Hillenbrand, *The Art of the Saljuqs in Iran and Anatolia* (Costa Mesa, CA: Mazda Publishers, 1994) delve deeper into various aspects of Seljuq architecture.

17. Naser Khosraw, *Safarnama*, trans. Wheeler M. Thackston Jr (Albany, NY: Bibliotheca Persica, 1986), 98.

18. Mofzil ibn Sa'd ibn al-Hossayn al-Mafarokhi al-Esfahani, *Mahasen Esfahan*, ed. Sayyed Jalal al-Din al-Hossayni al-Tehrani (Tehran: Eqbal, n.d.), 52–9.

19. Honarfar, *Ganjine*, 37–40; Golombek, "Urban Patterns," 25–6; Gaube and Wirth, *Der Bazar von Isfahan*, 35–6 and 260, for walls and citadel. See also Gaube, *Iranian Cities*, 65–98.

20. Shafaqi, *Joghrafiya-ye tarikhi-ye Isfahan*, 179; Honarfar, *Ganjine*, 37, relates the presence of two large natural cisterns that formed a moat for the Qal'e.

21. Essays in James D. Tracy, ed., *City Walls: The Urban Enceinte in Global Perspective* (Cambridge: Cambridge University Press, 2000) address different practices in urban wall enclosures, including some in the Islamic world. For a handy albeit general consideration of walls and fortifications, see Spiro Kostof, *The City Assembled: the Elements of Urban Form through History* (Boston; New York; London: Bullfinch, 1992), 26–38.

22. An old photograph of Isfahan's old walls is reproduced in Honarfar, *Ganjine*, 39. Jean Chardin's description is found in *Voyages du Chevalier Chardin*, vol. 7, 484–92; the English translation is from Ferrier, *A Journey to Persia*, 57–8.

23. Natanzi, *Noqavat al-asar*, 233 and 238–42. Farhad Beg had entered the Safavid court as a young slave (*gholam*) well before Shah Abbas came to power. During the reign of Soltan Mohammad Khodabande (1578–87), his deft handling of court intrigue earned him the governorship of the province of Iraq that included Isfahan. The chaos and civil war that preceded, and continued for a brief time into, the reign of Shah Abbas gave the wealthy and powerful Farhad Beg an opportunity to seize Isfahan as his personal dominion. Following a brief period of toleration, Abbas I set out to subdue the governor by having him imprisoned before the shah was to visit the city in 1587. This led to armed confrontation between Abbas' forces and Farhad Beg's brothers and supporters, who barricaded themselves into the Qal'e Tabarrok.

24. Gaube and Wirth, *Der Bazar von Isfahan*; Haneda, "Maydan et Bagh"; and Masashi Haneda, "The Character of the Urbanization of Isfahan in the Later Safavid Period," in *Safavid Persia: The History and Politics of an Islamic Society*, ed. Charles Melville, Pembroke Persian Papers, 4 (London: I. B. Tauris, in association with the Centre of Middle Eastern Studies, University of Cambridge, 1996), 369–88. See also Stephen Blake, *Half the World: The Social Architecture of Safavid Isfahan, 1590–1722* (Costa Mesa, CA: Mazda Publishers, 1999), 43 for a chart with the names of the gates and their locations on a map of the city that, unfortunately, is inaccurate.

25. Pascal Coste, *Monuments modernes de la Perse, mesurés, dessinés et décrits par Pascal Coste. Publiés par ordre de son excellence le ministre de la maison de l'empereur et des beaux-arts* (Paris: A. Morel, 1867), Pl. III and pp. 11–20; and Haneda's convincing assessment in "The Character of the Urbanization of Isfahan," 370–2.

26. Gaube and Wirth, *Der Bazar von Isfahan*, 44, 45 and 48 where the quotation from Chardin appears; Chardin, *Voyages du Chevalier Chardin*, 14.

27. Gaube and Wirth, *Der Bazar von Isfahan*, 43–9; Haneda, "The Character of the Urbanization of Isfahan," 370–2; Haneda, "Maydan et Bagh," 92–3.

28. Rosemarie Quiring-Zoche, *Isfahan im 15. und 16. Jahrhundert: Ein Beitrag zur persischen Stadtgeschichte* (Freiberg: Schwarz, 1980), 60–7.

29. The suspect *Jahangusha-ye khaqan*, a manuscript attributed to the reign of Shah Isma'il, edited by Allah Dotta Maztar (Islamabad: Center for Persian Studies of Iran and Pakistan, 1984), p. 304, is the only source I am aware of in which Isma'il is credited with architectural works or expansion at the Maydan-e Naqsh-e Jahan.

30. Ghiyas al-Din b. Humam al-Din Mohammad Khwand Amir, *Habib al-Siyar*, ed. J. Homa'i (Tehran: Khayyam Publishers, 1333/1954), 480 and Hasan Bek Rumlu, *Ahsan al-tavarikh*, ed. 'Abd al-Hosayn Nava'i. (Tehran: Bongah-e Tarjomeh va Nashr-e Ketab, 1978), 113 record the event at the "maydan-e balade-ye Esfahan" and "maydan-e Esfahan," respectively. While neither specifies the Naqsh-e Jahan, Eskandar Beg's reference to this event specifies the location as *maydan-e naqsh-e jahan-e esfahan*; Monshi, *Tarikh-e alam ara-ye Abbasi*, 31.

31. This comes from Eskandar Beg Monshi, a much later source; for the discussion of sources on the genesis of the Ali Qapu, see Sussan Babaie, "Safavid Palaces in Isfahan: Continuity and Change (1599–1666)" (PhD diss., New York University, 1994), 120–2.

32. The only exception is Stephen Blake's proposed map of Isfahan in 1722. It contains numerous errors and is based on an incorrect orientation. Moreover, he does not recognize a different configuration of gates and walls in the mid-seventeenth century (see his identification of gates in chart 43); rather, he draws the line on the south-southwesterly direction to include the Madrasa Soltani built by Shah Soltan Hossayn at the beginning of the eighteenth century.

33. Gaube and Wirth, *Der Bazar von Isfahan*, 34, where a chart suggests that the Daulat Gate may have pre-dated the Safavids; also see 43 and 48.

34. The other official entry point was the Toqchi Gate, near its namesake Maydan-e Toqchi, which Chardin identified as the northernmost end of the continuous bazaar artery that ended at the Hasanabad Gate; Gaube and Wirth, *Der Bazar von Isfahan*, 48. According to Lotf-Allah Honarfar, "Bagh-e Hezar Jarib va Kuh-e Soffe, behesht-e Shah Abbas," *Honar va Mardom* (Aban 1345/November 1966): 73–94, on p. 76, during Shah Abbas I's time, the first reception of visiting dignitaries and ambassadors took place at the Qushkhane Garden (Aviary Garden) located before this gate on the northeastern side of the old city. There, according to tradition, the shah would grant robes of honor (*khal'at*) to notable generals and others deemed worthy of such bestowals and would receive his honored guests. One example is the reception given by Shah Abbas II in 1646 to the ousted Uzbek ruler, Nadr Mohammad Khan; Mohammad Taher-e Vahid-e Qazvini, *Tarikh-e jahan-ara-ye Abbasi*, ed. Seyyed Sa'id Mir Mohammad Sadeq (Tehran: Pajuheshgah-e Olum-e Ensani va Motale'at-e Farhangi, 1383/2005), 424. See also Chapter 5 of this book for a consideration of the welcoming reception (*esteqbal*).

35. Pietro Della Valle, *Viaggi di Pietro della Valle il Pellegrino descritti da lui medesimo in lettere familiari* (Rome, 1658), 455 and Babaie, "Safavid Palaces in Isfahan," 90–1.

36. Engelbert Kaempfer, *Amoenitatum Exoticarum, politico-physico medicarum fasciculi, quibus continentur variae relations, observationes et descriptions rerum Persicarum et ulterioris Asiae* (Lemgovnia: Typis & impensis Henrici Wilhelmi Meyeri, 1712).

37. McChesney, "Four Sources," 124–5.

38. Chardin, *Voyages du Chevalier Chardin*, vol. 7, 310ff.

39. McChesney, "Four Sources," 125.

40. For a comparative consideration of walls and cities, see Tracy, *City Walls*, 1–15 and especially the article by Catherine B. Asher, "Delhi Walled: Changing Boundaries," 247–81.

41. Chardin, *Voyages du Chevalier Chardin*, vol. 7, 284. See also Haneda, "The Character of the Urbanization of Isfahan," 372, who notes the

Safavid disregard of walls in Isfahan but does not explore its meanings any further.

42. Rudi Matthee, "Unwalled Cities and Restless Nomads: Firearms and Artillery in Safavid Iran," in *Safavid Persia*, ed. Melville, 389–416, confirms the growing disregard of defensive enclosures in Safavid cities, albeit discussed in light of the use of firearms.

43. See Al-Azmeh, *Muslim Kingship*, esp. 189–219, and his difficulty in accounting for the strange ways of the Safavids.

44. The resistance is recorded by Mirza Beg Hasan Jonabadi, *Rauzat al-Safaviyye*, quoted and discussed by McChesney, "Four Sources," 117–18. For the Safavid political economy and silk monopoly in the early seventeenth century, see Ina Baghdiantz-McCabe, "Armenian Merchants and Slaves: Financing the Safavid Treasury," in *Slaves of the Shah*, Babaie, Babayan, Baghdiantz-McCabe, and Farhad, 49–79; Rudolph P. Matthee, *The Politics of Trade in Safavid Iran: Silk for Silver 1600–1730* (Cambridge: Cambridge University Press, 1999), esp. 61–118.

45. There are no inscriptions, decrees (*farman*), or any other recognizable marker of Shah Abbas' patronage at the Great Mosque of Isfahan. A portion of the sanctuary near the North Dome is popularly attributed to Shah Abbas the Great, but there is no evidence to that effect in epigraphic or historical sources. The only epigraphic reference to Shah Abbas is in the vicinity of this area, on the side of the north entrance hallway, and refers to the shah in terms of work done during his reign and not work sponsored by him; see Honarfar, *Ganjine*, 147–8. In contrast, earlier and later Safavid shahs lavished attention on the mosque, as witnessed by their epigraphic markers of patronage, Honarfar, *Ganjine*, 69–168.

46. Prior to McChesney's seminal study ("Four Sources"), most contended that the building began when the capital was officially transferred in 1598.

47. As yet, there is no monographic study of this important building, but see Honarfar, *Ganjine*, 427–64; Lisa Golombek, "Anatomy of a Mosque: The Masjid-i Shah of Isfahan," in *Iranian Civilization and Culture*, ed. Charles J. Adams (Montreal: McGill University, Institute of Islamic Studies, 1973), 5–15; Robert Hillenbrand, "Safavid Architecture," in *The Cambridge History of Iran: Vol. 6 The Timurid and Safavid Periods*, ed. Peter J. Jackson and Laurence Lockhart (Cambridge: Cambridge University Press, 1986), 786–9; Sussan Babaie, "Masjed-e Shah," *Da'erat al-ma'aref-e bozorg-e Eslami* (The Great Islamic Encyclopaedia) IX (Tehran, 1999): 198–201.

48. McChesney, "Four Sources," 117–18, followed by all subsequent scholarship, including my own earlier publications: "Building on the Past," and "Shah Abbas II, the Conquest of Qandahar, the Chihil Sutun, and its Wall Paintings," *Muqarnas* 11 (1994): 125–42. Blake, *Half the World*, maintains the same general sequence of building events but redates everything according to a faulty reading of a single passage; see also Sussan Babaie, review of *Half the World: The Social Architecture of Safavid Isfahan 1590–1722*, by Stephen Blake, *Iranian Studies* 33 nos. 3–4 (2000): 478–82.

49. These events are reported by Natanzi, *Noqavat al-asar*, and Molla Jalal al-Din Monajjem, *Tarikh Abbasi ya ruznama-ye Molla Jalal*, ed. Sayf-Allah Vahidniya (Tehran: Entesharat-e Vahid, 1366/1987); both are translated and analyzed by McChesney, "Four Sources," and Babaie,

"Safavid Palaces in Isfahan," 63–9. That the walls were there from the beginning may be deduced from the reference to whitewashing and decorating given in Natanzi, *Noqavat al-asar*, 577.

50. Both documentation and clearest exposé of the sequence are to be found in McChesney, "Four Sources," 124.

51. Monshi, *Tarikh-e alam ara-ye Abbasi*, 544–5. McChesney, "Four Sources," 124–5, compares the accounts by Monshi and Monajjem (*Tarikh Abbasi*) to arrive at what seems to be the most convincing building sequence.

52. Until recently, the bridge was thought to have been completed in 1602. It has been redated now to 1607 on the basis of evidence from a newly discovered source: the third volume of *Afzal al-tavarikh*; see Charles Melville, "New Light on the Reign of Shah ʿAbbas: Volume III of the *Afzal al-Tawarikh*," in *Society and Culture in the Early Modern Middle East. Studies on Iran in the Safavid Period*, ed. Andrew J. Newman (Leiden: Brill, 2003), 63–96.

53. McChesney, "Four Sources," 114–16; Babaie, "Safavid Palaces in Isfahan," 66–7 and 117–20.

54. Eugenio Galdieri, "Two building phases of the time of Šah ʿAbbas I in the Maydan-i Šah of Isfahan – Preliminary note," *East and West* 20 (1970): 60–9.

55. Babaie, "Safavid Palaces in Isfahan," 117–19 and 124–5.

56. Eugenio Galdieri, *Esfahan, ʿAli Qapu: An architectural survey*, Restorations 5 (Rome: IsMEO, 1979): 9–19; and Babaie, "Safavid Palaces in Isfahan," 117–25.

57. The subject has been extensively studied in three recent books: Amir Arjomand, *The Shadow of God*, Babayan, *Mystics, Monarchs and Messiahs*, and Abisaab, *Converting Persia*.

58. Notwithstanding the significance of the Safavid-Ottoman rivalry as a stimulus, it would be a mistake to interpret the Royal Mosque as a response solely to Ottoman pressure; nor is it justifiable to assume this rivalry was the sole or major motivating factor.

59. Babaie, "Building on the Past," 46.

60. According to a story by Chardin, the house of an old woman on the land posed a challenge, as confiscation was not permissible and the shah had ordered his supervisor of imperial building works to satisfy the demands of the owner. Furthermore, this same supervisor, Mohebb Ali Beg Lale, seems to have had a house or property somewhere in this area, since he and a few other court dignitaries benefited from the sale of their properties in favor of the mosque; for the various versions of the story of the mosque's lot, see McChesney, "Four Sources," 120–2, and Sussan Babaie, "Launching from Isfahan," in *Slaves of the Shah*, 90–1.

61. Roemer, "The Safavid Period," 267, and Monshi, *Tarikh-e alam ara-ye Abbasi*, 820–5. Safavid-Ottoman territorial conflict continued to flare up at intervals in Mesopotamia, where the shifting political fate of Baghdad and the holy cities of Najaf and Karbala remained unresolved until 1638/9, when Shah Safi permanently lost those cities to the Ottomans.

62. The historical and political significance of this cluster of important foundations – the first royal congregational mosque in Isfahan, the major refurbishments of the Shrine of Imam Reza in Mashhad and the brand new cities of Farahabad and Ashraf – is made evident in the way the official history is told by Shah Abbas' historian, Eskandar Beg Monshi in his *Tarikh-e alam ara-ye Abbasi*, 829–61.

63. Babaie, Babayan, Baghdiantz-McCabe, and Farhad, *Slaves of the Shah*, 1–19.
64. Mazzaoui, "From Tabriz to Qazvin to Isfahan," 514–22; Babaie summarizes these debates in "Safavid Palaces in Isfahan," 41–3.
65. The baffling measures taken by Shah Ismaiʿl II may have been related not only to the widespread Sunni presence, but also to the rising power of the Shiʿi doctors patronized by his father Shah Tahmasb; for aspects of Ismaiʿl II's reign see Roemer, "The Safavid Period," 250–3.
66. Shah Abbas married a daughter of Shaykh Lotf-Allah, one of the Shiʿi scholars imported from Jabal ʿAmil and the man in whose honor the chapel-mosque at the Maydan in Isfahan was named; see Roemer, "Safavid Period," 346.
67. For the silk trade and its place in Safavid politics and economy, see Matthee, *Politics of Trade in Safavid Iran* and Ina Baghdiantz-McCabe, *The Shah's Silk for Europe's Silver: The European Trade of the Julfa Armenians in Safavid Iran and India (1530–1750)*, ed. Michael Stone (Atlanta: Scholars Press, 1999).
68. The mosque and the Maydan-e Shah have been renamed as the Imam Mosque and Maydan since the establishment of the Islamic Republic in 1979.
69. Amir Arjomand, *The Shadow of God*, Part 2, gives an excellent account of the history of Shiʿism in this period. See also Babayan, *Mystics, Monarchs, and Messiahs*, 349–437.
70. Babayan, "Waning of the Qizilbâsh," has addressed the political and social unrest, especially with regards to the role of the Qezelbash in the sixteenth century and its aftermath into the seventeenth century. The religious crisis has been the subject of Abisaab's *Converting Persia*. For a recent discussion of the role of the *gholam*s or slaves of the household as one of the pillars of transformation, see Babaie, Babayan, Baghdiantz-McCabe, and Farhad, *Slaves of the Shah*.
71. McChesney, "Four Sources," 110.
72. Regardless, all these cities have exerted enormous power and influence by virtue of the rootedness of the clerical class in the political arenas of both modern Iran and Iraq. The profoundly influential role of Qom in the 1978–9 Revolution, which culminated in the formation of the Islamic Republic of Iran, and Najaf's place in directing the messy politics of Iraq during the American occupation since March 2002 are cases in point.
73. For the history of Shiʿism in Kashan, see Rasul Jafarian, "Pishine-ye tashayyoʿ dar Kashan (The Background of Shiʿism in Kashan)," in Jafarian *Maqalat-e tarikhi* (Qom: Ansarian Publishers, 1376/1997), 2: 341–67.
74. The history of the pre-Safavid religious scene and the place of Shiʿism in Isfahan remains largely untold. The exception is the work of the Iranian historian Rasul Jafarian, "Pishine-ye tashayyoʿ dar Esfahan (The Background of Shiʿism in Isfahan)," in Jafarian, *Maqalat-e tarikhi* (Qom: Ansarian Publishers, 1376/1997), 2:305–39. I rely chiefly on his research for the following discussion.
75. For the emerging scholarship on the Buyids, see, for example, John Jay Donohue, *The Buwayhid Dynasty in Iraq: 334 H./945 to 403 H./1012* (Leiden: Brill, 2003).
76. Jafarian, "Pishine-ye tashayyoʿ dar Esfahan," vol. 2, 313; Honarfar, *Ganjine*, 521–30 for Imamzade references, especially that of Imamzade Ebrahim.

77. Jafarian, "Pishine-ye tashayyoʻ dar Esfahan," vol. 2, 314–15.

78. Ibid.

79. For the Zaydis, see Mottahedeh, *Loyalty and Leadership*, 13, and Jafarian, "Pishine-ye tashayyoʻ dar Esfahan," 319ff.

80. Jafarian, "Pishine-ye tashayyoʻ dar Esfahan," 324ff.

81. Jafarian, "Pishine-ye tashayyoʻ dar Esfahan," 324–5.

82. Much is written on the advent of royal patronage of Shiʻism and its popularization in the sixteenth and seventeenth centuries, for which most of the supporting evidence is culled from literary sources. For the most recent and original interpretation of the Perso-Shiʻi trajectory of popularization, see Babayan, *Mystics, Monarchs and Messiahs*. A good measure of popularization and the role of the Persian language in this regard may also be deduced from the visual representations of Shiʻi sentiments and convictions, as conveyed through monumental epigraphic programs on buildings; See Sussan Babaie, "Epigraphy iv. Safavid and Later Inscriptions," *Encyclopaedia Iranica*, Vol. 8 (1998): 498–504.

83. Jafarian, "Pishine-ye tashayyoʻ dar Esfahan," 327.

84. On the many conversions of Öljeitu, see J. A. Boyle, "Dynastic and Political History of the Il-Khans," in the *Cambridge History of Iran*, Vol. 5, *The Seljuq and Mongol Periods*, ed. J. A. Boyle (Cambridge: Cambridge University Press, 1968), 303–421, and especially 401–2.

85. Jafarian, "Pishine-ye tashayyoʻ dar Esfahan," 329. See Alessandro Bausani, "Religion under the Mongols," in *The Cambridge History of Iran*, Vol. 5 *The Saljuq and Mongol Periods*, ed. J. A. Boyle (Cambridge: Cambridge University Press, 1968), 538–49, esp. 543.

86. For stabilization of Shiʻi theology in this period, see Bausani, "Religion under the Mongols," 543–4.

87. For a discussion of this addition and its significance to the mosque at large, see Oleg Grabar, *The Great Mosque of Isfahan* (New York: New York University Press, 1990), esp. 72–3.

88. For the inscriptions, see Honarfar, *Ganjine*, 116–20; see also Sheila Blair, *Islamic Inscriptions* (New York: New York University Press, 1998), 69.

89. Honarfar, *Ganjine*, 139–45 and 302–10, for example.

90. Jafarian, "Pishine-ye tashayyoʻ dar Esfahan," 332ff.

91. Abisaab, *Converting Persia*, gives a well-documented account of the profound role the clergy from Jabal ʻAmil played in the Shiʻification of Safavid Iran. Her analysis of how the institutionalization of a normative practice of Shiʻism coordinated with the formation of the Safavid state informs the following discussion.

92. For further consideration of this issue in light of Safavid sources, see also Rasul Jafarian, "Namaz-e Jomʻe dar daure-ye Safaviyye," in Jafarian, *Safaviyye dar ʻarse-ye din, farhang va siyasat* (Qom: Pajuheshkade-ye Hauze va Daneshgah, 1379/2000), 1: 251–334.

93. Babaie, "Building on the Past" 44–6.

94. Abisaab, *Converting Persia*, especially 53–87. Mir Damad's role in the architectural and urban articulation of Isfahan is not as visible as those of Shaykh Lotf-Allah and Shaykh Baha'i.

95. Abisaab, *Converting Persia*, 81–2.

96. For the differing clerical opinions see Abisaab, *Converting Persia*, 82.

97. Eskandar Beg Monshi, *Tarikh-e alam ara-ye Abbasi*, 157, does not name the mosque but states that the Shaykh was settled, on the orders of Shah Abbas the Great, at a madrasa that was next to the mosque the

shah had constructed across from the Daulatkhane gate. This has given McChesney reason to doubt whether the mosque was initially intended for Shaykh Lotf-Allah. Honarfar's assumption of the link between the Shaykh and the mosque has been recently supported by Melville's introduction of the third volume of *Afzal al-tavarikh*, "New Light on the Reign of Shah 'Abbas," 81. Also important is Abisaab's discussion in support of this conclusion in that she relies on a previously unknown source, Shaykh Lotf-Allah's treatise on the necessity and conditions of seclusion (*i'tikaf*); Abisaab, *Converting Persia*, 82–4. See also McChesney, "Four Sources," 123–4; Honarfar, *Ganjine*, 404–6; Blake, *Half the World*, 148–9.

98. As far as I know, the Farahabad Great Mosque remains unpublished. This substantial mosque is laid out on a four-ayvan plan, in style closer to the central Iranian mosque type, like those in Isfahan, for example, than to the Mazandaran vernacular. Its construction was part of the building of a new provincial capital city to which Shah Abbas had ordered large populations to be transferred for the purposes of silk production. With its twin city of Ashraf, a full-fledged royal retreat close to the shores of the Caspian Sea, Farahabad served as the principal resort for Safavid shahs, especially Shah Abbas I and his son and grandson, shahs Safi I and Abbas II, who frequently journeyed to Ashraf and Farahabad for hunting and restorative stays.

99. For the maqsura as an architectural feature in mosques, see Robert Hillenbrand, *Islamic Architecture: Form, Function and Meaning* (New York: Columbia University Press, 1994), 48–53.

100. For the maqsura at the Great Mosque of Cordoba, see Jerrilyn Dodds, ed. *Al-Andalus: The Arts of Isamic Spain* (New York: Metropolitan Museum of Art, 1992) 18–23; for the North Dome at Isfahan mosque, see Grabar, *The Great Mosque of Isfahan*, especially 38–40.

101. Babayan, *Mystics, Monarchs and Messiahs*, 57–108.

102. An example of such resistance was that of the merchants and nobility who owned land and shops around the Old Maydan and who vigorously opposed Shah Abbas's attempt to refurbish that area; see McChesney, "Four Sources," 117–18 and Abisaab, *Converting Persia*, 82–7.

103. For the blinding and killing of male contenders for the throne, see Roemer, "The Safavid Period," 276–7; for the elimination of the Nuqtavis, see Monshi, *Tarikh-e alam ara-ye Abbasi*, 476.

104. His name is also attached to the versified epigraphic bands on the façade of the Shaykh Lotf-Allah Mosque, a poem that was presumably composed by Shaykh Baha'i; Honarfar, *Ganjine*, 412–13. He also drew, on behalf of Shah Abbas I, the endowment deed for Maydan-e Naqsh-e Jahan and was likely closely involved with the development of the whole Maydan project.

105. For the epigraphic program, see Honarfar, *Ganjine*, 428–63.

106. For the waqf document, see McChesney, "Waqf and Public Policy: The Waqfs of Shah Abbas, 1011–23/1602–14," in *Journal of Asian and African Studies* 15 (1981): 165–90. For the role of the *gholam* Mohebb Ali Beg Lale in constructing the capital, see Babaie, "Launching from Isfahan," 89–92.

107. Monshi, *Tarikh-e alam ara-ye Abbasi*, 155–7; Abisaab, *Converting Persia*, 60.

108. Sa'id Nafisi, *Divan-e kamel-e Shaykh Baha'i* (Tehran, Nashr-e Chekame, 1361/1982), 10–82 provides a concise overview of Shaykh Baha'i's life and works. Amir Arjomand, *The Shadow of God*, consid-

ers Shaykh Baha'i in detail. See also Abisaab, *Converting Persia*, 59–61.

109. Amir Arjomand, *The Shadow of God*, 175–7.

110. Jonathan Brown and J. H. Elliott, *A Palace for a King: the Buen Retiro and the Court of Philip IV*. (New Haven: Yale University Press, 2003): 1–7; Ebba Koch, "The Mughal Waterfront Garden," and Catherine B. Asher, *Architecture of Mughal India* (Cambridge; New Delhi: Cambridge University Press, 1995), esp. 99–123.

111. Brown and Elliott, *A Palace for a King*, 2–3 and 33.

112. Brown and Elliott, *A Palace for a King*, 7.

113. Ebba Koch, "Diwan-i ʿAmm and Chihil Sutun: The Audience Halls of Shah Jahan," *Muqarnas* 11 (1994): 143–65

114. This is not to say, of course, that this aloofness is total and permanent. The visual and spatial links with other urban and monumental features of the city, especially with the Taj Mahal, which stands at a considerable distance from the Red Fort but remains within its visual field, so to speak, materialized over time, and especially under Shah Jahan; see the monumental work of Ebba Koch, *The Complete Taj Mahal and the Riverfront Gardens of Agra* (London: Thames and Hudson, 2006), esp. 23–33 The point here is that the Red Fort was not part of an overall urban scheme, as was the case of the 1630s Shahjahanabad in Delhi.

115. Necipoğlu, *Architecture, Ceremonial and Power*.

116. The Yeni Saray, which literally means "New Palace," was renamed the Topkapı Saray in the late eighteenth century.

117. Andrew McClellan, *Inventing the Louvre: Art, Politics, and the Origins of the Modern Museum in Eighteenth-century Paris*. (New York: Cambridge University Press, 1994) is one among many publications on the Louvre.

118. It was customary for the kings of Castile to hold court in principal cities of the central Castilian plateau to which the nobility was attracted; Brown and Elliott, *A Palace for a King*, p. 1, a practice comparable to Turco-Mongol conduct in Iran, especially during the fifteenth-century Timurid reign.

119. Gülru Necipoğlu, "The Suburban Landscape of Sixteenth-Century Istanbul as a Mirror of Classical Ottoman Garden Culture," in *Gardens in the Time of the Great Muslim Empires: Theory and Design*, ed. Attilio Petruccioli (Leiden; New York: Brill, 1997), 32–71.

120. Little has been done on Indian houses; for a generalized account, see Pavan K. Varma and Sondeep Shankar, *Mansions at Dusk: The Havelis of Old Delhi* (New Delhi: Spantech Publishers, 1992). A recent study of the *haveli* in Agra is found in Koch, *The Complete Taj Mahal*, 58–66.

121. Koch, "The Mughal Waterfront Garden," 140–5, and her *The Complete Taj Mahal*, 24, 27–8.

122. Some of the houses of Isfahan have been catalogued and published in recent years but none has been studied from a socio-cultural perspective. For a brief section on the houses, see Babaie, "Launching from Isfahan," fig. 5 and pp. 87–8. My research on the houses of the Armenians of New Julfa and of Isfahan has been developed through three unpublished papers and will be the subject of my next book.

CHAPTER FOUR

"The Abode of Felicitous Rule" or the *Daulatkhane* Royal Precinct

CHAPTER 3 FOCUSED on Isfahan's historical, social, and spatial trajectory and anchored the interventions in its built environment to the politico-religious adaptation of the city as the Safavid capital. Here, we turn from the macro image of the city to the micro landscape of the royal precinct, the conceptual and physical core of the capital and the empire envisioned in the seventeenth-century phase of Safavid rule. In keeping with this book's narrative structure of unfolding layers, this chapter attends to the royal ensemble (the Daulatkhane), reserving the architectural and social lives of the individual palaces for the next chapter (Figures 4.1, 3.7 and Plate 9).

With the collective (re)conceptualization of Isfahan as the center of the Safavid Perso-Shi'i imperium came the devising of a new formal seat of imperial authority. The Maydan-e Naqsh-e Jahan reconfigured and reinterpreted the Persianate urban conventions of the city square scheme to express clearly the centralization of imperial leadership. Similarly, the Daulatkhane ensemble projected a revised picture of authority and its urban rootedness. This chapter will explore how the Safavid palaces as a conglomerate of buildings in a unified precinct appropriated and reinterpreted conventional functional features of the early modern palatine paradigm. This is especially important in relation to the birun (public/male) zone of Islamicate palace complexes – including the judiciary and administrative buildings, kitchens, stables, and workshops – which served to house and represent the collective imperial machinery (Figure 3.7).

Isfahan palaces in the seventeenth century impart a compelling sense of transparency and accessibility in both their architecture and relationship to their sites. Despite considerable losses from among the original features of the Daulatkhane precinct, the visual and spatial logic of its interior is displayed in the ways that the building designs incorporate landscaping and open-air elements. Unusually massive in scale, the palaces in the Daulatkhane of Isfahan, as we shall see, defy the expectation of opacity or gravity by opening their architectural and spatial features to the interplay between their inner and outer zones and by allowing multitudes

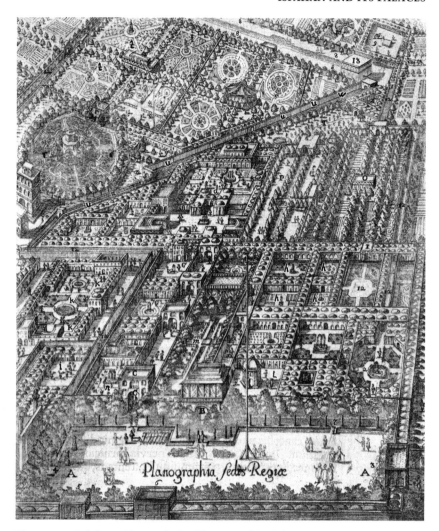

Planographia fedis Regiæ

Figure 4.1 *Isfahan, Kaempfer's "Planographia," from an engraving in his* Amoenitatum *(1712). Kaempfer's legend includes the following selection:*

A) Maydan-e Naqsh-e Jahan; B) Ali Qapu Palace; C) Harem Gate;
I) Daftarkhane (chancellery); L) Tauhidkhane; O) Chehel Sotun Palace;
d) main residence of the shah in the harem; h) royal workshops and
storehouses; i) royal kitchens; k) royal workshops of the jewelers,
goldsmiths and watchmakers; m) Talar-e Tavile Palace; n) apartments of
the shah's private chamberlains; t) Hasht Behesht Palace; u) private
routes inside the royal precinct; w) route to Dar-e Shahi, or royal
gateway, opening onto the north end of the Chahar Bagh Promenade;
2) royal caravanserai; 7) gateway from the Maydan-e-Naqsh-e Jahan to
Chahar Hauz Maydan; 8) Chahar Bagh Promenade; 13) Jahan Nama
Pavilion.

to be embraced from within or engaged from without.[1] The two operative concepts here are transparency and scale. Leaving the close analyses of individual palaces for the next chapter, here we will search for the ways in which the architectural vocabulary of the palaces in Isfahan mediates thresholds between royal and public spaces in a manner that represents the twin requisites of Perso-Shiʿi kingship: ritual accessibility – necessitated by the state-sponsored Imami creed of the Safavids – and *farr*, the ancient Persian notion of royal splendor.[2]

The positioning of the imposing palace of Ali Qapu at the threshold between the public maydan and the royal precinct signals precisely this sort of paradigm shift. Neither in Tabriz nor even in Qazvin, where the palace precinct was conceived afresh for the transfer of the seat of rule in the middle of the sixteenth century, was there a building of the same magnitude of both scale and function as that of the Isfahan Ali Qapu.[3] The Isfahan palace's namesake predecessor, the Ali Qapu at Qazvin, was architecturally formulated to serve as a monumental façade of the gateway into the royal precinct (Figures 2.3 and 2.4). Designed as a *pishtaq*, a framed ayvan or porch embraced a doorway that led to a vaulted crossing with small chambers in the flanking units and an opening toward the courtyard beyond (Figure 2.5). In contrast, the Ali Qapu in Isfahan grew as an integrated multipurpose structure, not just a façade to a gateway (Figure 4.2, Plates 9 and 10). In fact, similar comparisons may be made with other early modern palatine complexes. An impressively large gateway with flanking watchtowers mediated between the Topkapı and the city; the Mughal Red Forts, too, had similar gateway-watchtowers marking the liminal space between the city and the inner world of the palace (Figure 6.9).

Figure 4.2 *Isfahan, reconstruction rendering of the Maydan.*
The Maydan is shown as it developed between the 1590/1 initial building campaign by Shah Abbas the Great and before the 1644 additions during the reign of Shah Abbas II, when a structure with a *talar* (pillared terrace) was added to front of the Ali Qapu. Once past the Ali Qapu, one turned north (right) to access the domed Tauhidkhane, and south (left) to enter the garden of the pillared palace of Talar-e Tavile (1630s). The Harem Gate accessed the Maydan to the south of the Ali Qapu.

What does a palace such as the Ali Qapu tell us about the Safavid agenda? The established Islamicate practice was to surround the royal grounds with fortifications, to keep the most ceremonially prominent space limited to a single structure, to articulate this space in the form of an ayvan (Arabicized as *iwan*, the Sassanian architectural form of a vaulted space enclosed on all sides but the front), a pillared pavilion or a gate, and to veil and protect it by placing it deep inside the walled precinct. At the Topkapı in Istanbul, the Gate of Felicity and the Chamber of Petitions were located at the end of the second courtyard. Thus, well within the fortified compound, they provided degrees of ceremony and separation via the combination of an awning-like structure before a doorway that led to the single-roomed Chamber of Petitions (Figures 6.1, 6.2, 6.3 and 6.4). This structure was small, but strategically perforated and elaborately embellished to create an awesome effect in the context of Ottoman ritual performances of authority.[4]

The Mughal ceremonial public spaces, known as the Diwan-i Amm, at the Red Forts of Agra, Delhi, and Lahore were also placed deep inside the walled complex and consisted of a single, albeit large, stone-pillared hall closed on the back and open on three sides and with no other structure attached (Figures 6.7, 6.8, 6.10 and 6.12).[5] In other words, these were essentially free-standing, loggia-like structures set against the horizontal plane of a wall, the significance of which was marked by the central placement of the *jharoka*, the Mughal throne variously articulated as a dais, a royal box, or a seat raised and sheltered with a domical umbrella (Figures 6.13 and Plate 24).[6]

The Safavid model was somewhat different. As a monumental gate into a royal precinct, the Ali Qapu in Isfahan draws on a familiar formula. But as one palace among others in an imperial ensemble, the Ali Qapu is unusual in its architectural and urban articulation of the "seat of rule" paradigm. It does not follow the palatine conventions in the Islamicate world or most other comparable contexts in the early modern period. Moreover, and notwithstanding the singularity of the Ali Qapu as an architectural and functional solution to the problem of defining the threshold, the royal precinct in Isfahan presents us with a number of other uncommon approaches to the requisite ceremonial spaces. Two other palaces within the Isfahan Daulatkhane, the Talar-e Tavile and the Chehel Sotun, appear in successive campaigns during the first half of the seventeenth century, and each serves imperial ceremony in a rather specialized way (Figures 5.1 and 5.13). Their massive scale and the architectural transparency lent by ceremonial gardens and processional routes constituted the fixed features that contained the malleable and mobile theatrics of feasting and other rituals of Safavid kingship.

The fourth of the "four palatine paradigms" in the Islamicate world, discussed in the first chapter, may apply to the Safavid palaces in Tabriz and Qazvin but does not comfortably accommodate the

Isfahan palaces. The palatine ensembles of the post-Mongol period, including those of the Timurid, early Safavid (sixteenth century), Ottoman and Mughal domains, conform to a pattern in which an expansive enclosure – always walled, be it in masonry or cloth (tents) – collected in its midst clusters of smaller buildings subdivided according to their functions into the birun (without/male/public) and andarun (within/female/private) zones of the royal precinct. In all these examples, the space of public ceremony within the royal precinct remained aloof and veiled from the public eye. The royal precinct in Isfahan, by contrast, instead of concealing its constituent parts behind fortifications, flaunts the spectacle of its principal ceremonial building, the Ali Qapu (Plate 9).

In addition to several semi-private pavilions, the Safavid complex held within its perimeter three principal ceremonial palaces, each built on a scale several times larger than the largest of the ceremonial halls of their rivals or predecessors. The Islamicate palatine model proceeds from an outer "profane" world through successive courtyards towards an apex of "sanctity" at the most ceremonially rarefied and removed spot inside the gendered and enclosed birun or public zone of the palace complex. The separation of the profane outer world and the sacred inner world at the Isfahan Daulatkhane, the Ali Qapu, is marked with a ceremonial space of considerable significance in that it also functions for the administration of justice, a prerequisite of kingship in all its Persian and Islamic implications.

Far from positioning the holiest, most rarefied spot at the most removed reaches of the birun, the Safavid palatine ensemble in Isfahan brings that spot to the very threshold between the palace and the city (Figures 3.7, 4.2 and Plate 10). Given the addition of two more ceremonial structures to the Daulatkhane in the first half of the seventeenth century and the ways these structures are scaled and placed in the birun zone of the precinct, the Safavid Daulatkhane needs to be viewed from the perspective of a micro–macro palatine paradigm (Figure 3.8). It shows points of continuity in palatine traditions inherited from the shared Turco-Mongol past of these early modern Islamicate empires. More importantly, however, architectural analyses show us how the palaces in Isfahan embody and accommodate Safavid enunciations of a Perso-Shi'i notion of authority and legitimacy in contradistinction to those of their Sunni neighbors.

The building of palaces in Isfahan may be divided into three phases: the first spans the period between 1590/1, when the urban constructions began, and the death of Shah Abbas I in 1629. The second falls under the reigns of shahs Safi I and Abbas II from 1629 until 1666, when a new typology of the palaces institutionalizes the feasting ceremonials. The third extends from 1666, the beginning of the reign of Shah Solayman, until 1722, the collapse of the Safavids under Shah Soltan Hossayn, during which time the shahs increasingly retreated into the protective confines of the harem and relegated the conduct of kingship to the influential *gholam* (slave) officials of the court and administration and to the powerful clerical elite of the state. The structure of this chapter follows this periodization of the history of palace construction in Isfahan and comprises three interrelated units, each addressing the particularities of the architecture and social context during their respective periods of activity.

Abbas I inscribed on the face of Isfahan the principal features of its urban landscape as the new Safavid capital. His building campaigns focused on defining the boundaries between royal and public spaces and on endowing the city with major amenities such as its marketplace and congregational mosque, its residential quarters and caravanserais, its avenues and bridges. His project also articulated through architecture and space an iconic rendition of the Safavid notions of sovereignty and legitimacy. Safi I and Abbas II, the immediate successors to Shah Abbas I, sponsored the construction of a ceremonial type of palace that is especially suited to performing the ritual of feasting. Examples include the Chehel Sotun and the Talar-e Tavile, both positioned within the royal precinct, the Ayenekhane built in the royal retreat of Saʿadatabad on the banks of the Zayande River, as well as an addition to the Ali Qapu (Figures 3.7, 4.3, 4.6, 5.1, 5.5, 5.22, Plates 12 and 14). The most important architectural index of this Perso-Shiʿi imperial enterprise of the Safavids in the seventeenth century is embodied in the *talar* feature of these palaces – a flat-roofed pillared hall that abuts the front of the building of a palace and uses that building façade as the backdrop to the otherwise completely open area. The *talar*, discussed at length in this chapter, represents one of those architectural solutions of some antiquity that evolves to signify the symbolic and functional specificities of a cultural ethos, in this case the construction of a Safavid identity.

Despite enjoying relative safety from external invasions in the latter half of the seventeenth century, the reigns of the last two Safavid shahs were mired in economic destabilization, accompanied by a substantial growth in the power of the clergy at the court and within the ranks of the administrative machinery of the state, and marked by greater social constraints on important minorities, especially the Armenians, which contributed to the loss of international trading partnerships. The shahs' generally hands-off approach to the affairs of the state, so characteristic of this period, went hand in hand with their insularity and their tendency to disappear into the safety of the harem. The one public work of Shah Soltan Hossayn (the Chahar Bagh Madrasa) notwithstanding, it was in the harem zones, both inside the Daulatkhane and along the Zayande River, that Shah Solayman and Shah Soltan Hossayn built palaces and pavilions which served principally as playhouses for their concubine playmates.

Figure 4.3 *Isfahan, Ali Qapu and Tauhidkhane (Omidvar).*

The stairwell, on the palace's south side, is visible as three vaulted volumes of increasing height. Constructed along with the 1644 additions, it was brilliantly designed to accommodate a ceremoniously elegant and slow-paced ascent to the *talar* reception area through a sequence of vaulted rooms and sets of wide, shallow steps, without burdening the south side of the original tower with additional weight.

The Daulatkhane

The Daulatkhane of Isfahan, some 440,000 (about 610 × 720) square meters in area, constituted an expansive conglomerate: gateways and guardhouses (*dargah, darvaze*); administrative buildings such as the free-standing structure of the *Daftarkhane* or the Chancellery and the offices within the Ali Qapu of the *divan-begi* (judiciary), the *khwansalar-e a'zam* (grand master of the household), the Grand vizier, the *qapuchi-bashi* (commander of the special guards); and the Tauhidkhane, a ceremonial Sufi retreat serving also as a temporary refuge (*bast*) for the criminally accused (Figures 3.7, 3.8 and 4.1). It also comprised *karkhane-ha-ye saltanati* (royal workshops) and *makhazen* (storehouses), including the *ketabkhane* (a library-scriptorium-atelier for the production and storage of manuscripts), *khal'atkhane* (for tailoring and storing robes and cloths of honor), a *maykhane*, a pavilion where wine was stored but where a small group could also while away time in its delightful "wine bar," and storehouses for the court consumption of coffee (*qahvekhane*), tobacco (*chopoqkhane*), and tallow (*pihkhane*), among others. The Daulatkhane further housed the royal kitchens (*matbakh*), bakery and other food-related buildings; storehouses for carpets, tents, textiles, and dishware; royal workshops of goldsmiths, jewelers, and watchmakers; a royal bathhouse (*hammam-e shahi*); the ceremonial palaces of the Ali Qapu, the Chehel Sotun, and the Talar-e Tavile; the private or semi-private pavilions of Hasht Behesht, the Khalvatkhane, and the Goldaste, among others; and gardens of varying sizes and landscaping foci, including pools and ornamental lakes. Finally, it incorporated a vineyard (*angurestan*), an almond-tree grove (*badamestan*), and the harem complex of apartments, pavilions, and gardens, to which two extant buildings, the so-called Talar-e Ashraf and an octagonal tower, seem to have belonged.[7]

Such consolidation of diverse functions within a single royal precinct transcends the definition of the palace in the customary, European-centered usage of the term. This difficulty of transcultural pairings of terminology and typology in architecture may be gleaned from a description of the Daulatkhane provided by Jean Baptiste Tavernier, a Flemish jeweler who visited Safavid Iran in six voyages between 1632 and 1668 and served Shah Safi I and Shah Abbas II as a craftsman. In this descriptive passage, he claimed that

> for the King's palace, I cannot make any handsome description of it, in regard there is nothing of beauty either in the building or in the gardens. I think I have been as far in the house as a man can go, every time I was sent for by His Majesty; but excepting only four rooms which they call Divans, I saw nothing but pitiful low galleries, and so narrow that hardly two men could pass a-brest in'em.[8]

Tavernier's reduction of the vast royal precinct and its most prominent five-story palace to a house of pitiful rooms and narrow galleries exemplifies the inadequacy of European preconceptions of palatial design for elucidating an Islamicate royal precinct. Such linguistically mediated undervaluation of the impressive Isfahan ensemble may also be considered a strategy for European observers to deflate – self-consciously or unself-consciously – the challenge posed to the assumed superiority of the European models of empire, city, and palace. This would have been an especially compelling motivation, given the competitive landscape of imperial ambitions in this period.[9]

On another level, and setting aside the greater multiplicity of functions in the Islamicate palaces of the early modern age, the term "palace" does not adequately serve in the case of the Safavid Daulatkhane in Isfahan. In both the Topkapı and the Louvre, for example, series of interrelated architecturally articulated spaces – apartments, chambers, halls, pavilions, arcades, stables, kitchens, courtyards, et cetera – are composed in such a way that their collective is perceived, especially from the outside, as a single, large, multifunctional building. Whether they amass their spaces and functions across a horizontal plane of gardens and courtyards (the Topkapı) or in an uninterrupted sequence of vertical and horizontal blocks (the Louvre), they share the structure of a single, contiguous building we can call the palace or the *qal'e* (the fort, as in Topkapı or the Mughal Forts). The Isfahan precinct is harder to circumscribe within the terms "palace" or "fort" because it is a conglomerate of architecturally autonomous palaces in addition to the apartments, chambers, halls, pavilions, arcades, stables, kitchens, courtyards, and so forth and because the whole does not read from the outside as a walled enclosure.

The accounts of European visitors in the seventeenth century reveal the difficulty of applying terminology borrowed from their native architectural vernaculars to the Daulatkhane and its individual buildings. The Italian Pietro Della Valle calls the Daulatkhane "palazzo del re" or "casa realé," while his bafflement at what to name an independent high-rise building like the Ali Qapu comes through in his designation of the building as "il casino," a term more appropriate for a lodge than a palace on the scale and complexity of the Ali Qapu.[10] The Spanish ambassador Figuera's interchangeable "le Palais Royal" for the Daulatkhane and "le Palais ou la Maison Royale" for the Ali Qapu indicate the same difficulty in distinguishing between the two.[11]

Once the other principal ceremonial palaces of the Daulatkhane were in place, the fault lines of the European visitors' semantic inadequacy became even more pronounced. The "King's Palace" and French "Palais Royal," terms applied with no consistency, prevail in the chronicles of Thomas Herbert, Adam Olearius, Tavernier, and Chardin covering the period from the 1620s through the 1670s.[12] These authors use the same "palace" and a number of other incompatible terms to designate in their tongues the palaces in the Daulatkhane and elsewhere in Isfahan: Herbert's "the King's Palace" applies to both the Ali Qapu and the Daulatkhane, and he also uses "palaces" in general; Olearius conflates the Daulatkhane and the Ali Qapu in naming them as one "King's Palace"; the words "pavilion," "tabernacle," and "great hall of the palace," with accompanying Persian terms of *divan* and *divankhane*, demonstrate Tavernier's efforts to skirt the linguistic problem; Chardin's "le pavilion" for the Ali Qapu, "le salon de l'écurie" for the massive

Talar-e Tavile (see below), and the "corps de logis" for the Chehel
Sotun, the largest of all the palaces within the precinct, indicate his
grappling with the same problem (Figure 5.1, Plates 12 and 14).[13]
Engelbert Kaempfer is the most discriminating among the
Europeans in his terminology, distinguishing between the "Regiae
Urbis" or "Regiae" for the Daulatkhane and "Palatium" for all the
palaces.[14] Writing in Latin may have helped Kaempfer to better sort
building typologies without the overlay of the author's local vernacular, although his terminology, too, fails consistently to serve
his descriptive purposes, as in the case of the word *atrium* for the
talar or pillared porches of the palaces.

Given the inadequacy of "western" palace terminology for
the Islamicate ensembles in general and for Isfahan in particular,
the Persian term *daulatkhane* offers a compelling alternative.
Daulatkhane is most commonly used in Safavid chronicles and des-
ignates a specifically royal precinct associated with a city, be it within
a city's boundaries or in its suburbs.[15] Rarely does one encounter the
term in relation to royal palaces, pavilions, and hunting lodges outside
urban centers. The consistency and clarity of intentions undergirding
the use of the term *daulatkhane* to designate urban royal precincts
during the Safavid period, and especially after Isfahan became the
capital, denote a concretization of the urban seat of rule.

Furthermore, the composite word *daulatkhane*, from the Arabic
daulat (felicity and rule) and the Persian *khane* (abode or house),
avoids any allusions to the fortifications implied by the term *qal'e*. It
also serves to convey a sense of the uniqueness of the site in relation
to all other urban spaces, in contrast to, for example, the more generic
Turkish use of the term *serai* or *saray* (from the Persian *sara* or
house), which falls short of embedding the site, through language,
into a semiotics of power; in Ottoman usage, *saray/serai* refers to
many types of buildings in addition to a palace such as the Topkapı.

The Persian usage, itself already connoting divine fortune, often
tends to be accompanied with the qualifier *mobarake*, thus enunciating the sanctity of the precinct in the term *Daulatkhane-ye
mobarake*, the Blessed Abode of Felicitous Rule. Persian chronicles
written in the first couple of decades of the seventeenth century identify, at times, the Isfahan Daulatkhane with the famed gardens that
it occupied, hence the Daulatkhane-ye mobarake-ye Naqsh-e Jahan.[16]
This practice, however, seems to fall out of usage in subsequent
decades as the Daulatkhane of Isfahan steadily transformed from
gardens peppered with a few structures to a complex built environment dotted with gardens.

Before considering the constituent palaces of the Daulatkhane, it
will be helpful to gain a general picture of the royal precinct through
an overview of its parts, through the location and formal articulation
of its access points or gates, and through a general account of the
chronology and geography of its development. Given the scale of

destruction at the time of the Afghan invasion and afterward, any description of the Daulatkhane and its development is of necessity drawn mostly from textual sources and remains at least partly conjectural.

Moreover, it is clear that such a massive and complexly built area as the Daulatkhane did not materialize overnight. But, in fact, we do not know the sequence in which most of its constituent parts were built. With the exception of some reliable dating criteria available for such buildings as the Ali Qapu (1590/1–1617), the Chehel Sotun (1640s), or the Hasht Behesht (1669), much of our knowledge of the Daulatkhane is based on scattered contemporary Persian references and, especially, European descriptions, both visual and textual, of the precinct from the 1670s onward. It is therefore impossible to pinpoint the exact order in which various parts and functions were constructed. There should be no doubt, however, that essential functions such as the royal kitchens or stables must have been accommodated from the moment the court had moved to Isfahan, even if they were smaller in scale and housed in impermanent architectural arrangements (such as tents or tented walls). As the seventeenth century unfolded, the permanence of the royal household's presence and the increasingly sophisticated and aggrandized court ceremonials must have required the complex spatial articulation of their services, both administrative and ceremonial, at the Daulatkhane. The unresolvable dating of parts of the Daulatkhane does not affect our consideration of the palaces for which we have relatively reliable evidence. Architectural and historical milestones can safely be located on the landscape of the Daulatkhane. It is also possible to assign intentionality and significance to what may be conveyed by the absence or scarcity of building activity in the royal precinct. The following account of the ebbs and flows of construction in the Daulatkhane precinct takes the pulse of the actors, the motivations, and the clusters of meaning associated with building campaigns.

The early history

A chief concern in dealing with the earliest history of the Daulatkhane is the fact, often overlooked by Safavid scholars, that we can detect and document a very limited amount of building activity within the boundaries of the royal precinct between the beginning of construction of Isfahan as the capital in 1590/1 and the death of Shah Abbas I in 1629.[17] The addition of the Ali Qapu to the urban-palace ensemble of Naqsh-e Jahan (both the Maydan and the Bagh/garden) was indeed no small feat. Nevertheless, this was a building on the interface between the Maydan and the Bagh, the public and the royal zones, and it did not alter the inner composition of the Daulatkhane.

Little is known about construction at the Bagh-e Naqsh-e Jahan (the royal gardens) prior to the transfer of the capital to Isfahan, although one encounters its name in fifteenth-century chronicles.[18] Whatever buildings may have stood in this precursor to the Safavid Daulatkhane, the garden site was already identified as the Daulatkhane-ye Bagh-e Naqsh-e Jahan in at least two sixteenth-century sources: one dates to the 1505 visit by Shah Isma'il I, the other to the 1576 visit by Shah Isma'il II.[19] Soon after Shah Abbas I ascended the throne in 1587, some construction seems to have begun in the royal gardens, although these structures appear to have been unrelated to the transfer campaign that began in 1590/1.

During his 1587 visit, the newly installed Shah Abbas I did not have access to the lodging at the Daulatkhane-y Bagh-e Naqsh-e Jahan where his forebears had stayed earlier in the sixteenth century. According to Natanzi, a change of venue was necessitated because of the total destruction of the Bagh-e Naqsh-e Jahan, which he noted with great dismay for "nothing like its garden and building exists in Isfahan."[20] The destruction was inflicted by Farhad Beg, the *gholam*-governor appointed by Soltan Mohammad Khodabande to the province of Iraq-e Ajam (the Persian Iraq), which included Isfahan.[21]

Farhad Beg had gained great influence and amassed a vast fortune. In the midst of the political chaos preceding and immediately following Abbas's ascension, Farhad Beg had found an opportunity to annex Isfahan as his own dominion and to occupy and alter its royal garden precinct in order to inscribe his authority in contradistinction to that of the Safavid shahs, a course of events encountered also in Kerman and Fars during this period.[22] In an extraordinary expression of defiance, Farhad Beg destroyed the building (*emarat*) in the garden and took down trees both to provide materials for the construction of his own even more luxurious mansion and to diminish the significance of the royal association of the gardens. While we know nothing about Farhad Beg's rival mansion, we do know, thanks to his demolition activity and Natanzi's record, that a single, principal and permanent mansion was located somewhere within the garden precinct of Naqsh-e Jahan in Isfahan and that it was to serve as a royal lodging, no doubt supplemented with tents, as was the practice in the sixteenth century.

The Farhad Beg incident bears significantly on this discussion because it demonstrates the way in which the transfer of the capital and the construction of a royal abode wove together the same strands of political motivation that guided the centralizing enterprise carried out by Shah Abbas I. Instead of lodging at a mansion offered by one of the city's notables (a Qezelbash or *gholam* functionary, a wealthy landowner, a prominent Isfahani), a practice often encountered in such instances, the shah stayed at the Hossayniyye, where the city's chief theologians and especially the *sadat* (plural of *seyyed*, a descendant through the Shi'i Imams of the Prophet Mohammad) were lodged.[23] A Hossayniyye is dedicated to the memory of Imam Hossayn, the prince

of martyrs in Shi'i exegesis. It is also the place for repeated performances of ritual mourning and re-enactments of the martyrdom of the
Imam and his companions, a function of Hossayniyyes about which we
know more from nineteenth-century examples than any in the seventeenth century.[24]

The very existence of a Hossayniyye in Isfahan and the special
attention it received from the new shah are powerful reminders of the
deep roots Shi'i institutions had developed in Isfahan and the efficacy
of choosing the city as an imperial capital of Perso-Shi'i kingship.
Regardless of the state of disrepair or destruction in the royal gardens,
Shah Abbas's decision to lodge in one of the principal Shi'i institutions in Isfahan appears to have been his way of marking the fundamental importance of the religious pillar of Safavid authority. This
should, in other words, be seen in the retrospective light of the
repackaging of Isfahan as the seat of a fully realized and institution-
ally solidified Perso-Shi'i ethos of kingship.

The second visit of Shah Abbas I to Isfahan coincided with the
commencement of construction at the Maydan. During this sojourn
in 1590, the shah resided at the Bagh-e Naqsh-e Jahan, although it is
not clear whether a new building had already been raised for his visit
or whether he and his entourage stayed in tents within what one
assumes was a rehabilitated garden, even if only partially so.[25]
Nevertheless, it is clear from contemporary sources that the royal
gardens had been designated as the Daulatkhane of Isfahan.
Successive visits soon after, in the winter of 1591 and fall of 1592,
brought the shah again to the Daulatkhane-ye Bagh-e Naqsh-e Jahan.

A year later, Shah Abbas I ordered Alpan Beg, a ranking official at
the court in Qazvin (which remained the official capital until 1598),
to raise a residence next to the Daulatkhane-ye Bagh-e Naqsh-e Jahan
to temporarily house Hajem Khan, the exiled ruler of Khwarazm,
whom the shah had planned to bring to Isfahan for a visit.[26] From this
reference, one may surmise that there was at least one royal building,
probably of sixteenth-century provenance, still standing in the
Daulatkhane. Alpan Beg was dispatched to Isfahan in October of
1593, soon after which he completed the construction of a "lofty"
building in only twenty days. This feat so fascinated the historian
Natanzi that he devoted considerable attention to the details of
procuring building materials – but never described the building itself,
which he refers to as being next to the Daulatkhane.[27] Regardless of
whether Natanzi meant to convey that the new building was next to
the Ali Qapu (in its first phase of construction as the two-story
gateway of the 1590/1 campaign) or to another, perhaps sixteenth-
century, residence in the gardens, the fact remains that the Alpan
Beg/Hajem Khan residence had little to do with any official palace
building at this time.[28]

The most important signpost in the early history of the inner
zones of the Daulatkhane is associated with the construction during

the 1602 campaign, when the Maydan was formalized as the center of the new capital, representing the nucleus of authority for the empire. As noted earlier, this second Maydan campaign consisted principally of the addition of a second row of shops and a second floor to the square's periphery. This reduced the overall area of the Maydan but clarified its form, function, and meaning. More importantly, this second phase involved the construction of a new two-story unit above the Ali Qapu gateway-palace, as well as the raising of the royal chapel-mosque of Shaykh Lotf-Allah directly opposite on the eastern flank of the Maydan. The conclusion of the Maydan campaign, which provided the final architectural articulation of the eastern flank of the Daulatkhane, was supplemented by the completion both of the garden pavilions that lined the Chahar Bagh on the eastern boundaries of the royal precinct (mostly finished by spring of 1598) and the beginning in 1602 of the construction of the Allah Verdi Khan Bridge (completed in 1607).[29] In short, by 1602 all the principal pegs in the urban scheme of Isfahan as the capital had been anchored. Furthermore, with the peripheries of the palace precinct thus demarcated, Shah Abbas I's subsequent construction within the royal gardens focused on buildings in the andarun, where the harem was located.

The long-extinct harem zone was so restricted throughout the history of the occupation of the Daulatkhane that its architectural and functional components remain little known (Figures 3.7, 3.8 and 4.1).[30] The 1602 additions comprise one of the most important, albeit limited, pieces of evidence we have for aspects of the harem's architectural articulation.[31] This addition consisted of a Chahar Soffe, literally a four-platform, better understood from the description as a cluster of four structures, or four parts of a single structure, which straddled the harem.[32] There is no way for us to know exactly where this cluster of buildings was located, although I have posited elsewhere that the Chahar Soffe was immediately behind the inner side of the harem tunnel-gate (marked around the courtyard "d" in Figure 4.1).[33] Kaempfer's legend accompanying his "*Planographia*" identifies this cluster as the principal residence of the shah and his wives.

This link, however, presents many difficulties: one is the distance in time between 1602 and the 1684–5 visit of Kaempfer to Isfahan, a period during which much other construction may have taken place; another is the European visual and cultural biases apparent in the making of images such as the "*Planographia*," a point briefly considered in the first chapter. Moreover, it is not clear what Molla Jalal al-Din Monajjem, the court astrologer and historian of the reign of Shah Abbas the Great and our main Persian source here, may have meant by "soffe" in his "chahar soffe." He described a building with four flanks, ayvans or platforms that contained three pools (*hauz*) with fountains. One pool was positioned, according to Monajjem, at the exact center of the Chahar Soffe, while the other two were set on the eastern and western sides. Each of the side pools was equipped with some sort of stand (*dokkan*); one was for the display of foods and meats, the other for sweets. Presumably these were permanent features of the building's function, and their proximity to the harem, or placement inside the harem, served to bring into the andarun something akin to a "snack stand."[34]

Some fifty years after the first construction projects, Chardin recorded an intriguing description of a similarly composed quadripartite building with even more provocative water features.[35] These were, according to Chardin, four *emarat* or buildings composed at a distance from one another so that they need not have had walls – in other words, an integrated ensemble with sufficient space to provide some privacy and functional independence. Although Chardin's building seems more complex and larger than the Chahar Soffe of Monajjem, its location, some 120 feet behind the last gate of the harem tunnel-gate, conforms to Monajjem's reference and to Kaempfer's "*Planographia.*" As in Monajjem's record, Chardin's four-emarat cluster also provided places of entertainment. One was called the Mehmankhane, the guesthouse, and was reserved for the entertainment of female guests at the harem. A second was called Emarat-e Ferdaus, the Paradise Mansion. A third was known as the Divan-e Ayene, the Hall of Mirrors. The fourth, Emarat-e Daryache, was famous for the huge pool next to it; birds would flock to it, and one could sail in a boat to the small island in its middle. Chardin claims that each of these four buildings was constructed by one of the last four shahs, a statement so vague as to allow the possibility that the 1602 Chahar Soffe may have contained, at the very least, the embryonic version of this grander four-emarat seen by Chardin in the 1670s.

Despite the discrepancies in these accounts, a fundamental aspect of these clustered buildings in the Harem was the integration of aquatic architecture into buildings that were open to the world outside, throwing their inner and the outer domains into continuous dialogue. The extent to which they diverge from traditional architecture may be better understood by comparison with other conceptualizations of the harem. The prerequisite of extreme shielding and protection – a non-negotiable feature of the harem zone in all Islamicate palaces – has tended to result in a crammed and often cavernous aggregate of mostly small rooms, halls, and courtyards that look like deep wells because of their tall retaining walls. A relatively well-preserved example of this labyrinthine tendency in royal harems of the early modern age is at the Topkapı.[36] In contrast, a leitmotif of architecture at the Daulatkhane of Isfahan is precisely this capacity, or necessity, for the spatial choreography of access and remove.

The edifices in the harem zone of this early period appear modest in comparison to the impressive scale of Shah Abbas's building projects that defined the perimeter of the Daulatkhane and developed the urban works in Isfahan. The few structures of a residential or ceremonial nature are either limited in scope, such as the building to house a royal guest, or are entirely confined to the private realm of the harem. The Ali Qapu, as we shall see, served Shah Abbas I as the principal site of ceremonial functions in his new capital city. A suburban palace, the Hezar Jarib, also discussed later in this book, allowed for a space of retreat while still remaining connected with the city through the Chahar Bagh Avenue (Figure 3.2). The inner gardens of the Daulatkhane-ye Bagh-e Naqsh-e Jahan were otherwise used only occasionally, and in at least one instance with the supplement of temporary structures.

Nor did the inauguration of Isfahan as the capital and the massive building campaign of Shah Abbas I immediately translate into permanent lodging of the shah in Isfahan. In fact, Shah Abbas I spent considerably more time away from Isfahan than his successors would. His itinerancy seems to have been in direct response to matters of governance – the wars with the Ottomans and the Uzbeks, the rival claims of disaffected Qezelbash, the pockets of religious unrest, et cetera. Moreover, in attempting to consolidate the absolute authority of the centralized state, Shah Abbas I continued to campaign far and wide. For example, he performed two pilgrimages, on foot, from Isfahan to the Mashhad Shrine of Imam Reza; these public demonstrations of the shah's personal piety reiterated the allegiance of the household and state to Twelver Shi'ism.[37]

He also lavished a great deal of attention on the Caspian Sea provinces of Mazandaran and Gilan, visiting there frequently and for extended periods of time (Figure 1.2). This was an especially fertile region for the production of silk, one of the principal Safavid sources of trade on international markets and the state's major resource to exchange for European silver and gold.[38] Massive construction projects of Shah Abbas the Great in Mazandaran were part of the scheme of a planned economy, of which the exchange of silk for silver and gold was an important component (Figures 5.7 and 5.10). Thus, it is safe to say that economic development was a stronger motivation for his interest in the area than was the customary justification in scholarship of his love for the temperate climate and rich hunting ground or his matrilineal links to the region. He built two towns, Farahabad (a full-fledged new town with a congregational mosque) and Ashraf (principally a royal retreat), and populated them and their nearby silk-producing villages with people mostly from northwest Iran and the Safavid dominions in the Caucasus, especially from among the Armenians.[39]

The socio-political significance of the Isfahan-Mazandaran axis and the urgency of developing its economy, urban infrastructures and architecture undergirded the building preoccupations of the reign of Abbas I. Imperial energies pulsating from the core at Isfahan rippled through satellite centers of the imperium: Mazandaran and Kerman, for example, were closely bound to the centralizing planned economy of the Safavid state; Mashhad, with its Shi'i holy shrine, was targeted for special urban development so as to enhance its efficiency as a pilgrimage destination for the devotees of Twelver Shi'ism.[40] Construction in Mashhad, while not uniquely tied to Shi'i-motivated patronage, must be considered efficacious for the Safavids because it could potentially serve to divert attention from the contested territories of the holy shrines in Iraq, and indeed became a prime pilgrimage destination after their final loss to the Ottomans in the 1630s.[41]

Mazandaran construction was to play a transformative role in the architecture of the palaces in Isfahan during the reigns of Safi I and Abbas II, when the *talar* or wooden pillared halls, drawn from Mazandaran vernacular architecture, were introduced into the design of the palaces in the capital. Yet the palaces Shah Abbas I had built in Mazandaran remained architecturally rooted in earlier traditions that were established in Safavid Qazvin and Tabriz, as well as in the fifteenth-century Aqqoyunlu and Timurid pavilions discussed in Chapter 2 (Figures 2.1, 5.4 and Plate 3). It may also be surmised that the scarcity of Shah Abbas's palace buildings in the Daulatkhane of Isfahan was not so much associated with the presumed "nomadism" of the Safavids as with economic and political expediency.[42]

In the retrospective light of history, the conquest and consolidation carried out by Abbas I imposed a peripatetic existence on the monarch, but such a practical need does not negate the sedentary nature of the Safavid form of governance in this period. Indeed, Shah Abbas's battleground gains helped establish the conditions whereby his successors could remain immune from the need to don battle gear at far-flung corners of the Safavid realm. Although territorial battles – over holy cities in Iraq and over Qandahar – engaged Safi I and Abbas II in person, such military campaigns diminished in scale and frequency after Shah Abbas I and the court had become entrenched in urban life at the capital. Contrast this entrenchment with, for example, the frontier mentality that dominated the Mughal administration during this same general period. As Jos Gommans has demonstrated, the vast and largely Hindu landscape of the Mughal polity required the presence of the emperors at every corner of the empire; the court and administrative core of the Mughals remained indelibly attached to the person of the emperor and hence assumed centrality wherever the military camp was pitched. [43] And unlike Abbas I, shahs Safi I, Abbas II, Solayman, and Soltan Hossayn were not raised under the tutelage of a Qezelbash governor at an appendage far from the center. Rather, they grew up and learned to be kings in the harem in Isfahan and under the watchful eyes of the new aristocracy of the household – the concubine queen-mothers and the *gholam* tutors.[44] This reconfiguration of the household through the introduction of the slave elites and its centering in the new capital city contributed to the process of centralization so pivotal to an understanding of the urban and architectural strategies deployed in Isfahan.

Gateways and zones of operation

The location, architectural articulation, and functional regulation of the gateways into the Daulatkhane at Isfahan yield another glimpse into the semiotics of proximity and distance as developed in the Isfahan phase of Safavid rule (Figures 3.7 and 4.1). As urban-architectural strategies, the Daulatkhane gates further displayed the operational zoning of the precinct, and its subdivision of its vast conglomerate of buildings and functions, as already noted, into the *andarun* (within) and the *birun* (without). This typically Islamic, gendered designation of space served to distinguish the household and its residential quarter from its administrative, ceremonial, and manufacturing section. Entrance into these various segments in Isfahan was facilitated through gates on different sides of the Daulatkhane perimeter. Depending on one's "business" with the Daulatkhane, one's status and degree of access, or the wishes of the royal residents regarding relationships with the world of Isfahan beyond the precinct, gates assumed diverse architectural forms to accommodate equally diverse functions. Significantly, in comparison to the palace precincts in the earlier Safavid capitals of Qazvin and Tabriz – and in fact to those at Ottoman Istanbul, Mughal Delhi, Agra, and Lahore, for example – the staggering number, architectural variety, and siting of gates at the Daulatkhane in Isfahan signal a distinctive utilization of the symbolic load gateways can bear (Figures 2.1, 2.3, 3.7, 4.1, 6.1, 6.7 and 6.8).

At least four gates occupied the Maydan side; no fewer than three were on the Chahar Bagh flank; at least one served the northeastern side. The principal one at Isfahan was the Ali Qapu Palace-Gateway, a building to which we turn repeatedly and according to its multiple identities and lives. As in all comparable palatine examples, the significance of the principal gateway was made visible through the imposing scale of the building (Figure 4.2). Unexpectedly, however, this structure (which was without the pillared front portion until 1644) was articulated so as to accommodate multiple administrative and ceremonial functions, a major departure from the tendency in other palace complexes to treat the gate mainly as a glorified doorway (Figure 4.4 and Plate 11). Here on the first two stories of the building were housed the offices of the *divan begi* or "le président du divan" (the chief judge), the *khwansalar-e azam* or "le grand maître d'hôtel" (the grand master of the household), the *qapuchi bashi* or the "chef des maitres de la porte" (the chief of the gate keepers), and of the Grand Vizier (chief minister).[45] The spaces on the two lower stories of the Ali Qapu also served as the *qurchikhane* or "salles des gardes" for the special guards of the shah, who were composed of the loyal Sufi devotees of the Safavid household, a conciliatory nod in this age of centralization to the diminishing powers of the Qezelbash.[46]

Figure 4.4 *Isfahan, Ali Qapu, rear view from the Daulatkhane.*

Conceived as an integral part of the urban projects commissioned by Shah Abbas I in 1590/1, and built in preparation for the transfer of the Safavid capital in 1598, the Ali Qapu was initially a two-story gateway between the Maydan and the Daulatkhane. Expanded into a five-story tower by around 1615, it served as the station house for the shah's special guards, the offices of the judiciary, and a ceremonial palace.

In addition to the ceremonial functions of the Ali Qapu – audiences, feasts, and a viewing stage for parades, polo games, and the like at the Maydan – that justified its designation as a palace, the building as a gateway facilitated the flow from both directions of the threshold. On occasions when the shah or members of the inner household were to attend events at the Maydan-e Naqsh-e Jahan or visit the two mosques and the royal bazaar, a procession of the harem entourage would be delivered by the eunuch guards from the andarun to the Sufi guards (the *qurchi*) of the birun, who were housed precisely for such purposes at the Ali Qapu.[47] Conversely, too, the liminal space of this palace-gateway served as the transition from the profane to the sacred, from the Maydan to the Daulatkhane. Invited visitors to the court, guests and ambassadors, administrators and generals serving the provinces, local and foreign dignitaries, missionaries and prominent merchants – all passed through the Ali Qapu to enter the Daulatkhane.

It was through the braiding of potent Shi'i symbolisms associated with Imam Ali and those of an imperial flavor that the Ali Qapu acquired its aura of awesome sanctity. Several sources testify to the inviolability of the Ali Qapu as the threshold through which justice and kingship were to be dispensed.[48] Shah Abbas I had, reputedly, installed in the fabric of the gateway of the Ali Qapu one of the doors from the shrine of Imam Ali in Najaf that he had ordered brought to Isfahan. The transference of the inviolable holy shrine made it a breach of protocol to enter the gateway on horseback. Even the shah himself dismounted before the Ali Qapu Gate, while all others were also obliged to prostrate and kiss the marble doorsill that marked the threshold. The links with Imam Ali were further reiterated through the strategic placement of the 110 cannons – captured from the Portuguese at Hormuz in 1622 and from the Ottomans at Baghdad in 1623 (Figure 3.9). Flanking the gateway and facing the Maydan, the cannons conjured up in the minds of believers the numerical value of the name of Imam Ali in the Arabo-Islamic *abjad* system (the counting of the numerical value of letters).[49]

To many a denizen of Isfahan, for whose daily business the Maydan and its imperial structures formed the backdrop, such repeated performances of humility and obedience at the Ali Qapu Palace-Gateway tinged the imagination with the two-pronged religious and royal sanctity of the spot. This was the threshold blessed by Imam Ali himself, and the gate was therefore to be treaded reverently.

Moreover, Shah Abbas I had adopted, as part of the charismatic persona of kingship in its Twelver Shi'i enunciation, the posture of humility at the threshold of Imam Ali, calling himself *kalb-e astan-e Ali*, "the dog of the threshold of Ali" or *bande-ye shah-e velayat Abbas*, "Abbas, the slave of the threshold of the king of sovereignty."[50] The shah encouraged the widespread use of these titles. The effect of this is evident in the multiplicity of official sources in which he signs himself or is addressed as *kalb-e* (dog of) or *bande-ye* (slave of) *astan-e Ali* (the threshold of Ali) in royal seals, decrees, and correspondence as well as in poetic, epigraphic, and historical writings, either attributed to the shah himself or produced during his reign.

Here was, then, the upholder of Twelver Shi'ism, the Shadow of God (zell-Allah) on earth, and the reincarnation in farr of the ancient king of kings, who ritually renounced his august titles in utmost self-abasement to the exalted station of his master, Imam Ali.[51] For the Safavids to humble themselves before their spiritual master and (claimed) progenitor, on whose behalf they carried forth the banner of righteous and just kingship must have been read as a potent political gesture, especially given the Islamic view that dogs are unclean and slaves are abject because they fall outside the aura of Islam.

The indivisibility of the authority of the king and his public expression of humility were further displayed in the conceptual links between the sanctuary of Imam Ali and the Ali Qapu Palace-Gateway, from which the Safavid kings were to dispense justice in all its manifestations. After the reconquest of the holy cities of Iraq in 1032/1623 from the Ottomans, Shah Abbas made a royal visit first to Baghdad, where his name was included in the khotbe as a public statement of allegiance to his sovereignty, and then to Najaf and the shrine of Imam Ali. At a distance from the entrance to the city, the shah dismounted and proceeded on foot to the shrine, where he stayed for ten days in prayer, meditation, and service, including sweeping the sanctuary and grounds of the shrine and initiating repairs and beautifications of the holy sites.[52]

In popular imagination, the shah's public display of humility, such as his preferred titles as the dog or slave of the threshold of Ali, was fused with his personal deeds of humility, as at the sacred thresholds of the shrines in Najaf and Mashhad. The interweaving of complex images and concepts suggestive of the threshold, of holiness, of humility, and of the Shi'ification of justice and kingship made it possible for the denizens of Safavid dominions to imagine the Ali Qapu Palace-Gate as an equally sanctified threshold.

Dispensing justice from the locus of imperial authority and sanctity of the Daulatkhane was the obligation and prerogative of kingship. Here again, it is important to recall the significance of such prominent Shi'i scholars as Shaykh Baha'i, whose involvement in the overall project of making Isfahan the capital has already been discussed in Chapter 3. The close relationship between authority and sanctity, the shari'a-sanctioned Twelver Shi'i legitimization of sovereignty, was enunciated in the waqf (endowment) dedication of the entire Maydan, including its gates into the Daulatkhane, in the name of the family of the Prophet. It is worth recalling that Shaykh Baha'i, the great Shaykh al-Islam (jurist-consult) of the capital city and the shah's advisor and confidant in religious matters, drafted this waqf document.

Such linkages across the normative practices of Shi'ism and the conduct of imperial prerogatives and obligations were not only conceptually woven into the urban fabric of the Maydan but also manifested on a daily basis. The chief judge of the city, the divan begi, held

office at the Ali Qapu four days a week, hearing complaints and griev-
ances. Passage through the sanctified threshold of the Ali Qapu also
provided safe haven to those who were accused of a capital crime and
who sought justice through royal intervention. Both men and women
were allowed to take asylum (*bast neshastan*; literally sitting in
asylum) at the Tauhidkhane (Figures 4.2 and 4.3, Plate 10). This was a
polygonal domed building set in a garden that was subdivided, according to some sources, to accommodate male and female refugees.[53]

We get a glimpse of the workings of the judiciary at the Ali Qapu
from a litigious affair that took place during the 1637 visit of the
Holstein Embassy. Lion Bernoldi, a member of the embassy, had
sought refuge at the Tauhidkhane, beyond the Ali Qapu, in order
to escape Ambassador Brugman's wrath.[54] According to Olearius,
Brugman was furious that his domestic servant had been given refuge
and requested Shah Safi I to intervene and return Bernoldi to the
ambassador. The rejection of his request led the ambassador to turn
to other means to lure the hapless man out of the *bast*, with the
orders that he be killed immediately upon his exit. Evidently the
sordid matter led to a shouting match between representatives of
the embassy and the guards at the Ali Qapu. So loud was this
exchange that it awoke Shah Safi, who was in the private rooms on
the fifth floor of the Ali Qapu. Olearius relates that the shah, "desiri-
ous to prevent further disorder, commanded that Gate, through
which there was an entrance into the Sanctuary, to be shut, which
was more than had been seen in the memory of Man."

Besides the fascinating light that it sheds on legal proceedings,
such an episode indicates the range of judicial avenues of redress
and the universal nature of access to justice at the threshold of the
Daulatkhane and under the shadow of royal protection. The still
extant Tauhidkhane has lost its garden setting and its access
route, which reached from the alley behind the Ali Qapu (Plate 10).
Nevertheless, its general architectural configuration – a domed octagonal building – recalls the famed Jannat Sara (Paradisiacal Palace) of
the shrine complex of Shaykh Safi at Ardabil.[55] Built by Shah
Tahmasb around 1537–40, the Jannat Sara had served principally as a
place for prayer and devotional gatherings of the Qezelbash Sufi followers of the Safavid shahs and the royal household.[56]

The sixteenth-century cultic practices of the Qezelbash, so fundamental to the legitimizing representations of their allegiance to
the Safavid cause, were transformed into mimetic ritual performances with no real power or authority in the seventeenth century.
With the gradual but decisive shift in emphasis away from the
Qezelbash, implemented most effectively after Abbas I's reconfiguration of the household and his final consolidation of the *gholam*
elite into the Safavid power structure, the Tauhidkhane was all that
remained to represent the Sufi past of the Safavid royal household on
the grounds of the new Daulatkhane of the capital city. In fact, its

location inside the Daulatkhane, just beyond the sacred threshold of the Ali Qapu, signifies, in no uncertain terms, the connection between justice and kingship as well as between the Sufi past and the normative Twelver Shiʿi present of the Safavids in their new imperial home.[57]

At the Harem Gate, the second most important point of access to the Daulatkhane, the symbolic representations of kingship embodied in the palace-gateway of the Ali Qapu were reconfigured differently (Figures 3.9 and 4.2).[58] This too was a sacred threshold because it housed the protected Safavid bloodline and channeled access through bureaucratic layers of the imperial household. Located to the south of the Ali Qapu, the Harem Gate opened onto the Maydan with a series of gate-like structures positioned at regular intervals along an alley that led to the andarun zone of the Daulatkhane. Depending on the source, there were three (Chardin) or four (Kaempfer) successive gate structures. While Kaempfer's "*Planographia*" may be taken as a rough guide for the external shape of the gates, our understanding of the internal configuration of spaces of these gates remains vague. Nevertheless, Chardin's scattered descriptive notes on the Harem Gate, and especially his eyewitness description of the way in which the news of the death of Shah Abbas II and the succession to the throne of Shah Safi II (recrowned later as Shah Solayman) was delivered through the Harem Gate, can guide a tentative reconstruction of this important entry point into the Daulatkhane.[59]

The Harem Gate was marked on the Maydan-e Naqsh-e Jahan by a structure that was flush with the peripheral bazaar "wall" and that was the most fortified, formal, and heavily guarded of the series. If we were to take Kaempfer's distant view as a rough guide, the first Harem Gate structure resembled, on a smaller scale, the ayvan-opening-into-a-block configuration that constitutes the basic form of the first two stories of the Ali Qapu (the building in its initial phase). Beyond this publicly visible gateway stood a second, similarly shaped gate that was doubly shielded by corps of the *qurchi* guards from its outer side and by eunuchs of the household from its inner side. The third and possibly a fourth gate were occupied entirely by eunuch *gholam*s, with the black ones, considered the most abject, positioned at the sides closest to the harem site, as Chardin repeatedly informed his readers, and the whites at the farthest, that is, closer to the Maydan exit.

With the reconfiguration of the Safavid household and the rise to power of the *gholam*s in the course of the seventeenth century, black and white eunuchs came to assume increasingly central positions within the inner structure of the harem and the court hierarchy.[60] Their mediatory role here at the Harem Gate is not simply a matter of shielding access and providing security. Rather, and more importantly, these eunuchs were entrusted with the task of funneling all official business – requests, directives, and news of all kinds – pertinent to the shah and the household through the successive gates. The Harem Gate's political distinction was especially pronounced in the later seventeenth century. Starting with the reign of Shah Solayman, Safavid shahs tended to be more often found in the harem and were thus accessed, ordinarily, through the Harem Gate bureaucracy for all matters of state concern.

Besides the Ali Qapu Palace and the Harem Gate, the number of other gates into the Daulatkhane differs depending on the source, most of which are European chronicles.[61] Discrepancies regarding the number, locations, and functions of the gates make it impossible to assign dates of installation or to arrive at a fixed number for any slice of time during the period when the Isfahan Daulatkhane served as the nerve center of the empire. Nevertheless, some of the gates are relatively well documented. For instance, in addition to the Ali Qapu Palace-Gateway and the Harem Gate, there were at least three more gates on the Maydan side of the Daulatkhane. One was the Kitchen Gate or *darb-e matbakh*, whose name is given to an alley still open for traffic but now lined with tourist shops (Figure 4.1). According to Chardin, this "porte de la cuisine" gave access to the kitchens, the bakery, and various storehouses on the royal grounds.[62] Seemingly limited to providing prepared food for the court and for the ceremonial feasts, the royal kitchens at the Daulatkhane of Isfahan signaled to the public the other, well-established and universally acknowledged, symbolic value of feeding the king's subjects. Distribution of food from the royal table, presumably from this same Kitchen Gate, was not only considered a meritorious and generous dissemination of royal wealth but was also understood by many a denizen of Safavid Iran as a sacred offering, because food touched by the king acquired curative properties.[63]

Similar architectural and symbolic cross-references among generosity, justice, sanctity, and kingship were drawn elsewhere in the Islamicate world. At the Topkapı palace in Istanbul, the magnificent chimneys of the royal kitchens were as visible from a distance as the tower that marked the Council Chamber, the office of the judiciary-administration in the Second Courtyard, where the principal imperial ceremonials took place and where the tight bond between the sultan's generosity and his justice were illustrated through such strategic juxtapositions (Figure 6.2).[64] At the Isfahan Daulatkhane, too, the royal kitchens were positioned in proximity to the sites where the administration of justice and the orderly conduct of the empire were monitored.

In contrast to their contemporaries, however, Safavid shahs went further in institutionalizing the notion of generosity by incorporating the rituals of feasting into the very fabric of their performance of kingship. Viewed from the standpoint of the denizens of Isfahan, who could glimpse, albeit from a distance, royal feasts at the Ali Qapu, the prominent gate to the royal kitchens highlighted the prismatic nature of Shiʿi kingship as practiced by the Safavids in Isfahan. Buildings and the events that took place within them served as iconic markers of the multivalent aspects of Safavid kingship, with its symbols of generosity, justice, piety, politics, and commerce crisscrossing the Maydan.

The other gates along the Maydan side of the Daulatkhane are less clearly identifiable *in situ*. One of them may well be the same Kitchen Gate discussed above, but its descriptions are so muddled in the European chronicles that they appear as several independent entrances. The resolution of the meanings of this gate(s) matters because it reflects the "holistic" ways in which the Safavid ideology of kingship was represented through the clustering of select functions and urban locations, resulting in a carefully orchestrated encounter between the spheres of the sacred, royal, and private Daulatkhane and the profane, ordinary, and public Maydan.

Tavernier, for example, records an additional gate related to the Harem Gate, calling the latter "a great Portal that leads to a false gate of the King's Palace; near to which, as soon as you are enter'd, you meet with the apartment of the Great Treasurer, who is a white Eunuch."[65] Through this "false gate" presumably, he says that "all the King's provisions are carry'd into the Palace" and that this gate gave access to the workshops of fabric manufacturers, the most prominent artists, and the Europeans whom the shah employed. Indeed, a number of European craftsmen are recorded at the royal workshops in Isfahan during the reign of Shah Abbas II, including five "French artificers," a goldsmith, two watchmakers, and two musketmakers.[66] It should be clear that no such "false gate" could have been tucked inside the Harem Gate complex, and thus we must assume Tavernier is talking about a separate gate.

Similarly, Chardin refers to a small gate on the southeastern corner of the Daulatkhane (the southwestern corner of the Maydan) that, he says, was close to the Hammam-e Shahi, the Royal Bathhouse, and not far from the Kitchen Gate.[67] In another instance, Chardin refers to a gate watched over by Ishik Aqasi Bashi, the lord marshal of the household, in the general area of this southeastern corner of the Daulatkhane.[68] There were two branches of the latter office: one served as the master of ceremonies in state meetings and audiences, as well as the chief monitor of the gatekeepers and guards; the other performed similar tasks, but for the harem only.[69]

There is, however, no corroborating evidence that any of these other gates on this corner of the Maydan provided access to the Daulatkhane – no alleyways, doorways, or any other physical indication of another gate exists other than the Kuche-ye Matbakh, the kitchen's alley. Nor is there any indication in Kaempfer's "*Planographia*" of additional gates in this area. On the other hand, merging the archaeological evidence and the information provided by the "*Planographia*" yields what seems to be the most plausible conclusion: these descriptions most likely refer to the Kitchen Gate. In Kaempfer's engraving, the apartments of the private chamberlains of the shah (marked "n" in Figure 4.1) and the kitchens (marked "i") flank the only passageway (marked "12," a number used also to designate all such passageways in Kaempfer's scheme) on this corner of the Maydan-Daulatkhane confluence. This same passageway, which corresponds without a doubt to the Kitchen Alley, leads to another cluster of buildings around a courtyard (marked "k") that is identified by Kaempfer as the workshop of jewelers, goldsmiths, and watch-makers. What may be deduced from these references and other evidence is that the Kitchen Gate also housed two important offices that served inner court functions: one was the Lord Marshal or *Ishik Aqasi Bashi* of Chardin's description, who served as the master of ceremonies at royal feasts, among other duties. The other was the office of Tavernier's Great Treasurer, which may be the same as the *Saheb-e jam'* of the Royal Treasury that oversaw the royal workshops as well.[70]

According to the author of the *Tazkerat al-moluk*, the famous manual of Safavid statecraft written in the eighteenth century probably for the edification of the post-Safavid Afghan and other tribal rulers of Iran, a branch of this office "kept the sums and objects remitted to the Treasury, but also acted for the recovery of the remittances which were overdue." Among the goods remitted to this treasurer's office were "the more valuable objects of the Royal Household, such as jewels, precious textiles and presents consisting of books, sable marten furs, gold embroideries and other rare objects."[71] The proximity of the workshops of the jewelers, goldsmiths, and watch-makers, on the one hand, and the tasks performed by the Great Treasurer/Sahib-e jam', on the other, suggests that this office, too, was located at the Kitchen Gate, which also gave access to the workshops.

Equally important to note is the placement, as Chardin indicates, of the office of the Ishik Aqasi Bashi at this same Kitchen Gate. Given the primacy of feasting rituals, the proximity of the office of the master of ceremonies to the kitchens where the feasting provisions were produced seems all the more reasonable from not only a practical but, more importantly, a symbolic perspective. The clustering at the Kitchen Gate of such seemingly diverse but meaningfully interlaced functions invests this threshold between the public arena of the Maydan and the royal precinct with profoundly meaningful representations of the balance between the power to command riches and the will to dispense generously. The transport of culinary and other provisions for the feasts; the channeling of luxury goods remitted to the court treasury and its reciprocal "outpouring" of royal generosity from the kitchens; the gates that perforated the shared walls of the Daulatkhane and the Maydan – all of these enunciated the ways in which the Safavid Imami-Shi'i variant of kingship is predicated on the reciprocal relationship between the master and the subject. Like gifting, the dispensing of food from royal kitchens was universally practiced. But in this early modern age, Safavid authority was manifested especially through the visible symbols and proximate icons of its generosity. This was Imami rule on behalf of the Prophet Mohammad, who admonished His followers by saying, "The worst people are those who eat alone!"[72]

A fourth gate from the Maydan led to the royal chancellery and complemented, in fact completed, the cluster of functions that communicated between the ruler and the ruled. This was known as Dar-e Chahar Hauz, the Four-Ponds Gate.[73] In the legend accompanying Kaempfer's "*Planographia*," a gate marked "7" is located on the western side of the Maydan-e Naqsh-e Jahan to the north of the Ali Qapu and is identified as the "four gates of the Shah square" (Figure 4.1). However, neither Chardin's description nor Kaempfer's "*Planographia*" indicates a four-part gateway structure in this northwestern corner of the Maydan. Rather, the entrance into the chancellery complex from the Maydan seems to have been named after the Chahar Hauz Gate, which was placed "inside" the birun section of the Daulatkhane in its far northeastern corner.[74] Here, as the anonymous Persian author of the text known as *Dar danestan-e carevansara-ha-ye Esfahan* (On Knowing the Caravanserais of Isfahan) tells us, was a large, tree-lined square known also as the Maydan-e Chahar Hauz, which was linked through a covered alleyway to the Maydan-e Naqsh-e Jahan. Traces of this gate and the alleyway that led to buildings within the Daulatkhane are still extant in the silhouette of the bazaar of coppersmiths, the *bazaar-e mesgaran*.

The Daftarkhane (Secretariat or Chancellery), better known as the *daftarkhane-ye homayun-e a'la*, the Royal Supreme Secretariat (Figures 4.1 and 4.5, Plate 9), was at the end of the access road that came in from the "Chahar Hauz door" (*darb-e Chahar Hauz*), so named after the Maydan-e Chahar Hauz.[75] In addition to the Daftarkhane, the royal caravanserai and a cluster of buildings of the *karkhane* or royal workshops and storehouses also straddled the Chahar Hauz Maydan (marked "2" and "h" in Figure 4.1).

The Daftarkhane was the office charged with maintaining the bureaucratic machinery of the empire: keeping the books in general as well as the royal decrees "by which the Grand Vizier confirmed nominations, allowances, payments, et cetera." Its location, marked "I" in the "*Planographia*," corresponds to an extant building popularly known as Talar-e Taymuri, a structure often attributed to Timurid times (the fifteenth century) but still in need of systematic study to elucidate its materials and methods of construction and its stylistic relationship to Timurid architecture.[76] In plan, this building is rather unusual for Safavid Isfahan. It consists of a series of halls and rooms in two stories resting on a platform; the rooms and halls are joined to the back and flanking sides of a central ayvan. In other words, the

Figure 4.5 *Isfahan, Daulatkhane (Royal Precinct).*
The building on the right, now a natural-history museum, is popularly
known as the Talar-e Taymuri. It was the Daftarkhane or chancellery in
Safavid times. The structure on the left is what remains of the entrance
gate into the Chehel Sotun Palace, visible on the far left.

building is designed along a horizontal axis, with the ayvan porch
forming its principal façade. Neither the location nor the typology of
this building convincingly connects the building's function or the
configuration of its spaces and façades to Timurid parentage.
Moreover, repeated references by Khwajegi Esfahani, the historian of
Shah Safi I, to a palace of Hauzkhane may be related to this building
and its location at the Chahar Hauz.[77] We know nothing, nevertheless,
about this palace, nor is there any corroborating evidence for its location or form. It is also possible that the Hauzkhane Palace is the same
as the Chahar Soffe, noted above as one of the earliest structures in
the Bagh-e Naqsh-e Jahan.

The most likely hypothesis for the architectural shape of this
edifice is that the Daftarkhane was devised in a form that both accommodated the workings of the supreme secretariat and differed from
that of the "palaces." In other words, the clear delineation of branches
of the state and court bureaucracy and the ceremonial and practical
needs and duties contained in the Isfahan Daulatkhane had necessitated a totally different rendition of space and architecture for each of
these functions. As the analyses of the palaces will demonstrate, such
architectural specificity distinguishes the Daulatkhane of Isfahan
from its predecessors and contemporaries in significant ways.

Moreover, the location of the Daftarkhane marked the threshold between the externally orientated imperial secretariat and the

ceremonially central Palace of Chehel Sotun, marked "O" in the "*Planographia*," a building erected in the middle of the seventeenth century during the reign of Abbas II, to which we turn in the next chapter (Figure 4.1). The gateway visible to the left of the Daftarkhane is situated at the far end of the garden of the Chehel Sotun Palace, a fragmentary view of which can be seen as well (Figure 5.15). The Daftarkhane, it can be argued, mediated spatially between the ceremonial zone of the Chehel Sotun Palace and its garden, on the one hand, and the city on the other.

Just as gates and spaces braided a complex cluster of functions and symbolic meanings on the southeastern corner of the precinct (with the royal kitchens, treasuries, and workshops), this northeastern edge of the Daulatkhane signaled access through the Chahar Hauz Gate to the transitional space of the Maydan-e Chahar Hauz, where the Daulatkhane and the capital city merged and mingled most openly. As a forecourt to the imperial secretariat and the most ceremonial palace in the Daulatkhane, the Maydan-e Chahar Hauz and its name-sake gate continued to serve as a primary transitional space between the birun and the andarun of the royal precinct until the nineteenth century, when Mirza Hossayn Khan, a historian of Qajar Isfahan, observed in his 1877 description that it still had a lofty and excellent doorway "worthy of places of high quality."[78]

In their functions and architectural design, in their mediatory role between the Daulatkhane and the city of Isfahan, between the imperial household and the denizens of Safavid Iran, the gates along the shared "wall" of the Daulatkhane and the Maydan-e Naqsh-e Jahan stand out as distinctive interpretations of how access to a royal abode was conceptualized and monumentalized. Among the four gates, moreover, the hierarchical stratification of functions is rendered architecturally perceptible. Seen from the perspective of the symbolics of power, the gates can be ranked in terms of their monumentality: the most important were the ceremonial-judicial Ali Qapu Palace-Gate and the household directorate of the Harem Gate, whence "true" power emanated. The other aspects of the administration of authority were defined through the remaining two access points on the Maydan side: the Chahar Hauz Gate gave onto the supreme secretariat, which regulated the affairs of the empire, and the Kitchen Gate marked the threshold through which royal largesse was dispensed. Conceptually, the Daulatkhane–Maydan gates represented the two-pronged aspects of the administration of the Safavid Empire and its particular juxtaposition of notions of legitimacy and authority.

The gates on the Chahar Bagh side of the Daulatkhane, presumably numbering three, tend to recede in the shadow of secrecy and seclusion in contrast to the public locations, forms, and functions of the four principal gates on the Maydan side (Figures 3.6 and 3.8). All the gates opening onto the Chahar Bagh originate from the andarun zone of the harem and as such were designated for the exclusive use of the inhabitants of the harem – the royal women and children, as well as their female and eunuch guards, tutors, companions, and servants. Of these gates, one was located at the far southwestern corner of the Daulatkhane and has already been introduced, based on the little that we know.[79] About the other two we know much more.

Dar-e Khargah or Kaempfer's *horti Charga* opened onto the Chahar Bagh Avenue from Bagh-e Khargah, the "Tent Garden" (marked "S" in Figure 4.1).[80] Bagh-e Khargah was among the gardens of the andarun, and Kaempfer indicates that its gate was the exit point for the shah's afternoon rides and for the harem women's strolls in the Chahar Bagh. Chardin's reference to such a gate for the exclusive use of the women and eunuchs of the harem is without a proper name but appropriately located in the area near Bagh-e Khargah, which he, too, mentions, albeit with no further elaboration.[81]

The most important of the gates on the Chahar Bagh side of the Daulatkhane was the gate Chardin called "Impériale" or *Dar-e shahi* (Royal Gate) ("R" in Figure 3.6).[82] Nothing remains on the ground of this gate, but we know its general location because it gave access to the Jahan Nama royal pavilion, which stood at the beginning of the Chahar Bagh Avenue (Figure 3.8 and 13 in Figure 4.1). In the *"Planographia,"* the gate can be located at the Chahar Bagh end of a covered passageway marked partly "u" and partly "w" (Figure 4.1).[83] Kaempfer's legend identifies the first part of the passageway (u) as an "Enclosed route, one of the walls of the old city" and the second part (w) as "The station for forty ready horses for the Shah." This route, a tunnel in Pietro Della Valle's description, ran between two of the gardens of the Daulatkhane – the Angurestan, the vineyard, and the Khargah, the Tent Garden – and ended on the Chahar Bagh side just behind the Jahan Nama pavilion. Tavernier describes the exclusivity of the Dar-e Shahi by saying that "none but the King and his household pass that way into the walk [Chahar Bagh]. For they that go from Isfahan to Zulpha [New Julfa], find the way into the walk through a gate which is close adjoining to the tabernacle."[84] Moreover, the maintenance of "ready horses" on the route to the Shahi Gate clearly indicates its function as the exit point for the shah himself, a complement perhaps to the women's gate of the Khargah just to its south. Because the Shahi Gate opened onto the back of the Jahan Nama pavilion, the harem was further ensured safe access to the latter.

This pavilion too was an integral part of Shah Abbas I's urban planning ("13" in Figure 4.1). The Daulat Gate (Darvaze Daulat), one of the principal entry points into the city on its northwestern side, was connected through the architectural formality of the pavilion to the promenade of the Chahar Bagh.[85] Pietro Della Valle's "una piccola casa" and Chardin's "un pavillon carré" refer to the pavilion of Jahan Nama, which marked the start of the Chahar Bagh Avenue with imperial significance.[86] As is often the case, Europeans differ widely

Plate **9** *Isfahan, looking west over the Maydan-e Naqsh-e Jahan (Omidvar).*

The row of shops along the Maydan periphery is punctuated by the Shaykh Lotf-Allah Chapel-Mosque and by the Ali Qapu Palace-Gateway directly opposite. The Daulatkhane lies beyond the Ali Qapu. The Chehel Sotun Palace with its pillared terrace, talar, and the long pool in front is on the upper right-hand side.

Plate 10 *Isfahan, Ali Qapu and Tauhidkhane (Omidvar).*

This profile view from the north shows how far the 1640s addition of the talar building disrupted the original composition. The water-tower, a stepped two-unit structure leaning against the tower, was also added at that time, with clever pumping mechanisms that fed the fountain jets of the talar pool. An example of the composition of the internal subdivisions of work spaces of the Daulatkhane is presented in the courtyard of the domed, octagonal Tauhidkhane, a Sufi shrine and public refuge, and in the vaulted and arcaded structures surrounding it. A T-shaped building complex now occupies the site of the destroyed Talar-e Tavile Palace.

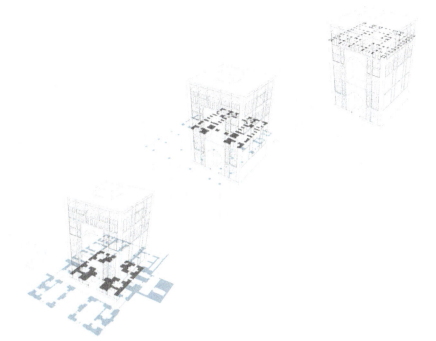

Plate **11** *Isfahan, Ali Qapu, exploded perspective renderings.*

The highlighted plans are of the main floors of the five-story tower (1590/1–1643/4): the ground floor gateway and offices of the guards and the judiciary (Figure 5.4 D); the fourth-floor audience hall (excluding the talar terrace); and the fifth-floor Music Room. From heavier piers, larger and fewer spaces of the ground floor, the building rises in ever lighter, more numerous but smaller rooms. The spatial composition of each floor responds to its function: from the public, martial/judiciary, to ceremonial, to private court leisure.

Plate **12** *Isfahan, Ali Qapu Palace-Gateway.*

In 1644 the ceremonial space of the talar front building was added to the five-story tower of 1590/1–1615. This multi-functional palace-gateway is most extraordinary for its location on the threshold between the public and royal domains of the city.

Plate **13** *Isfahan, Ali Qapu.*

The "Music Room" on the fifth floor of the tower was completed c.
1615. Its cross-shaped, high-vaulted central space opens onto a finely
proportioned cluster of rooms at its sides and corners. The lantern, also
devised on the forked-arch model, with thin membranes and glazed
surfaces, rises above the square room, creating the illusion of a rotating
well of light beams. The painted and gilded perforated plaster sheets feature
deeply carved shapes of drinking vessels. These cutout forms give the room
its good acoustics, hence its popular name. This elegantly appointed space
was reserved for the intimate gatherings of the shah and his harem.

Plate **14** *Isfahan, Chehel Sotun (c. 1647–50).*

Twenty slender wooden pillars, and their reflection in the pool, give the building its name (Forty Columns). The talar terrace forms the principal façade (facing east) of this palace to which royal guests were led through a formal gateway (Figure 4.5), the vast gardens and along the processional routes on either side of the long pool. This was the largest and most lavishly decorated of the ceremonial palaces in Isfahan and was entirely devoted to feasting and other imperial rituals of conviviality.

Plate **15** *Isfahan, Chehel Sotun.*

Looking from the southeastern corner, down the side of the building, this picture evokes the viewing angle available to the guests as they approached the talar. In both architectural and landscaping strategies, the palace was intended to be experienced through the drama of open and closed spaces.

Plate **16** *Isfahan, Chehel Sotun.*

The vast talar served as the principal gathering place for large feasts at the Safavid court in the middle of the seventeenth century. The pillared terrace was composed of a sequence of three spaces that shrank as they receded but were aggrandized in decoration and symbolic significance. The mirrored section in the back served as the throne ayvan.

in their descriptions of Jahan Nama: Della Valle's "piccolo casa" is a small building with windows and ayvans all around; Chardin's "pavillon carré" is three stories tall; and Tavernier refers to this building as "a pavilion or tabernacle forty feet square, which joins to the hinder part of the King's House, with a double story, to which several windows give light, clos'd with wooden lattices very artificially wrought."[87] Whatever its scale, the Jahan Nama was intended as an elegant place of repose for the women whose presence would have been veiled behind the finely wrought, trellised windows, while they could observe the goings on down the grand boulevard, that place of public strolls and picnics so singularly indicative of this early modern fetishization of leisure as a bequest of the absolutist imperial agenda.

As witnessed in the Royal Gate and Jahan Nama pairing with a city gate, or the Ali Qapu's multiple functions, the gateways into the vast Daulatkhane were carefully articulated for their composite architectural, functional, and symbolic import. Moreover, the "soft wall" approach to its boundaries allowed for the opening of a number of subsidiary gateways into the royal precinct for which there is hardly any comparison in either earlier or contemporary palaces and fortifications.

Negotiating the threshold: the Ali Qapu palace-gateway

The most extraordinary piece in the Daulatkhane ensemble is the Ali Qapu Palace-Gateway (Figures 4.2 and 4.4). We revisit it here and again in the next chapter in order to elucidate its complex building history over a 50-year span in relation to its almost organic functional evolution, and its physical and symbolic location between the public and royal arenas of Isfahan. Adam Olearius, the secretary of the 1637 embassy from the Duke of Holstein to the court of Shah Abbas the Great, observed that "The King's Palace is upon the Maydan. The Persians call it Dawlet-Chane or Der Chane Schach . . . Over the first Gate, there is a great square structure, which has large windows on all sides, and we were told that, within, it was carv'd all over and gilt."[88] The building he described was begun during the initial campaign at the Maydan-e Naqsh-e Jahan in 1590/1 and completed by about 1615 as a five-story tower (Figure 4.2, Plates 10 and 11).[89] Unlike all other Safavid palaces in Isfahan that had emerged from a single design and construction campaign, the Ali Qapu (the Lofty Gate) evolved over time from a two-story gateway into the royal precinct to "one of the most imposing palaces that can be seen in any capital."[90] By the time Chardin saw it in the 1660s, the Ali Qapu had been altered dramatically with the addition of a two-story fore-building that supported a *talar* in front of the original tower. Here our focus remains on the five-story building that was constructed during the reign of Shah Abbas the Great. Whereas the three gates on the Chahar Bagh side remained exclusively accessible to the family core of the royal household, the four on the Maydan side served multiple public functions. On the "business" end of the Daulatkhane, in other words, the Ali Qapu Palace-Gateway embodies, both conceptually and literally, the impulses toward access and visibility so character-istic of the gates.

The architectural transformations at the Ali Qapu appear, in ret-rospect, to reflect a refashioning of the practice of kingship in Safavid Iran in the seventeenth century. When in 1590/1 the Maydan had been leveled and its periphery demarcated by the single-story, single row of shops, the two principal buildings were two gateways – one into the royal gardens (the first phase of the Ali Qapu), the other into the bazaars (the Qaysariyye). Both rose to a height of two stories so that they remained proportionate to the one-story Maydan "wall." The Maydan project was reimagined in 1602 on a magnified scale of usage and ceremony, and the Ali Qapu thereby assumed an entirely new significance in the ceremonies of the Safavid household. Instead of retaining its functional definition as a gateway, as was the case in all other Persianate and Islamicate palace ensembles of its time and in the past, the building was redesigned on its upper levels to become the principal stage for the public performance of Safavid ceremonials.

The Ali Qapu's function as both a gateway and a ceremonial palace had been instituted by 1615, when Eskandar Beg Monshi listed the Ali Qapu, among buildings undertaken by Shah Abbas the Great, as the five-story gate of the Daulatkhane, *dargah-e panj tabaqe-ye daulatkhane*.[91] All European visitors recognized its dual function. Olearius, quoted above, obviously saw the building only from the Maydan, but his comments convey the fascination this architectural rendition of blended functions held for many European visitors to Isfahan. In the estimation of the Spanish ambassador Don Garcia Figuera, the Ali Qapu in 1618 was five or six stories tall and had mul-tiple rows of windows on the exterior, which he interpreted as the many rooms that "make it appear from the Maydan as a large tower with numerous openings around it."[92] In 1619, he was also received by Shah Abbas for nighttime festivities on the roof of the tower.[93] For the occasion, the shah had ordered the installation of a perforated low wall so that guests were protected but could also take in the views while still seated, a convenience admiringly noted by Figuera. Pietro Della Valle's account of 1617 corroborates those by others, adding that each floor of the Ali Qapu was composed of a large central chamber surrounded by numerous smaller rooms.[94] He also noted the presence of two ayvans: one overlooking the Maydan, and the other the palace compound.

The Ali Qapu is a surprisingly well-preserved palace, given the vicissitudes of history, especially the Afghan sack of Isfahan in 1722.[95] As it stands today, this palace-gateway preserves the princi-pal features of its structure as it developed over the period between 1590/1 and the 1640s. The building evolved through three major and two subsidiary phases of construction to become a massive edifice composed of two equally massive units welded, rather awkwardly, together (Figure 4.6 and Plate 11). These two distinct parts, the five-story tower and the four-story fore-building with the *talar*, correspond to two historical periods and the evolving public rituals of the Safavid household after it moved to the new capital of Isfahan.

The inception of the Ali Qapu Palace-Gateway dates to the first campaign at the Maydan itself, when, in 1590/1, the public square was demarcated into a rectangular space encased by a single row of shops behind an arcade. Two of the four monumental structures at the Maydan were constructed during this first campaign: the Qaysariyye (Royal Bazaar) and the Ali Qapu. At this stage in its evolution, the Ali Qapu rose as a two-story structure to serve principally as a gateway into the Bagh-e Naqsh-e Jahan, the royal gardens of pre-Safavid times that had been appropriated as the new Daulatkhane once the capital was transferred to Isfahan. As was also the case in

Figure 4.6 *Isfahan, Ali Qapu.*

The *talar* is a terrace that abuts the tower, leaving its other three sides open to views over the Maydan. Slender wooden pillars support the coffered and painted roof. Added in 1644, the *talar* updated the Ali Qapu by providing a sheltered stage for the enlarged court ceremonies. Polo games, parades, and other spectacles taking place in the Maydan enhanced feasting ceremonies, at which hundreds of royal guest were entertained. Simultaneously, royal events at the *talar* put the splendor of the Safavid court on display for the denizens of Isfahan.

the Ali Qapu in Qazvin, which was the key point of reference for that in Isfahan, the building was designed to house the office of the judiciary and the special guards and to serve as the formal gateway into and out of the royal precinct (Figures 2.4 and 4.2).

Setting aside, for the moment, the massive fore-building with *talar*, the first Ali Qapu was shaped as a square block, its eastern side flush with the internal façade of the periphery shopping arcade of the Maydan (Plate 10). In this first "block," the building measured about 19 by 20 meters at its base and about 13 meters in height. The block externally read as a *pishtaq* composition on its eastern façade, consisting of a tall ayvan rising to the full height of the two-story building and framed by two rows of niches on either side. Internally, it was composed like a *hasht behesht* (literally, eight paradises), a building type whose ground plan has a modified octagon of eight chambers or spaces rotating around a central open unit (Figure 5.4 and Plate 11). Not to be confused with palace-pavilions of the same ground plan that are also given the name Hasht Behesht (to these we shall turn later), the *hasht behesht* belongs to a Persianate architectural typology. Because of its formal allusions to the metaphorical paradise, it was equally adaptable to both royal and funerary structures that, moreover, were placed within a *chahar-bagh* (four-quadrant) garden. The Taj Mahal is the most famous example of the funerary application of the *hasht-behesht* plan. Less well known, but found throughout the region, were the *hasht-behesht* pavilions in royal gardens of Samarqand, Herat, and Tabriz of fifteenth-century Timurid and Aqqoyunlu times and of Qazvin, built by sixteenth-century Safavids.[96] The so-called Chehel Sotun of Safavid Qazvin is the sole extant example of these earlier *hasht-behesht* buildings, which are otherwise known only through descriptions. The initial block of the Ali Qapu gateway signaled precisely such a genealogy, continuing past traditions.

In contrast, the second block, the additional two stories of 1602, marked a radical departure in the conception of a royal seat, a palace. Here the third floor is principally given over to a rectangular audience hall the narrow sides of which face, through shallow ayvans (porches), the Maydan and the royal precinct (Figure 4.7, Plates 10 and 11). Flanking this audience hall are smaller rooms, reached by doorways, presumably for accommodating an overflow of guests at ceremonial events. The audience hall rises to the full height of the two stories, with its vaulted roof held aloft through an innovative forked-arch system that allowed for fenestration on the upper zone of the side walls.[97] An ingenious double-story mezzanine occupies the sides of the audience hall unit on the fourth floor. This little-known architectural feat, hidden in a space that corresponds to the entire fourth floor, was cleverly designed for women of the harem so that they could glimpse the ceremonial gatherings below through the windows that filled the intermediate squinch (triangular) surfaces of the forked arches.

Figure 4.7 *Isfahan, Ali Qapu.*
The audience hall on the third floor of the original tower was reached
through narrow winding staircases tucked into rear corners. The
rectangular hall occupies the greatest space on this floor, leading on its
narrow sides to shallow ayvans (porches) that open toward the Maydan
and the royal precinct. Smaller rooms, flanking the audience hall,
accommodated overflow of guests at ceremonial events. The audience
hall rises two stories high, with its vaulted roof held aloft through an
innovative forked-arch system that allowed for fenestration on the upper
zone of the side walls. These windows correspond to a mezzanine level
accessible to royal women for watching the ceremonial events in the hall.
Lavishly detailed textile-inspired patterns cover the vaulted ceiling.

Gorgeously detailed, textile-inspired patterns cover the vaulted
ceiling of the audience hall, while lesser versions of them fill the
vaults on the first two stories (Figure 4.7).[98] Interlacing stylized
floral and vegetal motifs with dainty birds perched on slender

tendrils of scrolling stems, all rendered in subdued earthy tones, dominate the upper surfaces of the audience hall. The patterns are made more textile-like by the introduction of a raised painting technique that seems to have become popular in the late sixteenth and early seventeenth centuries. Selected elements of the larger motifs were executed in relief, which, in combination with the chromatic definitions of forms, resulted in the illusion of a textured surface like a woven tapestry. Similarly sophisticated decorative schemes graced the walls of the women's "floors," as well as the architectural and decorative *tour de force* that is the top (fifth) floor of the Ali Qapu.

The addition of the fifth and final story (completed around 1615) concluded the first phase of the building's transition from a gateway into a ceremonial palace during the reign of Shah Abbas the Great (Figure 4.4, Plates 10, 11 and 13). This last floor displays an extraordinary array of new strategies in the layout of spaces, in the scaling of rooms, in their vaulting and fenestration, and in their mural decoration. Its cross-shaped, high-vaulted central space opens onto a finely proportioned cluster of rooms at its sides and corners. Light fills this floor in generous bursts coming from the pointed-arch windows placed at close intervals on the four sides of the floor, as well as through the windows of the lantern that forms the vault of the central space. This lantern, also devised on the forked-arch model, with thin membranes and glazed surfaces, rises above the square room, creating the illusion of a rotating well of light beams.

Paintings of youthful men and women embracing, lounging, frolicking, standing, and playing cover the surfaces of subsidiary rooms, while the principal (cross-in-square) space is overlaid, from the dadoes to the base of the lantern, with perforated plaster sheets that feature deeply carved shapes of drinking vessels, all painted and gilt. That these cutout forms have acoustically desirable properties (hence its popular name as the Music Room) was proven by experiment in the 1970s. They further contribute to the overall impression of this floor as an elegantly appointed space for entertaining in intimate gatherings. Figuera, among other observers, testified to this function of the fifth floor when, describing an evening reception on the roof, he noted his displeasure at hearing that the shah chose to entertain women of the harem on the floor just below rather than have them attend the festivities.[99]

The Ali Qapu of Isfahan is of singular importance in early modern Islamic architectural design for the distinctive way in which it marked the threshold between the public and the royal arenas of a capital city. Whereas the ceremonial seat of authority and its performance of kingship in the Ottoman Topkapı and the Mughal Red Forts were withdrawn deep inside the fortified royal precincts, the Daulatkhane of Isfahan placed its most ceremonial palace at the very threshold between the royal and the public (Figures 6.1, 6.2, 6.4

and 6.6). Not only did the gateway metamorphose into a multi-functional palace, it also communicated the most fundamental functions of a royal household through a radical reshuffling of the architectural expression of those functions. Instead of a horizontal stretch of buildings to signal the increasingly rarefied and sheltered nature of imperial authority, here at the Ali Qapu the fundamental armature of that authority was stacked vertically. The robust muscularity of forms in its first block articulated, as in gateways elsewhere, the martial powers of the *qurchi* who guarded the sanctity of the threshold and the uninterrupted issuance of imperial justice and authority.

Above this "foundation" rose the ceremonial stage of kingship, the hall for the performance of the feasts, the audiences, the gift-giving, and the coronation in 1629 of Shah Safi I. Here, Perso-Shi'i rules of the conduct of kingship necessitated visibility and access, or at least the illusion of such. The ayvan porch and the rows upon rows of windows on the second block accommodated that ceremonial imperative, while at the same time the hierarchical orientation of the rectangular audience hall conveyed the appropriate degree of imperial remove. Both in scale and in layout, the audience hall and its orientation eschewed the "democratic," spatially noncommittal *hasht-behesht* type of plan inside of which no place, except the very "exposed" center, is architecturally privileged. Lighter in its volumes, and brighter with its pointed-arch, glazed windows and their chromatically enlivened tiled spandrels, this ceremonial second block gave way to an even more luminous and elegant fifth floor. Through this strategy of stacking ever lighter forms, the building appears to soar. It exalted the social order it safeguarded and clarified the mediatory role of the imperial household for those standing in the Maydan-e Naqsh-e Jahan. The tower encoded, floor by floor, the workings of the imperial machinery.

The Ali Qapu, as constructed between 1590/1 and 1615, re-enacted in vertical terms and in architectural citations the functions that otherwise would have been laid out behind the gateway. As in a Persian painting where the ground is tilted up to make all motifs (from rocks and clumps of grass to people and animals) appear in their silhouetted fullness, here it is as though the building was conceived on a similarly inclined plane and stacked for complete transparency, which was, I argue, a principal ingredient of imperial authority. The Ali Qapu was the first and most important palace to have been built in Isfahan when the city became the capital. This political and physical transformation in the urban fabric was tantamount to the unambiguous authorization, based on Imami legal codes (*shari'a*), of the Safavid household's legitimacy to rule on behalf of the family of the Prophet. Viewed from this perspective, this is indeed a very different vision of authority, as well as a singular expression of that authority in architecture.

Notes

1. For a discussion of the political utility of façade designs, see Charles Burroughs, *The Italian Renaissance Palace Façade: Structures of Authority, Surface of Sense* (Cambridge; New York: Cambridge University Press, 2002).

2. For this Persianate definition of royal splendor (*farr* or *khvarnah*), see G. Gnoli, "Farr," *Encyclopaedia Iranica*, vol. 9 (1988): 312–19. Soudavar, *The Aura of Kings*, has studied the visual representations and symbolic meanings of *farr*; see esp. xi–xiv and 7–9.

3. See Chapter 2 of this book.

4. Necipoğlu, *Architecture, Ceremonial and Power*, 88–109.

5. These were conceived on the conflated models of the Diwan-i Amm at Fatehpur Sikri, the earliest of the Mughal palace complexes built by Emperor Akbar in 1587, and the stone-pillared halls of the Achaemenids at Persepolis, an ancient Persian architectural idea that will be discussed later in this chapter. For the Diwan-i Amm and the link with Persepolis see Koch, "Diwan-i Amm and Chihil Sutun." See also Ebba Koch "Mughal Palace Gardens from Babur to Shah Jahan (1526–1648)," *Muqarnas* 14 (1997): 143–65.

6. The most complex example of the Mughal jharokas is the one constructed for Shah Jahan at the Red Fort in Delhi with an Orpheus iconography and Italianate designs in inlaid marble technique of *pietra dura*; see Ebba Koch, *Shah Jahan and Orpheus* (Graz: Akademische Druck-u. Verlagsanstalt, 1988).

7. European descriptions of various parts of the Daulatkhane permit us to reconstruct the royal precinct. The most detailed and best informed are (in order of richness of observations): Chardin, *Voyages du Chevalier Chardin*, especially vol. 7; Kaempfer, *Amoenitatum Exoticarum*; and Jean Baptiste Tavernier, *The Six Voyages of John Baptista Tavernier*, English trans. (London, 1678). See also Babaie, "Safavid Palaces in Isfahan," 80–98. For functions and offices pertaining to the royal household and the Daulatkhane, see the principal Safavid administrative source, translation with commentaries by Vladimir Minorsky, as *Tadhkirat al-Muluk: A Manual of Safavid Administration*, reprint edn (London: Trustees of the E. G. Gibb Memorial, 1980). Willem Floor, *Safavid Government Institutions* (Costa Mesa, CA: Mazda Publishers, 2001) provides much-needed access to the *Dastur al-moluk*, the other major Safavid administrative manual.

8. Tavernier, *The Six Voyages*, 152.

9. In considering such linguistic translations and the valuation of superiority, I am grateful for the insightful comments made by my colleague, Professor Martin Powers, and also for pointing me to Lydia Liu, *Translingual Practice: Literature, National Culture, and Translated Modernity – China 1900–1937* (Stanford: Stanford University Press, 1995), esp. 1–42.

10. Della Valle, *Viaggi di Pietro della Valle*, 455, 458–9 and 461.

11. Don Garcia de Silva y Figuera, *L'Ambassade de Don Garcias de Silva y Figueroa en Perse*, trans. De Wicqfort (Paris: Lovis Billaine, 1667), 181, 183 and 329.

12. Herbert, *Travels in Persia*, 128; Adam Olearius, *Relation du Voyage* (Paris, 1666), 197, 201, 215, 220; Tavernier, *The Six Voyages*, 152, 178; Chardin, *Voyages du Chevalier Chardin*, vol. 7, 337, 343.

13. Herbert, *Travels in Persia*, 128,131; Olearius, *Relation du Voyage*, 200–1; Tavernier, *The Six Voyages*, 222, 152, 155, 178, 218; Chardin, *Voyages du Chevalier Chardin*, vol. 7, 343, 371, 377.

14. Kaempfer, *Amoenitatum Exoticarum*, 178, 180, 181, 184, 222.

15. Monshi, *Tarikh-e alam ara-ye Abbasi*, 438, 777, 1110–11; *Rostam-name-ye tarikh-e Bizhan* (British Library, London, Add. 7655): fol. 40a; Mohammad Taher-e Vahid-e Qazvini, *'Abbas-name* (British Library, London, Or. 2940): 199, 222, 307; Mirza Beg b. Hasan Jonabadi, *Rauzat al-safaviyya.* (British Library, London, Or. 3388): fols. 308b, 314b; Natanzi, *Noqavat al-asar*, 374, 452, 535; Qomi, *Kholasat al-tavarikh*, 902; Eskandar Beg Monshi and Mohammad Yusof Movarrekh, *Zayl-e tarikh-e alam ara-ye Abbasi*, ed. Sohayli-Khwansari (Tehran: Eslamiyye, 1317/1938), 198.

16. Monshi, *Tarikh-e alam ara-ye Abbasi*, 438; Jonabadi, *Rauzat al-safaviyye* (British Library, London Or. 3388): fol. 308b; Natanzi, *Noqavat al-asar*, 452, 535; Qomi, *Kholasat al-tavarikh*, 902.

17. McChesney's excellent account of this early history, in his "Four Sources," does not explore how this fact relates to the Safavid agenda in the new capital.

18. Quiring-Zoche, *Isfahan im 15. und 16. Jahrhundert*, 36 and especially fn. 1.

19. Quiring-Zoche, *Isfahan im 15. und 16. Jahrhundert*, 62, fn. 5 and p. 75.

20. Natanzi, *Noqavat al-asar*, 233.

21. For Farhad Beg's story, his fall from grace, his imprisonment, and the resistance put up at the Qal'e Tabarrok in Isfahan by his brothers and followers prior to Shah Abbas' first visit, see Natanzi, *Noqavat al-asar*, 238–42.

22. Farhad Beg's revolt represents an extraordinary case of blatant *gholam* disloyalty. The *gholam*s, unlike the Qezelbash officials, had yet to gain full ascendancy in the imperial household. In contrast, the Qezelbash governors of Kerman and Fars annexed their respective administrative territories and put up vigorous resistance against Abbas I's centralizing efforts. For the significance of the *gholam*s in securing centralized absolutism and on the prerequisite of loyalty to and inclusion within the royal household, see Babaie, Babayan, Baghdiantz-McCabe, and Farhad, *Slaves of the Shah*, 8–18; see also 92–7 for the Kerman and Fars *gholam* governors.

23. Natanzi, *Noqavat al-asar*, 233.

24. For the Shi'i martyrology of Imam Hossayn and the function of Hossayniyyes, especially in the nineteenth century, when they became a fixed feature of royal patronage, see Peter Chelkowski, "Popular Arts: Patronage and Piety," in *Royal Persian Paintings: The Qajar Epoch, 1785–1925*, ed. Layla S. Diba and Maryam Ekhtiar (London: I. B. Tauris, in association with the Brooklyn Museum of Art, 1998), 90–9.

25. Natanzi, *Noqavat al-asar*, 373–4; Monshi, *Tarikh-e alam ara-ye Abbasi*, 157 and 426–7.

26. Natanzi, *Noqavat al-asar*, 535; McChesney, "Four Sources," 119–20.

27. McChesney, "Four Sources," analyzes the significance of Natanzi's detailed report on the materials of construction, amounts and prices, and the harsh methods through which they were procured for this building.

28. For an analysis of the building's location and size in relation to the contemporary sources and the arguments advanced by McChesney, see Babaie, "Safavid Palaces in Isfahan," 74–5.

29. Monajjem, *Tarikh Abbasi*, fol. 121a; Monshi, *Tarikh-e alam ara-ye Abbasi*, 544–5. For the 1607 completion of the bridge, see Melville, "New Light on the Reign of Shah 'Abbas," 71 and fn. 30. See also McChesney, "Four Sources," 124–5.

30. Persian historians of the period are completely silent on the subject, although an early nineteenth-century text, *Rostam al-tavarikh* by Mohammad Hashem Asef, with its exceptionally imaginative and lurid details of life in the harem, should be given its own literary category since it examines a subject of considerable interest at its time of writing and well deserves serious scholarly analysis. Mohammad Hashem Asef, *Rostam al-tavarikh*, ed. Mohammad Moshiri (Tehran: Chap-i Taban, 1352/1973). European visitors had either no access or a very limited one, as is evident in the laments by Chardin, *Voyages du Chevalier Chardin*, vol. 7, 381 and by Kaempfer, *Amoenitatum Exoticarum*, 199.

31. For an account of the women's world, see Kathryn Babayan, "The 'Aqa'id al-nisa': A Glimpse at Safavid Women in Local Isfahani Culture," in *Women in the Medieval Islamic World: Power, Patronage, and Piety*, ed. G. R. G. Hambly (Basingstoke: Macmillan, 1996), 349–81.

32. Monajjem, *Tarikh Abbasi*, fol. 191a; McChesney, "Four Sources," 120; Babaie, "Safavid Palaces in Isfahan," 76–9.

33. Babaie, "Safavid Palaces in Isfahan," 78–9.

34. The gendered zoning of palace precincts in the Islamicate world had given birth to other similar attempts to bring inside some amenities that were available in the city; for an example, see the location of a small "bazaar" tucked inside a tunnel passageway that connects the successive gates at the Delhi Red Fort to the courtyard of the Diwan-e Amm, thus allowing women of the harem to peruse a selection of goods without having to leave the walled precinct; see the long bazaars in the plans of the Agra and Delhi Red Forts in Figures 6.7 and 6.8.

35. Chardin, *Voyages du Chevalier Chardin*, vol. 7, 383–4; McChesney, "Four Sources," 120 strongly suggests a link between the Chardin and Monajjem buildings.

36. Necipoğlu, *Architecture, Ceremonial and Power*, 159–83.

37. Charles Melville, "Shah 'Abbas and the Pilgrimage to Mashhad," in *Safavid Persia: The History and Politics of an Islamic Society*, ed. Charles Melville (London: I. B. Tauris, 1996), 191–230.

38. Baghdiantz-McCabe, *The Shah's Silk for Europe's Silver*, esp. 1–15; Matthee, *Politics of Trade in Safavid Iran*, esp. 1–32.

39. For the Mazandaran developments, see Babaie, "Launching from Isfahan," 98–101.

40. The notion of a planned economy is closely woven with other centralizing measures, implemented especially vigorously, beginning with the reign of Abbas I. These aspects of Safavid polity in the seventeenth century, however, remain a matter of debate, especially between the view that upholds a patrimonial, pre-capitalist, feudal, and "Oriental" system and one that argues for a planned economy intertwined with the socio-political trappings of an early-modern international network of trade and a centralization agenda. While no work of scholarship may be categorized as one type or another, it is fair to take Willem Floor, *A Fiscal History of Iran in the Safavid and Qajar Period, 1500–1925* (New York: Bibliotheca Persica Press, 1999), and to a lesser extent Matthee's *The Politics of Trade in Safavid Iran*, to exemplify aspects of the former view, and Baghdiantz-McCabe's *The Shah's Silk for Europe's Silver*, to

exemplify the latter. For a discussion of Safavid planned economy and its relevance to centralization, see also Baghdiantz-McCabe, "Armenian Merchants and Slaves," 49–79.

41. See May Farhat, "Islamic Piety and Dynastic Legitimacy: The Case of the Shrine of Ali al-Rida in Mashhad (10th–17th Century)," PhD diss., Harvard University, 2002.

42. The nomadism paradigm persists in such works as Necipoğlu, "Framing the Gaze," esp. 306–12 and O'Kane, "From Tents to Pavilions," 249–68.

43. Jos Gommans, *Mughal Warfare* (London and New York: Routledge, 2002); I thank Ahmed Azfar Moin for this reference.

44. Kathryn Babayan, "The Safavid Household Reconfigured: Concubines, Eunuchs and Military Slaves," in *Slaves of the Shah*, Babaie, Babayan, Baghdiantz-McCabe, and Farhad, 20–48.

45. Although these designations are from Chardin's 1670s account, the presence of the guards and the judiciary is recorded as early as 1617 in a description by the Italian Pietro Della Valle, *Viaggi di Pietro della Valle*, 458ff.

46. For the Safavid administrative structure, in general, see *Tadhkirat al-muluk: A Manual of Safavid Administration*, reprint edn, trans. and explained by V. Minorsky (London: Trustees of the E. G. Gibb Memorial, 1980). And see especially Chardin, *Voyages du Chevalier Chardin*, vol. 7, 368–70 and vol. 5, 342.

47. Chardin, *Voyages du Chevalier Chardin*, vol. 7, 370.

48. Honarfar, *Ganjine*, 420–2, discusses the traditional and popular assumption of sanctity of the Ali Qapu. See also, Blake, *Half the World*, 64.

49. Chardin, *Voyages du Chevalier Chardin*, vol. 7, 337–8 for the Portuguese cannons; Engelbert Kaempfer, *Am Hofe des persischen Großkönigs 1684–85*, ed. Walther Hinz (Tübingen: H. Erdmann, 1977), 209.

50. Monajjem, the historian of Shah Abbas I, used this title to refer to the shah in much of his *Tarikh Abbasi*. See also Nasr-Allah Falsafi, *Zendegani-ye Shah Abbas avval*, 4th reprint edn (Tehran: Entesharat-e Elmi, 1369/1990), vol. 1–2, p. 417 and vol. 3, pp. 871–2.

51. For an example of the commonly used phrase "the shadow of God" in Safavid sources, see Eskandar Beg Monshi, *Tarikh-e alam ara-ye Abbasi*, 545; and Amir Arjomand, who deals with the subject in detail in his book, *The Shadow of God*.

52. Monshi, *Tarikh-e alam ara-ye Abbasi*, 1004; Falsafi, *Zendegani-ye Shah Abbas avval*, 873.

53. Taher-e Vahid-e Qazvini, *'Abbas-name*, 220, 307; Chardin, *Voyages du Chevalier Chardin*, 369–70; Kaempfer, *Amoenitatum Exoticarum*, 183.

54. Olearius, *Relation du Voyage*, 215. A different version of such a story is recounted in Brancaforte, *Visions of Persia*, 10.

55. For the Ardabil Shrine and the Jannat Sara, see A. H. Morton, "The Ardabil Shrine in the Reign of Shah Tahmasp," *Iran* 12 (1974): 31–64 and Morton, "The Ardabil Shrine in the Reign of Shah Tahmasp (Concluded)," *Iran* 13 (1975): 39–58; and Kishwar Rizvi, "The Imperial Setting: Shah 'Abbas at the Safavid Shrine of Shaykh Safi in Ardabil," in *Safavid Art and Architecture*, ed. Sheila Canby (London: British Museum Press, 2002), 9–15, and Rizvi "Its Mortar Mixed."

56. For a summary of the debates on the functions of the Jannat Sara, see Babaie, "Building on the Past," especially 38.

57. Necipoğlu's assumption that "unlike the Topkapi the Isfahan palace projected an image of holiness through its domed octagonal shrine, known

as the Tawhid-Khana," should be modified to take note of the subtle but telling manipulation of distance and proximity in the Safavid case and its legitimizing significance. The Tauhidkhane was not a shrine, as she suggests, but a place of refuge made inviolable by virtue of its location within the Daulatkhane. Nor was it visible to the pedestrian in the Maydan; see her "Framing the Gaze," 309.

58. The most detailed description of the Harem Gate is by Chardin, *Voyages du Chevalier Chardin*, vol. 7, 368–70 and vol. 5, 342. Kaempfer, who provides us with the only visual indicator of its spatial and architectural composition, does not describe the Harem Gate but identifies four successive gates along the alley in his legend accompanying the engraving (Figure 4.1 in this book); Kaempfer, *Amoenitatum Exoticarum*, 177. See also Babaie, "Safavid Palaces in Isfahan," 88–90.

59. Chardin, *Voyages du Chevalier Chardin*, vol. 9, 453.

60. For a recent analysis of the *gholam* issue, see Babaie, Babayan, Baghdiantz-McCabe, and Farhad, *Slaves of the Shah*, especially chapters one and two.

61. Chardin and Kaempfer are the main sources for the Daulatkhane gates; Chardin, *Voyages du Chevalier Chardin*, vol. 7, 386–8; Kaempfer, *Amoenitatum Exoticarum*, 177. The gates have been discussed in Chapter 3 of this book.

62. Chardin, *Voyages du Chevalier Chardin*, vol. 7, 387.

63. Kaempfer, *Am Hofe*, 275. Such notions as curative powers of food from the royal table are found in many belief systems and cultural practices; for parallels to the symbolic and political significance of the distribution of food from a royal kitchen, see the discussion on the kitchens at the Topkapı in Necipoğlu, *Architecture, Ceremonial and Power*, 72. The bibliography on the semiotics of food has grown considerably over the past couple of decades; for further discussions of feasting and food and a sampling of the recent studies, see Chapter 6 below.

64. Necipoğlu, *Architecture, Ceremonial and Power*, 69–72.

65. Tavernier, *The Six Voyages*, 152.

66. Tavernier, *The Six Voyages*, 210.

67. Chardin, *Voyages du Chevalier Chardin*, vol. 7, 328. The spatial relations between the royal baths and the other ceremonial or governmental functions at the Maydan ensemble remain unclear but need further research since the pairings with the bathhouse assume great significance in other urban and palatine environments. Besides the early Islamic examples of princely residence–bathhouse in the Syrian desert, such contemporaries of the Safavid Isfahan as the Red Fort in Agra and the Maydan-e Ganj Ali Khan in Kerman demand probing.

68. Chardin, *Voyages du Chevalier Chardin*, vol. 7, 402.

69. For these offices, see Minorsky, *Tadhkirat al-Muluk*, 118.

70. These are indeed based on the analyses of the Russian scholar Vladimir Minorsky's *Tadhkirat al-Muluk*, 134–9.

71. Minorsky, *Tadhkirat al-Muluk*, 65.

72. Vaʿez Kashefi, *Fotovvatname-ye soltani*, ed. Mohammad Jaʿfar Mahjub (Tehran: Bonyad-e Farhang-e Iran, 1350/1971), 233.

73. Chardin, *Voyages du Chevalier Chardin*, vol. 7, 402.

74. Chardin, *Voyages du Chevalier Chardin*, vol. 7, 396–402. The above analysis is deduced from Chardin's tortuous jumble of turns and twists in alleys, roads, bazaars, and maydans, and has been traced in reverse in order to arrive at the reconstruction of this corner. See also Babaie, "Safavid Palaces in Isfahan," 94–7.

75. The British Library manuscript, Sloane 4094, is reproduced with German translation in Gaube and Wirth, *Der Bazar von Isfahan*, 262–85 especially p. 277 (fol. 21). See also the commentary by Minorsky in *Tadhkirat al-Muluk*, 140–1.

76. Honarfar, *Ganjine*, 327–8. To date, the most comprehensive study of this building is by Maryam Babashahi, "Barresi-ye manabeʿ-e tarikhi dar mored-e bana-ye Talar-e Taymuri (A Study of Historical Evidence about the Talar-e Taymuri) *Asar* nos 7, 8, 9 (Bahman 1361/January 1983): 187–231. She too is unable to confirm any date for this building prior to the Safavids. For the past few decades, the building has been used as the natural history museum of Isfahan.

77. Mohammad Maʿsum ibn Khwajegi Esfahani, *Kholasat al-siyyar*, ed. Iraj Afshar (Tehran; Entesharat-e Elmi, 1368/1989), 132–3, 135, 145, and 249–50.

78. Mirza Hossayn Khan Tahvildar, *Joghrafiya-ye Esfahan*, ed. Manuchehr Sotude (Tehran: Tehran University, Faculty of the Literature, 1342/1963), 23–4.

79. See Chapter 3 of this book.

80. Kaempfer, *Amoenitatum Exoticarum*, 190; Kaempfer, *Am Hofe*, 207.

81. Chardin, *Voyages du Chevalier Chardin*, vol. 8, 25.

82. Chardin, *Voyages du Chevalier Chardin*, vol. 7, 387.

83. Fragments of this passageway were still standing in the summer of 1992 when I visited Isfahan for my dissertation research but were subsequently destroyed in a misguided attempt to replace the unsightly "ruins" with parks. The initiative was spearheaded by the offices of the mayor and governor of Isfahan but was vehemently resisted by the officials of the Iranian Cultural Heritage Organization (ICHO). The ICHO's loss emboldened the civic leaders of the city to embark on other such beautification projects. The most tragic among them were the razing of the remains of a gateway structure that marked the Chahar Bagh entrance into the Hasht Behesht Garden and the clearing for a street of a magnificent Safavid bathhouse, the famed Hammam-e Khosro Aqa, for which, legend had it, Shaykh Baha'i's mathematical genius had devised a most efficient heating system.

84. Tavernier, *The Six Voyages*, 155.

85. Tavernier, *The Six Voyages*, 155; Chardin, *Voyages du Chevalier Chardin*, vol. 7, 387 and vol. 8, 23–5. See also Honarfar, *Ganjine*, 479.

86. Della Valle, *Viaggi di Pietro della Valle*, 455; Chardin, *Voyages du Chevalier Chardin*, vol. 8, 23.

87. Tavernier, *The Six Voyages*, 155.

88. Adam Olearius, *The Voyages and Travels of the Ambassadors sent by Frederick Duke of Holstein, to the Great Duke of Muscovy, and the King of Persia*, trans. John Davis, 2nd corrected edn (London: John Starkey and Thomas Basset, 1669), 220.

89. For a detailed analysis of the architectural development of the Ali Qapu see Galdieri, *Esfahan, ʿAli Qapu*. See also Priscilla Soucek, "Ālī Qāpū," *Encyclopaedia Iranica*, Vol. 1 (1988): 871–2. For an analytical synthesis of the archeological evidence with the historical towards a revised building history, see Babaie, "Safavid Palaces in Isfahan," 99–135.

90. Chardin is quoted in Ferrier, *A Journey to Persia*, 144.

91. Monshi, *Tarikh-e alam ara-ye Abbasi*, 1111.

92. Figuera, *L'Ambassade*, 183–4.

93. Figuera, *L'Ambassade*, 328–9.

94. Della Valle, *Viaggi di Pietro della Vallei*, 458–9.
95. This is also largely thanks to the efforts of the Italian team from the Istituto Italiano per Il Medio ed'Estremo Oriente (IsMEO), whose restoration work, under the leadership of Eugenio Galdieri, during the 1960s and 1970s and before the advent of the Islamic Revolution ensured the survival of an otherwise by-then fragile building. See Galdieri, *Esfahan, 'Ali Qapu*, for the record of this preservation project.
96. See above, Chapter 2 of this book.
97. Mario Ferrante, "Dessins et observations préliminaires pour la restauration du palais de 'Ālī Qāpū," in *Traveaux de Restauration de Monuments Historiques en Iran*, ed. Giuseppe Zander (Rome: IsMEO, 1968), 133–206; Galdieri, *Esfahan, 'Ali Qapu*, 101–2.
98. For the wall decorations at the Ali Qapu, see Babaie, "Safavid Palaces in Isfahan," 169–75.
99. Figuera, *L'Ambassade*, 184, 329–30.

CHAPTER FIVE

The Spatial Choreography of Conviviality: the Palaces of Isfahan

THIS CHAPTER EXPLORES the palaces as a series of interrelated structures for which, as with choices of form and function for the gateways at the Daulatkhane of Isfahan, accessibility and transparency proved central. The *talar*-fronted palace design emerges as the most practical spatial-architectural form for representing Safavid Perso-Shi'i authority. This chapter also considers the changing expression in architecture and urban space of that authority in the relationship between Isfahan and its suburbs.

The *talar* in Isfahan palaces

In the architectural evolution of the Ali Qapu, the most drastic intervention occurred in 1644, when, two years into the reign of the twelve-year-old Shah Abbas II, Mirza Mohammad Saru Taqi, the powerful Grand Vizier, was entrusted with the construction of the *talar*, the wooden-pillared porch in front of the Ali Qapu (*dar pish-e emarat-e haft asham-e Ala Qapi ru be janeb-e Maydan-e Naqsh-e Jahan talar saman namayand*) (Plates 10, 11 and 12). According to Vali Qoli Shamlu, the historian of Abbas II, this addition of the *talar* and its substructure was completed in a short time "under the supervision of the master of the noble emirs, Mirza Taqi, the grand vizier" (*be sarkari-ye makhdum al-omara al-akram Mirza Taqi vazir-e a'zam*).[1] The *talar* addition to the Ali Qapu was the third to have been built in Safavid Isfahan after the palaces of Talar-e Tavile and Ayenekhane, both datable to the 1630s (Figures 5.1, 5.3 and 5.5). Together with the Chehel Sotun Palace (1647), these Isfahani *talars* appropriated the established Persianate and Islamicate palatine architecture, turning it in a distinctly scenographic direction.

A *talar* palace is a building generally divisible into two parts: one consists of a cluster of rooms and halls of varying sizes; the other is anchored on the first and consists of a space open on three sides (the fourth is a wall of the room/hall cluster) with its roof held aloft by a number of pillars.[2] All the constituent elements of such an architectural assembly are universally recognizable motifs of building. Its ancient guises, as scholars have suggested, were the pillared-hall

Figure 5.1 *Isfahan, reconstruction rendering of the Talar-e Tavile (Hall of Stables).*
This was the prototype for the *talar* palaces, whose design of an open, wooden-pillared terrace in front of an enclosed structure was unique to Safavid ceremonial palaces in Isfahan. Built in the 1630s for Shah Safi I under the auspices of the Grand Vizier Saru Taqi, it was located in a long and narrow garden between the two alleyways that reached into the Daulatkhane through the Ali Qapu and the Harem Gate.

traditions that characterized the Achaemenid palace at Persepolis, the Greek house, the Sasanian palace and the Roman atrium-house (Figure 5.2).[3] Pillared halls were also evoked in the nomadic tentage of Central Asia and Mongolia, areas from which conquerors had swarmed into the Islamicate and, especially, Persianate worlds. Other traditions, both older and contemporary, near and far, may also have been available as inspiration for the configuration of the *talar* palace.

So detached from its historical base has the term *talar* become that, in its modern Persian usage, it has assumed a generic quality connoting grandness in space and decoration: an especially pretentious restaurant nowadays may be called a *talar*, just as the Talar-e Marmar (the Marble Hall) at the Golestan Palace in Tehran has been so named. By the time of the nineteenth-century Qajar palace, the name and a porch with a couple of pillars (the Talar-e Marmar is decidedly modest in comparison to the Isfahan *talar* palaces) sufficed to evoke a Safavid patrimony for a dynasty whose agendas were differently configured. By evoking the Safavid lineage, the Qajars visually and ceremonially indexed the deepened dependence of kingship on Imami

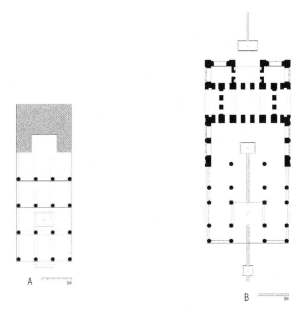

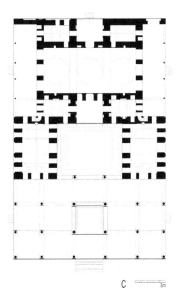

Figure 5.2 *Ground plans of the Safavid* talar *palaces of Isfahan.*

A) Talar-e Tavile, proposed reconstruction; B) Ayenekhane, after the plan
from Coste, *Monuments*; C) Chehel Sotun. This building type is the
quintessence of what may be called the architecture of conviviality.
Planned on its longitudinal axis and designed to progressively contract into
intimate spaces, *talar* palaces are unique to Safavid Isfahan. This was a
radical departure from the *hasht-behesht* type (Figure 5.4) that had
prevailed before and after these three structures.

Shi'ism and its legitimizing endorsement. This is a subject beyond our scope here, but it is worth noting that the Qajars cited the Safavid representations of authority – in city and palace as much as in small lacquered boxes and book covers – perhaps partly because the whole premise of the organized practice of Imami Shi'ism, and thus of its tolerated mode of kingship, was rattled by the religious upheavals that by the middle of the nineteenth century had welcomed the arrival of the Babi Dispensation.[4] The *talar* palaces in Isfahan, which were so particular in both their architecture and function, demand fresh consideration. As both a cluster and a building type, nothing quite like them was built before or after seventeenth-century Isfahan, and so they are also historically exceptional.[5]

Talar-e Tavile or Hall of Stables

Khwajegi Esfahani, the historian of Shah Safi I, tells us that the Nauruz (Persian New Year) celebrations of 1637 took place at "a *talar* built by the shadow of God [Safi I] in the midst of the stables" (Figures 4.2 and 5.1).[6] This is the first mention in contemporary chronicles of the *Talar*-e Tavile. In a later source, the *Khold-e barin*, Mohammad Yusof Movarrekh reports on this same Nauruz audience when a European embassy (most likely that of the Duke of Holstein with Olearius as its secretary) was also received at the *Talar*-e Tavile, noting that the celebrations were held there "according to order [of Safi I] and as was the custom."[7] Further corroborating evidence is culled from *Rostamname* or *Tarikh-e Bijan*, a history of the Safavid general Rostam Khan, who died in 1642, in which the author states that Talar-e Tavile was among Shah Safi I's buildings.[8]

Prior to 1637 no reference to this building exists, nor is there any description of a building in Isfahan that might possibly be this palace. Thenceforth, repeated references to the Talar-e Tavile in both Persian and European sources indicate that the palace had assumed a central role in the performance of the ceremonial functions of the Safavid household in Isfahan. Royal council meetings and nearly every important royal reception were held at the Talar-e Tavile until Shah Safi's death in 1642 (Figure 5.3).[9] Together with another extinct palace called Hauzkhane (noted above), the Talar-e Tavile served as the principal site for audiences celebrating Nauruz and the reception of ambassadorial convoys during the reign of Shah Safi I.[10] In addition, Chardin makes reference to at least one performance at the Talar-e Tavile of the religious rites commemorating the martyrdom of Imam Hossayn in the month of Moharram 1666.[11] The coronation of Shah Safi II in 1666 (recrowned in 1668 at the Chehel Sotun Palace as Shah Solayman) further underscores the ceremonial significance of this palace in the Daulatkhane of Isfahan.

Located just to the southwest of the Ali Qapu Palace-Gate, the Talar-e Tavile was reached through a ceremonial walkway extending

Figure 5.3 *Isfahan, "A Night Reception at the Talar-e Tavile" after an engraving from Kaempfer,* Amoenitatum *(1712), illustrating the seating order and protocol of proximity and distance in* talar *ceremonial palaces of Safavid Isfahan.*

from behind the Ali Qapu (Plate 10). Although no longer extant, its location and general configuration may be gleaned from the European visitors who have provided both visual and written representations (Figures 5.3 and 5.2 A). By the time Chardin described the walkway in the 1660s, the alley was shared by both the Talar-e Tavile and the Chehel Sotun for the ceremonial procession of guests to either palace. In Chardin's estimation,

> it seems as if there is a rather long passageway covered by the tallest plane-trees, along which, from the entrance to this room are stone mangers placed at intervals of 10 to 12 paces. They are made of lime and talc, are rather high, and are used to tether horses selected from royal stables, normally 12 to 15 [of them], and sometimes a larger number, on festive days, or when some ambassadors and other important foreigners are received in audience by the king.[12]

Olearius had seen in an audience given to the Holstein Embassy in 1637 similarly "excellent Horses" placed along this alley "with their covering-cloaths of Brocade, or Embroider'd with Gold and Silver."[13]

The presence of the choice horses along the alleyway, a common emblem of royal and ceremonial significance until modern times, alluded also to the interweaving in space of such symbolically charged relationships as the proximity of the seat of rule and the royal stables.[14] Such spatial and conceptual links, one may surmise from the historian Khwajegi Esfahani and others, were already established at the Daulatkhane during the time of Abbas the Great, when the royal stables stood in the vicinity of the Ali Qapu Palace-Gateway and at the site where the Talar-e Tavile was to be placed.

Through the equestrian display of pomp and ceremony, the walkway, as noted by nearly every European who received an audience at one of the ceremonial palaces inside the Daulatkhane, conducted the guests into the long and narrow garden of Talar-e Tavile. As in all such micro-palaces at the Daulatkhane, the garden was enclosed, richly landscaped and formalized with the aid of a long pool in front of the building (Figure 5.1). At the entrance to the garden, visitors faced the building from the far end of a long pool. Kaempfer noted, "The palace constitutes the end of the western side of the width of the park," and the dimensions provided by various observers confirm the narrowness of the lot and of the palace itself.[15]

Olearius described it as a

> hall . . . rais'd three steps from the ground, and was eight fathom broad, and twelve in length. There was at the entrance into it a Partition, like an Alcove, with curtains drawn before it, of red cotton, which were taken up and let down with silk strings. When they were drawn up, they rested upon the Chapters of certain

wooden Pillars, made Cylinder-wise, Embellish'd with Branch-work, Painted, and Gilt, as were also the Walls.[16]

An ornamental pool with jets of water stood at the center of this *talar,* and in Olearius's time the side walls of the enclosed area were adorned (at least on the left side) with European paintings of historical scenes.[17] Tavernier's "hall" was also a rectangle,

> being opened every way; the ceiling was sustained by sixteen wooden pillars of eight panels everyone, and of a prodigious thickness and height. As well the ceiling as the pillars were all painted with foliage-work in gold and azure, with certain other colors mix'd therewith. In the middle of the Hall was a vase of excellent marble, with a fountain throwing out water after several manners.[18]

The shah sat, according to Tavernier, on a "low scaffold" (throne) near the pool.

Later commentaries by Chardin and Kaempfer corroborate these descriptions, albeit with varying emphases and details.[19] Chardin's description is perhaps the most informative:

> This stable hall measures 400 paces in front, 26 in depth, and 25 feet in height; it is covered with a mosaic ceiling supported by painted and gilded wooden pillars. It is divided into three parts, of which the middle one is raised nine feet above the ground and the side rooms three feet only. Many-colored Venetian crystal glass frames form the divisions. The entire hall is hung with curtains all around, lined with the finest Indian chintzes, which extend along the side facing the sun, eight feet above the ground so as not to block the view. A large marble water basin, with waterspouts all around [its edge] and in the middle, occupies the center of the hall. It is here that Shah 'Abbas II's successor was crowned.

According to Kaempfer, the palace

> has an open terraced hall [*talar*] with four octagonal pillars, which bear the flat front roof. A three-foot-high wooden railing marks off the three levels of the terrace, which, like all such buildings, has been built above ground. In the middle is a large square marble basin, in which water rises fed by many pipes. Above it hangs a crystal candelabrum, a present from Venice to the shah. On the back side of the hall is a graceful iwan [portico], where the throne of the shah is placed for audiences. Everything has been embellished in a profligate manner with gold and mirrors. On festive occasions the space in front of the terrace is also included to

compensate for the narrowness of the hall. To that end a purple carpet is displayed, while to provide protection against the sun an awning is mounted.[20]

These descriptions provide clues for a reconstruction of the Talar-e Tavile in which the principal feature of the building was its openness to the landscaped environs (Figures 5.1 and 5.3). Several aspects of the palace's architecture are clear enough: The building was raised above the ground on a platform. It was long and narrow and laid out in plan on its longitudinal axis. Its principal space was given to a roofed open area – Olearius's "Partition," Tavernier's and Chardin's "hall," and Kaempfer's "terraced hall" – or what the Persian sources would call the *talar*. The roof was flat and made of wood. Polygonal wooden pillars (at least as many as sixteen) held up the roof. All woodwork was painted and gilded. The vast *talar* was subdivided into three sections with the help of low-rise, latticed banisters made of wood with (Venetian) glass infillings. An ornamental pool of marble with fountain jets was at the center of the *talar*, and all around red curtains were hung so as to modulate the light, especially during the morning hours, when the entire *talar*, facing east, would have been in the sun.[21]

The most puzzling aspect of this building, as described by European visitors, is the reference to some sort of enclosure within the structure (Figure 5.2 A). Rather than a roofed, pillared platform, as has been surmised from the descriptions, the building was composed, in my reconstruction, of a vast *talar* (pillared hall) that was subdivided into three zones by low balustrades and that concluded in a crescendo effect with an ayvan where the throne would have been placed. Kaempfer's unambiguous "On the back side of the hall is a graceful iwan [portico], where the throne of the shah is placed for audiences" must describe an integral part of the building from its inception. How else, one may ask, can Olearius's observation that "On the left side were three large European paintings of historical scenes hanging on the wall" be accommodated? An ayvan, furthermore, presupposes some sort of embracing structure or side walls into which the ayvan would be fitted. Chardin's "side rooms" indicates such an enclosed unit.

We shall probably never know with certainty how this building was configured, but determining its most likely configuration is fundamental to my contention that the palace architecture in Isfahan proclaims a distinctive Perso-Shiʿi performance of kingship. The Talar-e Tavile was the first palace in Safavid Isfahan to articulate in its built environment the shifting paradigm of kingship as it had evolved over the decades since the inception of the city as the imperial capital. That it was so far removed from the established typology of Persianate palaces, the time-honored nine-fold or *hasht-behesht* model, has scarcely sparked scholarly curiosity (Figures 5.2 and 5.4).

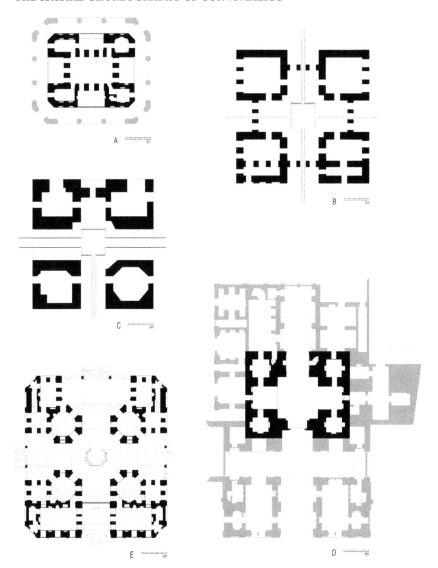

Figure 5.4 *Ground plans of the* hasht-behesht *types of palaces.*
A) Qazvin, Chehel Sotun; B) Ashraf, Cheshme Emarat; C) Kashan, Fin; D) Isfahan, Ali Qapu (1590/1–1644); E) Isfahan, Hasht Behesht. The *hasht-behesht* (eight paradises) building type is internally subdivided into eight chambers encircling a central, often domed unit. Probably the most adaptable building design in the Islamicate world, it is utilized for a variety of functions, ranging from palaces to tombs.

And yet, this was the palace that eclipsed the visible and imposing Ali Qapu for nearly two decades. Afterwards, the Talar-e Tavile was joined by two other "talared" palaces – the Chehel Sotun and the revised Ali Qapu, all completed by the middle of the seventeenth century – to become the principal ceremonial palaces within the

Daulatkhane. A third *talar*-palace type, the Ayenekhane, served ceremonial functions of the suburban royal precinct.

Mohammad Hashem Asef (also known as Rostam al-Hokama), the author in 1834 of *Rostam al-tavarikh*, compared the Talar-e Tavile with the *talars* at the Chehel Sotun and the Ali Qapu. By following this lead and comparing the Talar-e Tavile to the other similar palaces in Isfahan, we may propose a reconstruction of the Talar-e Tavile as a long and narrow building with a vast, longitudinally subdivided tripartite pillared hall and an ayvan with flanking rooms at the back (Figure 5.2 A).[22] Predating the other similarly configured palaces, the Talar-e Tavile, I propose, experimented with an architectural accommodation of altered ceremonial needs in Isfahan before its palatial kin, the Ayenekhane and the Chehel Sotun, recast those spatial principles and construction ingredients into an architecturally mature realization of the new *talar*-palace type.

The Ayenekhane or the Hall of Mirrors

Mirza Mozaffar Torke, a poet active during the reign of Shah Abbas II, eulogized the Ayenekhane as the *eshrat sara-ye Shah Safi,* "the pleasure palace of Shah Safi," noting especially its impressive mirror-work (Figures 3.7, 3.8, 5.5 and 5.6).[23] Shamlu, the historian of Shah Abbas II to whom we owe the poetic reference, further confirms the attribution of this palace to Shah Safi's reign when he introduces the building as the *"Ayenekhane-ye shah-e rezvan aramgah,"* the "Ayenekhane of the shah [who] rests in paradise," that is, the shah who was deceased by the time of Shamlu's writing between 1661 and 1674.[24] Unlike the Talar-e Tavile in the Daulatkhane, the Ayenekhane was built on the southern bank of the Zayande River, sufficiently distanced from the developments along the Chahar Bagh and the Allah Verdi Khan Bridge to have qualified as a suburban retreat. In fact, it is with this palace that the Safavid patrons seem to have first explored the riverfront potential of Isfahan. But unlike the Seljuq royal gardens discussed in Chapter 3, the Safavid appropriation of the riverbanks as a palatial haven served as the suburban pendant to a suite of urban palaces. As a retreat, its appeal must have been enormous, for it was located nearer the city, unlike the faraway, extra-urban garden-palace of Hezar Jarib that Shah Abbas the Great had built at the foot of the Soffe Mountain in the 1590s (Figure 3.2).[25] While there is some evidence suggesting mansions of the wealthy Armenian and Persian elite along the river farther to the west and in the vicinity of the Allah Verdi Khan Bridge, the Ayenekhane inaugurated the development (one that Shah Abbas II followed) of the Sa'adatabad palatial complex along the stretch between the Allah Verdi Khan and the Khwaju Bridges (Figures 3.5, 3.7, 5.21, and 5.22).[26] It was probably to accommodate this palace that Shah Abbas II built the Pol-e Ju'i (the Rivulet Bridge) to its west.[27]

Figure 5.5 *Isfahan, Ayenekhane Palace (Hall of Mirrors), after an engraving from Coste,* Monuments *(1867).*

Located on the south side of the Zayande River, the Ayenekhane was also built in the 1630s for Shah Safi. This profile image of the building represents the best example of this type of palace: a sequence of three sections, each smaller than the preceding one, implies a ceremonial crescendo effect. The Khwaju Bridge in the background was constructed for Shah Abbas II in 1651/2.

This indeed must have been the quintessential pleasure palace, because it also served as a restorative retreat for Shah Safi I, who suffered in his last years from severe illnesses (precipitated, presumably, by his excessive consumption of alcohol and opiates) and who spent much time in the suburban palaces. Late in 1641, according to Khwajegi Esfahani, the historian of his reign, "His majesty the shadow of God [Shah Safi I], after recovery [from illness], gave public audience at the *emarat-e* (palace of) Ayenekhane which is among this chosen of the world's constructions."[28]

Like the Talar-e Tavile, this was a palace distinguished by its prominent *talar*. Instead of adjoining an artificial pool, as at the Daulatkhane palace, the Ayenekhane stood on the southern bank of the Zayande River, turning its open *talar* onto river views and allowing for its faceted and mirrored surfaces, on the octagonal wooden pillars and the back wall of the *talar*, to reflect the play of light off the water and the surrounding gardens (Figure 5.6). Thanks to the renditions in engravings by Pascal Coste and Eugene Flandin, and at least one late nineteenth-century photograph taken before its destruction, it is easier to picture the Ayenekhane than the Talar-e Tavile, although its functions in the seventeenth century remain less clear than those of the latter.[29]

Figure 5.6 *Isfahan, Ayenekhane Palace, after an engraving from Coste,* Monuments *(1867).*

The view from inside out, comparable to Figure 5.15, indicates the ceremonial implications of seeing and being seen as articulated by the *talar* spaces of these palaces.

A sequence of ever-smaller architectural units ran from the front to the back of the building (Figures 5.5 and 5.2 B). Perched on what appears to have been a gently sloping embankment and built atop a platform, as was the case in all *talar* palaces, the Ayenekhane was composed of three units positioned along its longitudinal axis: the open (on three sides) *talar* of sixteen slender wooden columns and an ornamental pool at its center; the semi-open (on one side only) throne-ayvan flanked by two rooms, with a smaller pool and two wooden pillars at its opening; and the completely enclosed audience hall which was turned perpendicular to the main axis and was adjoined by two rooms on the farthest corners and three smaller verandah-ayvans on its sides. Such a sequential planning of space, gradually transitioning from vast and open to small and closed, from exposed to covered, from bright to dark, from public to private, articulates with architectural clarity the integrated and hierarchical organization of a building that explicitly privileges its ceremonial space.

The opulence of the palace was reinforced by its decorative mirrors, either in faceted pieces, especially on the pillars, or in large sheets on the back walls.[30] Mirror-work, interspersed with painted and gilded decoration throughout the open *talar*, created a constant dialogue of reflected and refracted light between the surface of the river and the *talar*.

The Ayenekhane represents the transitional stage between the architectural idea of a *talar* palace that was first tested at the Talar-e Tavile and the fully realized, large-scale version of that idea – the Chehel Sotun Palace. In all these palaces in Isfahan the diaphragmatic conceptualization of space along a longitudinal axis accommodates an architecturally predetermined hierarchy of the ceremonial. In fact, such buildings render the principal space of gathering so large and open as to preclude the possibility of intimate functions. In contrast, the nine-fold, *hasht-behesht* palaces of earlier and later times privilege the central, vaulted space, which is, moreover, flexible in both the scale and uniformity of its spatial parts and thus allows for a variety of uses (Figures 5.2 and 5.4). At the Timurid pavilions in Samarqand and Herat, the Chehel Sotun in Qazvin, or the 1669 Hasht Behesht in Isfahan itself, a formal audience could take place in the same space as that of a private gathering of the shah and his confidants or concubines.

Connecting with Mazandaran

Two aspects of the *talar* palace have escaped critical consideration: one is the fact that the *talar* is an architectural form fundamentally alien to the Isfahan region; the other is the question of its architectural genesis. The vernacular architecture of central Iran had been for centuries bound by the brick and mortar materials of construction and the pier and vaulting methods of building. Expansive, flat-roofed, wooden-pillared spaces had no precedent in the Isfahan region. Timber of the right height and density, the kind we find in the *talar* palaces, was not native or plentiful in this area – the scarcity of water imposed an agricultural economy that was focused on the cultivation of fruit trees rather than construction lumber. Instead, the Talar-e Tavile marked the first instance of an experiment with an architectural form and building materials that were appropriated in the 1630s from the Mazandaran region of Iran, where Shah Abbas the Great had developed, beginning in 1611, the two new cities of Ashraf and Farahabad.[31]

The provinces of Mazandaran and Gilan along the shore of the Caspian Sea had been especially important for both the production of silk in Safavid Iran, a precious commodity that Shah Abbas the Great exchanged for silver and gold as a key part of his restructuring of the Safavid economy, and its long-distance trade (Figures 1.1 and 1.2).[32] The annexation of these provinces into the *khasse*, or crown lands, during his reign had been a principal feature of the planned economy. The development of the cities of Farahabad (near Sari) and Ashraf (near Behshahr), the latter as a royal palace-city, and the populating of them with silk farmers from northwestern regions of Iran (including the

Armenians) were other crucial aspects of the 1611–12 project.[33] The Mazandaran transformations were part of the multifaceted projects of reform – in politics, economy, religion, and administration of the realms – and reconquest, especially in the face of Ottoman threats in the northwestern region and the Uzbeks in the northeast. Their corollary in the built environment was the construction of the infrastructure of the Safavid dominions and the enhancement of the capital city.

The Mazandaran region and especially its two Safavid urban centers were regularly visited by Shah Abbas the Great – the period of conquest required him to be mobile. His visits to Mazandaran, at first only during military campaigns, became increasingly prolonged and frequent toward the end of his reign.[34] Shah Safi I, much of whose reign was mired in conflict with the Ottomans over Baghdad and the holy cities of Najaf and Karbala in present-day Iraq, stopped in Ashraf only twice, while Shah Abbas II retreated to Mazandaran for several short restorative sojourns during his long and relatively peaceful years.[35]

Several palaces were built in Farahabad and Ashraf as part of its urban development. Only two of these palaces have survived, albeit in a very poor state. One is known as the Safiabad Palace and has long been appropriated by the military – both under the Pahlavi regime and that of the Islamic Republic – as a station to keep watch over the republics (Soviet and formerly Soviet) across the Caspian Sea. As far as can be ascertained, only the platform base of the pavilion belongs to the original structure, which was perched high on a hilltop overlooking the town of Ashraf. The other palace is the Cheshme Emarat (the Spring Palace), popularly so called because of the channels that direct, inside and around the building, the spring water that gushes from the mountainside (Figure 5.7). This latter building is the better preserved of the pavilions that once belonged to a conglomerate of buildings in the royal precinct at Ashraf.[36]

The Cheshme Emarat exemplifies the type of palace-pavilions that continued to be favored by the Safavids in the Caspian Sea shore region, just as they had been elsewhere in the Safavid realm throughout the sixteenth century; the Bagh-e Fin Palace in Kashan is one of the best preserved among them (Figures 5.8 and 5.9).[37] It was planned on the *hasht-behesht* scheme, with a slightly wider ayvan on its north side, which originally faced a pool and garden to distinguish it from the "back" of the building towards the mountain (Figure 5.4 B). The decoration consisted of glazed tiles, remnants of which are found mainly in the interior, and mural paintings with figural themes, noted by the Englishman Thomas Herbert (who visited Iran in 1627–9) to have made the hall "more resembling a gallery than a room of state; the ceiling was garnished with gold, and penciled with story in lively colours: all which seemed to strive whether art or nature to a judicious eye would be more acceptable."[38] Pietro Della Valle

Figure 5.7 *Mazandaran, Ashraf, Cheshme Emarat.*

The town of Ashraf was founded by Shah Abbas the Great in 1611/12 as
the royal retreat pendant to nearby Farahabad, the planned commercial hub
for the production of, and trade in, silk. Cheshme Emarat was one of many
pavilions built on the foothills of the Alborz Mountains that separated the
coast of the Caspian Sea from the Iranian plateau on its south side. Despite
its ruined state, including the loss of its second story, the general *hasht-
behesht* scheme and its four-quadrant garden setting (*chahar bagh*) are still
visible in the remains of two water channels that run through and intersect
at a pool in the central chamber of the pavilion (Figure 5.4 B).

observed that the painted decoration consisted of small, framed
paintings showing the shah in the midst of women playing music, as
well as at least one "portrait."[39]

Unlike the Mazandaran vernacular architecture in which wood,
open porches and thatched roofs predominated, this building was
made primarily of brick and mortar, was enclosed save for the four
smallish ayvans, and was probably topped (the building's original roof
is lost) like other *hash-behesht* types with a low-rise vault embedded
in a flat roof. Compared to the outward-looking and airy openness of
the local architecture, the Cheshme Emarat – and its now extinct
companions in Ashraf and Farahabad, known through descriptions to
have been similar – represents imported architectonic and design
concepts.[40]

Builders of the two towns and their palaces did, however, utilize
other aspects of the local vernacular. The historian Monshi's reference
to the construction at Farahabad includes that "the city was built
along the banks of the Tajine River" and that "people from every class
and tribe [presumably those transplanted communities] designed

Figure 5.8 *Kashan, Bagh-e Fin Palace.*
The construction of this building is generally attributed to the first two
decades of the seventeenth century, during Shah Abbas the Great's reign.
Situated at the crossing of two main water channels that subdivide the lush
gardens into four quadrants (a *chahar bagh* garden scheme), this pavilion is
designed as a typical two-story *hasht behesht* (Figure 5.4 C)

houses on each side and built *talar*s in such a manner that the river
runs through the actual heart of the city."[41] Furthermore, a year after
the Farahabad construction projects had begun in 1611–12, the building of the city of Ashraf had commenced with the royal ensemble of a
hammam (bathhouse), several houses and *talar*s.[42] While nothing in
these references helps us to describe the buildings, the "talars" appear
to have served either as the façades of the houses facing the river, in
the Farahabad instance, or as independent structures.

Such hypotheses can be supported by evidence of other *talar* constructions in Mazandaran during the first half of the seventeenth
century. A *talar* was built in 1618–19 at Mian Kale, a long, narrow
and uninhabited (then and now) peninsula near Ashraf that Shah
Abbas the Great frequented for its excellent potential for trapping
prey for the hunt. On that Nauruz of 1618–19, the shah celebrated the
New Year at Ashraf and enjoyed his favorite pastime of hunting at the
nearby Mian Kale.[43] Monshi tells us that the shah rested from
hunting and held conversations with his companions at "*talar-ha-ye
rafi'-e delgosha*," "lofty and pleasing talars" built in three locations
in Mian Kale.

The mid-seventeenth-century *Abbasname* history of Shah Abbas II
describes a similar hunting visit by the reigning monarch, providing
us with additional information about these structures.[44] According to

Figure 5.9 *Kashan, Bagh-e Fin Palace.*

The interior of the central unit rises to two stories in height and opens to the outside through ayvans and balconies. The gorgeous pool at the center of this space is fed by the gurgling sound of water in two intersecting channels; together they make this *chahar bagh* and pavilion justly famous.

Taher Vahid, advance parties were sent to Mian Kale to prepare the area for a hunting trip in 1658/9. In a short period of time, Taher Vahid tells us, two *talar*s were raised and their surroundings were cleared of trees and bushes before Shah Abbas II made his way from Natanz to Ashraf.

These references underscore a few essential aspects of the *talar* in its Mazandaran incarnation: they were built of light and easily transportable building materials, they could be raised rapidly, they were built as temporary edifices, and they served to create outdoor spaces with vistas (in *talar*s both at the Tajine River front and the Mian Kale hunting ground), intended, at least in the specified Mian Kale cases, for entertainment purposes. The fact that a *talar* was usually raised above ground level implies that one might have enjoyed a view while standing or sitting inside. An image of such a structure, albeit on a much smaller scale, may be glimpsed from a description by Pietro Della Valle.[45] During his 1619 visit to Ashraf, when Della Valle was pursuing an audience with Shah Abbas the Great, the Italian traveler noted with obvious delight the presence of a room in the middle of the garden where he was housed. This room was open on all sides but its roof and was raised above the ground to the height of a man. Stairs gave access to the room, which because of its height, he says, is called a *balakhane* (literally, raised or upper house). Furthermore, he confirms that such rooms were used primarily for entertainment.

Even more evocative of the scenic and festive potentialities of the *talar* is its association with a body of water. This is especially true in the semitropical Caspian Sea region. In fact, these concepts were so strongly intertwined that if a site was deemed especially advantageous, an artificial lake was constructed, along with a man-made island and a *talar* to form an architectural-scenographic package. Such was the case at Abbasabad in Mazandaran, considered the most delightful of retreats for Shah Abbas the Great, as Robert Stodart, a member of the English mission of Sir Dodmore Cotton and the Shirley Brothers, noted during his 1628 visit (Figure 5.10).[46] The site is placed at a considerable elevation on one of the forested mountains on the north side (along the Caspian Sea) of the Alborz range, which has an average height of 1,200 meters.[47] A vast clearing amid the thick forest, obviously made for the purpose of building the retreat, provided the space for an artificial lake with a man-made stone island at its center. Two watch- or water towers mark, at least in part, the boundaries on one side of the clearing. The intimate scale and plainness of a cluster of rooms to one side – known from archaeological remains that have yet to be properly studied – suggest that they mainly functioned as service facilities for the retreat.

The main attraction was the *talar* at the center of the lake, of which nothing remains. In Stodart's description, a room made of wood occupied the island and was reserved for the shah. At a later time, Mohammad Taher Vahid describes a more elaborate setting for a

Figure 5.10 *Mazandaran, near Ashraf.*
A man-made lake high in the mountains was the centerpiece of a retreat called Abbasabad, after its royal patron (1611/12). European and Persian descriptions indicate that a freestanding wooden-pillared shelter atop this platform provided a festive space in the middle of the lake. Such timber structures were native to the Mazandaran region and served as prototypes for Isfahan's *talar* palaces.

night of festivities hosted by Shah Abbas II in 1652 at this Abbasabad lakeside retreat. At this reception, the banks of the lake were illuminated with candles and torches, and the shah and his guests sat in the *talar* in the middle of the lake enjoying the flickering reflections of light on the lake surface.[48] The place must have indeed been beguiling – even in its ruinous state today it sparks the imagination to picture royal feasts under the shelter of a *talar* in the middle of the lake and protected by the thick green forest.

Another piece of evidence for the dedicated use of *talar*s in outdoor and leisurely settings is the description by the English traveler Thomas Herbert of the palace in Farahabad.[49]

This palace has two square large courts railed about, and the ground by the elaborate gardener was formed into grass-plots and knots of several sorts, and replenished with variety of trees and flowers, which makes the place seem exceeding pleasant . . . And amongst other trees the spreading chenaers, sycamores, and chestnuts surround the place with so much beauty, and every part of the house affords so amiable a prospect, as makes the eye and smell contend which shall surfeit soonest of variety.

Furthermore, as Herbert notes, "This house of the King's, though it be spacious yet is low; but the rooms are high enough, arched and of sufficient length, rather resembling galleries than rooms of State." Although the description does not specify a *talar* form, the fact that "the house affords so amiable a prospect, as makes the eye and smell contend" and that it resembled a gallery indicate that at least part of the palace consisted of a *talar*-type of building.

Whether the water and vegetative components were naturally present, as in the cases of the *talar* houses along the Tajine River in the city of Farahabad and the *talar*s on the Mian Kale peninsula, or were purposely fashioned, as in the Abbasabad lake retreat and the Farahabad palace, the *talar* building type appears to have been the local architectural means to commingle water and verdure with the built environment. When the *talar* design was transferred to Isfahan, where the vegetation had to be carefully cultivated as a garden and where the body of water had to be recreated in a vast pool, it was necessary to reconceptualize the typology of Persianate palaces.

The main examples of Persianate *chahar-bagh* garden-pavilion conventions are those in fifteenth-century Timurid Herat and Samarqand and Aqqoyunlu Tabriz, sixteenth-century Safavid Tabriz and Qazvin, and even early seventeenth-century Kashan (the famed Fin Garden) and Mazandaran (Cheshme Emarat among them). Such garden-pavilions called for at least one principal crossing of water channels to mark the four quadrants of the garden and prescribed the placement of the pavilion on the crossing (Figure 5.4).[50] The water channels were exactly that: narrow and shallow man-made canals. Their crossing was marked by a small square pool enclosed within the pavilion; extant examples are seen at the Chehel Sotun in Qazvin, the Fin Garden in Kashan, and the Cheshme Emarat in Ashraf.

In contrast, the *talar* palaces in Isfahan recreate the "natural" conditions of Mazandaran by aggrandizing the water component into a long and wide rectangular pool in front of the *talar* area (as at the Talar-e Tavile and the Chehel Sotun Palaces, the latter discussed below) or, in one instance, by building on a site where water is plentiful and visible (as at the Ayenekhane Palace). It is indeed the very indivisibility of the natural and the artificial in this triad of *talar*/water/verdure that distinguishes the Isfahan *talar*s from all other Persianate palace typologies – ancient or Islamic. Contrary to the assumption that these elongated rectangular garden palaces were only a Safavid variant of some timeless notion of Persianate gardens, the artificial conditioning of the built environment for ceremonially defined needs in the *talar* palaces of Isfahan underscores how the particulars of time and place affected the design and development of these palaces.[51] The Talar-e Tavile, the Ayenekhane and the Chehel Sotun were specific to mid-seventeenth-century Safavid Isfahan. Nowhere else did they emerge or could they have been appropriated. The intersecting webs of politics and practices that connected

Isfahan, Mazandaran, and the Safavid enunciations of Perso-Shi'i kingship at the beginning of the seventeenth century necessitated the specific ceremonial and architectural syntax of these palaces.

The Mazandaran linkage has an etymological dimension as well. Structures similar to Della Valle's elevated room in the garden are still found in Mazandaran, although none of the extant examples is in a residential context. These are essentially smallish rectangular spaces, made of wooden pillars and latticework holding up the roof while maintaining openness on all sides, and they are invariably built atop a tower-like base that houses a water container (Figure 5.11).[52] In local vernacular, they are known as *saqqānafār*, a composite word consisting of *saqqā* for the water tank or well and *nafār* for the type of open structure that sits on top of it.[53] *Nafār* is also a variant of *napār* and *talār*, the latter of which is clearly the same as the Isfahani *talar* with a slight twist of the vowel.[54] That the etymological link is indeed local is supported by the usage of the term *talar* in the early thirteenth-century *Tarikh-e Tabarestan* (the History of Tabarestan, as the Mazandaran region was called) in which Ibn Esfandiyar refers to a "talar" building, albeit of indecipherable shape.[55]

Figure 5.11 *Mazandaran, Saqqanafar in a village east of Amol.*
Nafār is a Mazandaran vernacular variant of the term *talār*, or *tālār*, indicating both the etymological and architectural genesis of the *talar* idea for Isfahan's palaces. The link between the two regions goes beyond the commercial and recreational centrality of Mazandaran to the Safavids. Saru Taqi, the Grand Vizier of Shah Safi, whose fingerprint is discernable and documented in Isfahan *talar* palaces, was the minister-governor of Mazandaran when the two royal cities of Ashraf and Farahabad were constructed.

The *talar*'s etymological roots in the Mazandaran region and its prevalence in that area's vernacular architecture have been ignored by scholars who favor a Central Asian link. Some evidence, albeit remotely relevant in architectural and functional terms, is traceable in the traditions of the nomadic worlds of Central Asia and has been uncritically assumed to have been the source for the *talar* in the Safavid architecture of Isfahan. The earliest usage of the term *talar*, ascertained by Dehkhoda, the celebrated Iranian lexicographer, appears in a twelfth-century poem by Mohammad ibn Ali Suzani, a native of Nasaf near Samarqand:

> *chandin ranj-o bala-o jor keshidam*
> *tash be balay khane bordam o talar*

"So much suffering I endured till I raised a house and *talar*."[56] From the context of Suzani's poem (and reading it literally), one has to deduce that his house and *talar*, built in such hardship, were modest in size and appearance. On the authority of this poem, and presumably on the evidence of actual *talar*s, older Persian dictionaries have defined the *talar* as a kiosk or house built on four or more columns, all of wood.[57] Such a description does indeed correlate with a reference in the 1509 *Mihmanname-ye Bokhara*, a chronicle of the reign of the Uzbek Mohammad Shaybani.[58] Here the khan is reported to have visited the Madrasa of Khaniyye in Samarqand, where he also paid his respects to the burial site of his deceased brother: *dar an talar ke bar bala-ye mazar baste-and dar amadand* (he entered the *talar* that was raised above the grave).

These kiosk-like structures – valued for providing shade like a tent awning – were, according to the above sources, located in Central Asia. In fact, scholarship has tended to assume that structures like the *talar* palaces could only have emerged from the nomadic Timurid cultural practices that were rooted in Central Asia. Clavijo, the Spanish ambassador to the court of Timur in 1403–6, described several instances of royal weddings and circumcision celebrations for which massive tents had been raised. Although not in any way spatially or architectonically relevant to the *talar* palaces in Isfahan, these and other such Timurid descriptions have come to serve as the fifteenth-century baseline of common cultural heritage from which, presumably, issued in varying reconfigurations all that the Safavids, the Ottomans, and the Mughals accomplished.[59] Setting the Mazandaran connection aside for the moment, it is worth considering the *talar*, in both architectural and etymological terms, in light of the traditions of the nomadic worlds of Central Asia, if only to "unthink" the Timurid determinism so prevalent in scholarship.

In his memoirs of the Indian expedition and conquest, the great Babur (1483–1530), the founder of the Mughal dynasty, used the term *talar* to refer in several instances to kiosks that he either saw or had built in his own gardens.[60] For example, Babur described the wooden *talar* in Rahimdad's garden in Gwaliyor near Agra as a squat and inelegant structure. He gives an account of another such kiosk, built by the same Rahimdad on top of a large dome in the palace complex of Rajah Bikramajit, that was clearly very small – he refers to it with the diminutive *talargine* or *talarak*.[61] More compellingly related to the Mazandaran version is Babur's own design of "a talar and a stone building in front of a pool" in a garden in Agra.[62]

In all these instances, the term *talar* as used by Babur seems to indicate a specific type of building of which a small version or a wooden version were options. Such variations did not visually deviate from the recognized form, and form did not imply a fixed, single function. Otherwise, it would be hard to explain the *talarak* on top of a large dome, even if in diminutive scale, as a multi-pillared hall or a suitable gathering place like the Safavid *talar*s in Mazandaran or Isfahan. Rather, these early Mughal references were probably to kiosk-like structures similar to the one described in Samarqand or to those ubiquitous *chatris* (Persian for umbrella) that appear in small scale and on elevated locations in buildings. There is, in short, no architectural or descriptive evidence of a Timurid prototype for the *talar* palaces of the Safavids.

Multi-pillared halls intended specifically for royal ceremonies and receptions did not appear in Mughal India until the reign of Shah Jahan (1628–58).[63] Within a few months after ascending the throne in 1628, Shah Jahan ordered the construction of wooden pillared halls in all three major fortified palaces (at Agra, Lahore, and Delhi) (Figures 6.7, 6.8, 6.10, 6.12 and Plate 24). These were meant to replace smaller, tented audience halls. Called *ayvan-e chubin* (wooden ayvan) by contemporary Mughal sources, these wooden halls, too, were soon supplanted by even larger stone versions. The grander variants were known as the Ayvan-e Chehel Sotun (the Forty-Columned Porch) or the Ayvan-e Daulatkhane-ye Amm (the Public [Amm] Porch of the Royal Precinct). A smaller version was the Diwan-e Khass (the Private Porch), placed deeper inside the public zone of the palace precinct and hence reserved for the emperor and the inner circle of court and government.

We shall return to the Shah Jahani pillared halls in the next chapter, when we will consider their architectural, functional, and ceremonial significations. Here a few important architectural and ceremonial aspects of these Mughal halls need be highlighted, especially with regard to the Diwan-i Amm examples, which are comparable to the *talar* palaces of Isfahan. First of all, these pillared halls were exactly that: rows of pillars in an elongated, flat-roofed rectangular space with one wall to its back and the other three sides left open (Figure 6.10). They were not attached to any other structure, nor were the pillared halls part of a larger building. Such halls were laid down with their central axis on the short side of a long and narrow rectangle that measured, in length, to about 54 meters in Delhi and Lahore and about 61 meters in Agra (Figures 6.10 and 6.12). In Agra, for example, the building's appearance as a horizontally stretched rectangle was reinforced by its location in a vast courtyard that was accessible immediately after one passed through the complex of multiple gateways – hence, the public ceremonial function of the Diwan-i Amm (Figures 6.7 and 6.9). The considerably shorter central axis (around 25 meters in Agra and 24 in Delhi) marked the placement of the *jharoka*, the imperial throne that was variously treated in the pillared halls of Shah Jahan as a viewing balcony (in Agra) or a full-fledged Europeanized throne (in Delhi) (Figures 6.10 and 6.13). The pillars of stone, carved and painted, supported ornamental, scalloped arches and shallow-rise vaults upon which rested the flat roof.

The relative length and position of the axes express the shape of the ceremonies that took place within these pillared Mughal halls. The distinctive feature of their spatial articulation is the foreshortened sight line cast onto the emperor's throne. During the ceremonial performance of an audience, for example, a person standing or seated at either end of one of the horizontally stretched Shah Jahani Diwan-i Amm would have had limited visual contact, if any, with the jharoka. Shah Jahani pillared halls exploited the rectangular shape of the hall and its horizontal layout perpendicular to the throne to define the relationship between the individual and the emperor according to status and privilege.

This layout informed the spatial rendition of the ceremonial at Isfahan as well, but Shah Jahan's "ayvan-e chehel sotun" or pillared hall was conceptually antithetical to the *talar* palaces of mid-seventeenth-century Isfahan. The Safavid manner of manipulating space and representing hierarchies of access and remove, of the privilege of falling within the royal gaze, assumed a processional character. The throne at the *talar* palaces of Isfahan stood at the visual and spatial conclusion of an approach that commenced from the vast gardens and gradually narrowed and became rarefied in the social rank of the attendees as one reached the *talar* and advanced inward. At all points along this processional route one never fell outside the visual arc of the imperial gaze. The king's commanding view was ensured by his placement at an ever-so-slightly-elevated spot, architecturally accommodated through the gradual rise of the levels, from the garden and pool area to the platform of the talar, to the slightly stepped-up next level and then the throne ayvan positioned another step up. One could imagine the *talar* palace composition as a spatial-functional-symbolic triad made visible and navigable through the triangular arc of the two main vantages: one, located at the apex of the arc, emanated from the throne outward with open arms; the other came from the wide arc of the outer arena of the *talar* and converged onto the throne at its far end. In such a space, all – from the outer rungs of service workers to the inner circle of confidants – fell into the visual embrace of the king, whose role it was to regulate with vigilance and justice the affairs of the mundane world of humanity on behalf of the Twelfth Imam and the Family of the Prophet Mohammad. The Perso-Shi'i variant of kingship required just such an enunciative spatial order of visibility and access.

As Ebba Koch has suggested, Shah Jahan and his architects took their inspiration for the Diwan-i Amm pillared halls not from some Central Asiatic model, of which none existed, but from the fifth-century BCE Achaemenid Apadana and other pillared halls of the great royal complex at Persepolis.[64] More importantly, the typology of an ayvan, a vaulted space open only on one side, did not serve as the inspiration of the Mughal variant; the ayvan was a completely alien concept to Achaemenid architecture of the fifth century BCE. Instead, the ayvan as a charged royal space was ubiquitous in Sasanian architecture from the sixth century CE, especially in the palaces and, most famously, in Ctesiphon in present-day Iraq.[65] The Mughal ayvans (iwans) seem to have been generated by a desire to adopt the heritage of an ancient Persianate kingship. The resulting conflation of Achaemenid architectural and conceptual ancestry also incorporated that of the Sasanians, at least in evocations of their celebrated might, whose legendary Palace and Ayvan-e Kasra (Ctesiphon) had been so widely emulated and evoked by Muslim rulers from Cairo to Kashmir.[66]

Notwithstanding the feebleness of the notion that Central Asian Timurid models mediated the pillared halls in the palaces of the Mughals and the Safavids alike, the compelling evidence of the Mazandaran lineage and the spatial and ceremonial particularities of the Isfahan *talar* palaces decisively separate the Talar-e Tavile and the Chehel Sotun from their Mughal Diwan-i Amm counterparts. Each derived from a source meaningful to its own political, ideological, religious and cultural agendas; each was composed and choreographed to enunciate kingship in its own variant. The Perso-Shi'ism of the Safavids was distinct from the Mughal legitimizing hybrid occasioned by the braiding of Hinduism, Sunni Islam as well as Persianate and Caliphal forms of kingship.

The etymologically and architecturally persuasive linkage between Mazandaran and Isfahan is further supported by the presence of a "protagonist" who helped transmit to the imperial capital city of Isfahan the architectural idea and functional practices – the spatial syntax – associated with the *talar* and the palace. This was, as discussed elsewhere, the Grand Vizier Mirza Mohammad Saru Taqi.[67] Saru Taqi joined the Safavid military in his youth as a commoner. His rapid rise in the Safavid political and administrative hierarchy was aided by the fact that he was a eunuch, a condition forced upon him by Shah Abbas the Great as a punishment for alleged sodomy.[68] His ascent in the ranks began when he was appointed in 1611/12 as the governor of Mazandaran, and thereafter of Gilan, and was charged with building and populating the cities of Farahabad and Ashraf in Mazandaran. When under Shah Safi I he was made the Grand Vizier in 1634, the eunuch-*gholam* assumed a uniquely powerful and influential position because of his capacity to penetrate the inner sanctum of the court and to forge alliances from within the household. Saru Taqi's pervasive authority and vast and distinguished experience in urban, infrastructural, and architectural patronage (exercised in Mazandaran as well as in the holy city of Najaf, where he repaired the Shiʻi shrine) all point to his agency in bringing the building technology and ceremonial potentialities of the *talar* to the design of the ceremonial sites in Isfahan's *talar* palaces.

Restoring the Ali Qapu

It must not have been a coincidence that Saru Taqi himself was given the charge in 1644 of supervising the addition of a *talar* section to the Ali Qapu Palace tower. Two years into the reign of the twelve-year-old Abbas II, the powerful Grand Vizier, who together with the shah's mother held the reigns of authority, was entrusted, according to Vali Qoli Shamlu, with the construction of the *talar* in front of the Ali Qapu palace (Plate 12).[69] Shamlu, the historian of Abbas II, tells us that the *talar* and its substructure were completed in a short time "under the supervision of the master of the noble emirs, Mirza Taqi, the grand vizier" (*bi sarkari-ye makhdum al-omara al-akram Mirza Taqi vazir-e aʻzam*).[70]

With the construction of Shah Safi's Talar-e Tavile on the site of the stables, the Ali Qapu seems to have yielded its ceremonial primacy to the new palace. Persian and European chronicles clearly demonstrate the shift to the Talar-e Tavile for the staging of kingship.[71] As has been suggested earlier and will be discussed further in the next chapter, the shift away from the Ali Qapu, where the five-story tower had for two decades served as the premier ceremonial palace in the Isfahan of Shah Abbas the Great, was occasioned by considerable change in the ritual performances in the capital city. The centralization agenda largely accomplished, the Safavid court and polity had already begun to assume an increasingly settled and urbanized posture of kingship. Unlike their forebears, who were dispatched to the provincial capitals and raised under the tutelage of Qezelbash governors, Safi I and Abbas II grew up in the harem under the supervision of eunuch-*gholam* tutors at the Daulatkhane of Isfahan.

Despite their relatively frequent absences from Isfahan, especially during Safi I's reign when war loomed larger, neither shah remained distant from the capital for long. Nor did the conduct of the administrative affairs of the state and the reception of envoys require travel beyond the Daulatkhane and Isfahan. The state machinery was sufficiently rooted in Isfahan not to need to be displaced when circumstances required a king to travel. In fact, none of the Safavid practices of kingship in the seventeenth century can be considered peripatetic in nature. Safavid kings, like their brethren in rule, traveled, of course, to quell unrest, to defend territories, to conquer territories, to oversee development projects, to hunt, and to rest. In the seventeenth century, however, they did not pitch massive tent cities outside major urban centers or in favorite meadows for celebrations of major "national" festivals, for victories, or for the reception of ambassadors and the like, as had been the norm in the sixteenth-century phase of Safavid rule or the fifteenth-century Timurid past. Those and such Turco-Mongol necessities as the royal weddings and circumcisions that forged familial bonds and sealed tribal loyalties were customs discarded by the Safavids in this period and replaced with a sedentary and urban conduct of the rituals of royalty that was concentrated at the palaces and the public spaces of Isfahan, the capital city.

In place of the tribal confederacies of the past, the empire was held together through the agency of the *gholam*-governors, who were administrator-generals who served as if they were blood members of the royal household stretching out from the nucleus of authority. The enactment of ceremonies of kingship at Isfahan and its palaces in the seventeenth century implied the centralization of royal authority and its power over the entire Safavid dominion. The aggrandized scale of ceremonies, their revised hierarchies of access and remove, and the emergence of feasting as a principal enunciative form for Safavid kingship were paramount to the maintenance of this Perso-Shi'i grid of authority and legitimacy; to stage them required vastly different kinds of spaces for which the old Ali Qapu no longer sufficed.

After the coronation in 1629 of Shah Safi I at the Ali Qapu, Persian and European chronicles make little reference to events there, in comparison to the increasingly important role they assign to such palaces as the Talar-e Tavile and the Hauzkhane.[72] Already in the 1630s, the five-story Ali Qapu tower of Shah Abbas the Great must have fallen short in providing an adequate stage. Its ayvan porch could accommodate no more than a few people, and its elegant audience hall was too intimate in scale for the enlarged receptions described by European travelers and envoys to the courts, especially those of Shah Safi I and Shah Abbas II. Moreover, the ayvan was hidden from the view of the multitudes for whose consumption the royal command of resources, both material and spiritual, was enacted in feasts and audiences (Figure 4.6).

The *talar* appendage to the Ali Qapu radically transformed the building and altered the visual-spatial experience of the Maydan. Like the Qaysariyye and the portals of the two mosques, the original entranceway of the Ali Qapu receded from the bazaar façade of the Maydan and created a transitional entry space. The addition of the *talar* and its substructure projected the building into the space of the Maydan, thus permanently disrupting the harmonious pattern of solids and voids drawn from the march of the shops around the periphery of the Maydan and interspersed with the inviting hollow in front of each monumental marker on the four sides. Instead, the *talar* thrust forth, as if on a tray, the spectacle of royal feasts and receptions. Once it was altered to serve as a venue for highly visible staged events with hundreds of attendees – their colorful costumes and the accoutrements of feasting reflected in the mirrored surfaces of the "forest" of pillars and the painted and coffered ceiling – the Ali Qapu again became the important ceremonial palace that it had been at the time of Shah Abbas the Great.

Much of the Ali Qapu's architectural integrity was sacrificed for the sake of restoring it to full function. In order to make the *talar* area vast enough, its back wall extended in width beyond the block of the five-story tower, making the *talar* appear as a paper-thin stage set when the projection of the back wall beyond the original tower was viewed from the sides or behind (Figure 4.3). But the public were not privy to either of those sight lines, and therefore the visual experience of the newly refashioned Ali Qapu (as of 1644) struck an awesome architectural and ceremonial chord. The fact that the *talar* was to serve as a platform from which to view the pageantry at the Maydan, or its parallel function for the staging of events to be seen from the public arena, may be too obvious an explanation for the awkward architectonics of the joints. Yet it was precisely the urgency of refreshing the functional and symbolic articulation of this most visible of the ceremonial palaces that justified the "quick" solution. Saru Taqi, from this perspective, seems all the more a logical choice to have headed the refurbishing of the Ali Qapu since he may indeed have had a hand in conceptualizing of the two earlier and more fully realized *talar* places in Isfahan, the Talar-e Tavile and the Ayenekhane.

Notwithstanding the inelegant junction of the old and the new at the Ali Qapu, the *talar* and its functionality were enhanced by the addition to the sides of the structure of two tall units: one was a water tower, the other a stairwell (Figure 4.3 and Plate 10).[73] Both replaced smaller, similarly functioning units that had ceased to be sufficient for the expanded needs of the *talar* palace that the Ali Qapu had become. The first, on the north side of the building, employed an ingenious pumping mechanism that brought water to the considerable height of four stories so that, upon its descent, it would burst forth from the spouts in the copper-clad fountain pool in the middle of the *talar*. The complex mechanics of such a task underscores the inseparability of the aqua-cultural dimensions of the *talar* and its architectural-functional form. Equally impressive is the stairwell, on the south side, which rises through consecutive units of stairs-and-landings. Where the water tower is purely mechanical in function, the stairwell is brilliantly designed to accommodate a ceremoniously elegant and slow-paced ascent through a sequence of vaulted rooms and sets of wide, low-rise steps without burdening the south side of the original tower with additional weight. Three vaulted volumes of increasing height constitute the landing rooms, while flights of steps are tucked into the space between each two volumes.

The originality of the architectural solution in this stairwell partly rests in the fact that its vaulting ribs run parallel to the side of the tower and allow for the building simply to abut the Ali Qapu and not burden it. The stairwell is also a very clever architectural solution to the emerging need to conduct royal guests to the site of the festivities at the *talar* level via a climb that was relatively easy and yet still embodied suitable pomp and ceremony. Each landing room and set of steps offered an opportunity to perform the rituals of *esteqbal* or welcoming, to heighten the pitch of anticipation but also to rest. The landing rooms, undoubtedly carpeted and furnished when decked out for events at the *talar*, were decorated with murals representing curtains, parted and waving in the wind, that appear now in badly damaged condition on the dado level of the plastered walls beneath the windows or flanking the fireplace niches. Each set of steps was covered in glazed tiles with vegetal motifs in brilliant yellows, blues and greens, all appearing as flowers strewn underfoot. The uppermost set of stairs turned thrice before facing the low-rise opening onto the *talar*. One came out of this "hole" to the spectacle of light, colors, and forms. The visual excitement of the painted and mirrored *talar* pillars and ceiling as well as the textiles, accoutrements, and furnishings used at feasts and receptions, was accompanied by vistas, on the south side and immediately to one's right, of the towering blue-tiled minarets, ayvans, and dome of the royal congregational mosque, while directly in front soared the golden yellow dome of the Shaykh Lotf-Allah Mosque (Plate 6).

The transformation of the Ali Qapu into a *talar* palace propelled the building back onto the roster of ceremonially indispensable palaces of the Daulatkhane at Isfahan. Immediately after the completion of the *talar*, Nadr Mohammad Khan attended a sumptuous reception at the Ali Qapu in September 1645 (Sha'ban 1055).[74] In deference to the aged khan, Shah Abbas II had ordered splendid welcoming rituals to conduct the ousted Uzbek ruler from his entry point into the Safavid dominions all the way to Isfahan's Maydan-e Naqsh-e Jahan. From the *talar* of the newly refurbished Ali Qapu, Shah Abbas II hosted the Uzbek Khan and his entourage in wondrous ceremonies, an awesome part of which were the illuminations (*cheraghani*) with fireworks (*atashbazi*) and thousands of torches (*mash'al*) and lamps (*fanus*) installed around the Maydan. All at once the lamps, torches and candles were lit and the fireworks began, and the Maydan, which, according to the contemporary historian Taher Vahid, was in breadth and spread like the sky (*ke dar vos'at va foshat*), was illumined like the stars (*kavakeb mesal*) by these countless lights.[75]

The *talar*, then, had restored to the Ali Qapu its capacity as the uniquely multifunctional palace-gateway that it had been intended for from the beginning. The architectural solution of the *talar* palaces – implemented in the Talar-e Tavile and the Ayenekhane – addressed the ceremonial needs and ideological impulses of the seventeenth-century Safavid performances of kingship. Just as the newer rituals of hospitality were taking shape, the *talar* addition to the Ali Qapu seems to have been calculated to transform those ceremonial performances into fully public spectacles.

Crowning of the palaces: the Chehel Sotun

In the eulogizing words of Sa'eb-e Tabrizi, the poet laureate of the court of Shah Abbas II, under whose patronage the Chehel Sotun was erected, this palace is likened to a "new world" (*jahan-e nau*) that has "made Isfahan the envy of the eternal Paradise" (*ghayrat afza-ye behesht-e javdan*).[76] To the French traveler Chardin, this "largest and most sumptuous building in the entire royal palace" represented the quintessential Safavid setting for the stagecraft of kingship.[77] He used this palace to exemplify how state ceremonies were conducted in Safavid Isfahan. His recounting of the place and its events reveals especially the links between such vast *talar* palaces and the centrality of feasting for the conduct of kingship, and also provides us with a window onto the semiotics of feasting and hierarchies of access and remove that so characterized the Perso-Shi'i Safavid notions of legitimacy and authority. This paradigmatic convergence of the city, the palace, the grand feasting-audience ceremonies, and the heavenly realms of paradise permeates much that contemporaries tell us about the Chehel Sotun (Plate 9).

Set in a vast garden of its own with a long pool in front, the Chehel Sotun is a rectangular building (57.80 × 37 meters) composed of three spatially, formally, and functionally interrelated zones: the *talar* front, the pseudo-*talar*-ayvan and its flanking rooms, and the cluster of the throne ayvan-audience hall with attendant closed and open units (Figures 3.7, 3.8, 5.2 C and Plate 14). Like all such *talar* palaces, the building progressively rises above the ground level – from 0.80 meters in height at the *talar* platform, to 1.00 meter at the throne-ayvan cluster, to the 1.45 meters at the audience hall section (Figures 5.12, 5.2 C and Plate 15). Such tapering of the building's profile signals the telescoped effect of space that one is led subtly to experience from within. It is this ceremonially mediated march – performed on foot and perceived visually – that characterizes the *talar* palaces of Isfahan as a coherent phenomenon and separates them from former and contemporaneous palatine traditions.

As in the other mid-seventeenth-century ceremonial palaces of the Daulatkhane (the Talar-e Tavile and the revised Ali Qapu), the Chehel Sotun is oriented on an east–west axis with the open *talar* articulating its principal façade.[78] Here, also, the *talar* forms the widest and loftiest space in the palace (Plate 16). Like a massive awning, the intricately painted, mirror-faceted and coffered wooden ceiling of the *talar*, projects forth from the building (Figures 5.13, 5.14 and Plate 15).

Figure 5.12 *Isfahan, Chehel Sotun.*
The building is raised above a platform, with each section opening and closing as they advance through internal spaces of the palace. The exterior of the large audience hall is seen here from the southwest, with its triple window openings onto the pillared veranda, and its back onto an ayvan.

The massive ceiling is held aloft by eighteen painted, tall and slender wooden columns that rise from heavy stone bases to delicately faceted and painted wooden capitals. An ornamental pool, originally outfitted with fountains, rests at the center of the platform (Plate 16). Four of the eighteen columns peg down the pool, with their exceptional stone bases carved into shared bodies of lions in the corners, an allusion, no doubt, to the well-established Solomonic iconography of kingship in the traditions of Islam.[79] The outward-facing sides of the platform are delineated with low, grated wooden banisters. Allowing unencumbered vistas on three sides and shielding guests from the elements, the *talar* serves visually and spatially to mediate between the indoors and the outdoors.

Pillared spaces partially open to the elements are indeed universal – the classical Greek or Persian hypostyles of antiquity or the loggias and balconies of medieval and early modern architecture serve as comparisons. And we have already discussed some of the formal, functional, and etymological aspects of the *talar* as an architectural building type. Yet the extraordinary visual and spatial experience of the *talar* at the Chehel Sotun stems from the fact that an enormous area is roofed at a considerable height without the visual encumbrance of its weight-bearing architectural elements (Figures 5.15 and

Figure 5.13 *Isfahan, Chehel Sotun Palace, after a photograph from
Dieulafoy,* La Perse *(1887).*

The photograph conveys the effect of light playing on the mirrored, painted
and gilded surfaces of the wooden pillars and back walls of the *talar*, and
their reflections in the pool. All mirror and painted work is lost except for
that of the throne ayvan (Plate 16).

Plate 16). Neither the abbreviated pillared awning of the Gate of
Felicity at the Topkapı, nor the horizontally stretched, vast stone-
pillared halls of the Red Fort Diwan-i Amms generates the same experience of simultaneous lightness and solidity as to the Chehel Sotun
Palace and its *talar* (Figures 6.4 and 6.11). It is this monumentally
scaled soaring lightness – so extraordinary in view of the pre-modern
architectural obsession with articulating the logical relationship
between weight and its support – that distinguishes the *talar* palaces
of Safavid Isfahan. At the Chehel Sotun the *talar* acts as a dialogic
space for nature–culture elements in architecture, decoration, and
landscaping. To picture how the *talar* shapes both architectural and
ceremonial space, it may help to imagine the solidity and regulated
pace of the *talar* pillars as the remains of an otherwise hollowed-out
structure, as if the *talar* zone were to have been a building with four
walls. Conversely, the same solidity and regulated pace of the pillars
in the *talar* zone may be perceived as the continuation of the march
of the trees in the surrounding gardens (Figure 5.13 and Plate 14). The
visual threads of this dialogue may be extended to the elements of
water as well: The long pool before the palace structure finds its footprints first in the smaller ornamental pool of the *talar* and then again
in the second, even smaller ornamental pool that sits on the platform
of the next unit, behind the *talar* zone.

Figure 5.14 *Isfahan, Chehel Sotun.*
Detail of the southeast corner of the *talar* ceiling with remnants of painted wooden coffers. The *talar* portion of the palace burned down in 1706 during a supper at which Shah Soltan Hossayn and Safavid grandees were present. According to one of the resident Carmelites, it was replaced "similar in everything to that burnt and destroyed."

Figure 5.15 *Isfahan, Chehel Sotun.*
The view from the *talar* toward the pool and the gateway into the palace gardens.

Moreover, such an extraordinary architectural conceptualization of the liminal space between nature and culture, between unrestrained airiness and protective enclosure, between the space within and the space without, exploits all kinds of natural potentialities. Because of the lofty rise of the roof and hence the exposure of the *talar* space to light, and allowing for seasonal variations, the interior of the east-facing *talar* begins to be shielded from the rays of the sun only in the afternoon. Given that the height of outdoor festivities and activities in Isfahan would have coincided with the most temperate seasons in the region – beginning with Nauruz (vernal equinox) through early summer and culminating with the Mehregan Festival, the ancient Persian celebration of the autumnal equinox – the light-shade sequence would have allowed the *talar* to fall outside the harshest hours of sunlight during outdoor feasts and audiences, which tended to begin, according to European descriptions, after noon and continue into the early hours of the morning. Massive curtains, hung from the edges of the *talar* roof (the rings are still in place) and operated with ropes, were noted by many European visitors.[80] Since royal receptions were usually held during later afternoon or evening, the curtains served to keep the *talar* from heating up and could also have been raised just enough to allow for views at eye level.

Immediately behind the open space of the *talar* at the Chehel Sotun lies what may be called a pseudo-*talar* area, a space with a smaller footprint, opened to the *talar* in front by two wooden columns (Plate 16). It housed a smaller ornamental pool, gave way to the throne-ayvan behind and was linked through its flanking walls to rooms that appear to have served as additional spaces of ceremony. The dropped ceiling of this pseudo-*talar* and its smaller proportions serve to visually mediate hierarchies of significance and ceremony. It is a space for the eye to transition, in its perception of the built environment and perceived ceremonial, from the vastness and accessibility of the *talar*, where the lower rungs of court society sat, to the intimacy and remoteness of the royal seat in the throne ayvan behind. This pseudo-*talar*, in other words, is an element of spatial and ceremonial tempering that could telescope the conceptual and optical view of the shah as much as of the world that stretched before the shah.

The next cluster in the spatial sequence at the Chehel Sotun revolves around the throne ayvan and the indoor audience hall (Figure 5.2 C, Plates 16 and 17). Here the transition from the *talar* area to the interior is marked by a shrinking of the space to concentrate attention on the place of honor. This is molded as a proper ayvan, an architectural profile emblematic of a throne space made even more throne-worthy by its heightened decorative value, visible in the traces of royal images in two mural panels flanking the throne space and the painted Venetian mirror-work that fills the inner vault of the ayvan. A triple-arched doorway behind the throne ayvan opened into the audience hall that stretched perpendicularly to the main axis of the building.

The audience hall is a magnificent triple-vaulted space (c. 25 × 15 meters) that is made bright and airy by the placement of glazed openings in the upper zones of its longer east and west walls and by rows of doors and windows on its north and south sides (Figures 5.12 and 5.2 C).[81] The north and south doors open onto verandas that run the length of this throne-ayvan–audience hall cluster. Four slender wooden columns, of the kind used in the *talar*, visually integrate the verandas into the whole (Figure 5.12). Access to the verandas can be gained only from the inside, for there are no steps ascending to their considerable height from the ground level. The verandas are also linked to four vaulted rooms of an intimate scale on each corner of the audience hall.[82] Their mural decoration – of scenes recalling episodes from well-known romance poetry, or intimate princely gatherings and leisure activities – and their location on the edges of the public-ceremonial zones of the palace indicate their private function as an auxiliary space for the harem women, as was the case in the mezzanine level of the Ali Qapu. These rooms were furthermore articulated on two levels, with the upper floor of each opening onto a wooden "balcony" in the veranda that was held aloft in the space between the veranda's corner walls and one of the pillars. These little "balconies," unsafe as they may appear, commanded a view over the sides of the Chehel Sotun gardens and were perhaps intended for taking in the breezes without being in view of the guests.

The audience hall, baroque in its sensory excitement, is entirely sheathed with materials ranging from painted murals to tile panels to fabric arts featuring a multiplicity of decorative techniques (Plate 17).

The triple-vaulted ceiling is complexly subdivided into painted and gilded triangular squinches that emanate from a central motif at the peak of the vaults and appear as sunbursts of floral and vegetal motifs. Upper walls of the hall are further covered in painted clumps of flowers in rows against rich red and green backgrounds, collectively evoking the fashionable textile patterns worn at the time in Isfahan. The textile impression of the overall decoration found its counterpart in a single carpet that legendarily covered the entire floor.[83] The overall extravaganza of colors and patterns was further enhanced with the placement of an elaborate mixture of painted dadoes and tiled and paneled fireplaces on the lower walls, interspersed with smaller mural panels portraying scenes of men and women engaged in leisurely outdoor activities (reclining in the shade of a tree, passing cups of wine to one another, gazing with lovelorn eyes into a beloved's face, and the like).[84]

The most striking decorative portion of this audience hall is the large narrative mural paintings that occupy the four principal walls (Figures 5.16–5.17, Plates 17–20). Each depicts a scene from Safavid dynastic history: the defeat of the Uzbek armies by Shah Isma'il, and

Figure 5.16 *Isfahan, Chehel Sotun audience hall.*
"Shah Tahmasb hosting the Mughal emperor Homayun," is one of the four large mural paintings that depict scenes from Safavid dynastic history. Representations of royal feasts, in which the Safavid shahs extend hospitality and refuge to deposed neighboring monarchs, give these paintings their political charge and reiterate through iconography the building's function as a ceremonial palace. The fact that Safavid monarchs personally hosted such convivial rituals distinguishes their imperial ceremonies from those of their contemporaries.

Figure 5.17 *Isfahan, Chehel Sotun audience hall.*
The scene of "Shah Abbas II hosting the Uzben Nadr Mohammad Khan," alludes to a banquet that was held at the *talar* of the Ali Qapu Palace soon after its completion in 1644. These feasting scenes were chosen to fit a uniquely Perso-Shi'i enunciation of kingship that had crystallized by the mid-seventeenth century in Isfahan. Although heavily restored, this painting helps us imagine the immediacy of the paintings as seen during audiences and feasts at the Chehel Sotun itself.

three banquet scenes representing the offer of refuge, hospitality, and assistance to deposed rulers from neighboring territories of the Uzbeks and the Mughals.[85] One of the banquet scenes depicts Shah Tahmasb's extension of such royal munificence towards his fellow king, the emperor Homayun, whose temporary loss of the Mughal throne in the middle of the sixteenth century brought him to the then capital of Qazvin in 1544 (Figure 5.16). Tahmasb's generosity defined the imperial scale and range of influence, power, and authority for the Safavids, as the constructed narrative at the Chehel Sotun announced (Plate 18). The other two banquet scenes represent Shah Abbas the Great and Shah Abbas II hosting two deposed refugees from Uzbek Central Asia (Figure 5.17, Plates 19 and 20).

Notwithstanding some curious, and as yet unresolved, iconographic details in these large panels, the focus of the mural program at the Chehel Sotun on episodes of historical contact with Central and South Asia and the choice of the feasting theme to signal the centrality of the Safavids' Perso-Shi'i authority in this vast region of the Islamicate world seem to also have been intended to represent the balance of powers in territories lying to the east of the Ottomans. With the Safavid-Ottoman peace Treaty of Zuhhab (1639) in place – its significance was underscored by the later Safavid refusal to break the agreement despite considerable European pressure for (re)new(ed) alliances against the Ottomans – the narrative program focused on making crystal clear the place of the Safavids on the political map. In the eyes of those who perceived Asia as the embodiment of a First World – in retrospect, waning no doubt but still indispensable to world trade and diplomacy – such a construction of the nexus of power and authority served to highlight the Safavids at the apex of a practice of kingship that integrated Persianate cultural "norms" and Twelver Shi'i religious precepts.[86] Hospitality to and feasting of companions in rule seamlessly declared the synthesis that had matured by the middle of the seventeenth century into rituals of kingship particular to Isfahan, its urban spaces, and its palaces.

Despite damage and later alterations – inflicted by a fire in 1706, by nineteenth-century mural interventions, by later disfigurements and whitewashings – this audience hall preserves in its variety of materials and techniques of decoration as well as its complex iconographic scheme the most complete and compelling representation of the Safavid penchant for braiding architectural theatricality with the ceremonial staging of kingship. In fact, it is the representational glimpse of feasting in this hall's murals that confirms the functional significance of the building and its place in Safavid ritual performances of kingship. One wonders whether the feasting scenes in the audience hall were not also visual reminders, during wintertime gatherings, of the more sumptuous feasts held at the *talar* of this same palace during the warmer seasons.

Chardin describes the experience of one such festive occasion at the Chehel Sotun.[87] Royal guests, Chardin tells us, entered the palace precinct of the Daulatkhane from the formal gateway at the Ali Qapu, where they were made to wait their turn, sometimes for several hours. Having already crossed the threshold, the liminal experience of "cleansing" and transformation – at times also requiring the donning of robes of honor bestowed and sent in advance – was enhanced by the march along the tree-lined alley that extended from behind the Ali Qapu. There, one was dazzled by the "excellent Horses" from the royal stables "with their covering-Cloaths of Brocade, or Embroider'd with Gold and Silver."[88]

Contrary to the abbreviated processional ritual for events at the garden and palace of Talar-e Tavile, to reach the Chehel Sotun required deep penetration through additional alleys into the birun zone (public/ceremonial) of the Daulatkhane. More displays of sumptuous accoutrements of power, including a larger number of those gorgeously robed and decked-out horses and their youthful attendants, accompanied the guests to the formal garden entrance of the Chehel Sotun. As the recent reshuffling of access into the gardens has finally made clear even to tourists, the Chehel Sotun was intended to burst unexpectedly into one's field of vision. Hidden behind the tree-lined walls of the alley on the western side of the palace (its footprint is still a street), the Chehel Sotun would have been first glimpsed after guests had stepped into the entrance gateway at the far western end of the Chehel Sotun garden. There, and suddenly, appeared this vision of the "Eternal Paradise" (behesht-e javdan), as the poet Sa'eb would put it.[89]

The long rectangular pool, stretched between the entrance gate and the palace at the far end, imposed a stately pace in the march toward the talar along which one could observe, reflected on the shimmering surface of the water, the delights of the flanking gardens. The pool served to heighten the illusionistic effect of the gardens and the talar as one approached the palace. In characteristically extravagant poetic language, Sa'eb complicates the allusive theatricality of the visual and spatial artifice.[90] He says that what is reflected on the surface of the pool is nothing but ferdaus-e barin (Eternal Paradise) which has had to hide in the sweat of shame [the waters of the pool] at the sight of this palace (manzel) and from this [ocean] glides, by extension, the ship of Noah whose sails have opened up like wings in the image of the awning-like talar.[91] It was with the anticipation of feasting in the shade of this talar that guests would have been guided to walk along the pool to the palace.

The processional theatrics of the Chehel Sotun, so singular even in Isfahan, brought into the farthest reaches of the birun at the Daulatkhane what had been ordinarily relegated to the public spaces of city squares (the Maydan-e Naqsh-e Jahan in Isfahan, the Hippodrome in Istanbul) and vast courtyards (the Diwan-i Amm courtyards in the Red Forts at Agra, Delhi and Lahore, the Second Courtyard in Istanbul's Topkapı). In so doing, the practice of feasting, especially as staged in the talar and witnessed by nearly all the Europeans who visited Safavid Isfahan, formed the apex of the rituals of kingship by the middle of the seventeenth century and gave Shah Abbas II's Chehel Sotun its raison d'être.

Some controversy surrounding the dating of the Chehel Sotun must also be addressed here. The historiography of the Chehel Sotun tends to be rather slim, and the dating criteria for the building have been devised with little support.[92] Earlier scholars dated the "back" building (the audience hall and its attendant rooms, verandas, and two ayvans) to the reign of Shah Abbas I (1587–1629) and the *talar* front of the building to 1646/7, which is recorded both in the epigraphic band on the front of the *talar* roof and in contemporary chronicles and panegyrics. My earlier work has challenged such a patchwork construction of the building on the basis of an integrated re-evaluation of all the architectural, decorative, and historical evidence on the Chehel Sotun. Accordingly, the Chehel Sotun was constructed in a relatively short span, with the date of 1646/47 as a *terminus ante quem*. More recently, it has been suggested that the Chehel Sotun was rebuilt completely after a fire broke out in the *talar* in the winter of 1706, when Shah Soltan Hossayn was hosting a feast in the *talar*.[93] This assertion is based on a report dated 12 March 1706, and written by one of the Carmelite priests in Isfahan:

> The king being with his grandees at a sumptuous supper in the finest and most magnificent of his palaces – called that of the forty Columns . . . fire . . . attacked the base of one of those pillars and with the greatest velocity mounted to the top of it and set alight the ceiling and in turn all the other columns. So in a short space of time it was completely burnt out – the whole of that immense hall . . . had been reduced to ashes . . . the new hall, which is already being built once more, . . . similar in everything to that burnt and destroyed.[94]

What this passage indicates is that the *talar* of the Chehel Sotun burned down as a result of this fire. The rest of the building – that is, everything but the wooden columns and ceiling of the *talar* – survived that terrible fire. The archaeological evidence of the rest of the building unequivocally affirms its survival, although murals were darkened and damaged. For example, the Italian restoration of the wall paintings in the 1960s and 1970s uncovered, under grimy layers of varnish and later retouching, a layer of soot left by the fire in the *talar*.[95] Far from being exact copies of "original" paintings from the reign of Shah Abbas II, these large historical mural paintings can be dated through discursive (Sa'eb's panegyric and Chardin's descriptions, among others) and visual evidence (in paintings on paper), on stylistic and iconographic grounds, to the mid-seventeenth century, when the Chehel Sotun was completed. To this evidence we can also add a tinted drawing in the Museum Rietberg in Zürich, which is dated and signed by the celebrated late seventeenth-century painter Shaykh Abbasi.[96] The painting, an enthusiastic rendition inspired by one of the feasting scenes at the

Chehel Sotun, records an image in the style not of an eighteenth-century copyist but of an admired and emulated contemporary painter whose work still graces the wall of the audience hall in the Chehel Sotun.

It is likely that work on the Chehel Sotun lasted into the early 1650s; its extensive program of mural paintings makes iconographic references to events related to the conquest of Qandahar by Shah Abbas II.[97] Even before its wall decorations were finished, an ambassadorial reception was held in the building, and thereafter it continued to serve as one of the principal sites for feast-audiences of succeeding shahs, as witnessed in the Carmelite passage quoted above.[98] Its centrality is, furthermore, visible in the choice of the Chehel Sotun for the second coronation in 1668 of Shah Solayman, who began his reign as Shah Safi II in 1666 with a coronation ceremony at the Talar-e Tavile but then fell into a two-year period of personal illness, earthquakes, famines, and severe inflation.[99] The second coronation was intended to break the grip of the ill omen and to usher in a new, cleansed beginning, and the Chehel Sotun provided the only other suitably large space for such an auspicious event. The continued importance of the Chehel Sotun may also be gleaned from the fact that when fire broke out in 1706, Shah Soltan Hossayn ordered repairs to the building that restored its original *talar*. The shah and his grandees were "at a sumptuous supper" in the *talar* when the fire, in all likelihood started by the candlesticks and torches that provided illumination during such night banquets, probably ignited the carpets and cushions and then set the columns aflame. Although Tadeusz Krusinski, the Polish Jesuit priest resident in Iran from 1707 to 1725, says that Shah Soltan Hossayn let the fire burn itself out, presumably on some religious ground, it is nevertheless clear that the *talar* was the site of great festivities through the remainder of its life in Safavid Isfahan.[100]

Like all the other ceremonial palaces in the Daulatkhane of Isfahan, the Chehel Sotun was conceived as a massive building with varied and interrelated ceremonial functions. In scale, both actual and conceptual, it far surpassed its counterparts in the sheltered imperial stages of the Gate of Felicity at the Ottoman Topkapı or the Diwan-i Amm at the Mughal Red Forts. As the largest of the micro-palaces of the macro-palace of the Daulatkhane in Isfahan, the Chehel Sotun served as the principal site for ambassadorial receptions, audiences, feasts, and at least one coronation throughout the remainder of the Safavid dominion. Its centrality in crafting and disseminating a Safavid imperial identity is discernible not only in its seventeenth-century role within the life of the Daulatkhane, the capital city, and the empire at large, but also through the reverberations of its architectural, artistic, and ceremonial programs in the visual production of the succeeding dynasties and especially that of the nineteenth-century Qajars.[101]

Paradise contained: the Palace of Hasht Behesht or Eight Paradises

In Kaempfer's words about the Hasht Behesht, "we must say that one has to have a hundred eyes to be able to grasp the incomparable variety of excellences and luxuries of this palace."[102] As Kaempfer's conclusion to his description of the Hasht Behesht Palace suggests, this was an exceptionally elegant and impressive building (Figures 3.7, 4.1, 5.18 and 5.4 E). Chardin deemed its recesses and alcoves to be "more cheerful and pleasant than our [European] most lavish palaces."[103] The Hasht Behesht became one of the most famous of Safavid monuments and one of the most admired of all the palaces in Isfahan largely because of its perfectly cogent and transparently legible architectural composition, for its intimacy of scale and refinement of decoration, and for its superb landscaping.[104]

Following the pattern of palace building set by his predecessors, Shah Solayman embarked on the construction of a new palace soon after he assumed the throne in 1666. The Hasht Behesht was completed in 1669, a year after his second coronation. Many of the details

Figure 5.18 *Isfahan, Hasht Behesht Palace.*
This palace was constructed for Shah Solayman in 1669 in a harem garden of the Daulatkhane, famed as Bagh-e Bolbol (The Garden of the Nightingale), just where its water channels intersected. The building's perfect *hasht-behesht* plan (Figure 5.4 E) is the most famous and sole survivor of a common architectural practice in the fifteenth and sixteenth centuries: to name a *hasht-behesht* palace a Hasht Behesht!

of the early years of Shah Solayman's reign come from Chardin's *Le Couronnement De Soleïmaan*, published in 1671.[105] Chardin's account is indispensable for his descriptions of events, people, and places, but it should also be read with caution. Despite his long and repeated sojourns in Isfahan, his extensive travels within Safavid domains, his undisguised appreciation for Isfahan, and his enthusiastic observations of local customs and norms, Chardin remained a true product of the discourse of European superiority. As he stated, his accounts were not simply chronicles of the Safavid world but were also meant to illuminate the difference between Louis XIV, "the greatest King in the world," and "the superb arrogance of the Persian Kings."[106] To further underscore the differences, Chardin and others inform us that in order to reverse what was deemed to have been an infelicitous omen caused by the conjunction of the stars, the second coronation of Solayman was fixed at a propitious moment by the court astrologers.[107] The recoronation and renaming of the shah in 1668 at the Chehel Sotun was followed by the appearance of Halley's great comet, which, according to Chardin, further exacerbated the fears of more calamities to come. Nevertheless, the reign of Shah Solayman was largely peaceful and not as devoid of cultural interest or economic vitality as has been generally assumed.[108]

Shah Solayman's new palace was constructed not in the birun or public zone of the Daulatkhane but in the vast garden area located in the andarun (private) area associated with the harem apartments (Figures 3.7 and 4.1). As such, the Hasht Behesht manifests in both its location and its architectural and decorative strategies the priorities of a more private function than the feasting rituals and ceremonial events held at the Talar-e Tavile or the Chehel Sotun.[109] The broader implications of such a shift in palace design for the architectural representations of Safavid royal ideology will be discussed later. Suffice it here to note that while the *talar* palaces continued to serve for audiences and occasional ceremonial functions, the frequency and scale of the rituals of conviviality, the feastings, declined in the reigns of Shah Solayman and his successor. The choice of a *hasht-behesht* type of palace over a *talar* variety signals a transformation in the way Safavid royal authority was staged. Nevertheless, and while the Hasht Behesht as a palace denotes its functional significance as a place of courtly leisure, the edifice's historical and architectural particularities do not warrant its dismissal as "an ornamental masterpiece of colourful extravagance and decorative indulgence appealing to the superficial luxury, characteristic of the contemporary court."[110]

The Hasht Behesht was set at the center of the large and richly landscaped Bagh-e Bolbol, the Garden of the Nightingale, in the harem zone of the Daulatkhane. During the early phases of the development of the Daulatkhane, the Bagh-e Bolbol was among the garden-parks that filled the south side of the palace precinct. It was demarcated by the Chahar Bagh Promenade to its west, the Tent Garden or Bagh-e Khargah to its north, the Rose Garden or Golestan to its east, and the Mulberry Garden, Bagh-e Toot, to its south. Until the early 1990s, the remains of an arched gateway at the Chahar Bagh side of the Garden of the Nightingale preserved the memory of the spatial relationship between the palace–garden ensemble and the public promenade.[111]

The landscaping, based on the chahar-bagh scheme (four-quadrant garden), drew universal admiration. Kaempfer notes that the building "is set in the middle of a vast and open space that is paved with square stone slabs, [with] a row of marble benches at regular intervals and a water channel [running] around [the building]."[112] He continues that

> from all sides of the garden, walkways, lined with beautiful banisters and plane trees on both sides, lead to the palace [at the center] . . . Rows of paved alleys that run from north to south intersect with delightful mini-gardens [beds] while the rows from east to west carry to the garden the water that comes from the subterranean source under the Chahar Bagh.

This water, Kaempfer says, "is used to fill the pool that is eleven feet in width and is built of square stones; duck and swans float on the surface of the pool."

As a type of building, the *hasht behesht*, essentially an octagon inscribed in a square, was based on a centralized nine-fold plan of two stories in elevation consisting of an open unit at the core with eight volumes (solid or hollow; massive piers or actual rooms) around it (Figures 5.4, 5.18, 5.19 and Plate 21). Associations of paradise with this type of building in the Persianate world contributed to the ubiquity of the plan in both funerary-commemorative and palatine traditions. In its funerary-commemorative genealogy, the mausoleums in Delhi (sixteenth-century Tomb of Homayun) and Agra (seventeenth-century Taj Mahal) mark the apogee of a tradition that harks back to the domed octagonal mausoleums in Iran and Central Asia – at Kharraqan (twelfth-century Seljuq), at Soltaniyye (fourteenth-century Ilkhanid), and at Samarqand (fifteenth-century Timurid).[113] Domes of increasing monumentality emblazoned onto the profile of such *hasht-behesht* mausoleums the paradisiacal connotations that were further reiterated by the buildings' *chahar-bagh* (four-quadrant) garden settings.[114]

In its palatine taxonomy, several *hasht-behesht* palaces precede the one in Isfahan in both their architectural configuration and, in at least one case, in its proper name (Figure 5.4). Ruy Gonzalez de Clavijo, the Spanish envoy to the court of Timur in 1404, described a square pavilion at the center of the Bagh-e Nau (the New Garden) in the outskirts of Samarqand that seems to have resembled a *hasht-behesht* type of building.[115] Also near Samarqand, in the foothills of

Figure 5.19 *Isfahan, Hasht Behesht Palace.*
Interior after an engraving from the *Atlas* volume of Chardin's, *Voyages*
(1811). Notwithstanding the artist's unnaturally elongated impression of
the building, he conveys why Chardin deemed its recesses and alcoves to
have been "more cheerful and pleasant than our [European] most lavish
palaces."

Kuhak where the famous observatory of Ulugh Beg was constructed
in 1420, there was a garden called Bagh-e Maydan at the center of
which was located the pavilion known as Chil Sutun (Chehel Sotun)
for its multiple pillars.[116] Babur describes the edifice as "a superb
building" at the center of the garden that was "two stories high with
columns of stone," which lined the upper story in one row to create
a portico on each of its four sides. In the middle of the building, Babur
continues, is "a *chardara*," a "four-door," which indicates "a roofed
or domed pavilion open on all four sides."[117] Despite its designation
as a Chehel Sotun, which in Central Asiatic terms is justified by the
row of columns of the pillared portico, the actual shape of the building was not like the Chehel Sotun or other *talar* palaces in Isfahan
but closely related to the *hasht-behesht* pavilion form. In this regard,
the fifteenth-century Samarqand Chil Sutun constitutes the architectural ancestry of the sixteenth-century Chehel Sotun in Qazvin.
Both are *hasht-behesht* (nine-fold) in plan, and both had at least one
ring of columns (on the lower, upper, or both floors). The ubiquity of
the *hasht-behesht* type is evidenced in the countless representations of such octagonal pavilions in the miniature paintings of late
fifteenth- and sixteenth-century manuscripts, which, even though

cast in certain pictorial conventions, are remarkably consistent in the portrayal of this "favorite" pavilion type.

Most famous, however, was the Aqqoyunlu Palace of Hasht Behesht in Tabriz, completed in 888/1483 (Figure 2.1).[118] According to the anonymous Venetian merchant-traveler, that renowned Hasht Behesht too was situated at the center of a magnificent garden and was lavishly decorated, although it rose to only one story. With the conquest of Tabriz and the annexation of the Aqqoyunlu dominions into the new Safavid empire, Shah Isma'il I continued to use this most prominent of the palaces in his capital city of Tabriz. The recycling of old palaces, especially of conquered rulers, into the ceremonial spaces of a new dynasty was rare indeed. Yet, Shah Isma'il appropriated the Aqqoyunlu palace not solely as a symbol of victory over his fallen predecessor but as a palace, and more importantly a capital city, to which he could legitimately lay claim. After all, Isma'il was the grandson of the Aqqoyunlu Uzun Hasan and grew up in the courtly environment of Tabriz.

Nearly all of these Hasht Behesht and *hasht-behesht* style palaces have disappeared. The Qazvin Chehel Sotun, the Fin in Kashan, and the Hasht Behesht in Isfahan represent the only surviving examples of the palatine application of this long-established building type, with the latter representing the largest and most elaborately articulated specimen (Plate 3).[119] Two stories tall and raised on a 1.60 meter-high platform, the Hasht Behesht in Isfahan reads as a square (of about 10.30 meters per side) (Figure 5.18). Like a molded sculptural assembly of solids and voids, massive pylons and open porches alternate to make visible on the exterior the octagonal configuration of the interior spaces (Plates 22 and 23). This clarity of subdivisions is rigorously maintained on the ground level, where the nine units consist of a single large, central space with four openings on its cardinal points and four solids on the diagonals.

The multiplicity of rooms on the second floor, the balconied walkways that linked the sections of the upper floor, the two winding staircases, and the rich variety in which the rooms were articulated moved Chardin to say:

> A hundred of the most delightful little places were set up and arranged in a false light, but sufficiently clear for what is essential for pleasure and for which these places are designed. None of them resembled each other either in form, architecture, decoration or size. Everywhere is something different and new: in one are fire places, in others basins with fountains which can be turned on by pipes let in to the columns. This marvellous salon was a real labyrinth, as one loses oneself almost everywhere, and the stairs were so hidden that they were not easily recognizable. The base up to ten feet high was covered all round in jasper (Figure 5.20 and Plate 23).[120]

Figure 5.20 *Isfahan, Hasht Behesht Palace.*
This view of the small south porch on the back of the palace records the presence of a waterfall that poured into the small pool below; from the interior side of this very pier, flames would have risen from a fireplace. This sensualization of architectural space made the Hasht Behesht that perfect palace of private courtly leisure so at odds with the earlier, ceremonially-charged *talar* palaces.

Although in principle a centrally planned structure, the building rests on a main north-south axis. The chief outwardly oriented space of the Hasht Behesht faces north and is delineated as a wide and deep porch with two slender pillars at its opening and a shallow pool at its center (Plate 22). On the opposite side, the porch shrinks considerably to make space for larger flanking rooms on the south side of the building, while at the same time accommodating a waterfall that rises nearly to the full height of the inner two stories on its exterior and pours into a small but deep pool (Figure 5.20).[121] This tall water unit is paired on its back – that is, its interior face – with a chimney chute that serves as a fireplace on the interior side of the little pool.

The sensory experience of architecture in this building – so intensely choreographed in the fire-water juxtaposition of the waterfall and chimney – extends to the entire structure and its dialogue with its surroundings. Internally, the building is anchored on the great octagonal space that tapers as it rises into a magnificent mirror-faceted lantern at the very center of the inner building (Plate 23). This lantern casts beams of refracted light back onto the inner core, where the fountain(s) in the shallow rectangular pool just below countered the play of light through rippling effects of delicately carved marble patterns underneath the water surface.

The two stairwells, so carefully tucked into the southeastern and northwestern pylons that they disappeared from sight, as Chardin commented, reached to the more labyrinthine second story. Rooms of various sizes and decorations on this floor were clustered at the corners and linked by way of balconied walkways. Chardin describes the marvel of this second floor:

> The banisters are made of gilded wood, the frames of silver and the panes are of crystal or fine glass of all colours. The decoration is magnificent, unsurpassed. It is coloured only in gold or blue. As for the paintings many of them are full of scenes of enjoyment and nudity, which have an abundance of astounding beauty and animation, with crystal mirrors here and there. Little chambers have mirrors on the walls and in the domes. The furnishings of each place are the most magnificent and sensual in the world. There are niches with only a single bed. Oriental beds are set on the ground without curtains. There were many plaques on which voluptuous verses or moral sayings were written.[122]

As is clear from Chardin's description, the sensuality of the volumetric alternating of solids and voids within the structure of the Hasht Behesht itself was contrasted with the rich surface articulation through murals, perforated woodwork, and prismatic mirrors. The allusions to themes of paradise in the interior decoration are also dominant on the exterior façade, where extensive tile-work on the spandrels of the arched niches represents scenes of leisure and hunt, and assemblages of birds and flowers.[123]

The rhythm of alternating solids and voids, as read on the building's exterior, depends on the remarkable system of stacking pointed-arch niches in rows to tie the building together. These perforated niches and their tiled spandrels act as belts that pull the projecting and receding surfaces of the pylons and the porches into a unified whole. Equally significant in harmonizing the building is the judicious use of tall and slender wooden pillars. Their appearance in pairs at the opening of three of the porches – the principal one on the north, the west one facing towards the Chahar Bagh entrance into the gardens, and the east one facing the great pool – recalls through mimesis the great ceremonial spaces of the *talar* at the palaces of Talar-e Tavile, the Ali Qapu, and the Chehel Sotun. But unlike the ceremonial palaces at the Daulatkhane of Isfahan, the Hasht Behesht was conceived and articulated in every respect – its garden site, architectural specificities, and decorative strategies – to serve a different purpose. As its siting, landscaping, architecture, and decoration indicate, its intended uses ranged from housing the most intimate of harem gatherings to accommodating the entertainment of select guests, but it could not meet the ceremonial needs better served at the palaces in the birun/public zone of the Daulatkhane.

In its architectural nomenclature, as much as its proper name, the Hasht Behesht embodied the Persianate concept of palace-paradise. As such it occupied the center of what was self-consciously composed as a paradisiacal setting – the intersecting of channels of running water with long marches of stately plane trees, the fountains and the pools that attracted resident birds, the planted beds filled with flowers and ornamental bushes. These delights were to be enjoyed from the marble benches around the building of the Eight Paradises or in leisurely strolls down those rows upon rows of tree-lined alleys.

The construction of this building in Isfahan further exemplifies the lasting significance of that most commonly utilized architectural configuration of Persianate palace types, the *hasht-behesht* plan. In its revival here, it also marks a departure from what had become the Safavid practice in which each shah, up until the reign of Shah Solayman, had constructed at least one new ceremonial palace. The reversion to the sixteenth-century, and even earlier, practice of building a *hasht behesht* to serve multiple functions coincides with and accommodates a shift in Safavid ceremonials of kingship as the shahs became increasingly isolated and removed from public performances, especially feasts and audiences. Moreover, the convergence of energies back into the inner court and royal retreats may also be retraced in the fact that many royal commissions for painting during Shah Solayman's reign are attributed, in their dedicatory inscriptions, to the city of Ashraf in Mazandaran, indicating a revivification of the mobility of the court commensurate with the re-emergence of the *hasht-behesht* pavilion design.[124] The age of *talar*s had ended.

This significant absence of the architectural adaptation of accessibility and the processional conduct of proximity in the *hasht-behesht* types of palace-pavilions contrasts sharply with those features that distinguished the primary "façade" of the *talar* palaces. The point here is not simply the diagnostic typologies of palaces. Rather, the fact that the *hasht-behesht* pavilions are so decidedly unconcerned with public display of accessibility heightens the different social and political motivations that mediated the Ali Qapu Palace-Gateway and the *talar* palaces in the Daulatkhane. Even more removed were the suburban palaces that followed Shah Solayman's reign.

Moving away from the city: palaces and gardens of Shah Soltan Hossayn

By 1722, Shah Soltan Hossayn, then twenty-eight years into his reign, had earned a reputation, at least among some European observers, for his peaceful and moderate nature and his deep devotion to religious orthodoxy. Others, however, viewed the shah's pacifism as an expression of his indolence and cowardly disposition. Contemporary views also point out the paradoxical contrast between the shah's bigoted religiosity and his lavish taste for personal pleasure. Jan Oets, the last director of the Dutch East India Company (the *Vereenigde Oostindische Compagnie*, VOC) in Safavid Iran, thought that the king was "a great squandermaniac and lover of building and demolishing mansions and pleasure-gardens."[125] This was, in Oets's words, "about the only thing he occupies himself with."[126] Oets's comment is especially intriguing in that he associates the shah's preoccupation with mansions and pleasure gardens not only with their building but also with their destruction. What did the last Safavid shah build, destroy, replace, change, assimilate, or appropriate; and why?

Apart from his most famous and truly grandiose madrasa opening onto the Chahar Bagh Promenade and its adjoining caravanserai and bazaar in Isfahan, we know little about palace projects during the reign of Shah Soltan Hossayn (Figure 3.7 and Plate 4).[127] Nevertheless, and taking into account discrepancies among sources, the shah probably did devote a handsome portion of the royal building resources to the construction of the Farahabad palatial ensemble, the place where he handed his crown, throne, and empire to the Afghan tribal chief, a subject to which we shall turn in the last chapter of this book.[128] As with all Isfahan royal retreats, the complete destruction of the physical evidence and the paucity of information makes it impossible to reconstruct Farahabad at this point.[129] Yet the few sketchy references in contemporary sources allow us, at least, to observe that it was located on the lower, eastern slopes of the Soffe Mountain, and that it was conceived as a garden retreat at the farthest distance from the city of all the seventeenth-century Safavid suburban and extra-urban royal palace-gardens.

Its predecessors, the Sa'adatabad (The Abode of Felicity) ensemble of Shah Abbas II (1642–66) and the Abbasabad (The Abode of Abbas), also known as the Hezar Jarib (Thousand Acres) gardens of Shah Abbas I (1588–1629) remained functionally and formally integrated into the urban landscape (Figures 3.3, 3.1, 3.2, 3.7 and 3.8). Shah Abbas I's Abbasabad or Hezar Jarib garden-palace was built near the foot of the Soffe Mountain to mark the conclusion of the great promenade of the Chahar Bagh, the principal artery that served to connect the new urban functions clustered around the Maydan to the residential quarters and satellite centers of Isfahan, to provide the women of the royal harem a playground, as well as to constitute a place of public leisure in the city. The entertainment and leisure value of the Chahar Bagh Promenade, together with the famed terraced gardening scheme of the Hezar Jarib (or Abbasabad), lent the palatial retreat the twin distinction of being a suburban palace while remaining within the purview of royal spaces of the capital city.

Furthermore, the emblematic and functional network between the garden-palace retreat of Abbasabad and the royal city center both granted and gained significance when the name Abbasabad was also given to the quarter on the southwestern corner of the Chahar Bagh Promenade where it connects with the north bank of the Zayande River. This was the residential quarter built to house the merchants relocated from Tabriz (the wealthy families from the center of the frontier province of Azerbaijan). The new housing development was begun in 1611 on the orders of Shah Abbas I by Mohebb Ali Beg Lale, the chief of the royal *gholam*s and the principal supervisor of royal building projects in Isfahan (*sarkar-e emarat-e khasse-ye sharife-ye Sifahan*).[130] Built soon after the construction of its namesake suburban palace-garden, and also considered a suburban residential quarter because of its location, the Abbasabad neighborhood spread north of the river and to the west of the great avenue in a stretch that is popularly known (in both historical sources and modern times) as the Lower Chahar Bagh or *Chahar Bagh-e payin*.

The two Abbasabads in the urban topography of Isfahan represent two important latitudinal spheres of authority in an interactive series of concentric circles that bring together politics, religion, and commerce, the inseparable elements constituting the Safavid symbolics of power in Isfahan. With the Abbasabad extra-urban garden-palace and the Abbasabad suburban residential quarter, the urban topography, once again, makes visible the conceptual and practical relationships between the center and periphery, between the ruler and the ruled, or the capital and the empire.

Developments along the western side of the Zayande River were the crowning jewels of Shah Abbas II's urban building campaign.

Figure 5.21 *Isfahan, Khwaju Bridge (1651/2).*
Shah Abbas II sponsored a promenade, bridge, and palace retreat to the southeast of the city. The Khwaju Bridge was the centerpiece of the project as well as the principal artery in this part of the city, linking the new Chahar Bagh-e Khwaju to the suburban retreat of Sa'adatabad.

Inspired by his grandfather's urban–suburban scheme, Shah Abbas II sponsored a promenade, bridge, and palace retreat. The Khwaju Bridge (1651/2) appears to have been the centerpiece of the project as well as the principal artery in this part of the city (Figures 3.7 and 5.21). As was the case with the Allah Verdi Khan Bridge, this bridge linked a promenade, called Chahar Bagh-e Khwaju, to a suburban retreat, the Sa'adatabad. In several of the contemporary sources, the Khwaju Bridge is also known as the Hasanabad Bridge, so named after the neighborhood just north of the river. This bridge also linked newly developed residential quarters (*mahalle*) to the palace retreat of Sa'adatabad (Abode of Felicity), a formula we have seen in the initial phases of urbanism in Isfahan.

The mid-century Sa'adatabad stretched along the southern shore of the Zayande River between the two bridges of Ju'i and Khwaju, both also built by Shah Abbas II (Figures 3.7, 3.8 and 5.22).[131] This royal retreat included several new pavilions that were collectively known as the Haft Dast (Seven Buildings), and that included the Ayenekhane Palace of Shah Safi I (c. 1630s), an octagonal pavilion of indeterminate date famed as Namakdan (Salt Cellar), and other buildings.[132] The so-called Daryache Garden (Lake Garden) stood directly across the river on the northern bank, along with other royal gardens. These two gardens formed one axis that was intersected by the river as a second axis, forming a veritable *chahar bagh*, a cross-axial, four-quadrant

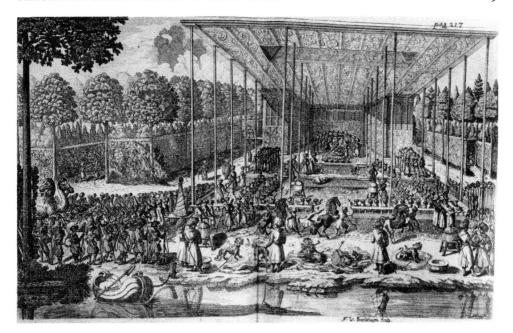

Figure 5.22 *Isfahan, Sa'adatabad palace, engraving after Kaempfer*, Amoenitatum *(1712)*.
The ceremonial event at the *talar* of this structure, with the parade of the diplomatic gifts
of exotic animals along the riverbank, makes this an especially good visual indication of
the range of convivial rituals that were accommodated by the *talar* palaces.

garden. Sa'adatabad, thus linked with the central zones of the city
through the bridges, through the formal dialogue across the river, and
through the analogy of a *chahar-bagh* scheme, became an accessible
suburban pleasance, both literally and figuratively.

In contrast to Abbas II's Sa'adatabad and Abbas I's Abbasabad/Hezar
Jarib, where the royal retreats were formally and functionally interwoven into the fabric of the city, Shah Soltan Hossayn's Farahabad was
only tangentially linked to older arteries and was so far from the city
that it fostered the development of its own surrounding settlement.[133]
Its isolation and distance from cosmopolitan Isfahan accommodated
the shah's reclusive habits. And in contrast to the urban consciousness
of the palace construction projects of his forebears in Isfahan, Shah
Soltan Hossayn appears to have focused his palatine campaign on a
cluster of "playhouses," pavilions of dainty scale and delicate disposition planted in the midst of pleasure gardens in Farahabad.

The new royal madrasa, the Madrese-ye Jadid-e Soltani (also
known as the Chahar Bagh Madrasa and the Madrese-ye Madar-e
Shah) – ordered in 1116/1704/5, near completion in 1118/1706/7, and
occupied in 1122/1710 – was ceremonially opened on 10 Rajab 1122
(6 September 1710).[134] A year later, the shah visited the newly developed garden of Farahabad and soon after, in Ramadan 1123 (October
1711), ordered the construction of a palace (*emarat*) on the site.[135] The

magnificent madrasa, an apt representation of the emphasis on orthodox teaching of Imami Shi'ism during the reign of Shah Soltan
Hossayn, seems to have served as the ideological anchor of royal
authority comparable to Shah Abbas the Great's congregational
mosque on the south side of the Maydan-e Naqsh-e Jahan. Similarly
deliberate in political alignment with the past is the conception of
Farahabad.

Despite his apparent detachment from the city and his apathy
toward personal involvement in governance, Shah Soltan Hossayn
and his advisors must have also been acutely aware of the social and
political memories that his new garden-palace would conjure. First of
all, his new royal city-retreat recalled the Farahabad in Mazandaran
that Shah Abbas the Great had ordered built in 1611/12. More tangi-
bly, however, his command for the development of the royal precinct
at Farahabad took into account the necessity of engaging the upper
strata of the realm. His illustrious forebear Shah Abbas the Great had
required the participation of the elite in the early seventeenth-
century development of the new suburban settlements along the
Chahar Bagh Promenade. Those whose prominence was deemed
symbolically revealing of the structure of power in Shah Abbas's
capital and court, especially the *gholam* or slave elite, were granted
land upon which they were required to build garden-mansions and
gateways according to a given architectural canon.[136]

Whereas Shah Abbas the Great's circle of power pivoted on the
slave elite of the household, that of Shah Soltan Hossayn was predicated upon his extreme religiosity and his reliance on the *ulama* (religious doctors) to maintain his base of power. A telling example of the
intensity of Shah Soltan Hossayn's relationship with and dependence
on the *ulama* comes from a royal donation made in 1708–9 in
Mashhad.[137] In this instance, the shah outperformed his predecessors
by extending his patronage of the holy city and its clergy-custodians
of the shrine of Imam Reza to include some of the property of the
daulatkhane at Mashhad. While all Safavid shahs had extravagantly
donated to the shrine complex and made endowments (*waqf*) of a
variety of income-producing properties, none, as far as I know, had
authorized the leasing of land in the royal precinct, the privileged site
of imperial power.

At Farahabad in Isfahan, these relationships are made more tangible. Among the royal confidants (*moqqareban*) required to purchase
land and build a garden-mansion was Amir Mohammad Baqer
Khatunabadi, one of the most learned of the *ulama* and the dean of
the new royal madrasa of Chahar Bagh. The great doctor of theology
suppressed his discontent and succumbed to the shah's order. On its
own, such acquiescence underscores the exceptional circumstances of
rule that colored the reign of Shah Soltan Hossayn whereby the clergy
wielded enormous power and remained at the core of the circle of
authority. Farahabad imparted a picture of authority not dissimilar to

that of Shah Abbas the Great in its coercion of loyalty through architectural engagement and through urban patterns of development. This, however, was different in that the aloofness of the shah was made all the more visible by the way his new royal precinct retreated farther away from the traditional Safavid center of power, both geographically and metaphorically.

Whatever may have guided the internal composition of Farahabad, it is probably reasonable to assume that architecture here was not used to emphasize ritually charged spaces as had been the case with the vast and open audience halls and banqueting spaces of the *talar* palaces built earlier in Isfahan. The politics of governance as defined and practiced in the time since Isfahan had become the capital of the empire held little sway for Shah Soltan Hossayn. This shah was much criticized by contemporary observers and later historians for relinquishing the reins of state into the hands of the harem eunuchs from the inner sanctum of the household (*gholaman-e khwaje*) and the aristocracy of the clergy, the two-pronged power base that upheld the last two Safavid kings on the throne. The dynamics of power in this period need a great deal of further study and analysis.[138] Yet, with the shah apparently absent from nearly all affairs of the state, the household and the empire were represented by proxy through the agency of the eunuch *gholam*s and the *ulama*, thereby changing the structure of power and necessitating rituals of kingship different from those of the earlier Isfahani phase.

Rarely does one read in sources contemporary with Shah Soltan Hossayn of the kinds of royal gatherings performed in the capital of Isfahan that served publicly to represent Safavid authority. In retrospect, the decision to hold Shah Soltan Hossayn's coronation at the Ayenekhane, where the ceremonial gestures of investiture were performed exclusively by the Shaykh al-Islam of Isfahan, 'Allame Majlesi, presaged the shah's extreme religiosity, his aversion to politics, and his aloofness toward his capital city.[139]

Notwithstanding the significance of the suburban retreats to a fuller understanding of the range of palatine architectural works of this period, this consideration of the palatine retreats of Isfahan reinforces the impression of the important rebalancing of the dialectic of Safavid rule in the course of the seventeenth century. As is evident in the palace campaigns within the Daulatkhane, the urban–suburban dialogue also remained preoccupied with the architectural and spatial enunciations of the presence and hence authority of the king in the period spanning the reigns of Abbas I through Abbas II. In comparison, the reigns of Shah Solayman, increasingly, and Shah Soltan Hossayn, entirely, reconfigure the balance between the two sides of the dialogue: the former locates his "urban" palace of Hasht Behesht deep inside the harem zone, while the latter shifts attention to a new suburban enclave farther removed from the city. Neither ceases to utilize the enunciative powers of architecture. Rather, there is a shift from a dialogue between urban and suburban palaces to one that is set between an urban institution of religious teaching and a suburban palace.

In fact, by the second decade of Shah Soltan Hossayn's reign, the traditional Safavid fabric of governance had unraveled to such a point that the capital was temporarily transferred from Isfahan back to Qazvin for a period in 1717–18.[140] The pretext was to assemble troops to battle grave challenges rising throughout the land: Afghan tribal revolts and efforts to secede from the empire, Russian attacks on the southwestern coast of the Caspian Sea, Kurdish skirmishes in the west, and unrest instigated by the Imam of Oman in the Persian Gulf. Such a scheme, even if temporary, would have been unthinkable in the time of Shah Abbas the Great, Shah Safi I, Shah Abbas II and Shah Solayman. Granted, Shah Abbas the Great did indeed spend a great deal of his reign away from Isfahan either on military campaign or in leisure retreat.[141] In many such instances, especially hunting expeditions and summer or *yaylaq* temporary relocations, he took the court along as well. Nevertheless, the task of centering the empire, which was most effectively engineered and implemented under his direction, presumed the permanence of a capital city. Isfahan, unlike any other Persian city of rule before the seventeenth century – but resembling Paris and Istanbul in this early modern age – was purposefully molded to perform as the singular center of rule through its spatial, architectural, functional, and symbolic components of urban life.

During the first decades of the seventeenth century, the peripatetic existence became increasingly archaic as the centralizing agenda – in the making since at least the middle of the sixteenth century – crystallized in the restructuring of the household, the government, and the empire at large, as Isfahan's royal precinct developed into a livable environment for kings and the performance of kingship, and as Isfahan's urban scheme assumed its full measure as a capital city. The waning of the itinerant practice of rule coincided, at least temporarily, with the resolution of major territorial struggles, especially in terms of external threats to Safavid lands, but also to some extent with regard to internal challenges to Safavid authority; much of this was initiated and accomplished by Abbas I before his death in 1629 and consolidated thereafter by shahs Safi I and Abbas II. The mobility in the period of Shah Abbas the Great represents the last vestiges of the old Turco-Mongolian habits that by the early seventeenth century were well along in the process of transition from an itinerant household, court, and government apparatus to an urban form of kingship ensconced in a permanent capital city.

The palaces built over the course of the seventeenth century in Isfahan serve as the architectural and urban correlatives of the shifting paradigms of kingship. The *hasht-behesht* buildings, those one-shape-fits-all-functions palaces associated with the earlier capitals of the Safavids and with their Aqqoyunlu and Timurid predecessors,

ceased to serve the needs of a centralized polity that deployed aggrandized rituals of feasting to articulate the charisma of kingship
through studied proximity to and conviviality with the shahs. *Talar*
palaces both represented and accommodated those ritual practices as
they fully enunciated the Perso-Shi'i performance of kingship in the
period after Shah Abbas the Great. The addition of the *talar* to the Ali
Qapu was an especially revealing signifier of these changes. The *talar*
clinched the building's functionality as the most publicly visible site
for such ceremonials. It also helps us to conceptually bridge between
the gateway and the palace by transitioning from royal accessibility,
so central a point in the urban design of Isfahan and the opening links
between the Daulatkhane and the city, to royal hospitality and rituals
of conviviality, the key to understanding the architectural implications of the ceremonial shifts. Considerations of the royal retreats in
Mazandaran and in the outskirts of Isfahan further underscore the difference in representations of authority between the palaces in urban
versus suburban, capital versus peripheral, arenas of Safavid political
culture. And finally, it is in both design and landscaping that the specialized *talar* palaces of Isfahan – the Talar-e Tavile, Ayenekhane, and
Chehel Sotun – demonstrate the realization of the Safavid phenomenon I have called the architecture of conviviality.

Notes

1. Vali Qoli Shamlu, *Qesas al-khaqani* (British Library, London, Add.
   7656): fol. 280. Saru Taqi's life and career has been discussed by Willem
   Floor, "The Rise and Fall of Mirza Taqi, the Eunuch Grand Vizier
   (1043–1055/1633–1645)," *Studia Iranica* 26 (1997): 237–66. For Saru
   Taqi's patronage and its political agency, see Babaie, "Launching from
   Isfahan," 97–108.
2. A preliminary consideration of the *talar* as a distinctive architectural
   form is found in Babaie, "Safavid Palaces in Isfahan," esp. 245–54.
3. Arthur U. Pope, "Isfahan Palaces," in *A Survey of Persian Art*, ed. Arthur
   U. Pope and Phyllis Ackerman, new edn (Tokyo and London: Oxford
   University Press, 1964–5), 2:1192; Ingeborg Luschey-Schmeisser, "Čehel
   Sotūn," *Encyclopaedia Iranica*, (1988), 113; Galdieri, *Esfahan, Ali Qapu*,
   28 and Hillenbrand, "Safavid Architecture," 797.
4. See Abbas Amanat, *Resurrection and Renewal; the Making of the Babi
   Movement in Iran, 1844–1850* (Ithaca and London: Cornell University
   Press, 1989).
5. No specialist in the fields of Islamicate or Persianate architecture has
   ever connected the particularity of the *talar* to a specific time, place
   and cultural matrix, as will be discussed here.
6. Khwajegi Esfahani, *Kholasat al-siyyar*, 245. Another Talar-e Tavile is
   also referenced by Khwajegi Esfahani to have existed near the Zayande
   River and was presumably associated with royal stables of the suburban palace area; ibid., 249. Floor is probably right to conclude that this
   and another such reference (in *Zayl-e alam ara-ye Abbasi*) were mis-
   takes by the authors; Floor, "The Talar-i Tavila," 151 and fn. 17.

7. Mohammad Yusof Movarrekh, *Khold-e Barin* (British Library, London, Or. 4132), fol. 209.
8. *Rostamname-ye tarikh-e Bizhan*, fol. 77r. This manuscript was copied in 1693.
9. Floor, "The Talar-i Tavila," 150–1, and his important assemblage of documents pertaining to the uses of this palace, 154–6.
10. Babaie, "Safavid Palaces in Isfahan," Appendix II, 311–12. For a recent and more comprehensive documentation of its history, see Floor, "The Talar-i Tavila," 149–63.
11. Jean Calmard, "Shi'i Rituals and Power II. The Consolidation of Safavid Shi'ism: Folklore and Popular Religion," in *Safavid Persia: The History and Politics of an Islamic Society*, ed. Charles Melville (London: I. B. Tauris, 1996), 139–90, esp. 164, 174–5, notes this event during the reign of Shah Solayman. Babayan, *Mystics, Monarchs and Messiahs*, 229, misreads this note and extends the use of the Talar-e Tavile for this purpose to the reign of Shah Abbas II as well, whose particular interest in directing the mourning rituals lasted the entire ten days and was carried out in the Maydan-e Naqsh-e Jahan. According to Calmard's translation of the chronicle of these events by De Montheron, a lay companion of the Carmelite mission in Isfahan, Shah Safi I held such an elaborate ceremony in the Maydan in 1641; see "Shi'i Rituals and Power," 173–4.
12. As his description of the garden and palace at the end of the road indicates, Chardin was using the walkway in relation to the Chehel Sotun and not to the Talar-e Tavile, as Floor has assumed; Floor, "Talar-i Tavila," 152. Nevertheless, this alley was used for access to both palaces.
13. Olearius, *The Voyages and Travels of the Ambassadors*, 201.
14. Similar parallels are found at the Topkapı's second court; Necipoğlu, *Architecture, Ceremonial and Power*, 53–75.
15. Olearius measured the *talar* area in front to be 48 × 72 feet; Chardin's measurements of the entire building are 26 × 104 feet. Such discrepancies do not detract from the basic impression one gets of the building as long and narrow.
16. Olearius, *The Voyages and Travels of the Ambassadors*, 202.
17. Floor, "The Talar-i Tavila," 152.
18. Tavernier, *The Six Voyages*, 178. Tavernier is describing the Talar-e Tavile and not the Chehel Sotun as some had concluded, for example, Luschey-Schmeisser, "Čehel Sotūn," 111.
19. The following passages are quoted from Floor, "The Talar-i Tavila," 152–3.
20. Quoted in Floor, "The Talar-i Tavila," 153.
21. See also Floor, "Talar-i Tavila," 153 for his summary, in part, of the building's descriptions.
22. Asef, *Rostam al-tavarikh*, 72–3, for his description of the Talar-e Tavile and the Chehel Sotun. Floor's reading of the passage on Talar-e Tavile – "It [Talar-e Tavile] is located next to the ʿAlī Qāpū palace and is built in the style of the *Chihil Sutūn*" – supports my argument but is not an accurate translation; Floor, "Talar-i Tavila," 158. Instead, the following analysis aims to situate the *"talar"* typology within a network of related architectural and cultural criteria.
23. Quoted by Honarfar, *Ganjine*, 576–8. See also Shamlu, *Qesas al-khaqani* (British Library, London, Add. 7656): fol. 16v; and Shamlu, Vali

Qoli, *Qesas al-khaqani*, ed. Hasan Sadat Naseri (Tehran: Vezarat-Farhang va Ershad-e Eslami, 1374/1995), 1:81.

24. Shamlu, *Qesas al-khaqani*, ed. Hasan Sadat Naseri, vol.1, xi–xii (yazdah-davazdah).

25. Honarfar, "Bagh-e Hezar Jarib," 73–94; Mahvash Alemi, "The Royal Gardens of the Safavid Period: Types and Models," in *Gardens in the Time of the Great Muslim Empires: Theory and Design*, ed. Attilio Petrucciolo (Leiden; New York; Köln: Brill, 1997), 72–96. See also Alemi's "Il giardino persiano: tipi e modelli," in *Il Giardino Islamico: architettura, natura, paesaggio*, ed. Attilio Petrucciolo (Milano: Electra, 1994), 39–62.

26. For a preliminary consideration of the mansions, see Babaie, "Launching from Isfahan," 87–8.

27. Honarfar, *Ganjine*, 576–8 where he also attributes, without evidence, the completion of the Ayenekhane to Shah Abbas II.

28. Khwajegi Esfahani, *Kholasat al-siyyar*, 295.

29. Coste, *Monuments modernes de la Perse*.

30. In addition to the poetic description by Mirza Mozaffar Torke noted above, Mirza Hossayn Khan Tahvildar, the nineteenth-century historian of Isfahan, also left a description of the building in which he emphasizes the mirrors and the overall grandeur of the building; Tahvildar, *Joghrafiya-ye Esfahan*, 27.

31. Little has been done on these royal cities in Mazandaran about which Eskandar Beg Monshi has quite a bit to say; Monshi, *Tarikh-e alam ara-ye Abbasi*, 849–51 and 855–6. For a few general and preliminary considerations see the following: Donald Wilber, *Persian Gardens and Garden Pavilions*, 2nd edn (Washington, DC: Dumbarton Oaks, 1979), 55–64; and his "The Institute's Survey of Persian Architecture; Preliminary Report of the 8th Season of the Survey," *Bulletin of the American Institute for Iranian Art and Archaeology* 5, no. 2 (December 1937): 109–36, esp. 114–21. See also the sections on Farahabad and Ashraf in the monumental work of Manuchehr Sotude on the Mazandaran and Gilan region: *Az Astara ta Astarabad* (Tehran: Vezarat-e Farhang va Ershad-e Eslami, 1366/1987), vol. 4, pt. 1, pp. 580–663.

32. Opinions vary as to whether the Safavid imperial machinery had a planned economy. All evidence seems to point in that direction but on the link between silk, the economy, and the politics of Safavid Iran, see Matthee, *The Politics of Trade in Safavid Iran*, and Baghdiantz-McCabe, *The Shah's Silk for Europe's Silver*, and her article, "Armenian Merchants and Slaves."

33. For the links between these urban-architectural projects and the politico-economic reforms, see also above, Chapter 3 of this book.

34. Charles Melville, "From Qars to Qandahar: The Itineraries of Shah 'Abbas I (995–1038/1587–1629)," in *Etudes Safavides*, ed. Jean Calmard (Paris–Tehran: Institut Français de Recherche en Iran, 1993), 195–224; for an analysis of the movements of the shahs and their relevance to the palaces and Isfahan, see Babaie, "Safavid Palaces in Isfahan," 308–10.

35. Babaie, "Safavid Palaces in Isfahan," 311–14. As far as I know, Shah Solayman and Shah Soltan Hossayn rarely left Isfahan, if at all, especially in the latter's case.

36. Wilber, *Persian Gardens and Garden Pavilions*, 55–64 and figures 39, 40, and 41. These important reconstructions, helpful as they are, remain tentative, at best. See also the study by Yves Porter, who utilizes

previously unpublished photographs; Porter "Les jardins d'Ashraf vus par Henry Viollet," in "Sites et monuments disparu d'apré les témoignes de voyageurs," *Res Orientales* 8 (1996): 117–38.

37. The following description is based on field research by the author.

38. Herbert, *Travels in Persia*, 154–5. There, Herbert also mentions "One John, a Dutchman (who had long served the king)," to have "celebrated his skill here to the admiration of the Persians and his own advantage." The evidence of wall paintings in Safavid Iran has been studied by Basil Gray, "The Tradition of Wall Painting in Iran," in *Highlights of Persian Art*, ed. R. Ettinghausen and E. Yarshater (Boulder, CO: Bibliotheca Persica, 1979), 312–29; Eleanore Sims, "Late Safavid Painting: The Chehel Sutun, The Armenian Houses, The Oil Paintings," in *Akten des VII. Internationalen Kongresses für Iranische Kunst und Archäologie* (Berlin: D. Reimer, 1979), 408–18. For the most recent consideration of the tradition of Safavid wall paintings see, Babaie, "Shah Abbas II, the Conquest of Qandahar."

39. Della Valle, *Viaggi di Pietro della Valle*, 637–8.

40. There is no reliably analytical or general study on the architectural traditions of the Caspian Sea area. A very important survey, however, is Sotude's *Az Astara ta Astarabad.*

41. Monshi, *Tarikh-e alam ara-ye Abbasi*, 849–50.

42. Monshi, *Tarikh-e alam ara-ye Abbasi*, 855–6.

43. Monshi, *Tarikh-e alam ara-ye Abbasi*, 945.

44. Mohammad Taher-e Vahid-e Qazvini, *Tarikh-e Vahid* (British Library, London, Or. 2940), fol. 277. This important history of the reign of Shah Abbas II was published, in part only, under the title of *'Abbasname* by Ebrahim Dehqan (Arak: Davudi Publishers, 1329/1951). More recently, Seyyed Sa'id Mir Mohammad Sadeq has expertly edited and annotated the complete manuscript and published it with a very useful introduction under the title, *Tarikh-e jahan-ara-ye Abbasi.* See Taher-e Vahid-e Qazvin, *Tarikh-e jahan-ara-ye Abbasi*, 692–3 for the Mian Kale preparations of buildings and the hunting grounds.

45. Della Valle, *Viaggi di Pietro della Valle*, 635–6.

46. Quoted in Sotude, *Az Astara ta Astarabad*, vol. 4, p. 616; on the mission's reception in Ashraf, see also Laurence Lockhart, "European Contacts with Persia, 1350–1736," in *The Cambridge History of Iran.* Vol. 6, *The Timurid and Safavid Periods*, ed. Peter Jackson. (Cambridge: Cambridge University Press, 1986), 373–411, especially 396.

47. This description is based on my own field research.

48. Taher-e Vahid-e Qazvini, *Tarikh-e jahan-ara-ye Abbasi*, 548–9. This may have been the same as the Homayun Tappe noted by Taher-e Vahid.

49. Herbert, *Travel in Persia*, 174.

50. Qasem b. Yusof Abu Nasri Haravi, *Ershad al-zira'a*, ed. Mohammad Moshiri (Tehran: Daneshgah-e Tehran, 1346/1967) is a manual of agriculture that provides, in its chapter 8, an outline of a standard Persianate *chahar bagh.* For an important study of this treatise, see Maria E. Subtelny, "Making a Case for Agriculture: the *Irshād al-Zirā'a* and its Role in the Political Economy of Early Safavid Iran," in *Proceedings of the Second European Conference of Iranian Studies held in Bamberg, 30th September to 4th October 1991 by the Societas Iranologica Europaea*, ed. Bert G. Fragner, et al. (Rome: Istituto Italiano per il Medio ed Estremo Oriente, 1995): 685–700; and her "Agriculture and the Timurid *Chahārbāgh*."

51. It is unfortunate that an important discovery, such as the sketches by Engelbert Kaempfer in the British Library, and its publication by Mahvash Alemi – "The Royal Gardens," and its Italian version, "Il giardino persiano" – have given credence to such an ahistorical typology by categorizing Safavid garden pavilions into formal groups without regard for the political and sociocultural parameters of patronage, production, or consumption. As noted in the introduction to this book, such essentializing methodologies and their resultant monolithic architectural continuum have characterized much of the study of Persianate and especially Safavid palaces.

52. These structures are scattered among remote villages tucked within the forests in Mazandaran. They tend to be hard to reach and, notwithstanding the local residents, remain largely unknown except to the local researchers and restorers of the Iranian Cultural Heritage Organization office in Sari, the provincial capital.

53. Ali Akbar Dehkhoda, *Loghatname*, new edn (Tehran: Tehran University Press, 1373/1994), 4:5499.

54. Some sources also refer to a river in Mazandaran called Talar; Taher-e Vahid-e Qazvini, *Tarikh-e jahan-ara-ye Abbasi*, 749.

55. Quoted in Sotude, *Az Astara ta Astarabad*, vol. 4, 339

56. Dehkhoda, *Loghatname*, 4:5499. On Suzani, see Jan Rypka, *History of Iranian Literature*, ed. Karl Jahn (Dordrecht, Holland: D. Reidel, 1968), 214–15.

57. In addition to Dehkhoda, see the following dictionaries: Hossayn ibn Hasan Inju Shirazi, *Farhang-e Jahangiri* (Mashhad: Daneshgah-e Mashhad, 1351/1972), 127; Mohammad Qasem Soruri, *Farhang-e majma' al-Fors* (Tehran: Elmi, 1338–41/1960–3), 1:249.

58. Fazl-Allah ibn Ruzbehan-e Khonji, *Mihmanname-ye Bokhara*, ed. M. Sotude (Tehran: Bongah-e Tarjomeh va Nashr-e Ketab, 2535/1976), 284.

59. While the Uzbek Shaybanids, who in fact inherited the Central Asian side of the Timurid world, have been largely ignored, this widely held perspective on the grip of Timurid common heritage has been especially damaging to scholarship on Safavid and Mughal cultural production. For the exceptional inclusion of the Uzbeks, see Sheila Blair and Jonathan Bloom, *The Art and Architecture of Islam 1250–1800* (New Haven and London: Yale University Press, Pelican History of Art, 1994), 199–211. For one example of the impact of selective "liberation" from the Timurid nomadic past on scholarship on the Safavids and Mughals, see Necipoğlu, "An Outline of Shifting Paradigms." In contrast, see Koch, "Diwan-i 'Amm and Chihil Sutun."

60. Babur, *The Baburnama*, 726–7

61. *Talargine* is in Babur's Chaqatay Turkic, the language of the *Baburname*, while Abd al-Rahim Khankhanan's late-sixteenth-century Persian translation of the emperor's memoir used the Persian diminutive form of *tālārak*.

62. In the Mughal context, most of these have been expertly analyzed by Koch in her article, "Diwan-i 'Amm and Chihil Sutun."

63. Koch, "Diwan-i 'Amm and Chihil Sutun," 143.

64. Koch, "Diwan-i 'Amm and Chihil Sutun," 147–9.

65. For a general consideration of the Sasanian Ctesiphon, see G. Hermann, "The Art of the Sasanians," in *The Arts of Persia*, ed. R. W. Ferrier (New Haven and London: Yale University Press, 1989), 61–79, esp. 75.

66. For the Cairene evocations in Mamluk architecture, see Bernard O'Kane, "Monumentality in Mamluk and Mongol Art and Architecture," *Art History* 19, no. 4 (1996): 499–522.
67. For a study of the architectural-patronage linkage between Saru Taqi in Mazandaran and in Isfahan, see Babaie, "Launching from Isfahan," 97–108. A preliminary version of this subject also appears in Sussan Babaie, "Building for the Shah: The Role of Mirza Muhammad Taqi (Saru Taqi) in Safavid Royal Patronage of Architecture," in *Safavid Art and Architecture*, ed. Sheila Canby (London: British Museum, 2002), 20–6. For a biographical account of Saru Taqi, see Floor, "The Rise and Fall of Mirza Taqi."
68. In addition to the references in the previous footnote, see Babayan, "The Safavid Household Reconfigured," 42–7.
69. Vali Qoli Shamlu, *Qesas al-khaqani*, edited by Hasan Sadat Naseri, 2 vols (Tehran: Vezarat-e Ershad-e Eslami, 1371/1992), 280.
70. For the significance of Saru Taqi's doubly charged status as a *gholam* and grand vizier and analysis of the terminology and syntax implied in the phrasing of Shamlu's reference and in the epigraphic programs of Saru Taqi's own foundations (his two mosques and a caravanserai among others), see Babaie, "Launching from Isfahan," 103–7.
71. See above and Babaie, "Safavid Palaces in Isfahan," 234–44.
72. Babaie, "Safavid Palaces in Isfahan," 245–53.
73. Galdieri, *Esfahan, 'Ali Qapu*, 28–9. See also Babaie, "Safavid Palaces in Isfahan," 107–16 for a summary and revision of Galdieri's conclusions.
74. Shamlu, *Qesas al-khaqani*, 299–306 on the events of Nadr Mohammad Khan's visit to Isfahan.
75. Shamlu, *Qesas al-khaqani*, 300–1; Taher-e Vahid-e Qazvini, *Tarikh-e jahan ara-ye Abbasi*, 425.
76. Sa'eb-e Tabrizi, *Kolliyyat-e Sa'eb-e Tabrizi*, ed. Amiri Firuzkuhi (Tehran: Khayyam, 1333/1954), 834–7. For the long panegyric in Persian and its paraphrased and provisional translation, see Babaie, "Safavid Palaces in Isfahan," 315 and 321–8.
77. Chardin, *Voyages du Chevalier Chardin*, vol. 5, 468–76.
78. Galdieri has argued that the audience hall with its two ayvans and two verandas constituted the original building the construction of which he attributed to the reign of Shah Abbas I. That initial structure was, according to Galdieri, orientated along its north–south axis. The refutation of that argument appears in Babaie, "Safavid Palaces in Isfahan," 152–8.
79. Soucek, "Solomon's Throne/Solomon's Bath;" Koch, "Diwan-i 'Amm and Chihil Sutun."
80. For example, see Chardin's description of the curtains at the Talar-e Tavile in his *Voyages du Chevalier Chardin*, vol. 7, 372 and vol. 9, 469–71.
81. For scale comparison, note the measurements of the well-trodden Sistine Chapel at 40.93 × 13.41 meters.
82. Babaie, "Shah Abbas II, the Conquest of Qandahar," for the mural decoration at the Chehel Sotun.
83. Mohammad Hasan Jaberi Ansari, *Tarikh-e Esfahan va Ray* (Isfahan: Hosayn Emamzade, 1322/1943), 346.
84. Tile panels flanking the fireplaces were removed long ago. A number of such tile panels – depicting men and women in scenes similar to those found on the smaller wall paintings above the dado level of the audience hall – are now in museums and private collections. See, for example, the tile panels at the Metropolitan Museum of Art in New York, discussed

and reproduced in Stefano Carboni and Tomoko Masuya, *Persian Tiles* (New York: Metropolitan Museum of Art, 1993), 40–1.

85. For an interpretation of the murals based on the political dimension of the banqueting scenes, see Babaie, "Shah Abbas II, the Conquest of Qandahar," 125–42.

86. A recent study of these Asian networks, with a consideration of the Safavid place in them, is offered by Muzaffar Alam and Sanjay Subrahmanyam, *Indo-Persian Travels in the Age of Discoveries, 1400–1800* (Cambridge: Cambridge University Press, 2007).

87. Chardin, *Voyages du Chevalier Chardin*, vol. 5, 468–70.

88. Olearius' description was for a reception at the Talar-e Tavile along the same alley behind the Ali Qapu as that used for the Chehel Sotun; Olearius, *The Voyages and Travels of the Ambassadors*, 201.

89. My current reading of the poems of Sa'eb differs from my provisional translation of the panegyric on the Chehel Sotun in Babaie, "Safavid Palaces in Isfahan," 321–8; see especially line #1 for this particular reference.

90. Paul Losensky's publications on Safavid poetry have recovered for this tradition, beleaguered by the "decadence and decline" paradigm for so long, its rightful place within the great literary pantheon of Persian poetry; see especially his *Welcoming Fighani: Imitation and Poetic Individuality in the Safavid-Mughal Ghazal* (Costa Mesa, CA: Mazda Publishers, 1998). For considerations of the Safavid "new style" in visual cultures, see Babaie, "Epigraphy iv. Safavid and Later Inscriptions," and Sussan Babaie, "The Sound of the Image/The Image of the Sound: Narrativity in Persian Art of the Seventeenth Century," in *Islamic Art and Literature*, eds. Oleg Grabar and Cynthia Robinson (Princeton: Marcus Wiener, 2001), 143–62.

91. Babaie, "Safavid Palaces in Isfahan," 321–8, lines #24 and 25 with modifications in translation made here.

92. For a survey of the scholarship up until the early 1990s, see Babaie, "Safavid Palaces in Isfahan," 151–62, with an account also of the Italian (IsMEO) campaign in the 1960s and 1970s of excavations and restorations. My revised building history is also found there.

93. This point is made by Blake, *Half the World*, 68–9. For the fire, see *A Chronicle of the Carmelites in Persia and the Papal Mission of the XVIIth and XVIIIth Centuries*, ed. H. Chick (London: Eyre and Spottiswoode, 1939), 1:473 and Father Judasz Tadeuz Krusinski, *The History of the Late Revolutions of Persia*, reprint edn (New York: Arno Press, 1973), 125–6.

94. Exactly as quoted in Blake; see previous footnote.

95. Paolo Mora, "La restauration des peintures murales de Čihil Sutūn," in *Travaux de restauration de monuments historiques en Iran*, ed. Giuseppe Zander (Rome: IsMEO, 1968), 323–8.

96. I wish to thank Axel Langer for this information. I have not seen the painting in person and cannot therefore be certain of its authenticity. Regardless, my argument here depends on more than one piece of evidence in painting.

97. Babaie, "Safavid Palaces in Isfahan," 151–62 for an analysis of the dating controversies; Babaie, "Shah Abbas II, the Conquest of Qandahar," 125–42, for the decorative scheme and its iconography.

98. In 1646/47 and soon after the completion of the building the ambassadors from Bukhara, Russia, and India were received at a reception in this new building; Shamlu, *Qesas al-khanqani*, 305.

99. Chardin's account of the coronation is in his *Le Couronnement De Soleïmaan Troisiéme Roy de Perse*, Paris, 1671. Roemer, "The Safavid Period," 304–10; Floor, "The Talar-i Tavila," 154. Rudi Matthee, "Politics and Trade in Late Safavid Iran: Commercial Crisis and Government Reaction under Shah Solayman (1666–1694)" (PhD Dissertation, University of California, Los Angeles, 1991), is still the only critical analysis of the history of Shah Solayman. Amy Landau's dissertation, "*Farangi-Sazi* at Isfahan: The Court Painter Muhammad Zaman, The Armenians of New Julfa and Shah Sulayman (1666–1694)," (PhD dissertation, University of Oxford, 2007), represents the first large-scale art-historical consideration of this period in Safavid visual culture.

100. Notwithstanding the uncritical assumption of "truth" in Krusinski's report in much of Safavid scholarship, the priest attributed the shah's decision to an unspecified religious conviction. The reputation of Shah Soltan Hossayn as an extremely superstitious man does not necessarily explain why such a decision may have been religiously informed.

101. The Qajar claim to legitimacy drew from Safavid patrimonial legacy, among other resources, in the visual culture and built environment of Isfahan and especially the Chehel Sotun. The murals in this palace were harvested extensively for images of kingship in portable luxury arts in the Qajar era. For a discussion of the Qajar appropriations of the Safavid iconography of kingship and the relevance of the murals at the Chehel Sotun to Qajar visual culture, see my article, "In the Eye of the Storm."

102. See Kaempfer, *Am Hofe*, 221; and 219–21 on his description of the Hasht Behesht and its Garden of the Nightingale.

103. Chardin, *Voyages du Chevalier Chardin*, vol. 8, 43; and translation quoted from Ferrier, *A Journey to Persia*, 150.

104. Among contemporaries, Chardin was the most admiring, Chardin, *Voyages du Chevalier Chardin*, vol. 8, 39–43; Kaempfer, *Amoenitatum Exoticarum*, 191–2. For modern considerations of the Hasht Behesht see, for example, Honarfar, *Ganjine*, 622–6; Mario Ferrante, "Le pavillon des Hašt Bihišt, ou les Huit Paradis, a Ispahan: Relevés et problèmes s'y rattachant," in *Travaux de restauration de monuments historiques en Iran*, ed. Giuseppe Zander (Rome: IsMEO, 1968), 399–420; and Hillenbrand, "Safavid Architecture," 804–5.

105. Quoted by Ferrier, *A Journey to Persia*, 1 and taken from Jean Chardin's preface to *Le Couronnement De Soleïmaan Troisiéme Roy de Perse*, (Paris, 1671), which was published as a separate account of the shah's second coronation (discussed below). *Le Couronnement* was intended for the finance minister, Jean-Baptiste Colbert, as part of a larger effort to inform the French in their trade policies with Muslim empires.

106. Ferrier's study of Chardin's journey and his book are gratefully used here, but it is also works such as his *A Journey to Persia* that remind us of the persistence of the Orientalist perspective into the present, as exemplified in his uncritical reading of Chardin's Franco-centric judgment on Safavid society and the Persians as points of fact.

107. For Chardin's account of Persian obsession with superstitions, see Chardin, *Voyages du Chevalier Chardin*, vol. 10, 84–97. For an anachronistic commentary on the relationship between the failures of the Safavid state and the superstitions of the Persians, see Ferrier, *A Journey to Persia*, 106–7.

108. Landau's dissertation, "*Farangi-Sazi* at Isfahan," represents a convincing alternative to the doom and gloom narrative of Solayman's reign. Her research into Persian, European, and most importantly, Armenian sources, has greatly advanced our knowledge of the cultural world of Safavid Isfahan in its last decades in the seventeenth century.

109. Revelries of a very private nature, with the shah and chosen beauties from his harem, are described in the early nineteenth-century *Rostam al-tavarikh*, a text that presents a new and remarkably modern literary genre and that awaits critical analysis and careful consideration as a cultural document. Nevertheless, its "stories" deserve attention for what they may tell us about the principal function of such pavilions as the Hasht Behesht as a place of leisure and not of the business of kingship.

110. Ferrier, *A Journey to Persia*, 150.

111. Unfortunately, I failed to photograph and study this gateway when I visited it for the first time in 1992, and it was destroyed by the time of my subsequent field research. One hopes, nevertheless, that some record of those remains has been kept at the archives of the Iranian Cultural Heritage Organization.

112. Kaempfer, *Amoenitatum Exoticarum*, 191–2.

113. The commemorative shrine of the Dome of the Rock in Jerusalem stands as the first monumental domed octagonal building to have been built for Muslim patrons (completed 691 CE). For the paradisiacal iconography of the dome, see Oleg Grabar, "From Dome of Heaven to Pleasure Dome," *Journal of the Society of Architectural Historians* No. 49 (1990): 15–21.

114. These have already been discussed in Chapter 2 above.

115. Clavijo, *Embassy to Tamerlane*; Golombek and Wilber, *The Timurid Architecture of Iran and Turan*, 176.

116. For Babur's brief description of this pavilion and its garden, see *The Baburnama*, 86 (fol. 47). For the Timurid pavilions and gardens around Samarqand, see *The Baburnama*, 83–6.

117. Wheeler Thackston gives this definition of the *chardara*; *The Baburnama*, 86, fn. 115.

118. See Chapter 2 for my discussion of the Tabriz Hasht Behesht.

119. Ferrante, "Le pavillon des Hašt Bihišt," 399–420.

120. For Chardin's description of the Hasht Behesht, see Chardin, *Voyages du Chevalier Chardin*, vol. 8, 39–43. This passage is translated and quoted in Ferrier, *A Journey to Persia*, 150.

121. Eugenio Galdieri has brilliantly, if preliminarily, addressed the agency of water in the architecture of Isfahan, a topic of considerable importance that has received little scholarly attention; Eugenio Galdieri, "L'acqua nell'antico aspetto di Isfahan attraverso le pitture parietali degli ultimi due secoli," in *Gururājamanjarikā: Studi in Onore di Giuseppe Tucci* (Naples: Istituto Universitario Orientale, 1974), 1–15.

122. This is translated and quoted in Ferrier, *A Journey to Persia*, 150–2.

123. The tilework at the Hasht Behesht has been studied, especially for its iconographic scheme, by Ingeborg Luschey-Schmeisser, *The Pictorial Tile Cycle of Hašt Bihišt in Isfahān and its Iconographic Tradition* (Rome: IsMEO, 1978).

124. I thank Dr Massumeh Farhad for bringing this connection to my attention. The corpus of paintings made in Ashraf includes several key pieces commissioned by the provincial administrator, vizier, in the name of

the shah. Among those are large, single-sheet paintings intended for albums and the additions to the famous Shah Tahmasb *Khamse* made by Mohammad Zaman. That Mohammad Zaman, one of the greatest masters of the royal workshops, was also active in Ashraf needs further probing. For one of the paintings from Ashraf, see Abolala Soudavar, *Art of the Persian Courts* (New York: Rizzoli, 1992), 374–5. For a discussion of Mohammad Zaman and his work for Shah Solayman on this manuscript, see Landau, "*Farangi-Sazi* at Isfahan," 76–80 and 177.

125. Willem Floor, *The Afghan Occupation of Safavid Persia, 1721–1729* (Paris: Association pour l'avancement des etudes iraniennes, 1998), 19.

126. Ibid.

127. The caravanserai has been restored for reuse as Hotel Abbasi; the adjoining bazaar, also much restored, is a functioning market for fine jewelry and handcrafts. The entire complex needs monographic study, but for an overview, and especially the epigraphic program of the madrasa, see Honarfar, *Ganjine*, 685–722. See also Hillenbrand, "Safavid Architecture," 808–811 for the madrasa, caravanserai, and bazaar complex and a list of minor building works during the reign of Shah Soltan Hossayn. The shah continued the Safavid tradition of extending patronage to important Shi'i shrines by having also contributed to the refurbishments at the holy city of Karbala; Abd al-Hossayn Khatunabadi, *Vaqayi' al-sanin v-al-a'vam*, ed. M. B. Behbudi. (Tehran: Ketabforushi-ye Eslamiyye, 1352/1973), 553.

128. As in most Safavid architecture, this ensemble remains to be studied, although the complete absence, as far as I know, of visual evidence makes this a daunting task. For brief overviews and introductions see Honarfar, *Ganjine*, 722–5; and Hillenbrand, "Safavid Architecture," 808–11.

129. The willful destruction of the Safavid retreats is recounted, through local histories, personal memoirs, and legal deeds, by the Qajar-era historian Jaberi Ansari; see his *Tarikh-e Esfahan va Ray*; and the new edition, *Tarikh-e Esfahan*, under the supervision of Jamshid Mazaheri. See Khatunabadi, *Vaqayi' al-sanin*, 562–3 on the construction of Farahabad and its endowment as *waqf*, as was the custom in Safavid Isfahan. See also Shafaqi, *Joghrafiya-ye tarikhi-ye Esfahan*, 314–15.

130. Monshi, *Tarikh-e alam ara-ye Abbasi*, 949–50.

131. Honarfar, *Ganjine*, 576 and 582–5, for a general discussion of the Khwaju and Ju'i bridges; Heinz Luschey, "The Pul-i Khwāju in Isfahan: a Combination of Bridge, Dam and Water Art," *Iran* 23 (1985), 143–51; and Hillenbrand, "Safavid Architecture," 801–3.

132. Honarfar, *Ganjine*, 575–81.

133. Honarfar, *Ganjine*, 484, 575, and 723.

134. Khatunabadi, *Vaqayi' al-sanin*, 559–61. In honor of this grand religious gesture, the shah is also credited with the invention of a new religious holiday (*'Id*) marking the birthday of Ali, the first Shi'i imam.

135. Khatunabadi, *Vaqayi' al-sanin*, 562–3. Roemer, "The Safavid Period," 320, dates additional buildings in Farahabad after the court's return to Isfahan in April 1721 and before the Afghans reached the outskirts of the city.

136. The historian Jonabadi notes that the interior gardens where the mansions of the elite lined the Chahar Bagh were laid out according to the *qanun-e tarrahi* or the canon of design; see Jonabadi, *Rauzat al-safaviyye*, fol. 315r and McChesney's translation, "Four Sources," 113.

137. Khatunabadi, *Vaqayi' al-sanin*, 558. A very useful source on the collapse of the Safavids, and especially its aftermath, is Mohammad Shafi' Tehrani, *Mer'at-e varedat*, ed. Mansur Sefat-Gol (Tehran: Miras-e Maktub, 1383/2004), esp. 15–16. The excellent introduction by Dr Sefat-Gol addresses some aspects of the complex psychology of the pietistic and superstitious reign of Shah Soltan Hossayn and the Safavid–Afghan dynamics that led to the capture of Isfahan.

138. Much of the excellent work on this last phase of Safavid rule concerns the collapse of the empire and the rise of the Afghans. As far as I know, there are as yet no comprehensive studies of the reign of Shah Soltan Hossayn.

139. Jafarian, *Safaviyye az zohur ta zaval*, 405, is quoting from *Dastur-i Shahryaran* by Nasiri.

140. Roemer, "The Safavid Period," 310–324.

141. Patterns of use, residency at or absence from Isfahan are discussed in Babaie, "Safavid Palaces in Isfahan," 234–44.

CHAPTER SIX

Feasting and the Perso-Shi'i Etiquette of Kingship

> Foreign envoys gain audience with the shah only on occasions when all courtiers participate in splendor at major gatherings which the Persians call *majles*. Every year, several of these festive occasions take place, be it according to the wishes of the shah or because of political necessities. The king does not feel obligated to give audience to ambassadors at a designated place. Rather, and according to his wishes, he chooses one of his garden palaces for this purpose. Clearly, this building should have a space that would be suitable for the reception of a large number of guests.[1]

THIS BOOK OPENED with Chardin's account of a feast at the Chehel Sotun; the Frenchman intended to describe a typical Safavid ceremony at the largest of the ceremonial palaces in the Daulatkhane of Isfahan. Our discussion will close with a consideration of the practice of feasting, the micro-universe of social action that animated the relation between the palaces and the politics of Perso-Shi'i kingship. As Kaempfer's observations on the formal court receptions indicate, the feasting of multitudes constituted the principal ceremonial at the Safavid court in Isfahan to which foreign envoys were invited, and for which only certain of the palaces could be considered a suitable venue. My aim has been to set forth the political utility of feasting, something that has been dismissed in scholarship on the Safavid world as an indiscriminate adoption of unchanging traditional practices associated with ancient and tribal polities and modes of social behavior. Indeed, a statement such as Kaempfer's "The king does not feel obligated to give audience to ambassadors at a designated place" has been cited out of context to support the assumption that such political and ceremonial "informality" befitted a confederate system of rule. The argument also assumes that feasting, along with combat, is a Persianate cultural trope memorialized in the *Shahname*, and in many other literary and visual representations, as *bazm u razm*, the Manichaean pairing of conviviality/hospitality on the one hand and battle/hostility on the other. Prowess on the battlefield (*razm*) legitimated victory, which the feast (*bazm*) commemorated in an opulent fashion. What tied them together was the prerogative of kingship.

Yet the paired concepts gain their cultural currency from the inventive ways in which their authorizing powers have been activated in particular historical contexts. In Safavid Iran, these ancient and Persianate concepts had to merge with the rationalist articulation of Imami Shi'ism in order for kingship to maintain legitimacy. These same Persianate concepts played an important role in the Ottoman and Mughal constructs of centralized and absolutist kingship as well, but in each of those cases the Sunni religious elements had to merge with caliphal notions of authority and its locally meaningful representations. Thus, the dramatic Safavid feasting rituals are far from being a continuation of the nomadic-inspired practice whereby the king was expected to appease his partners in rule through his accessibility and his performance of the prerequisite ceremonies of sharing. They fuse charismatic and absolutist notions of rule and reveal the reconfigured household and its centralizing vision. The splendor of feasting had a political purpose that required a particular type of ceremonial space, the *talar* palaces. The present chapter focuses on how the Safavid politics of splendor sensualized power through the visual and aural iconography of the feast, an enunciation of authority that recognizes and appropriates the transcultural value of pomp and ceremony and the symbolics of dining and its accoutrements, yet fundamentally differs in both method and meaning from its predecessors and its contemporaries. All evidence – from buildings and urban spaces, to paintings and luxury objects, to descriptions and chronicles – testifies to a change in the Safavid "style" of feasting that demarcates the Isfahan period, especially after the reign of Shah Abbas the Great, from the eras of its precursor capital cities, and the seventeenth century from the preceding phase of Safavid rule, from its Persianate and Islamicate past, and from its contemporaries.

Hospitality and magnanimity were indispensable trappings of rule in the early modern age, and all imperial courts in this period recognized the political value of splendor (Plate 2.1). The element that distinguishes Isfahan, however, was the practice of banqueting in the company of the shah, at his table, in the palaces of the sacred abode. How did such a performance articulate the unprecedented Perso-Shi'i (of the Twelver variety) vocabulary and performance of kingship? What were the feasting practices of their predecessors and their contemporaries? The premium placed on feasting rituals – for which architecture engineered a special place within the divinely ordained paradisiacal city – conveys the symbolic charge of the ritual for the Safavid rule in its Isfahan phase. As performative procedures, moreover, Safavid feasting rituals and the kinetic vision of space present a *tableau vivante* of authority and legitimacy. This representation needs to be situated within the historical and cultural matrix of the early modern practices that provoked, and were predicated upon, centralization and absolutism. The structure of power in Safavid Iran was made tangible by repeated performances of the feasting rituals, a royal ceremony whose function was paralleled by the processional festivals of the Ottomans at the Hippodrome in Istanbul (Figure 6.1) and the daily appearances of the Mughal Emperors at the *jharoka-ye darshan*, "the throne of beholding," at the Red Forts in Agra and Delhi (Figure 6.11). The following pages consider in a comparative light the microcosmic realm of menus, dining utensils, seating, and spatial choreographies, as well as the macro-stage of the politics of proximity and distance and the imperial iconography of feasting.

The microcosm of feasting

Persian chronicles praise the splendor of the feasting events, which they often call *ziyafat* and only occasionally *majles*, but they do not record the proceedings in detail (Figures 5.3, 5.16, 5.17 and Plate 19). Chardin's account of the feast at the Chehel Sotun, and Kaempfer's notes on the one at the Ayenekhane, thankfully do linger on descriptions of these ceremonies and make it clear that feasting provided the proper ceremonial format for the receipt of diplomatic missions and for the conduct of imperial affairs in the international arena.[2] Europeans who attended royal feasts at the *talar* palaces in Isfahan testify to a highly choreographed procedure with prescribed hierarchies that permeated every action and every apparatus: from the menu to the manner of serving; from the changing of serving cloths to the bowls, dishes, and cups; from the intervening rituals of drinking and conversing to the performances of dancers and musicians (Plate 18).

The meal began with what Europeans considered to be dessert: candied and fresh fruits, sweet breads and pastries, and cool sherbets – presented in large gold, wooden, or ceramic dishes and bowls over richly decorated silk spreads – were set out as starters. Wine was served at the discretion of the shah (Plate 19). If he was not refraining from alcohol, on doctor's advice or out of repentance, the master of ceremonies offered wine on the shah's command, further heightening the effect of his bestowal of generosity and favor.[3] Nonetheless, European reports are unanimous that wine was abundant; it was consumed in small quantities over a long period of time, and its ultimate effect was a low level of intoxication conducive to good cheer but not disruptive of order.[4]

Thomas Herbert's observations on the matter of drinking, albeit generalized, point to another significant aspect of the feasting rituals. "Wine they also drink, having (as they pretend) a peculiar privilege from Ally and from the indulgence Siet Gunet in his Commentary afforded them, which the Turks are not worthy of."[5] Reflecting perhaps popular justifications for the consumption of wine, Herbert's note refers to a specifically Safavid-manufactured privilege derived from no less an authority than Shaykh or Seyyed Junayd (Siet Gunet),

Figure 6.1 *Istanbul, Topkapı Palace site plan (after Necipoğlu).*

Soon after the Ottoman conquest of Constantinople in 1453, the Yeni Sarai, popularly known as the Topkapı, was commissioned. It remained the principal residence and administrative heart of the Ottoman Empire until well into the nineteenth century. Built on the site of the Byzantine acropolis, it stands majestically on the promontory overlooking the intersection of the Golden Horn, the Sea of Marmara and the Bosphorus. The heavily fortified Topkapı is forbiddingly distant from its urban matrix. Moreover, the ceremonial particularities of the Ottomans necessitated a high degree of seclusion for the sultans. This map is adapted to highlight the imperial posture of transcendence that the Ottoman palatine complex articulates: A) Imperial Gate, Bab-i Homayun or the first gate accessing the complex; B) the Byzantine Church of Hagia Sophia, converted into a mosque after 1453; C) the direction of the Byzantine Hippodrome, which served as the principal public space for the ceremonial spectacles of the Ottoman court; 1) the first court, the most public space within the fortified palace precinct; 2) the second court, the administrative center of the complex and the empire; 3) the third court, containing the Chamber of Petitions (audience hall) and the sultan's residence, the harem; 4) the terraced gardens of the inner court.

the grandfather of Shah Isma'il and the spiritual link between the Safavid dynastic power and Shaykh Safi al-Din, the founder of the Safaviyye Sufi order.[6]

Although this sort of linkage may not be what prompted the wine-drinking component of the receptions, the feasting ceremonies in the *talar* palaces in Isfahan did include other performances that reactivated the memory of the Safavids' mystical lineage, from which the shahs drew their legitimacy. An especially charged presentation was the ritual beating of young applicants to mark their initiation into the Safaviyye Sufi Order (Plate 20).[7] In an instance described by Kaempfer, two eligible and willing youths were brought to the middle of the *talar*.[8] When the shah turned his gaze toward them and gave a nod of approval, the *yasavol bashi-ye sohbat* (aide de camp) who served as the master of ceremonies left the *talar* in order to exchange his regular turban for a Safavid *taj*, the special hat associated with the Sufi Brotherhood of the Safaviyye. Returning clad in his Sufi costume, he commanded the youths to lie face down on the ground with their arms straight and to their sides. He then raised the stick, *chub-e tariq* (the cane of, or the cane that leads to, the path), holding the pose until the shah gave him the signal, at which point he struck the youths three times on their buttocks. To conclude the ceremony the youths rose to kiss, three times, the *chub-e tariq* which had initiated them into the fold, placed the Safaviyye *taj* on their heads and left, fully aware, as Kaempfer said, of their newly conferred status and their responsibilities as members of the order. An allusion to this initiation ceremony, along with other puzzling vignettes, seems to have been included in the mural at the Chehel Sotun Palace of Shah Abbas the Great feasting Vali Mohammad Khan the Uzbek (Plate 20).

Javanmardi and the obligation of generosity

The theatrical reconfiguration of the initiation ceremony, its repeated performance under the protection and command of the shah, and its representation – both actual and pictorial – at the public and ceremonial feasts sparked the memory of Safavid mystical origins and kept the Safavid source of the charisma of kingship alive and visible without jeopardizing its absolute and centralized structure. Theoretically, the shah occupied the seat of the master, inherited from his forebear Shaykh Safi al Din, in the master-disciple relationship of the mystical brotherhood. In that capacity, he was also bound by the code of conduct by which all members of such spiritual brotherhoods – be they artisan guilds, soldiers, or bureaucrats – abided.

There is also a long tradition in the Islamicate world, especially its Persianate side, of committing to writing the code of behavior and attitude befitting a *javanmard* (literally, a youthful man) or a man of honor in such social groups.[9] *Javanmardi*, with its martial connotations of a struggle against injustice, especially in defense of the family of Imam Ali, denoted chivalry and gallantry in the battleground of life for the devotees of the Twelve Imams. It implied gentility, consideration, valor, decorum, justice, piety, and generosity, among other virtues desirable for a member of any society or brotherhood.[10] Such a code belongs to the literary genre known as *fotovvatname*, a kind of manual of *javanmardi* of which numerous versions are known.[11] An example of the genre, and one that is close to our time frame, is the *Fotovvatname-ye soltani*, a handbook of chivalry written by the mystic eulogist Vaʻez-e Kashefi early in the sixteenth century for the last Timurid ruler, Soltan Hossayn Bayqara, and translated from Chaghatay Turkish into Persian for Shah Ismaʻil I.[12]

As in all examples of the *fotovvat* genre, this manual delineates in minute detail a range of topics: carrying arms; hosting and attending feasts; patronizing and participating in religious rituals; the decorum of greeting, clothing, eating, drinking, and sitting; and other facets of social conduct. The culture of *javanmardi*, summarized in this *Fotovvatname*, emphasized the propagation of piety through cultivating skills of storytelling as much as through wrestling. Properly knotting one's waist sash was as important as preparing and presenting rice dishes. Performing Shiʻi rituals of mourning for the martyred imams was as essential as feasting and conviviality. The Prophet Mohammad's statement that "the worst people are those who eat alone" (*sharr al-nas man akala vahdahu*) would resonate with all who had a stake in upholding *javanmardi*, and was especially applicable to the shah as the spiritual master of the entire community of the devotees of Imam Ali.[13] Similarly, to be a *javanmard* meant to "share in one's bowl of food," for *barekat* [blessing] was in *ejtemaʻ*, the collective.

In fact, given the wide membership from among artisan groups, it is conceivable that many serving the Safavid court would have followed such directives while taking part in the preparation and performance of feasts. Nur-Allah, the royal chef at the court of Shah Abbas the Great, whose assemblage of recipes is among the most intriguing sources on Persian cookery in the early modern age, characterized the art of the cook (*sanʻat-e tabbakh*) to be his ability to cook well with speed and agility. He admonished those rival master chefs who advised their apprentices to "cook badly, but serve beautifully," thus disdaining the exaggerated emphasis on the serving of food over its taste but also recognizing the significance of the former.[14]

The authority of the Prophet was invoked to inculcate the rules and etiquette of eating and drinking and to elevate cooking and the presentation of foods to the level of performance. In so doing, Safavid culture braided together dining rules and values with notions of generosity, piety, and justice in its courtly milieu. The *fotovvatname* manual of chivalry assembles the characteristic features of a Persianate cult of heroes that was appropriated by Safavid monarchs.

It merges ancient Iranian symbols of valor with Shi'i Muslim notions of piety. In the Safavid context, it was the shah, the loyal devotee of Ali, who was the ceremonial spiritual master. Thus the ideals of piety, gallantry, justice, and generosity became inseparable from the person of the shah and found their expression in the feasting rituals in Isfahan.

The politics of generosity

The *Fotovvatname-ye soltani* belonged to the formative stage of the Safavid authority. This was the period when power and legitimacy sprang from the shah's (Isma'il and Tahmasb, in particular) association with the locus of spiritual energy. At this time, the devotees, the Qezelbash as well as members of the urban guilds, found in the promise of the Safavid household the fulfillment of their expectation of justice under the Shadow of God, who was believed to be the upholder of Shi'ism, the true religion. In the Isfahani age, this mystical and messianic past was replaced with a normative and imperial practice that put the shah at the apex of a centralized power structure. From the perspective of the king and the *ulama*, this was indeed the age of fulfillment of an empire whose foundations rested on the rationalist and legalistic practice of a Perso-Shi'i mode of kingship. It could be said that the inclusion of the initiation ceremony during a feast at one of the *talar* palaces in Isfahan encapsulated the memory of the Sufi past of the Safavids and constituted a nod to that locus of power from which the shah drew one strand of legitimacy.

   The other, more fundamental source of legitimacy rested in the Twelver Shi'i doctrine and its application to the conduct of kingship. For that purpose, Shah Abbas the Great had commissioned his trusted advisor and confidant Shaykh Baha'i, the great Shi'i doctor of religion, philosopher, and mathematician, whose role in the urban renewal of Isfahan has been discussed, to compose his *Jame'-e Abbasi*.[15] This codification of Twelver Shi'i jurisprudence and its provisions for an ethical life systematized the proper and legal requirements of social relationships and the maintenance of justice in a way that is not dissimilar to the "unofficial" *fotovvat* genre. Shaykh Baha'i's ethico-legal manual and its codes of conduct – including the etiquette of hosting, feasting, eating, and drinking – contain a rigorous interpretation of the Twelver Shi'i reading of Islamic law (*shari'a*). As an official legal document, moreover, it carried political implications that bring to mind such manuals of kingship as the eleventh-century *Siasatname* by Khwaje Nezam al-Molk, the vizier of the Seljuq Malek Shah, which, however, stressed the maintenance of justice more than religious laws (Sunni, in that case).[16]

   Shaykh Baha'i's manual rejected the messianic zeal of the early Safavid phase and subjugated the exaggerated and esoteric Sufi

practices of the Safaviyye and the Qezelbash to the legalistic structure of Imami Shiʿism. It thereby signaled the complete institutionalization of an imperial religious posture exemplified by such
members of the *ulama* as Shaykh Bahaʾi and Shaykh Lotf-Allah in the
early decades of the seventeenth century, and later by Mohammad
Baqer-e Majlesi the Younger (d. 1699), under whose leadership as the
Shaykh al-Islam of Isfahan during the reign of Shah Solayman the
process of normalizing orthodox Shiʿism congealed.[17] The royal commission of a manual of social conduct that conformed to Twelver
Shiʿi laws at the same time that Isfahan was being transformed into
the capital of the restructured empire reflected the shift in emphasis
that began with Shah Abbas the Great and solidified under his successors. Integrating the initiation ceremonies into the feasts and performing them at the *talar* palaces in the capital city rather than at a
shrine (as in sixteenth-century Ardabil) or in temporary tent encampments and garden pavilions in provincial centers underscores the centrality of the feasts as a means both to conduct and legitimate the new
politics of the Safavid state.

In fact, the entire feasting event accomplished a number of official
matters of state, the astounding range and variety of which is especially well represented at the feast described by Kaempfer. Not unexpectedly, the German doctor paid particular attention to the
reception of the Swedish ambassador – Ludwich Fabritius, himself a
Dutchman – detailing the special treatment the ambassador received
and the content of the letter that was officially translated for Shah
Solayman by Father Raphaël du Mans, the highly respected resident
Capuchin missionary.[18] Ambassadors from Poland, France, Moscow,
and Siam were also invited to present their diplomatic credentials
and their royal epistolary charge. Two tribal chiefs from Iraq seeking
protection from their Ottoman overlords, a Carmelite priest bearing
an old Ottoman letter, and nineteen Georgians who had recently converted to Islam were also received. The multinational nature of the
assembly at the court of a Muslim ruler strikes a familiar chord, but
the king's attendance as host is indeed exceptional in this early
modern age.

As Kaempfer noted, a regular component of these feasts was the
exchange of gifts: those brought in the diplomatic train and those
bestowed by the shah. We shall return to the gifting again, but here
it is worth noting the presentation of robes of honor on such public
and ceremonial occasions. The case of the converted Georgian elite
is especially striking: the nineteen men and women present at this
occasion were incorporated into the Safavid household slave system
as *gholam*s and concubines but also as hostages in order to maintain the political balance against the Ottomans.[19] In other words,
these feasting ceremonies embodied and represented the complex
network of social groups that made up the Safavid structure of
power.

Food and the ritual

Courses of food bracketed the changing moods, scenes, and activities. The flavor of an event depended on whether or not drinking wine was part of that feast. According to Chardin and other travelers, "A feast takes much less time when no wine is drunk for no side-dishes are served and the main meal is brought in just an hour or so after the fruits." Following the first course, as Chardin noted,

> When the time comes that the Shah decides the meal should commence, he signals for it to be served. Then, the fruits are lifted, the table cloths removed and others are laid as wide as the room woven in finely painted cloth or taffetas with golden flowers. On these are served a variety of stews which consist of lean roasted or highly seasoned meat, plain or smoked fish with all kinds of sauces. We would call that a side-dish, for these stews are only served to stimulate the appetite. Each person has fifteen or twenty little plates set in front of him and large porcelain or gold bowls which hold about two pints of sherbet and in each of which is a box-wood spoon with a handle 14 to 16 inches long.

Lasting up to three or four hours, this part of the meal featured convivial conversation accompanied by music; the large number of appetizing small dishes made it possible to consume wine over a long period of time without becoming inebriated.[20] As Chardin also stated, it was the shah who regulated the pace of drinking and hence the length and mood of the feast:

> One of the young equerries present or a young eunuch acts as the cup-bearer. He only offers drink to those authorized by the Shah and after he had done so, he takes it round again without stopping until the Shah gives him a sign. It is, nevertheless, a fairly slow proceeding, for nobody dares put down the cup. The bottles are round with long necks, enameled or covered in precious stones as are the cups.

Then,

> When everyone has drunk sufficiently and the Shah wishes to retire, he calls for the services to be taken away. So the side dishes are lifted, the table cloths removed and others no less beautiful put in their place. The last service consisting of soups, boiled dishes, stews and many different kinds of delicious rice, called Pilo, is served.

To initiated guests, the conclusion of the feast was signaled by the arrival of an infinite variety of rice preparations, a specialty of Persian

cuisine that prompted an ill-tempered comment from Thomas
Herbert: "But in that dish express they think a witty invention,
setting before you sometimes forty dishes called by forty names, as
Pelo, Chelo, Kishmy-pelo, Cherry-pelo, etc., albeit indeed it differ but
in the cookery."[21] In any event, the rice and meat dishes served in
large platters, in contrast to the small bowls of the appetizers, clearly
marked the winding down of the feast, as Chardin's observation indicates: "This only lasts half an hour and as soon as the Shah has eaten
his guests are offered facilities for washing, large hollow basins of
solid gold or enameled with warm perfumed water. Once the Shah
leaves, everyone withdraws."

The feast and its spatial grammar

Court ceremonials did of course extend beyond feasting. Nauruz
audiences – when paying homage to the king included the offering of
nauruzi, the gift in celebration of the Persian New Year – took place
annually in these palaces. There is also evidence that, after a night of
feasting, the shah and his officials gathered at the *talar* of the Chehel
Sotun to move from light conversation that had begun at the feast to
more serious "business" negotiations. The two coronations of Shah
Solayman occurred at the *talar* of the Talar-e Tavile and the Chehel
Sotun. In 1661/2, after a popular protest took "the enfeebled poor
and anxious empty-pocketed" men and women to the gateway of the
Daulatkhane to voice their complaints over an inflation in prices and
shortages of food, Shah Abbas II ordered key officers of the state to be
present and available (presumably every morning) at the Talar-e
Tavile so that people's petitions could be brought to them with
greater efficiency and the shah himself would be able to access the
right official while he held his daily *divan* hearing of state affairs.[22]
And at least one recorded instance of the *Ashura* ceremony, lasting
ten days in 1666, brought the ritual mourning that commemorated
the martyrdom of Imam Hossayn and his companions in Karbala to
the Talar-e Tavile, indicating that the *talar* of that palace occasionally
served as the setting for the performance of this religious ceremony.[23]
In none of those ceremonial occasions, however, did the spatial
organization of the *talar* play as integral a role in activating the ritual
or in coordinating its performance as it did in feasting events.

For these events, seating arrangements appropriated the tripartite
organization of the *talar*. Chardin and Kaempfer describe the position
of the actors – hosts, guests, attendants, entertainers, and servants –
during feasts at the *talar* palaces as though drawing the ground plan
of the space, measuring its capacity, and painting the visual effect of
the decorated surfaces.[24] The glitz and glamour increased as the space
telescoped toward the throne ayvan: from the openness of the widest
section, to the painted and mirrored walls that bracketed the second,
smaller zone, to the ayvan porch in the very back, where only a few

people could stand and where figural wall paintings on either side and faceted mirror-work inside the vault of the ayvan intensified the hierarchical value of this most rarefied part of the *talar* front. At the archetypal seventeenth-century Safavid feast that Chardin witnessed at the Chehel Sotun, he observed (Plates 17–19):

> The royal throne is at the back of the first great room. It is square, about 8 feet across and 2 or 3 inches high, covered with a white fabric on which were embroidered pearls, and gold and silver very richly woven in the centre. A large high cross-bar covered with precious stones served as the back of the seat having two cushions at the sides, also covered with precious stones. The covering on the throne is held in place in the front by two solid gold knobs which are similarly decorated as were the spittoons which were placed between them. The Shah is adorned with the finest jewelry in the world, valued at millions, mostly in coloured precious stones, because they were most esteemed in Persia. Behind him were ranged nine or ten small eunuchs between ten and twelve years old who were the most attractive children imaginable, richly clothed, making a semi-circle behind the Shah. They seemed to resemble real marble statues, so clearly were they motionless folding their hands across their stomachs, their heads turned to the right and eyes fixed. Behind these were older eunuchs with muskets on their shoulders, decorated with gold and precious stones. On the right of the Shah is the Chief Eunuch, called the Mehter or Grand, who is the Chamberlain of the Shah, having at his waist a little golden box full of handkerchiefs and scents for the use of the Shah if requested. Along the sides of the room are the royal officials in rank.[25]

Those included the Grand Vizier (*vazir-e a'zam*), the financial officer (*nazer al-mamalek*), the commander of guards (*qurchi bashi*), the royal squire (*qullar aqasi*), the head of the finance chamber (*mostaufi al-mamalek*), the head of the stables (*mir akhor bashi*), the official chronicler (*vaqaye'nevis*), the royal physician (*hakim bashi*), the royal astronomer (*monajjem bashi*), and the chief of firearms (*tofangchi bashi*), an assembly of officials alluded to in the murals of the Chehel Sotun (Figure 5.16, Plates 19 and 20).[26] Kaempfer further underscores the formality of the scheme by subdividing the list of guests according to their location in the *talar* palace and concluding that even though Persians claim all are equal in the presence of the shah (a statement that parallels the Quranic view on the relationship of people to God), there is indeed a strict rule regarding proximity to the shah that is especially enforced when it comes to ambassadors.[27]

As in the feasting scenes on the walls of the audience hall at the Chehel Sotun, and as contemporaries observed, the honored guest – an ambassador or a ruler – was placed close at hand beside the shah (Plates 18 and 19). The seating order replicated social distinctions through degrees of proximity or distance from the shah, through positioning to his right or left, and through placement immediately next to him or separated by other people. Descending from the already nuanced social order of that first tier was the assembly in rows of governors, chief members of the clergy, mid-level officials, and foreign visitors such as members of the ambassadorial retinue, tradesmen, missionaries, and the like.[28] Dancers, musicians, and servants were positioned on the third level, in the space farthest from the shah and his entourage (Figure 5.3 and Plate 18).

In summary, the three-tiered hierarchy of importance that dominated the seating order synchronized with the sequence of spatial delineations in the *talar* front of the palaces of Talar-e Tavile, Ayenekhane, and the Chehel Sotun (Figures 5.1, 5.6, 5.15 and Plate 16). The rarefied throne-ayvan housed the shah and a small entourage of his personal youthful attendants and honored guests. As the space enlarged, the numbers swelled, and the rank of the occupants diminished.

No other court ritual assumed the kind of symbiotic relationship with architecture that we find between the feasting ceremonies and the *talar* palaces. The *talar* front's role in spatially regulating the social relationships and the conduct of the ceremonial is evident in Chardin's description of a feast at the Chehel Sotun; in Kaempfer's account of a feast at the Ayenekhane; in the engraving of the "Night Reception" at the Talar-e Tavile, of which Kaempfer's version is the best known; and in the pictorial allusions to spatial hierarchies of feasts depicted on three of the walls of the Chehel Sotun's audience hall.

Depending on the perceived significance of the guest, the diplomatic and trade value of the negotiations, and the politico-military relations between the host and the guest, hierarchies of seating performed in a spatial vocabulary the social order that was imposed by the Safavid shah through the agency of the household of slave elite and loyal functionaries. These feasts were not about sharing the throne with the tribal chiefs of a confederate state. The feast and its semiotic charge enunciated the Perso-Shi'i structure of kingship infused with the charismatic absolutism that undergirded the centralization project of the Safavids in Isfahan.

Spatial choreography of the ritual

Processionals were an integral part of the feasting rituals in Isfahan, further delineating the contours of the Safavid social order. Chardin's archetypal feast was accompanied by a very carefully choreographed processional. As he and other European travelers noted, strict protocol dominated not only the order of seating, drinking, eating, and entertainment, but also the ritualized walk toward the site of such feasting events. Guests had to wait, sometimes for hours, at a designated room on the ground floor of the Ali Qapu, a practice that sharpened the perception of the guest's status relative to that of his royal host and heightened the expectation of resplendent might to which one must pay homage through such ceremonials (Figure 4.4).[29]

The processional approach to the palace and its *talar*, the site of feasting, was regulated by an elaborate and prescribed series of movements through space: "Those invited were made to come through gardens by an avenue of large trees under which a dozen horses were to be seen making one of the main spectacles of royal celebrations."[30] According to Olearius, guests were led through the display of the "excellent Horses" from the royal stables "with their covering-Cloaths of Brocade, or Embroider'd with Gold and Silver."[31] To these observations from the 1630s, Chardin adds that "all the stable equipment, everything was in solid gold such as the buckets, hammers, nails, combs, trappings and chains and harness which were spread out to view. The harness was covered in precious stones, each one quite different from the other with diamonds, pearls, rubies, emeralds, sapphires and turquoises."[32]

Having traversed through gates and gardens of the royal precinct, the retinue entered the palace at a gateway located at the opposite end of the long garden and pool (Figures 4.5 and 5.13). Thus turned to face the *talar* of the Chehel Sotun Palace, kings, ambassadors, and other visitors marched in the company of appointed *mehmandars* (hosts) along the pool, taking in the shimmering sight of the *talar*: its painted, gilded, and mirrored pillars; their reflection on the surface of water; and the competing visual echoes in the stately trees that lined the garden pool path (Plate 14).[33] The massively scaled *talar* space, clad in colorful and richly patterned textiles, stood at the end of the processional path. The whole ritual procession and its artifice – its spatial articulation through the strategic positioning of movable and immovable objects that ranged from horses and grooms to landscape elements such as trees, shrubs, and pools – was orchestrated to heighten the visual impact of the staged feast at the *talar* of the appointed palace.

Just as the palace articulated the spatial and ritual conclusion of the processional, the feasting ceremony constituted the apex of the entire ceremonial event at which the shah granted favor – of an audience, of robes of honor (*khal'at*), of gifts given and received. The parade of gifts and of wild and exotic animals depended on the location of the audience and feasting event (Plate 2 for a Mughal parallel). Kaempfer's engraved image of the *talar*-fronted palace at Sa'adatabad, with its procession of many leopards, camels, and Arabian horses, evokes something of the processional component of a palace whose *talar* led out to a wide open space, in this case the riverbank (Figure 5.22). Olearius's description of a reception in the 1630s at the Talar-e Tavile indicates a similar use of the *talar* front: "The Presents were brought in, which were carried, close by the King, into an apartment designed for the treasury, on one side of the Hall, at the entrance of the Palace."[34] Allowing for Olearius's misreading of distances and spatial relations among buildings, it is well documented that the inanimate gifts to the shah ended up at the *Jobbekhane* (the royal treasury and arsenal), where they were stored and rarely seen again except when precious items such as jewels, gems, or the gold and silver were removed for use elsewhere.[35]

When the event included a public display at the Maydan-e Naqsh-e Jahan, the *talar* at the Ali Qapu served as a viewing stage as much as it was a stage to be viewed. There, too, the entire event peaked with the feasting ritual at the *talar* during which the shah granted what must have been the ultimate gift, proximity to his person and the privilege of sharing at his table. According to established social rules of gifting and reciprocity, the shah also promised favorable treatment and patronage in political and commercial realms.

Besides its commercial and other urban functions, the vast and open space of the Maydan served as a stage for spectacles that not only entertained the public but informed them of the relative socio-political position of the royal household within both local and inter-national arenas of imperial operation (Figure 3.9). Military parades, mock battles with towers and fortifications built like a stage set for an opera – including, presumably, one instance of a naval combat for which a vast portion of the Maydan was filled with water and ships were floated – and equestrian sports and shows (a game of polo being supreme among them), elaborate fireworks, and displays of sudden and simultaneous lighting of thousands of torches and lamps number among the staged spectacles. Some of these preceded the banquet at the *talar* of the Ali Qapu, and others, especially the fireworks and the synchronized lighting of the Maydan buildings, took place during and after the meal.

After the *talar* was added to the Ali Qapu Palace in 1644, it became a principal stage for major ambassadorial receptions, in which a royal banquet was also the high point. These ceremonies also took advan-tage of the spatial and theatrical potential of the Maydan–*talar* rela-tionship. One such event, recorded by Chardin, illustrates the visual mediation of the ceremonial and its stage-managed choreography. In a spectacular reception given to the ambassadors from Muscovy and "Lesqui," a mountainous region near the Caspian Sea, Shah Solayman and a retinue of over three hundred courtiers stationed themselves at the *talar* before the parade of the envoys and their gifts were to begin.[36] In full view of the public gathered around the Maydan, the ambassa-dors, one after another, arrived on horseback into the great public square from an eastern corner (Chardin does not specify whether from the northeastern or southeastern corner). At about one hundred feet from the entrance of the Ali Qapu, presumably directly facing the gateway, the envoys were helped off their horses and were conducted on foot toward the palace and through the great ceremonial stairwell on the south side of the building to the *talar* level, where the shah and his court were awaiting their guests.

Once all were in place, the theatrical performance shifted its focus to the parade of ambassadorial gifts in the Maydan. Notwithstanding its widespread practice throughout history, the public display of diplomatic offerings has an especially distinguished and long tradition in the Persianate world.[37] The most famous visual rendition of its socio-political significance as a form of submission to imperial power is found in the magnificent relief panels of tribute bearers on the walls of the grand staircases that lead to the Apadana Palace at Achaemenid Persepolis.[38] Contemporary examples include representations of gift-bearing ambassadors in Mughal and Ottoman paintings that chronicle the reigns of emperors and sultans.[39]

The distinctive aspect of the gifting parade in Isfahan lies in how space was choreographed in such a way as to load the already freighted symbolics of gifting with a religious iconography that was specific to Safavid kingship in its Isfahani phase. Before the parade toward the Ali Qapu Palace-Gateway was allowed to begin, servant-carriers bearing ambassadorial gifts stood for a time in front of the new imperial congregational mosque, the Masjed-e Jadid-e Abbasi (the Royal Mosque) on the south side of the Maydan. Chardin notes that during such events, the offerings from the envoys were always held waiting at this designated spot in front of the mosque. He clarifies the logic of such a procedure by adding that, according to religious doctors (the *ulama*), the bearing of gifts from the east side (the area in front of the Shaykh Lotf-Allah Chapel-Mosque) and from in front of the Royal Mosque in the Maydan signified to the viewing public, and no doubt the donor, that worldly riches emanate from a divine source. In the instance described by Chardin, the Russian ambassador's gifts alone had to be carried by seventy-four men.[40] Both the abundance and the splendor of the gifts and the tactical procedure of the parade aggrandized in visually palpable form the exalted status of the monarch among foreign potentates, a point that Chardin underscores in his account of gifting ceremonies in Safavid Isfahan.[41]

More importantly, however, the bearing of rich gifts and tribute was incorporated into a larger ceremonial fabric in which the act of paying homage with gifts transcended its material basis just as it was about to be reciprocated, even more grandly, with the bounty of the feast, which assumed the character of a spiritual practice as well. The fact that the shah was present at both the gifting and the feasting that followed emphasizes the centrality of the ceremonial in this Perso-Shi'i articulation of charismatic absolutism and its obligations. The architectural and spatial engineering of the ceremony turned the event of paying tribute into a privilege afforded to the Safavid shahs alone in their deputized role on behalf of the Imams as masters of the heavenly feast on earth. In presiding over the ceremony, the shahs were performing their part of the covenant. Riches flowing from the

Plate **17** *Isfahan, Chehel Sotun.*

The audience hall is a triple-vaulted rectangular space positioned behind
the throne ayvan. Most unusually for a palace in the Islamic world,
the audience hall is sheathed in painted decorative patterns and figural
paintings, especially four large historical scenes on the upper walls.
Originally, tile panels with scenes of outdoor entertainment flanked
fireplaces on the lower walls of the piers. Small painted panels of similar
scenes, visible on the lower edges of the picture, fill the spaces above.
Colorful, gilded floral and vegetal patterns cover all the surfaces of the
shallow vaults and their triangular pendentives. Similar motifs demarcate
the friezes and frame the larger paintings on the upper walls. The large
central painting is of nineteenth-century date; the one on the right side
is dateable to 1647–50 and depicts a battle that took place between Shah
Isma il and the Uzbeks early in the sixteenth century.

Plate **18** *Isfahan, Chehel Sotun audience hall.*

In this detail of "Shah Tahmasb hosting the Mughal emperor Homayun," the viewer is invited to visualize, through the pictorial strategy of foreshortening the scene of feasting, and the placement of the accoutrements, the attendants, and the entertainers, the ceremonial order of such events. The historical event had taken place in 1544, when Homayun was in Qazvin; the artists of the mural remember it, however, in the contemporary guise of the imperial feasts and their architectural setting at the Chehel Sotun. The stylistic contrast between the historical scenes (utilizing European representational conventions) and the decorative patterns that cover the rest of the interior of the audience hall sharpens the impression of immediacy.

Plate **19** *Isfahan, Chehel Sotun audience hall.*

Detail from the scene of Shah Abbas the Great hosting the Uzbek Vali Mohammad Khan, who took refuge in Isfahan. Shah Abbas, recognizable for his famous handlebar moustache, and clad in the finest gold-embroidered Safavid textiles, offers a cup of wine to his guest, whose status as the recipient of the shah's protection and hospitality is made visible by the way the Uzbek cowers and hides his right hand under the long sleeve of his robe. The loving embrace of the two young women on the lower left side adds a curious note of sensuality to the scene. Gold and silver bottles and dishes on richly embroidered cloths, colorfully enrobed pages, attendants, musicians and dancers intensify the impression of grandeur in such ceremonies of conviviality.

Plate **20** *Isfahan, Chehel Sotun audience hall.*

Detail from lower right-hand side of the "Shah Abbas the Great hosting the Uzbek Vali Mohammad Khan." This ensemble of puzzling vignettes includes a young man who seems to have fallen in ecstasy into the lap of an older man who suggestively holds a fruit to his parting lips and looks directly at the viewer. The standing figure in regal costume separates this group from one behind in which an inebriated young man is helped out by a youthful pair. The corner detail of a man about to strike a boy with a stick refers to the initiation ceremony through which young boys were admitted into the Safaviyye Sufi Order.

Plate **21** *Isfahan, Hasht Behesht Palace (1669).*

Unlike the earlier talar palaces of Isfahan, this building pivots on a vertical central axis. The subtle expansion of the porch on the north side (right side in this picture) relative to the other three indicates the north as its main façade. Slender wooden pillars on three sides of the building mediate between its inner and outer spaces, while glazed tile panels framing the pointed niches provide color accents to the exterior.

Plate **22** *Isfahan, Hasht Behesht Palace.*

This view of the interior of the north porch affords a glimpse of its ornamental pool and its elaborately painted and mirror-inlaid coffered ceiling. Unique to this building is the complex beehive of rooms, alcoves and walkways on the upper floors.

Plate **23** *Isfahan, Hasht Behesht Palace.*

This view illustrates how the architects of this palace lightened the
massive solidity of such forms as the pylon or the dome, making them
appear to dissolve before our eyes. The concave pieces filling the famous
muqarnas covered lantern lead up to a latticed ring of high windows
that filter and refract light beams before the latter touch myriad painted
and gilded surfaces. Kaempfer was so impressed by the intensity of the
building's visual impact to have said "that one has to have a hundred eyes
to be able to grasp the incomparable variety of excellences and luxuries of
this palace."

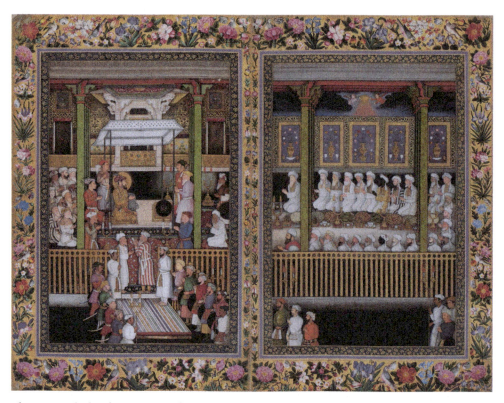

Plate **24** *"Shah Jahan Honors the Religious Orthodoxy" Album folio from the St Petersburg Album, Shah Jahan, 1628–58, India, Mughal dynasty, c. 1635; opaque watercolor and gold on paper, 30.5 × 23.1 cm (12 × 9⅛ in).*

Shah Jahan is seen seated on a raised platform underneath a canopy set up in front of the jharoka. The emperor presides at this feast, but does not partake of it. His transcendence is accentuated by his and his immediate companions' rigidly formal stances and their positioning away from the sumptuous display of fruits and food in the right half of the picture. The choice of a double-page composition further heightens the pictorial evocations of ritual and architectural distance.

gates to the second Ka'ba (Isfahan) and reciprocated with riches emanating from its heavenly throne (the palaces) made the contours of
the covenant visible to all present.

Such giving and receiving illustrate the power relations between
the donor and the recipient. Similar parades of gifts received and displays of largesse bestowed in ceremonials aggrandized the authority
of Mughal emperors and Ottoman sultans, as well as their Hindu and
Christian counterparts, for example. As in other instances, what was
received was made to appear exceedingly grand – a mere few gifts,
regardless of actual value, would probably not have been paraded
around in public. In the case of Safavid Isfahan, the Maydan parade
magnified the effect of the ceremony. In return, what was received by
the gift-giver – whether in the material terms of *khal'at* (which
included a horse, its gilded rein and saddle, daggers and swords, as
well as money in addition to the robe of honor) or in terms of hospitality and the granting of favors – depended on the status of the recipient and the significance of the negotiations that were to follow.[42]
Their value as "business" transactions notwithstanding, all such
exchanges presupposed a well-defined social code of power relations
that reflected, in visual and conceptual terms, relative degrees of
loyalty and patronage.

Through the subtle spatial and architectural articulation of the ceremonial nuances, the presence of and access to the shah were coded
and activated. The visual effect and symbolic value of the presentation of gifts was maximized by a parade composed of seemingly
endless rows that issued from the side of the mosque as if from a transcendental source. In turn, the shah's position at the impressively
scaled and elevated site of the *talar*, with its gilded, painted, and mirrored pillars and its coffered ceiling shielding him and his entourage
like a canopy of heaven or "the envy of the heaven's nine roofs"
expressed with visual eloquence the balance between presence and
absence, between proximity and distance.[43] The shah was neither
rigidly formal and aloof beyond reach, nor carelessly informal and
overly available. His personal presence at the spatial apex of the ceremonial (the *talar* when viewed from the Maydan, or the ayvan at the
back of the *talar* in other palaces) enunciated a studied proximity that
was in sharp contrast, for example, to the studied distance of the
Ottoman sultan or the Hapsburg emperor.[44]

Toward a definition of difference

Feasting had a long history in Turco-Mongol constructs of kingship.
It signified the tribal structure of authority in which the king was
elected from among chieftains of the confederate tribes, as in the case
of Genghis Khan and the Mongols and Timur, whose own Barlas
tribe was a minor player among various Turkic and Mongolian
groups. In both instances, the leadership role presupposed a powerful

personality if not some measure of megalomania. Theoretically, such confederate structures are predicated on the sharing of power and demand ritual performances of that sharing. Just as the tribesmen joined forces in the conquest of resources, they also shared in the fruits; banqueting rituals expressed the political and social bonds of the partners in rule.

A great many descriptions of feasts at Timurid, Aqqoyunlu, and early Safavid courts point to the crucial place this performance of sharing and hospitality held in the schema of kingship in the fifteenth and sixteenth centuries. Josafa Barbaro's 1474 arrival in Tabriz and his first audience with the Aqqoyunlu Uzun Hasan took place at the Daulatkhane, where the Hasht Behesht palace was the principal hall for ceremonial occasions (Figure 2.1).[45] His descriptions of the assembly in this and his subsequent audiences illustrate a certain degree of informality in conducting such events and illuminate the difference between the feasting ceremonials of the Safavid Isfahan period and those that preceded it. He was conducted to the place of audience through a sequence of gates, but the distances he traversed and the scale of ceremonies were much smaller:

> The place wheare I had this accesse to the King was on this maner. First, I had a gate w'hin the which was a quadrant of iiij or v paces square, wheare sate his chief astates that past not eight or ten in nombre. Than was there an other gate neere to the first, in the which stoode a porter wth a little staffe in his hande. Whan I was entered that gate I passed through a grene garden like a meadowe full of trufles, wth mudde walls, in the which on the right side was a pavement. About xxx paces further was there a lodge, volte wise, after o maner, iiij or v steppes higher than the foresaid pavement. In the middest of this lodge was a fountaigne like vnto a little gutter, alwaies full of water, and in thentrie of it the king himself sate on a cushion of cloth f gold, wth another at his backe, and besides his was his buckler of the Moresco facon with his scimitarra, and all the lodge was laied wth carpettes, his chiefest Princes sitteng round about.[46]

After having presented his credentials, Barbaro was awarded a robe of honor but was dismissed without spending much time in the company of the shah. He was called repeatedly to join various festivities in the palace as well as the adjoining maydan.

On one of those occasions, he was taken to the maydan to watch, along with the royal children and their tutors who were seated at "certain wyndowes," a shocking pastime in which men battled wild wolves.[47] Afterward, the European guest was invited to join a drinking *majles* with the shah at the same Hasht Behesht, where he observed the presentation of a coterie of wild and exotic animals brought as gifts by the Indian ambassador. Up to this point, parallels may be seen with the seventeenth-century descriptions by Kaempfer and others of Safavid ceremonies. Yet, the reception the Venetian traveler attended concluded with him dining alone: "Than was I taken vp and brought into a chamber, wheare I dyned, and whan I had doon he that attended on Ambassadors bade me farewell and willed me to departe."[48] Soon after he reached his lodging, Barbaro tells us, he was called back to the presence of Uzun Hasan, who was so dismayed at the mistake made by his appointed host that he had the man brought in and bastinadoed on the spot.

As this and other accounts of such receptions indicate, feasting and hospitality were indeed an important component of the court rituals in the fifteenth century, but they did not proceed according to strict rules of conduct or a prescribed spatial and ceremonial structure as developed in the Isfahan period of the Safavids. It is also inconceivable, for example, to hear of an incident in which the Safavid shah would be admonished for excessive pomp, as was Soltan Yaqub, the son of Uzun Hasan.[49] According to the historian Khwandamir, the sight of Soltan Yaqub in gold-embroidered robes and enthroned in majesty at an audience given to the Mamluk and Ottoman envoys provoked the chief theologian of his court to declare, in the presence of all, that "wearing gold-decorated garments is contrary to the Sacred Law." In this case the sultan actually allowed the offending tunic to be removed from him and be replaced with "a plain, coarse cloak."

The ambivalence toward such bombastic luxuries may have been partly due to the declining economies of the late fifteenth century, the impact of which also seems to have slowed large-scale construction and the production of luxury manuscripts at the later Timurid court.[50] Indeed, the *majles* receptions, often represented by depictions of Soltan Hossayn Bayqara hosting drinking parties, appear to have been private and rarefied gatherings of the courtiers when compared to the massive receptions and festivities that characterized Timur's own time.[51] Much like the ones Barbaro experienced in Tabriz, the Timurid rituals in Kesh and Samarqand point to splendid but unstructured procedures. The most spectacular of the court ceremonials of the Timurid world are associated with Timur himself. His megalomania permeated everything, including wedding and circumcision celebrations at his court. In 1404 in Samarqand, the Spanish ambassador Ruy Gonzalez de Clavijo was summoned to daily royal feasts, none of which was especially arranged for ambassadors. He describes in great detail the numerous and magnificently appointed tents that were pitched either in the palace garden outside the city or in the encampment meadows further beyond, where he and his companions and other ambassadors were called repeatedly.[52] At his first audience, Clavijo and several other ambassadors were taken through a number of thresholds inside the palace and were made to wait at different intervals before they were taken, held under their arms, into Timur's presence.

Then coming to the presence beyond, we found Timur and he was seated under what might be called a portal, which same was before the entrance of a most beautiful place that appeared in the background. He was sitting on the ground, but upon a raised dais before which there was a fountain that threw up a column of water into the air backwards, and in the basin of the fountain were floating red apples.[53]

Notwithstanding the magnificence of the architectural setting, visible in the remains of the Aq Sara palace near Samarqand, Clavijo's note clearly demonstrates that the reception was held in front of one ayvan, with at least one other visible in the background. Moreover, many such audiences were combined with wedding and circumcision ceremonies in movable feasts that were held in huge and sumptuously decorated tents outside the city or within royal gardens.

At all these events, conventional symbols of hospitality abounded. Indeed, the ambassadors dined in Timur's presence, following the presentation of letters and some conversation about various envoys and their sovereign lords. As Clavijo observes,

The attendants began to bring up viands for the feast. These consisted of a quantity of mutton, roast, boiled and in stews, also horse-meat roasted. What they thus brought before us was laid out severally on very large circular dishes of leather, such as we in Spain call Guadameci [of Cordovan leather], and these had handles whereby the attendants could move them from place to place. Thus when Timur had called for any particular dish, that leather dish would be dragged along the ground to him, for the attendants could not lift them, such was the quantity of meat with which each was charged.

According to this account, large pieces of horsemeat were cut up and distributed in large gold, silver, glazed ceramic, and porcelain vessels topped with broth. They were carried by two or three men who placed these dishes before each guest, setting them to the side while the next course was served, so that the guests could take the leftovers home. The "viand" was followed by side dishes, fruits, melons, and so forth, and the meal concluded with a sweetened mare's-milk drink that Clavijo found to be "an excellent beverage" for the summer. The event as a whole ended with the presentation of the gifts to Timur. All of this stands in sharp contrast to what Chardin and Kaempfer tell us about the feasts at the palaces in Isfahan.[54] In other audiences, Clavijo's observations allow us to see the rather undisciplined structure of the audience and feast: robes of honor were granted indiscriminately, guests were showered with silver coins, wine was drunk in cups that were filled nonstop, boiled sheep and horse meat were piled up so high in leather vats they had to be dragged around the tent, the music and party chatter were loud, and dust clouded the entire camp. He further emphasized that "no feast we were told is considered a real festival unless the guests have drunk themselves sot."[55] Indeed, Clavijo's impressions vividly convey Timur's largesse and the tribal habits and rituals upheld by him and his clan, but they also emphasize the fact that such events were not tamed by the same codification of the ceremonial that developed in a post-Timurid imperial era.

The early Safavids

The desire to tone down the mega-feasts of Timur is traceable in the later fifteenth-century Timurid *majles* and especially in the Aqqoyunlu ambivalence toward ceremonial bombast. By the sixteenth century, the rather undisciplined Turco-Mongol traditions of hospitality had already been transformed into the more refined form of the *majles*, the intimate drinking parties that began at the princely courts of Timur's heirs and continued in the courts of the early Safavids (Plate 1). Yet, as the sources attest, stately banquets of the scale and ceremonial order we now associate with Isfahan were rare indeed.

In a celebration held in Tabriz in 1508, Shah Isma'il participated in a series of games set up in the maydan, where he and his companions took turns shooting arrows at silver and golden apples placed on tall staffs.[56] As the Venetian traveler Angiolello observed, "Between the knocking down of each apple, Ismael rested a short time, drinking several confections and delicate wines; and while he was amusing himself, there stood before him two beautiful boys: one of whom held a vase of gold with a cup; and the other, two jugs of refreshing drinks." Thousands of courtiers, soldiers, and citizens of Tabriz stood around while the shah carried on with these games and then, "After his recreation he goes with his lords to sup in a palace in the country built by Sultan Assambei, but the lords sup apart." Domenico Romano, another of the Venetian merchants in Tabriz at this time, confirmed Angiolello's observations and added, "At the entrance of the garden nearest the palace there is a large saloon, where a supper is prepared for the lords who have joined in the sports, while Ismael retires to his repast in the palace Astibisti," that is, the famous Hasht Behesht of Uzun Hasan.[57]

In both Tabriz and Qazvin of the Shah Tahmasb era, feasts were held in tents in the maydan or at the main audience pavilion inside the Daulatkhane in Qazvin (Figures 2.1, 2.3 and Plate 3). The descriptions of these feasts also point to the sumptuous display of foods, dishes, and textiles and thousands of attendants, games, and shows, but none involved the formal choreography of processions and feasting spaces seen in the events that transpired in the *talar* palaces in Isfahan. For a religious festival in 1540 (probably the *'Id al-fitr* or the

Festival of Sacrifice that marks the end of the Muslim month of fasting), Shah Tahmasb hosted a huge feast at the Maydan in Tabriz where he and his companions played the same game of shooting the apples before he retired to

> the pavilion where is his usual place, on a seat of gilded wood, covered with velvet; and they place on the ground in front of him dishes full of rice and mutton, which come to perhaps 3 or 4 thousand, so many that the said dishes take up 40 or 50 ells of the ground . . . The Lords his vassals are seated all around in the pavilions. It is already in the evening when they eat. And then the King goes into his house and all go their ways.[58]

As Gulbadan Begum, the sister of Homayun, the Mughal emperor, also noted, richly varied and luxuriously supplied feasts and ceremonies were held in honor of the deposed emperor while he was in Safavid territories seeking refuge with Shah Tahmasb.[59]

It was with Shah Abbas the Great and early in the seventeenth century that the small *majles* gatherings grew large and became increasingly elaborate feasts with the concomitant ordering of the rituals. Shah Abbas's mobility – his constant travel from battle to hunting ground, from Isfahan to Mazandaran, from palace to encampments – was necessitated by the restructuring of the empire in the wake of the last civil war and the ongoing conflicts with the Ottomans, the Mughals, and the Uzbeks.[60] Unlike the case of his successors, whose audience-feasts were almost invariably held at the *talar* palaces in the capital city, diplomatic and mercantile missions followed Shah Abbas I from region to region in the hope of gaining a reception. In the process they endured arduous journeys that many recorded in grim detail. Pietro Della Valle, the Italian traveler, had to follow Abbas from Isfahan to Ashraf and then to Qazvin, only to be called to Farahabad in Mazandaran, where he was kept waiting on the bad advice of the court astrologer, before he was finally granted an audience in Ashraf.[61] The Spaniard Figuera arrived in Isfahan in April 1618 after a three-year journey only to find out that the shah had left for Qazvin. He hastened there and was received briefly, only to be sent back to wait in Isfahan for another ten months before he could receive an official audience.[62] Thomas Herbert and the English Embassy of Sir Dodmore Cotton and Robert Shirley endured even more hardship as they tried in vain to receive a proper audience first in Ashraf and then in Qazvin, where the ambassador and Shirley died.[63]

Scholars have seized upon Shah Abbas's itinerant conduct of the state as evidence that the Safavids needed to maintain an unbroken alliance upheld by the confederacy of the Qezelbash. This assumption is further buttressed by Shah Abbas's famous walks around the Maydan in Isfahan, or his offering of a cup of wine or a morsel of food to an envoy, which shocked many and especially the Ottomans, whose own court ceremonies were deafeningly silent and obsessively codified. Della Valle observed, for example, that unlike European princes, Shah Abbas never gave audience at his palaces, and that he preferred to hear from his subjects while walking or riding in public squares.[64] Figuera recorded at least one occasion when Shah Abbas granted an audience to a number of ambassadors in the Maydan-e Naqsh-e Jahan in Isfahan.[65]

The point to emphasize here is that neither the accessibility of Shah Abbas the Great nor his itinerant habits can be interpreted as the reverberations of an ancient practice. Equally untenable is the assumption that instituting distance between the ruler and the ruled and rigidly codifying ceremonials were the sole means of constructing and maintaining a centralized and absolutist empire in the early modern age. Instead, one must consider the processes of adaptation and transformation through which social life shapes itself and emphasize the malleability of the ceremonials and their structures of meaning. The Safavid agenda, in the politico-religious arena as much as in any other of its social universes, transitioned from an age of experimentation to one of fulfillment; the period of the reign of Shah Abbas bridges the two. In keeping with the sanctified aura of the warrior king, modeled after Imam Ali, Abbas's style, so to speak, was a more charismatic variant of absolutism than its petrified modes in contemporary courts. By the time we enter the urbanized court of his heirs, the state banquet had assumed the full realization of its ritualized meaning and had established its particular brand of etiquette as an index of the Perso-Shi'i mode of kingship.

The architectonics of feasting

In the Islamicate world, palaces (and houses) did not have an architecturally distinct or fixed hall, chamber, or space that was designed or designated for dining. The subject deserves a separate study and needs to be addressed in terms of regional cultures and histories.[66] Suffice it here to state in very broad terms that any space of honor in the public (birun) zone of a palace or house – the main courtyard, the principal reception hall, an arcade, and so forth – could be used for dining purposes. Similarly, tents and awnings in royal gardens or encampments served as multifunctional spaces where a host of activities took place, ranging from the conduct of the affairs of the state, to audiences, receptions, and grand dining, to entertainment and even sleeping.

Another area of investigation that needs further probing is that of the palaces in the Ancient Near Eastern and late classical worlds from which the Islamicate cultural world emerged.[67] Notwithstanding the voluminous literature on the culture of communal dining and food and their indications of local attitudes and practices vis-à-vis authority in antiquity, little remains in the archaeological evidence to firmly ascertain the existence of architectural forms designated for dining.[68] There is, for example, no clear sense of a discrete dining space at the palace of Persepolis even though banqueting scenes on cylinder seals in Achaemenid Iran, as well as in the Ancient Near East in general, are both numerous and complex.[69]

Furthermore, and taking into account the distinct political meanings that an imperial feast may establish in contrast to those of a "republican" polity, the late antique traditions of dining and architecture need to be considered as well, albeit here in brief. The Greek dining hall, usually a round room, had given way over time to the Roman era's specially constructed and appointed room, the *triclinium*, which served as the setting for the dinner party, the *convivium* or *cena*.[70] This, however, was the room designed with couches strategically organized to accommodate the fashion of eating while reclining.[71] Otherwise, the earlier Roman dinners were served in the all-purpose open *atrium*. In fact, in Europe, too, the need for a separate dining room for communal eating did not find architectural expression on a grand scale until later in the Renaissance and the early modern period.[72]

Dining halls in the palaces and mansions across the Islamicate world do not materialize until the later eighteenth and nineteenth centuries, when Muslim rulers and elite looked to what had become by then a culturally sophisticated Europe for inspiration. Even though a vast audience hall in the Ottoman Dolmabahce in Istanbul and in the Qajar Golestan Palace in Tehran, for example, could also serve as a dining space, neither hall was especially planned to accommodate imperial banquets, despite the fact that both were inspired by European palatine models.[73] The former, dating to the first half of the nineteenth century, was designed as a Turkish-Rococo extravaganza; the latter, built over a hundred-year period, had mid-to-late nineteenth-century parts inspired by the glitz and glamour of European palaces.

Among the Muslim empires contemporary with the Safavids, grand dining took place in spaces for which feasting was an incidental function. At the Topkapı, large gatherings of ambassadors and special guests were feasted as they sat on benches lined behind long tables and set along the back wall of the arcade that ran on two sides of the Second Court (Figures 6.1, 6.2 and 6.3).[74] This was the most ceremonial courtyard of the palace ensemble, the place where the highly codified and grandly choreographed ceremonies of the Ottoman court took place. The arcade, a modular row of vaulted spaces that opened onto the courtyard by the march of slender stone columns, linked the Gate of Felicity and the Council Chamber on the north and west sides of the courtyard. It served as a shelter for waiting dignitaries and functionaries, as a place for audiences to gather, as well as a place to seat the sultan's dinner guests.

Figure 6.2 *Istanbul, Topkapı Palace (after Necipoğlu).*
The numbers in this aerial view correspond to the large divisions of the
inner palace into courtyards (Figure 6.1). More specifically, these are: a)
Second, Middle gate; b) Third gate or the Gate of Felicity; c) the Chamber of
Petitions, which served as the formal audience hall; d) the Council Hall
and the Tower of Justice.

Figure 6.3 *Istanbul, Topkapı Palace.*
The Council Chamber and the Tower of Justice, located diagonally across
from the Second Gate, sum up the remarkably centralized imperial
structure of the Ottomans. Ambassadors were often formally received
under the arcades.

Figure 6.4 *Istanbul, Topkapı Palace.*
The Gate of Felicity was the third of the gates within the fortifications.
A ceremonial marker and guard post for the most sacred spot in the whole
complex, the Chamber of Petitions, this gate also served as a throne ayvan
on those rare occasions when the Ottoman sultan appeared in all his
majesty before a select group of people.

In the almost complete absence of the sultan from public view
within the fortified palace ensemble, the Gate of Felicity – where the
sultan appeared twice a year in majestic public audiences on two religious holy days – served as the hallowed seat of imperial authority
(Figures 6.2 and 6.4). Similarly rich in associations was the Council
Chamber, where the daily affairs of the state were conducted by the
sultan's agents – his grand vizier, ministers, generals, bureaucrats,
and courtiers. There too, as Necipoğlu has argued, a screened window
placed high above the main hall suggested the omnipresent gaze of
the sultan, a gaze that was perceived as a symbolic gesture of authority regardless of whether he himself could be detected in silhouette
watching over the events. Ambassadors also ate in the Council
Chamber, making this the more intimate and likely the more presti-
gious site for extending hospitality to the highest-ranking members
of a diplomatic mission (Figure 6.5).

In all events, guests dined in the company of ministers and designated hosts but never in the presence of the sultan, whose status was
deemed according to the Ottoman theory of kingship to be exalted
beyond all mortals, and whose earthly needs, eating among them,
were not to be visible to any but the closest members of the household. Even when the chosen few gained access to the sultan, as on the
very rare occasion of an audience in the Chamber of Petitions (the

Figure 6.5 *"The banquet of the Austrian ambassador at the Council Chamber," from the travels of Hans Ludwig von Kuefsteins in 1628 (after Teply).*

With the sultan in such awesome seclusion, and access to him so severely restricted, the Ottoman reception of ambassadors and other dignitaries was usually held either along the arcades in the second court (Figure 6.3), or in this chamber where the routine affairs of the state were also conducted. Written descriptions and other similar images show that while guests were lavishly dined, they were never honored with the sultan's presence.

one-room audience hall of the Topkapı located just beyond the Gate of Felicity), the guests were led by guards, who held them under the arms, to see the sultan clad in a massively scaled and magnificently tailored robe of bold colors and patterns, and immobile like a statue before the honoree (Figure 6.6). Rigidity and silence dominated all encounters with the sultan and in fact reigned over all ceremonial affairs at the court. This sort of compartmentalization, so typical of the architectural and ceremonial functions at the Topkapı, was utterly alien to the integrated rituals of the Safavids in Isfahan's Daulatkhane.

In large part, the fragmentation of the ceremonial procedure encoded the social discriminations upon which the Ottoman discourse of authority depended. Sultanic legitimacy was predicated upon vivid comparisons with the early history of the caliphate, especially that of the Abbasids, and with Byzantine imperial codes of conduct. Although he was not the spiritual master in the same way that the shahs in Safavid society were (at least until the institutionalization of the normative religious practices), the sultan in the

Figure 6.6 *Istanbul, Topkapı Palace.*
This view looks through the Gate of Felicity toward the doorway and
grilled window of the Chamber of Petitions, the formal audience chamber.
The constricted passageway, the narrow corridor behind it and the
relatively small audience chamber underscore the extreme rigidity of the
Ottoman ceremonies, in sharp contrast to the architectural and ceremonial
accommodation of proximity and conviviality in Safavid Isfahan.

Ottoman discourse of kingship represented the divine authority embodied in the ideological trappings of the caliphate as a system of governance; especially after Selim I (1512–20) took over Cairo and the holy cities and assumed the mantle of the Prophet, the sultan was the Prophet's deputy on earth. Sanctity in the case of the Ottomans drew from the political, ideological, and religious context of caliphal rule and lacked the blood legitimacy that the Safavids had claimed. Yet, like the Safavids, the Ottoman sultans appealed to a mystical past, in their case to the Naqshbandiyye Sufi Order to which they paid homage and provided patronage as a means of securing legitimacy on a popular level. Nevertheless, the distance between these two ways of conceptualizing imperial authority points to the difference in how the Imami Shi'ism of the Safavids had accommodated an alternative form of religiously sanctioned legitimacy. The Holy Roman Emperor received his nominal stamp of legitimacy from the pope; the Ottoman sultan appealed to direct custodianship of the mantle of the Prophet; the Safavids claimed to have the blood of the Imams, and hence of the Prophet, running through their veins.

Similarly complex and distinctive was the Mughal conceptualization of kingship and its centralizing project.[75] Founded by Babur in 1526 as a continuation of the house of Timur, the Sunni Empire of the Mughals also had to accommodate the expectations of kingship as practiced and understood by its majority Hindu subjects. And just as the centralization of an absolutist empire and its legitimating syntax took time to crystallize in the Ottoman and Safavid worlds, so it was also an evolving project in the Mughal period.

To confine this discussion to the period of the sixteenth and seventeenth centuries, there is a considerable disparity between the way in which Babur conducted the empire – a phase that was preoccupied with conquest – and the highly codified and systemized imperial posture of Shah Jahan (1628–1657). In between, the perilous reign of Homayun (1530–40 and 1555–6) gave way to the consolidation of the empire under Emperor Akbar (1556–1605), who completed the Indicization of the Mughals by adopting a brilliant syncretic religious premise that harmonized the diverse and conflicting elements of an empire that served Hindus, Buddhists, Jains, Christians, Jews, and Zoroastrians, as well as all branches of Islam. No other imperium – in the Islamicate world and Asia, much less in Europe – sheltered such a diversity of belief systems. Akbar's *Din-e Elahi* (the Divine Creed) and the principle of *Solh-e Koll*, his declaration of Universal Peace, aimed to accommodate such multiplicity of faiths and practices. As articulated by Abu'l Fazl, the great historian and confidant of Akbar, there is a "social contract" between the king and his subjects that is not tied to a particular faith.[76] Akbar and Abu'l Fazl's concept of an agreement that transcends religious identity precedes by a wide margin of time any similar attempts at theorizing the relationship between the king and his subjects in European history.

Akbar's syncretic religion and its underlying structure of imperial power articulated a different sort of enunciation of legitimacy. The palace of Fatehpur Sikri holds the architectural-visual key to this assemblage of the constituent parts of the empire.[77] Hybrid both in architectural and functional forms and in stylistic choices (materials, techniques, and motifs), Fatehpur Sikri illustrates the architectural syncretism of Akbar's politico-religious syntax of authority. The council chamber of the Diwan-i Khass, for example, is an exceptionally tall and square building whose interior is formed by the hollowness of the cube and the single pillar at the center that rises to meet at the crossing of two elevated passageways or corridors. There, at the central space of the pillar and at the core of the building, Akbar sat in attendance while affairs of the empire were discussed and negotiated. In this case, the architectural rendition and accommodation of the Indic notions of *axis mundi* express the imperial posture of the Muslim ruler.

Equally important to note was the merging of the Persianate and Hindu symbols and practices of kingship.[78] For example, the ancient Persianate notion of *khvarnah*, or what was in Abu'l Fazl's words *farr-e izadi* (the divine light), emanated onto and through the king and rendered him "the Sun, the illuminator of the universe."[79] The Mughal emphasis on the Persianate Sun-King construct fit well with some Hindu beliefs in the status of kings as the semi-divine incarnations of the sun. Accordingly, the Mughal emperors adopted the ritual of *darshan*, appearing after sunrise before a palace window from which the public would receive "a ray from the sun" of "royalty," that is "a light emanating from God," just as the physical sun had risen.[80] The cyclical and infinitely repeating appearance of the emperor at the *jharoka-ye darshan*, "the throne of beholding," expressed notions of authority, its permanence, and its obligation to maintain justice.

As Necipoğlu has aptly noted, this Mughal ritual and its articulation of the reciprocity of the gaze conveys the symbolics of power, as do the assumed omnipresent eye of the sultan represented by the royal windows at the principal gate into the Topkapı and at the Council Chamber and the appearance of the Safavid shahs at the Ali Qapu Palace-Gateway on the Maydan in Isfahan. Windows and the performance of the daily and perpetual framing of the sun or the eye, however, scarcely convey the palpable immediacy that the feasting rituals of the Safavids did. Moreover, and like the Ottomans, Mughal emperors did not attend the kind of large banquets that the shahs in Isfahan hosted. There too, eating in the company of mere mortals did not suit the Mughal discourse of kingship – so painstakingly refined and articulated, by the emperors Jahangir and Shah Jahan in particular during the first half of the seventeenth century – which positioned the emperor, the sun-king, the light of God, in a transcendental realm.

The internal layout of the Red Forts as they were rebuilt or built afresh by Shah Jahan represents the institutionalization of kingship

rituals in which the emperor remained both visible and aloof
(Figures 6.7 and 6.8). The formidability of the outer walls and towers
of the Red Forts was reflected in the spatial regulation and layered
sequencing of the interior (Figure 6.9). Our focus here will remain on
the public zone, where a vast courtyard and an equally impressive
audience hall constituted the arena of encounter with the emperor
(Figures 6.10 and 6.11). And as in the Ottoman case, foreign visitors
and envoys, local vassal kings, and the *mansabdars* (the officials of the
imperial household whose loyalty was secured through grants of land
and office) lined the courtyard and gathered under the roof of the pillared hall in a hierarchical order in which relative proximity and distance from the emperor reflected an individual's status (Figures 6.12,
6.13 and Plate 24). In no instance, however, did the ceremonial transform into a convivial scene.

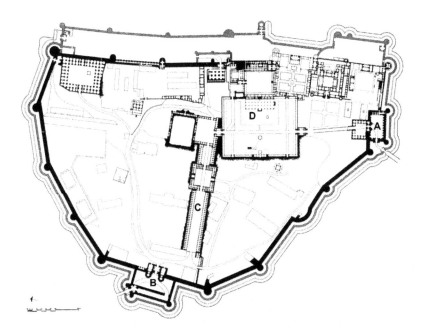

Figure 6.7 *Agra, Red Fort, site plan (after Koch).*
Massive walls and watchtowers in red stone give the Mughal palatine
establishments their name. There is little spatial-urban relationship
between the city and the palace-fort, which looms as a massive and
impenetrable structure on the western bank of the Yamuna River. Access
to the interior is through multilayered gateways. While successive
emperors constructed the Agra Fort, it was Shah Jahan's additions in the
1630s that formalized its ceremonial features and the procedures that
governed access to the emperor. A) Amar Singh Gate and Akbari Darwaza;
B) the Elephant Gate, the principal ceremonial gate into the fort; C) the
Bazaar, which served the needs of the harem and the court; D) Diwan-i
Amm, the audience hall and its courtyard.

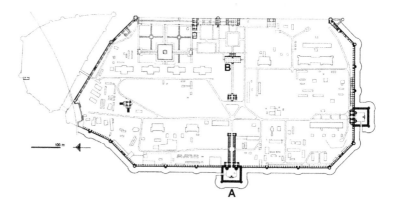

Figure 6.8 *Delhi, Red Fort, site plan (after Koch).*

Shah Jahan's construction of the Red Fort along the bank of Yamuna River in Delhi was linked to the founding of his new city of Shahjahanabad (begun 1638). Inspired in part by Isfahan, the principal artery of the city extended straight outward to meet the main gate of the fort. However, the palace precinct remained heavily fortified. The internal layout of the complex's principal ceremonial features exemplifies the strict bilateral symmetry imposed on all Shah Jahan's architectural projects. A) the Lahore Gate, followed by a bazaar; B) the Diwan-i Amm and its courtyard.

Figure 6.9 *Agra, Red Fort, Amar Singh Gate and a view of the fortifications.*

Figure 6.10 *Agra, Red Fort, Diwan-i Amm.*

Shah Jahan's addition in the 1630s of the pillared audience hall to the Red Fort at Agra introduced a new era in Mughal imperial ceremonials. Shah Jahan's Diwan-i Amm buildings, including those at the Red Forts of Delhi and Lahore, were constructed as almost freestanding buildings, which were horizontally stretched, with the *jharoka* throne at the center of the rear wall. The spatial proximity and distance from the throne dictated the hierarchical order of guests and dignitaries relative to the emperor. Neither the architectural configuration of these halls nor the ceremonial procedures of the Mughals, however, allowed for public displays of conviviality.

Figure 6.11 *Agra, Red Fort, Diwan-i Amm.*

This view from the *jharoka* throne out to the courtyard demonstrates the deliberate limits placed on the emperor's arc of vision. Conversely, those who were standing or seated in the hall but towards its outer flanks were entirely outside this visual zone of privilege.

Figure 6.12 *Delhi, Red Fort, Diwan-i Amm.*
The massive, stone-pillared hall is entirely turned to the vast courtyard and is oriented toward the formal walkway leading from the main gate to it.

Figure 6.13 *Delhi, Red Fort, Diwan-i Amm.*
View of the interior arcade with its magnificent scalloped arches and carved sandstone pillars. The *jharoka*, visible on the left-hand side and against the back wall, is a free-standing carved and inlaid marble throne emulating European examples.

The Mughals and the Ottomans inherited the same traditions of feasting. They, too, dined and wined their guests, but in open court-yards, tents, and arcades and never in the company of the sultan or the emperor. Neither in Istanbul's Topkapı nor in the Delhi, Agra, and Lahore Red Forts, is there any building comparable in size and func-tion to the Talar-e Tavile or the Chehel Sotun. The presence of the Safavid shahs at feasts sharply contrasted, as Europeans inform us, with the Byzantine-inspired seclusion of the Ottoman sultans or the aloofness of the Mughal emperors, whose minority rule over a majority Hindu populace entailed different rituals of appearance and invisibility.

Prescribed patterns and practices of communal eating are so plainly pregnant with meaning, especially to the anthropologist, as to hardly need repeating. Yet, to the historian of architecture, and espe-cially of that which pertains to the Islamicate world, feasting, its presence or absence, its sites and rituals of performance, its accou-trements and procedures, have acquired little localized significance. Situating the ritual in its context, so obvious as to need no prosely-tizing, privileges variability over an assumption of indolence in the upholding of traditions. While feasting among the Turco-Mongol predecessors of the Safavids was vigorously charged, mobile, and undisciplined, their contemporaries who shared the same Turco-Mongol heritage manipulated those traditions differently. Thus the Ottoman premium on the sultan's transcendence and the cultivation of an aura of absolute distance and inviolable superiority severely cur-tailed the privilege of even a glimpse of the royal visage, much more the chance for sharing a meal in his presence. The Mughal emperors appeared and disappeared in mandated daily intervals and sat in audi-ence, yet never personally feasted any but a select company, and only in private.

In a more geographically distant comparison, but one that shares the absolutist mandates and procedures of the early modern era, Louis XIV summoned his courtiers to Versailles to share in the sumptuous royal *fêtes* thrown by the monarch. There they attended balls and theatrical performances where watching the king gorge himself on quantities of diverse foods must have counted as a highlight of the evening festivi-ties.[81] In such instances the guests were fed, but their meal was a ritual conducted separately from that in which the public observed the king dining. Louis XIV ate in public with great gusto and from a stupefying array of dishes, yet: "Being alone at the table did not mean that the king was literally alone; in addition to the servants, a group of high-ranking nobles and court officials would always stand at a respectful distance looking on."[82] Similarly, the Burgundian-Spanish protocol of Louis's court maintained a strict division between the king's private and public life, and eating was considered part of the latter. On the other hand, the pope never ate in public view, a fact directly related to his transcendent status in Christendom as the embodiment of spiritual authority. Papal authority was indeed invoked to lend sanctity to the absolutist kings of the early modern age in Europe – witnessed through such alliances as that between Charles V and Clement VII in the middle of the sixteenth century. And nowhere was this link between Christ and the king more carefully cultivated as a symbol of consecrated kingship than in the case of the Hapsburgs, whose studied seclusion, especially in regards to eating, resembled Ottoman practices.[83]

Ziyafat or feasting in Safavid Isfahan was not about consuming grand meals. Nor was it intended to showcase a confederacy of rule. Rather, it was predicated on an imperial form of communal dining that presupposed the personal attendance of the king as host, his active command of the events, and a ranking system and a social scheme that was woven into the codes of hospitality and treatment of guests. It seems too obvious to state, but given the fundamental significance of feasting in this early modern Safavid example of absolutism and centralization, it is worth underlining the fact that on the level of a royal household it was the religio-political station of the king that mattered the most: he remained the master of ceremonies, regardless of his presence, his absence, or the degree and nature of his engagement.

Feasting in Isfahan punctuated the spectacle of the court ceremonials with its display of material splendor and its implied politico-spiritual largesse. The host was no less than the shah himself, present in the flesh on the throne of kingship, which stood as the proxy for the throne of heaven, where his masters, Imam Ali and the Prophet Mohammad, were to be seated. The multitudes of people feasted on the bounty symbolizing the heavenly grant of beneficence as understood and enunciated in the Perso-Shi'i personification of kingship. The richly colored and patterned textiles and carpets; the opulently varied array of costumes worn by servants, eunuchs, dancers, and dignitaries as they moved about the space; the light shimmering off of gold, silver, copper, brass, and bronze candlesticks, torches, basins, pails, bottles, and cups; the sound of gurgling water fountains, of music and singing, and of sotto voce conversations; the mingling of the fragrances of foods, flowers, and perfumes – the whole was displayed as a *tableau vivant* whose task it was vividly to represent "the alliance between eating and power."[84]

Conclusion

This book has aimed to recover a lost Isfahan, to repopulate it at its apogee, and to change the conventional, albeit adulatory, views of the city as the capital of the Safavids. In so doing, the book has challenged received notions about the conventions of palatine architecture and urban design in the Islamicate world. It has argued that the Safavid practice of kingship drew from the interlaced principles and practices of a two-pronged cultural authority: the Persianate tradition of kingship and the ancient notions of the king's aura of splendor or *farr*, on the one hand, and the Imami Shiʿi extractions from the Qurʾan and the *hadith* (sayings and deeds attributed to the Prophet) on the points of legal- or *shariʿa*-based legitimacy of authority, on the other. This final chapter has aimed to see, through the lens of feasting and the ritualized movement and repose that activated the palaces, the "aesthetic" of built space as it came to embody and accommodate the Perso-Shiʿi mode of kingship in Safavid Isfahan. In interrogating the construction of a "throne-worthy-abode," this chapter has explored the place of feasting in the Safavid etiquette of kingship and its articulation of a social behavior that denotes inviolable authority.

In its codified script and its designed plentitude, feasting and its accoutrements – dinnerware, furnishings, food, dress, gifts, entertainment, and associated spaces – convey, fashion, and amplify the particularized Safavid notions of charismatic absolutism and its Perso-Shiʿi definition. Amid the spatial and visual splendor of the ceremonial palaces, surrounded by hundreds of attendants and guests, and stimulated by the sensory spectacle of sights, sounds, and tastes, Safavid shahs enchanted the beholders and those beyond. They acted as the masters of their own ceremonies, sharing food and entertainment as subtle yet unmistakable emblems of their absolutist imperative. The hierarchies of distance and proximity, activity and passivity, enacted at royal feasts and festivals situated the king as the ideal personification of the Shiʿi and Iranian conceptions of justice and generosity – principles mandated by the divine cosmic order and mediated through the Prophet Mohammad and Imam Ali, the First Shiʿi Imam. Spiritual and chivalric impulses informed the development of the Safavid language of kingship, whose constancy and perpetual relevance were displayed through the architectural medium of the palaces in the ceremonial of feasting.

The nascent Safavid era in the early part of the sixteenth century was rife with social, cultural, and political spasms and upheavals. This chaos spurred the centralization and institution of an idealized vision of the kingdom of God on earth as it was conceptualized in Persianate Twelver Shiʿism. Isfahan, the city "whose rank is that of Paradise," represented in the totality of its built environment, and especially the palaces in the Daulatkhane, the terrestrial rendition of this utopian paradise.[85] This was the capital city whose character the pre-eminent historian of Shah Abbas the Great so ingeniously encapsulated in the couplet:

They say Isfahan is half the world
[By so saying] They describe [only] half of Isfahan.[86]

Notes

1. Kaempfer, *Amoenitatum Exoticarum*, 223; *Am Hofe*, 246. Kaempfer provides a long and detailed description of the ceremonial events at the court of Shah Solayman when he accompanied the Swedish ambassador in 1684–5. Translations are mine.

2. Chardin's passage quoted at the beginning of the book is enhanced with even greater detail by Kaempfer, *Amoenitatum Exoticarum*, 223–50 and in *Am Hofe*, 246–83, where he describes the minutiae of what took place during a feast-audience in 1684 when several ambassadors were received at once. These richly detailed accounts of *objets de luxe* will need to be culled for another study.

3. The prohibition on wine was enforced periodically throughout the Safavid period; see Taher-e Vahid-e Qazvini, *Tarikh-e jahan-ara-ye Abbasi*, 412–16, for example, for the 1645 one imposed by Shah Abbas II along with prohibitions on prostitution, the making and sale of *pustin* coats by the Armenians, and other religiously unlawful activities.

4. The subjects of drinking and drugs in Safavid Iran are most recently studied by Rudi Matthee, *The Pursuit of Pleasure. Drugs and Stimulants in Iranian History, 1500–1900* (Washington, DC: Mage Publishers, 2005), especially 37–96. Indeed, excessive drinking and addiction among the courtiers and the shahs is well documented; see Matthee, *The Pursuit of Pleasure*, 48–66. The point here remains that the etiquette of drinking was integrated with the rest of the feasting rituals at the *talar* palaces. On wine and wine-drinking in the Islamic context, see also, among others, Richard Tapper, "Blood, Wine and Water: social and symbolic aspects of drinks and drinking in the Islamic Middle East," in *Culinary Cultures of the Middle East*, ed. Sami Zubaida and Richard Tapper (London and New York: I. B. Tauris, 1994), 215–32. On the literary dimensions of food, see Geert Jan van Gelder, *God's Banquet: Food in Classical Arabic Literature* (New York: Columbia University Press, 2000).

5. Herbert, *Travels in Persia*, 260.

6. See William Foster's notes in Herbert's travel account, *Travels in Persia*, 260, fn. 2 and 266, fn. 1.

7. On this subject, see A. H. Morton, "The *chūb-i tarflq* and *Qizilbāsh* Ritual in Safavid Persia," in *Etudes Safavides*, ed. J. Calmard (Paris-Tehran: Institut Français de Recherche en Iran, 1993): 225–45.

8. Kaempfer, *Am Hofe*, 274.

9. Babayan, *Mystics, Monarchs and Messiahs*, 165–74 on *javanmardi* and related concepts such as *fotovvat*.

10. Dehkhoda, *Loghatname*, 5:6931.

11. Seven such *fotovvatname*, all dating to pre-Safavid times, are collected in Morteza Sarraf, ed. with an introduction in French by Henry Corbin, *Rasa'el-e javanmardan* (Tehran and Paris: Department D'Iranologie de L'Institut Franco-Iranien de Recherche, 1973). A useful study of the subject is Mohammad Ja'far Majzub, *A'in-e javanmardi ya fotovvat* (New York: Bibliotheca Persica Press, 2000).

12. Babayan, *Mystics, Monarchs and Messiahs*, 165ff., where she makes extensive use of this text in constructing her argument on the brotherhoods formed around devotion to Ali. This manual may also be considered as belonging to an instructional genre of which the *Ershad al-zira'a* is well known. The latter condensed the Timurid knowledge and traditions of agriculture as well as horticulture at a time when their

successors, especially in Central Asia and India, sought to invoke the
Timurid heritage as a means of claiming legitimacy. For the agriculture
manual and its significance for garden designs of the sixteenth century,
see Subtelny, "Agriculture and the Timurid Chahārbāgh."

13. This and the next quotation are from Kashefi, *Fotovvatname-ye soltani*,
233.

14. *Ashpazi-ye daure-ye Safavi, matn-e do resale az an daure*, ed. Iraj Afshar
(Tehran: Entesharat-e Seda va Sima, 1360/1981), 210–11.

15. The copy I have used is Shaykh Baha'i, *Jame'-e Abbasi* (Tehran: Farahani
Publishers, n.d.). This copy was reprinted under the patronage of
Ayatollah Najafi Mar'ashi from the 1319AH/1280SH/1901/2CE Bombay
printed version. It includes five chapters by Shaykh Baha'i, while the rest
were added by Shaykh Nezam al-Din Savoji, one of the disciples of the
Ayatollah. For the significance of this manual in matters of jurispru-
dence and its centrality to seventeenth-century Iran, see Amir
Arjomand, *The Shadow of God*, 207–9.

16. On medieval manuals of kingship, see A. K. S. Lambton, "Justice in the
Medieval Persian Theory of Kingship," *Studia Islamica* 16 (1962): 91–
119; see also Amir Arjomand, *The Shadow of God*, 94–5.

17. On Majlesi's role, see Amir Arjomand, *The Shadow of God*, 151–5 and
175–8.

18. For du Mans, his long stay in Isfahan, and his richly documented
memoir, see Francis Richard, *Raphaël du Mans, missionaire en Perse au
XVIIe s.*, 2 volumes (Paris: Société d'Histoire de l'Orient–L'Harmattan,
1995).

19. The significance of the conversion of the Georgian aristocracy and their
incorporation into the *gholam* system and the Safavid household is discussed by Babayan, "The Safavid Household Reconfigured."

20. These small dishes are now associated with the Turkish and Greek *meze*
that accompany the drinking of alcohol.

21. Herbert, *Travels in Persia*, 257. Little scholarship exists on the history
of Persian food and culinary arts; for a couple of examples, see Bert
Fragner, "Social Reality and Culinary Fiction: the perspective of cook-
books from Iran and Central Asia," in *Culinary Cultures of the Middle
East*, ed. Richard Tapper and Sami Zubaida (London; New York: I. B.
Tauris, 1994), 63–71; and M. R. Ghanoonparvar, "Culinary Arts in the
Safavid Period," in *Iran and Iranian Studies. Essays in Honor of Iraj
Afshar*, ed. Kambiz Eslami (Princeton, NJ: Zagros Press, 1998), 191–7.
Although the number of rice recipes in seventeenth-century cookbooks
far exceeds those offered in modern cookbooks, the variety in the living
cuisine of Iran is remarkable; see, for example, Najmieh Batmanglij,
*New Food of Life; Ancient Persian and Modern Iranian Cooking
and Ceremonies* (Washington, DC: Mage Publishers, 1992), especially
141–208.

22. Taher-e Vahid-e Qazvini, *Tarikh-e jahan-ara-ye Abbasi*, 733–4, and 728–
9 on the popular protest.

23. For the *nauruzi* gifting, see Rudolph Matthee, "Gift and Gift-giving in
the Safavid Period," *Encyclopaedia Iranica*, Vol. 10 (2001), 609–14, esp.
609. The occurrence of the *Ashura* in 1666 has been noted by Calmard,
"Shi'i Rituals and Power," 164, quoting Chardin, *Voyages du Chevaliers
Chardin*, vol. 9, 57. Like Calmard, Babayan sees in the link between the
Ashura performances and palace site evidence for the imperial appropriation of popular devotion and the synthesis of Imami religious

doctrines and the symbols of authority. While I agree with this assessment, I do not think that the Talar-e Tavile's principal purpose was to serve for such religious ceremonies.

24. Chardin, *Voyages du Chevalier Chardin*, vol. 5, 470–3; Kaempfer, *Amoenitatum Exoticarum*, 227–30.

25. Translated and quoted by Ferrier, *A Journey to Persia*, 66–7; Chardin, *Voyages du Chevalier Chardin*, vol. 5, 469–70.

26. Chardin, *Voyages du Chevalier Chardin*, vol. 5, 471–2; Kaempfer, *Amoenitatum Exoticarum*, 226–31. For the significance of these offices in Safavid bureaucracy, see Floor, *Safavid Government Institutions*.

27. Kaempfer, *Am Hofe*, 258–62.

28. Chardin, *Voyages du Chevalier Chardin*, vol. 5, 472–3; Kaempfer, *Amoenitatum Exoticarum*, 228–30.

29. Having an audience with the Aqqoyunlu shahs in the fifteenth-century Palace of Hasht Behesht at the Daulatkhane in Tabriz and with Timur at his tented encampments outside Samarqand also required waiting in designated areas to accommodate the wishes of the ruler. For the former, see Chapter 2 in this book; for the latter, see Clavijo, *Embassy to Tamerane*, 257, for example.

30. Jean Chardin, translated and quoted in Ferrier, *A Journey to Persia*, 66; Chardin, *Voyages du Chevalier Chardin*, vol. 5, 469–70.

31. Olearius, *The Voyages and Travels of the Ambassadors*, 201–3, where he describes the alleyway leading from the Ali Qapu to the Talar-e Tavile Palace, a route that served also to conduct guests to the Chehel Sotun, albeit continuing further past the entrance into the former palace. See also Tavernier, *The Six Voyages*, 178–80.

32. Translated quote is from Ferrier, *A Journey to Persia*, 66; Chardin, *Voyages du Chevalier Chardin*, vol. 5, 469–70.

33. The *mehmandar* served as a guide and host to an ambassador and his retinue; nearly all European visitors to seventeenth-century Isfahan note their guide-host; see for example, Chardin, *Voyages du Chevalier Chardin*, vol. 5, 372.

34. Olearius, *The Voyages and Travels of the Ambassadors*, 203.

35. Matthee, "Gift and Gift-giving," 609.

36. Chardin, *Voyages du Chevalier Chardin*, vol. 3, 175–7.

37. For the classic study of the social significance of gifts and gifting, see Marcel Mauss, *The Gift* (New York; London: W. W. Norton, 1967). For the Persianate context of gifting, see Ann Lambton, "Pishkash: Present or Tribute?" *Bulletin of the School of Oriental and African Studies* 57, no. 1 (1944): 144–58.

38. For the Persepolis iconography of kingship, see Margaret C. Root, *The King and Kingship in Achaemenid Art: Essays on the Creation of an Iconography of Empire*. Acta Iranica 19 (Leiden: Brill, 1979), especially 300–11 and 227–67 for the tribute procession reliefs at the entrance into the Apadana palace. See also Pierre Briant and Clarisse Herrenschmidt, eds, *Le Tribut dans l'empire perse* (Paris: Peeters, 1989) and Heleen Sancisi-Weerdenburg, "Gifts in the Persian Empire," in *Le Tribut dans l'empire perse*, ed. Pierre Briant and Clarisse Herrenschmidt (Paris: Peeters, 1989), 129–46.

39. The gifting parades in the famous *Padshahnama* of Shah Jahan are among the most striking paintings in that magnificent manuscript; see Milo Beach and Ebba Koch, *King of the World; The Padshahnama, an imperial Mughal manuscript from the Royal Library, Windsor Castle* (London;

Washington, DC: Azimuth Editions and Sackler Gallery, 1997), especially "Europeans Bring Gift to Shah-Jahan," 56–7, where Europeans carry their own gifts and "Shah-Jahan Receives the Persian Ambassador, Muhammad Ali Beg," 52–3, where servants carry the gifts for the ambassador and his retinue. For an Ottoman example, see the presentation of the Austrian ambassadorial gifts to the sultan from the Album of Lambert Wyts, in Necipoğlu, *Architecture, Ceremonial, and Power*, 65, fig. 40.

40. An excellent survey of gifts in the Safavid period and analysis of their social and especially economic value in that period of Iranian history is offered by Matthee, "Gift and Gift-Giving."

41. Chardin, *Voyages du Chevalier Chardin*, vol. 3, 170.

42. The social and symbolic value of the gifting of robes of honor was recognized across Eurasia; see Stewart Gordon, ed., *Robes and Honor: the Medieval World of Investiture* (New York: Palgrave, 2001).

43. The quote from Sa'eb-e Tabrizi, the court poet of Shah Abbas II, is about the *talar* at the Chehel Sotun; for the poem and its translation, see Babaie, "Safavid Palaces in Isfahan," 317–18.

44. The failure in scholarship to recognize the calculated nature and synchronized choreography of access and proximity in the Safavid case has contributed to the misunderstanding of the seventeenth-century rituals in Isfahan as a mere extension of tribal practices.

45. Barbaro describes several audiences, *Travels to Tana and Persia*, 51–60.

46. Barbaro, *Travels to Tana and Persia*, 52.

47. Barbaro, *Travels to Tana and Persia*, 53. This was, perhaps, not unlike bull-fighting as entertainment.

48. Barbaro, *Travels to Tana and Persia*, 55.

49. The following passage is quoted by Woods, *The Aqquyunlu*, 137.

50. Such a scenario of economic decline and its impact on artistic production in late Timurid Herat is developed by Lisa Golombek, "Discourses of an Imaginary Arts Council in Fifteenth-Century Iran," in *Timurid Art and Culture; Iran and Central Asia in the Fifteenth Century*, ed. Lisa Golombek and Maria Subtelny (Leiden: Brill, 1992), 1–17.

51. The cultural habits formed in the Timurid *majles* are discussed by Maria Subtelny in "Scenes from the Literary Life of Timurid Herat," in *Logos Islamikos: Studia Islamica in honorem Georgii Michaelis Wickens*, ed. Roger Savory and Dionisius A. Agius (Toronto: Pontifical Institute of Medieval Studies, 1984), 137–55, and Subtelny, "Art and Politics in Early Sixteenth-Century Central Asia," *Central Asiatic Journal* 27, nos. 1–2 (1983): 121–48.

52. Clavijo, *Embassy to Tamerlane*, especially 218–56.

53. Clavijo, *Embassy to Tamerlane*, 220.

54. Clavijo, *Embassy to Tamerlane*, 224–5.

55. Clavijo, *Embassy to Tamerlane*, 231, describes the manner of serving wine and the expectation that all guests drink regardless of their wishes or capacity.

56. Giovanni Maria Angeiolello in *A Narrative of Italian Travels in Persia*, 110–11.

57. Romano in *A Narrative of Italian Travels in Persia*, 201–2.

58. Membré, *Mission to the Lord Sophy of Persia*, 32–3.

59. Gulbadan Begum's *Homayunname* is translated with introduction and notes by Annette S. Beveridge as *The History of Humāyūn (Humāyūn-Nāma), by Gul-Badan Begam* (New Delhi: Oriental Books Reprint Corporation, 1983); see especially 168–74.

60. Persian sources are especially important on this subject; for a chart showing the movements of Shah Abbas the Great, see Babaie, "Safavid Palaces in Isfahan," 308–10.

61. Della Valle, *Viaggi di Pietro della Valle*, 638–73.

62. Figuera, *L'Ambassade*, 4–5 and 299–305.

63. Herbert, *Travels in Persia*, xxvii–xxxi and 154–7.

64. Della Valle, *Viaggi di Pietro della Valle*, 673.

65. Figuera, *L'Ambassade*, 330.

66. Disciplinary demarcations have tended to consider dining and food habits as a separate subject from the spatial and visual dimensions of the practices of communal eating. This makes a comparative study much more challenging than I can manage in this book but I hope to return to it at a later time. For a discussion of some aspects of dining and architecture in an early modern context, see Samuel John Klingensmith, *The Utility of Splendor; Ceremony, Social Life, and Architecture at the Court of Bavaria, 1600–1800* (Chicago: University of Chicago Press, 1993), especially 159–69.

67. A thought-provoking overview of palaces in the Ancient Near East, with a start-up bibliography for the non-specialist, is found in Irene Winter's " 'Seat of Kingship'/ 'A Wonder to Behold': The Palace as Construct in the Ancient Near East," *Ars Orientalis* 23 (1993): 27–55.

68. The literature on food in antiquity is dauntingly large for this space. For a few examples, see John Wilkins, David Harvey and Mike Dobson, eds, *Food in Antiquity* (Exeter: University of Exeter Press, 1996), and Jean-Louis Flandrin and Massimo Montanari, eds, *Food; A Culinary History from Antiquity to the Present*, translated edition of *Histoire de l'alimentation* (New York: Columbia University Press, 1999). See Strong, *Feast*, 8–43 for a useful overview of the Greek and Roman banquets with many references. For the Achaemenid side of food and further references, see Heleen Sancisi-Weerdenburg, "Persian Food: Stereotypes and Political Identity," in *Food in Antiquity*, 286–302. See also the collection of essays in *La sociabilité à table: Commensalité et convivialité à travers les ages*, Actes du colloque de Rouen (Rouen: University of Rouen Press, 1992).

69. For examples of banqueting scenes in the arts of the Ancient Near East, see the famous Standard of Ur in the British Museum and cylinder seals found in the royal tombs at Ur, Mesopotamia, all from the Early Dynastic period (c. 2550–2400 BCE.); Joan Aruz with Ronald Wallenfels, eds, *Art of the First Cities: The Third Millennium B.C. from the Mediterranean to the Indus* (New York, New Haven and London: Metropolitan Museum of Art and Yale University Press, 2003), 97–100 and 103. For a recent and exhaustive study of the Persepolis seals, see M. B. Garrison and Margaret C. Root, *Seals on the Persepolis Fortification Tablets* (Chicago: University of Chicago Oriental Institute Publications, 2001).

70. In the context of a house, rooms were designed for dining from as early as the fifth century BCE; see, for example, Brigitta Bergquist, "Sympotic Space: A Functional Aspect of Greek Dining-Rooms," in *Sympotica. A Symposium on the Symposion*, ed. Oswyn Murray (Oxford: Clarendon Press; New York: Oxford University Press, 1994), 37–65. For a good survey of the Roman practices and their Greek inspiration, see Strong, *Feast*, 3–43, esp. 28. For the architectural study of the houses and their dining areas, see Andrew Wallace-Hadrill, *Houses and Society in*

Pompeii and Herculaneum (Princeton: Princeton University Press, 1994), especially 8–16 and 17–37.

71. The Roman banqueting couch implies an architectural and spatial form that could accommodate the needs of seeing and being seen. A point to interrogate further is the relationship between the ancient Near Eastern traditions of *banquet couchant* and architectural forms.

72. A distinction should also be made between private or family chambers for dining and the ceremonial banqueting halls of imperial palaces. As Strong, *Feast*, 147–57, suggests, the classical dining room re-emerged in the context of the Renaissance villa and its emulation of such life that was inspired by the writings of Pliny the Younger. Otherwise, grand dining took place, along with other ceremonial events, in the state halls and antechambers to the throne rooms of such palaces as the Louvre, Versailles, and the Kremlin.

73. For the Dolmabahce, see Celik Gülersoy, *Dolabahce* (Istanbul: İstanbul Kitablığı, 1984); for the Golestan Palace in Tehran and its late nineteenth-century additions (especially the so-called Talar-e Ayeneh, a stately hall of mirrors without any pillared section), see Yahya Zoka', *Tarikhche-ye sakhtemanha-ye arg-e saltanati-e Tehran va rah-nama-ye kakh-e Golestan* (Tehran: Entesharat-e Anjoman-e Asar-e Melli, 1349/1970; and Jennifer Scarce, "The royal palaces of the Qajar dynasty; a survey," in *Qajar Iran; Political, Social, and Cultural Change 1800–1925*, ed. Clifford Edmund Bosworth and Carole Hillenbrand, reprint edn (Costa Mesa, CA: Mazda Publishers, 1992), 329–51, esp. 339–40.

74. Necipoğlu, *Architecture, Ceremonial, and Power*, 79–84.

75. Given the long period of Mughal rule, from 1526 to 1858, and its great upheavals, it would be unwise to generalize on this subject. For a history of the Mughals, see John Richards, *The Mughal Empire* (Cambridge and New York: Cambridge University Press, 1996). See also Koch, "Diwan-i 'Amm and Chihil Sutun," for a consideration of the palaces and ceremonies of kingship in the classical period between the reigns of Akbar and Shah Jahan from 1556 until 1657.

76. See, for example, S. A. A. Rizvi, *Religious and Intellectual History of the Muslims in Akbar's Reign* (New Delhi: Munshiram Manoharlal Publishers, 1975).

77. Brand and Lowry, *Akbar's India*, especially 35–54.

78. Catherine Asher, "Sub-Imperial Palaces: Power and Authority in Mughal India," in *Ars Orientalis* XXIII (1993), 281–302 is an especially important opening on this subject. Necipoğlu's discussion of kingship in the Mughal classical period has also informed my brief consideration here; "Framing the Gaze," especially 312–17.

79. As quoted in Necipoğlu, "Framing the Gaze," 314 from *A'in e akbari*, vol. 1, 3; 1, 163.

80. Ibid.

81. On feasting at the French court and especially that of Louis XIV at Versailles, see Strong, *Feast*, 258–62. Strong's book offers a very useful comparative study of feasting and eating habits of European courts.

82. Strong, *Feast*, 250.

83. For the Hapsburg practice, see Fernando Chesa, "The Court of the Spanish Habsburgs 1500–1700," in *The Princely Courts of Europe: Rituals, Politics and Culture under the Ancien Regime 1500–1750*, ed. John Adamson (London: Weidenfeld and Nicolson, 1999), 43–65.

84. Strong, *Feast*, 209 uses the phrase in relation to Louis XV and the changes in dining rituals at his court in the first half of the eighteenth century.
85. Natanzi, *Noqavat al-asar*, 376.
86. Monshi, *Tarikh-e alam ara-ye Abbasi*, 544.

CHAPTER SEVEN

Epilogue: The Fall of Isfahan

ON THE TWENTIETH of Jamadi al-Avval of the year 1134 (8 March 1722), a helter-skelter contingent of Safavid troops made a desperate attempt to stop the Afghan assault on Isfahan. Afghan hordes had come menacingly close to the Safavid capital since they set out from Herat some months earlier and were on the verge of entering the suburban palace of Farahabad, Shah Soltan Hossayn's preferred seat of rule. Here, the cool, paradisiacal environs, lined with tall trees and flowing waters and protected by little more than flimsy walls, were to become the nerve center of Afghan operations that would unleash a campaign of bloody murder on the world-famous Safavid capital. Farahabad's architectural and logistical vulnerability – in retrospect, a sign of naïve confidence in the immunity of the Safavid kings – had already forced Shah Soltan Hossayn into abandoning his favorite retreat for the Daulatkhane inside the walled city.

Emboldened by their earlier conquest of Kerman, Afghans arrived from the southeastern side of the city, where they rounded the Zayande River and met the Persians in battle. The Safavids suffered a crushing defeat at the hand of Mahmud and his soldiers in the village of Golunabad near Isfahan. The shah had asked the Armenians to send three hundred of their young men to protect the palace in Isfahan while his men were deployed to fight off Mahmud.[1] On Nauruz 1722 (21 March, the spring equinox and the Persian New Year), Mahmud occupied *shahr-e mobarak-e Farahabad*, the exalted city of Farahabad.[2] From there he dispatched his troops to subdue and conquer villages around Isfahan, including the prosperous New Julfa, the Armenian suburb. Now camped in comfortable proximity to Isfahan, their ultimate target, Afghan troops plundered the suburb, took dozens of its young women, and forcibly procured provisions from residents of New Julfa while laying siege to Isfahan from Jamadi al-Avval 1134 until Muharram 1135 (March–October 1722). During this time they made several attempts to cross one of the numerous bridges into the city. In one instance, they took over the Marnan Bridge and occupied portions of the famed Abbasabad quarter to the southwest of the city.[3] For those months, their efforts remained limited to minor skirmishes that nonetheless were harrowingly close calls for the Isfahanis.[4]

When Isfahan finally fell, between the eleventh and fifteenth of the month of Muharram 1135 (October 1722), seven months and twenty-three days had elapsed since the Afghans had laid the city under siege.[5] The blockade had taken a heavy toll on the denizens of Isfahan; refugees from surrounding villages and suburbs filled "not only the Houses, but even the Gardens, Streets, and Publick Squares."[6] Shortages were thereby aggravated, and there came a state of famine so intense that people began eating dogs and cats and even the flesh of the dead.[7] According to Father Krusinski, the suffering, already comparable to that of Jerusalem when besieged by Titus and Vespasian, was made even more unbearably frightful because of the daily flow of rumors.[8] The terrified residents traded tales of imminent Afghan entry, the brutal massacre and plunder of nearby villages and other cities (especially Kerman), and dashed hopes for reinforcement troops and rescue missions – Tahmasb Mirza, the eldest prince, was sent out to gather troops but ended up assuming a temporary throne in Qazvin, with no success in procuring help.[9]

Having failed to protect his beloved Farahabad despite all efforts, including the placement of cannons at the entrance into the royal precinct, Shah Soltan Hossayn must have been keenly aware of the extreme vulnerability of the capital city. The inadequacy of the city's defenses, so brilliant a symbol of politico-military confidence in the earlier part of the seventeenth century and so horrible a liability a hundred years later, forced the shah to order the preparation of rooms in the Qal'e Tabarrok (the fortification, arsenal, and treasury) and to dig and fill moats (*khandaq*) with water around the old fortress.[10] All proved of no avail.

According to the diaries of the Dutch East Indies Companies (VOC), on 13 October 1722, the grand vizier left Isfahan for the Afghan encampment at Farahabad to begin negotiations.[11] Sensing desperation, Mahmud demanded that the shah himself come to Farahabad and "hand over to him his person and crown, and therewith the kingdom itself." Mahmud's threat to annihilate the city, should the shah choose to do otherwise, forced Shah Soltan Hossayn and his council to submit to the harshest terms. Before surrendering to Mahmud, the shah donned all-black clothing, removed all royal insignia, and walked through the principal streets of the city, taking one last look, in his capacity as the sovereign king, at his capital and commiserating in shared wretchedness and defeat with his subjects.[12] At eleven o'clock on 21 October, the shah rode out in darkness, accompanied by a small contingent of servants.[13] "This departure was witnessed by the Dutch dispenser, Mr. Lypsig, the English divine, Mr. Fraast, I myself (Friar Alexander of Malabar) and some 12 Iranian men and women, the King asked a napkin from one of his servants to wipe his sad eyes."[14] In this tragic twist of fate, Shah Soltan Hossayn had to march in shame, riding over the dead bodies strewn along the streets of Isfahan as he made his way to his beloved Farahabad palace to personally hand the capital city and his royal crown (*jiqqe* or plume) to the reviled Afghan conqueror.

As though these humiliations were not enough, four days later Mahmud forced the shah to ride with only a few of his servants, under bright morning light, at the tail end of a cortege of four to five thousand troops marching to the triumphal tune of trumpets and drums into the city. The march was preceded by twelve soldiers cursing the shah's religion, an exclamation of the Sunni conquerors' newly acquired supremacy that stabbed at the very heart of Shi'i imperium. Under the protection of his ancestors Shah Isma'il and Shah Tahmasb, the cursing of the Sunni caliphs of early Islam had been turned into ritualized performances by the *tabarra'iyan* (those who dissociated themselves from the Sunnis who were the enemies of the Twelve Imams), who were employed to march through the streets of Tabriz and curse the first three caliphs.[15] One hundred and fifty years later, nothing could have been more humiliating than to parade the Safavid shah, the sole imperial bearer of the flag of Twelver Shi'ism in the early modern period, through his capital city to the chanting of Sunni curses!

Mahmud and his troops chose to make their ceremonial entrance over the Khwaju Bridge. Soon after, the shah was separated and sent off quietly to the Daulatkhane, while Mahmud rode his horse over the precious gold-embroidered textiles that the people of Isfahan had laid in his path. He entered the palace precinct from the Chahar Hauz Maydan, the square on the northeastern corner of the precinct that was associated with administrative functions and was located before the Daftarkhane or chancellery.[16] Three days after his triumphal entry (on 28 October 1722), Mahmud had the royal treasury opened and was surprised to find less than he expected. Notwithstanding the terrible effects of the long months of siege, the treasury had already been depleted over the previous decades of economic mismanagement, and then spiraled dangerously downward during the reign of Shah Soltan Hossayn.[17]

The deposed shah was subsequently given the Ayenekhane Palace for his residence during captivity, while Mahmud, inveterate tribal chieftain that he was, chose to reside in a tent pitched by one of the city gates (the Tuqchi Gate). The Afghan then set out to inflict a period of terror on the capital by sending small contingents into different corners of the city to plunder homes and murder their inhabitants. He invited some fourteen hundred of the shah's grandees and slaves for a killing orgy that was followed by exhibiting the victims' naked bodies in front of the palace (presumably the Ali Qapu, and hence in the Maydan) for all to see, extorted money in exchange for safety from murder from the representatives of the East India companies and the Indian merchants (Banyans), killed prominent Armenians of New Julfa and confiscated their belongings, and refused to contribute to the city's depleted coffers, which worsened the horrific famine that had hung over the city for the long months of siege.[18]

Plunged into deep shock and beset with chaos, Isfahan (and much of Safavid Iran) remained hostage to Mahmud and his successor, Ashraf (in Isfahan between 1725 and 1730), until 1736, when Nader Qoli, a general in the service of the surviving Safavid princes, whom Nader himself had planted on a whim on the fledgling Safavid throne during the interregnum period, finally assumed the Persian throne for himself.[19] Meanwhile, both Mahmud and Ashraf continued to eliminate the Safavid threat in an effort to clear the way for a legitimate Afghan assumption of the throne in Iran. Mahmud kept Shah Soltan Hossayn imprisoned but opted to kill a majority of the incarcerated princes, reportedly with his own hands.[20] Ashraf set his troops loose in Isfahan, and they managed to massacre some seventeen hundred of its denizens in a single afternoon, on the twenty-eighth day in June 1726.[21] And finally, provoked by an Ottoman ambassador's letter in which he had called the Afghan a usurper, Ashraf chose to strike the final blow and, despite earlier assurances to the contrary, ordered his soldiers to behead Shah Soltan Hossayn on 9 September 1727.

With the last legitimate Safavid shah out of the way, Ashraf negotiated a truce with the Ottomans and convinced them to recognize him as the king of Iran, suggesting that, as a fellow Sunni, he was particularly acceptable to the Turks. In order to confer this recognition, the Ottoman envoy was soon to be received in pomp and ceremony in Isfahan.[22] Already stretched to their limits, the textile merchants of Isfahan and New Julfa were ordered to donate copious lengths of red cloth so that the Afghan soldiers could be attired for their requisite parade before the "shah." Gold and silver dishes, to be held and carried by the young pages during the royal feast, were forcibly procured from the people of Isfahan. In so choreographing a ceremonial event, Ashraf was enacting a familiar type of sovereignty, one that had been performed until not so long ago in the palaces of Isfahan. Young pages arranged closely behind the shah, their role as cupbearers offering drinks and foods to the king, the march of sumptuously clad soldiers – all of these elements were drawn from Safavid practices in Isfahan. Curiously, however, Ashraf had to force Isfahanis to provide the accoutrements for these ceremonies. Where, one must ask, were the finely tailored and richly embellished costumes that used to be produced and stored in the *karkhanes* (workshops) of the royal precinct? Where were the stores of Chinese porcelain, Persian ceramics, and gold and silver dishes that were used to bring food to the Safavid feasts?

The massive destruction and pillaging of the palaces entailed enormous losses, especially of imperial records. All evidence of the empire's administration – its inventories and bookkeeping implements, its documents and decrees – were thrown into the river, according to a later source.[23] The fact that Isfahan was so brutally plundered has contributed to the dearth of documentation that stands

in such sharp contrast to that of the Ottomans. An obvious but necessary point to reiterate is that an imperial structure requires copious
and obsessively detailed records for its maintenance and dominion.
The accidents of history have preserved some with greater fullness
than others; there is no reason to assume a greater complexity of
imperial structure where records had never been removed from their
shelves in the chancellery.[24]

Between the patched-together audiences of Ashraf and those of the
mid-seventeenth century for which special palaces had been built and
masses of furnishing and feasting accoutrements had been produced
lies a period of lull in public ceremony, a calm brought about by the
fact that the last reigning Safavid shah chose to retreat to the comfort
of the harem. His predilection for building playhouse palaces, situated far from the traditional halls of ceremony in the city, seems to
have been, curiously, emulated by his nemesis Ashraf in the so-called
"one-hundred-sided building" in the Daulatkhane, a building that is
impossible to identify, if it indeed was ever built.[25] The edifice known
as Talar-e Ashraf, a building on the former grounds of the harem zone
of the Daulatkhane and without anything in it remotely resembling
a *talar* structure, may have been one of the structures that issued
from Ashraf's presumed love of building palaces. Not much can be
said about the meaning of this love of palace building, but the Talar-
e Ashraf – in its plan and architectural articulation of spaces, vaults,
and surfaces – is closer to the aristocratic mansions in Isfahan and
New Julfa than to the palaces of even the later Safavids.

Nevertheless, it was Ashraf's order of destruction that was more
typical of the Afghan period in Isfahan. Caravanserais, shops, and
houses located at the center of the city were razed and replaced by a
new, fortified and moat-surrounded "city" for the exclusive occupation of Afghans and Banyans (Indian merchants). Moreover, neither
Mahmud, who conquered Isfahan, nor his successor Ashraf, who
ruled Isfahan for a short period, chose to occupy the Daulatkhane in
any way that allowed the palaces to function as they had under the
Safavids. In fact, soon after the plunder of the city, Ashraf and his
close circle of generals kept moving about town, so to speak, from
encampments to palaces that stood outside the "inner" city. For
example, Ashraf took temporary lodging in the Sa'adatabad palatine
complex on the south side of the Zayande River from 8 August until
10 September 1728.[26]

More than signaling disdain for the symbols of a defeated foe, the
Afghan abandonment of the ceremonial palaces and permanent structures that served the machinery of Safavid governance indicates the
particularities of the cultural matrix that gave rise to the uniquely
Safavid architecture of conviviality. In contrast to the established paradigms of Muslim kingship, be it confederate tribal or absolutist
imperial, the Safavid synthesis of Imami Shi'i and ancient Persian
notions of authority accentuated the charisma of conviviality for the

maintenance of power. The ceremonial palaces of Isfahan represented the conceptual unity of that form of statecraft.

Notes

1. Petros di Sarkis Gilanentz, *Soqut-e Esfahan*, trans. Mohammad Mehryar (Isfahan: Omur-e Farhangi-e Shahrdari-e Esfahan: Entesharat-e Golha, 1992), 53. Another heartbreaking rendition of life during the tumultuous fall of Isfahan is provided by Babai ibn Farhad in his Judeo-Persian chronicle of the second forced conversion of the Jewish community in Kashan; Vera Basch Moreen, *Iranian Jewry during the Afghan Invasion: The Kitāb-i sar Guzasht-i Kāshān of Bābāī b Farhād* (Stuttgart: Franz Steiner Verlag, 1990), 29–33, chapters V and VI.
2. Floor, *The Afghan Occupation*, 24.
3. Gilanentz, *Soqut-e Esfahan*, 59–60.
4. One such effort was an assault on the Abbasabad bridge. Krusinski attributes the initial Afghan failure to enter the city to a combination of resistance by the Isfahanis and the Afghan miscalculation in prematurely disbanding troops; see Krusinski, *The History of the Late Revolutions*, 13–14.
5. Jafarian, *Safaviyye az zohur ta zaval*, 448.
6. Krusinski, *The History of the Late Revolutions*, 32.
7. Jaberi Ansari, *Tarikh-e Esfahan*, ed. Jamshid Mazaheri, 25. According to *Majm' al-tavarikh*, by Mar'ashi Safavi, some adults would sit in wait for children to come by in the alleys so as to kill and eat them; Mohammad Khalil Mar'ashi Safavi, *Majma' al-tavarikh*, ed. Abbas Iqbal (Tehran: Sherkat-i Sami Chap, 1328/1949), 57. See also Krusinski's description, *The History of the Late Revolutions*, 33–4.
8. Krusinski, *The History of the Late Revolutions*, 31.
9. Dutch VOC records in Floor, *The Afghan Occupation*, 83–172. Krusinski portrays the prince with much adulation and notes that he was invested with the title of the presumptive heir to the throne by his father before setting out to gather troops; *The History of the Late Revolutions*, 19.
10. Floor, *Afghan Occupation*, 83–4 and 88.
11. Floor, *Afghan Occupation*, 173.
12. Krusinski, *The History of the Late Revolutions*, p. 36.
13. VOC's date differs from that given by Krusinski, 23 October; *The History of the Late Revolutions*, p. 35. Also note that Gilanentz and others relate the shah going out to Farahabad around noon and being made to wait for a while before Mahmud would see him; Gilanentz, *Soqut-e Esfahan*, 70–1. Evidently the only non-Muslim present was Joseph Apisalaymian, whose account others seem to repeat; Gilanentz, *Soqut-e Esfahan*, 72, n. 1.
14. A Carmelite priest residing in Isfahan at the time of the siege; Friar Alexander of Malabar, "The Story of the Sack of Ispahan by the Afghans in 1722," *Journal Cras* 1936, 649–50; quoted in Floor, *Afghan Occupation*, 173.
15. Membré, *Mission to the Lord Sophy*, 24. Rosemary Stanfield-Johnson has extensively studied the Sunni-Shi'i public tensions and performances; see her "The Tabarra'iyan and the Early Safavids," *Iranian Studies* 37, no. 1 (March 2004): 47–71.

16. Gilanentz, *Soqut-e Esfahan*, 73.
17. Gilanentz, *Soqut-e Esfahan*, 74. Earlier scholarship on the political and economic history of Safavid Iran has generally characterized much of the period after the death of Shah Abbas the Great as a long trajectory of economic decline. The fall of Isfahan has served as the end towards which Safavid Iran was presumably destined to move! Recently, greater historical nuances have been introduced into the debate and while the reigns of Shah Solayman and Shah Soltan Hossayn demonstrate a detrimental decline in trade for and maintenance of reserves of gold and silver, we can no longer see post-Abbas Safavid Iran as a century of continuous downward spiral in economic and political terms. Matthee's *The Politics of Trade in Safavid Iran* offers the most recent overview of the literature and an excellent study of the economic history of the Safavids.
18. Floor, *Afghan Occupation*, 179.
19. Roemer, "The Safavid Period," 327–8; Peter Avery, "Nadir Shah and the Afsharid Legacy," *The Cambridge History of Iran*, Vol. 7, *From Nadir Shah to the Islamic Republic*, ed. Peter J. Jackson and Laurence Lockhart (Cambridge: Cambridge University Press, 1986), 3–62. For the most recent study of Nader, see Ernest Tucker, *Nadir Shah's Quest for Legitimacy in Post-Safavid Iran* (Gainesville, FL: University Press of Florida, 2006).
20. Roemer, "The Safavid Period," 326.
21. Willem Floor, *Ashraf Afghan dar takhtgah-i Esfahan: be revayat-e shahedan-e Holandi*, trans. Abu al-Qasim Sirri (Tehran: Tus, 1367/1988), 17.
22. Floor, *Ashraf Afghan*, 22.
23. Jaberi-Ansari, *Tarikh-e Esfahan*, ed. Jamshid Mazaheri, 26.
24. Scholarship has much too often placed the blame for the tipped balance on the absence of "serious" bookkeeping strategies by the Safavids in a comparison between the Ottoman Topkapı and the Safavid Daulatkhane. An insidious, albeit unspoken, assumption of a "*laissez-faire*" attitude in Safavid bookkeeping is part of the broader assumption of more nomadic and less "civilized" imperial practice, for which feasting the multitudes has also been taken as evidence.
25. Floor, *Ashraf Afghan*, 23.
26. Floor, *Ashraf Afghan*, 27.

Select Bibliography

Primary Sources

Ashpazi-ye daure-ye Safavi, matn-e do resale az an daure. Edited by Iraj Afshar. Tehran: Entesharat-e Seda va Sim, 1360/1981.

Asef, Mohammad Hashem. *Rostam al-tavarikh*. Edited by Mohammad Moshiri. Tehran: Chap-i Taban, 1352/1973.

Babur, Zahiruddin Muhammad. *Baburnama: The Memoirs of Babur, Prince and Emperor*. Translated by Wheeler Thackston. Washington, DC; New York; Oxford: Freer Gallery of Art and Oxford University Press, 1996.

Barbaro, Josafa and Ambrogio Contarini. *Travels to Tana and Persia*. Translated by William Thomas and S. A. Roy. Edited with an introduction by Lord Stanley of Alderley. Works issued by the Hakluyt Society 49 pt. 1. New York: B. Franklin, 1964.

de Bruyn, Cornelis. *Voyages au Levant, c'est-à-dire, dans les principaux endroits de l'Asie Mineure*. 5 vols. *Voyages de Corneille Le Bruyn par la Moscovie, en Perse, et aux Indes Orientals*. Volume 4. Paris: J. B. C. Bauche, le fils, 1725.

Chardin, Jean. *Le Couronnement De Soleïmaan Troisiéme Roy de Perse*. Paris, 1671.

——. *Voyages du Chavalier Chardin, en Perse, et autres lieux de l'Orient*. Edited by L. Langlès. 10 vols. Paris: Le Normant, 1811.

A Chronicle of the Carmelites in Persia and the Papal mission of the XVIIth and XVIIIth centuries. Edited by H. Chick. London: Eyre and Spottiswoode, 1939.

Clavijo, Ruy González de. *Embassy to Tamerlane, 1403–1406*. Translated by Guy Le Strange. New York and London: Harper and Brothers, 1928.

Coste, Pascal. *Monuments modernes de la Perse, mesurés, dessinés et décrits par Pascal Coste. Publiés par ordre de son excellence le ministre de la maison de l'empereur et des beaux-arts*. Paris: A. Morel, 1867.

Dar danestan-e carevansara-ha-ye Esfahan (On Knowing the Caravanserais of Isfahan). British Library, London, MS Sloane 4094.

Della Valle, Pietro. *Viaggi di Pietro della Valle il Pellegrino descritti da lui medesimo in lettere familiari*. 3 vols. Rome, 1658.

——. *The Pilgrim. The Travels of Pietro Della Valle*. Translated, abridged and introduced by George Bull. London: Folio Society, 1989.

Dieulafoy, Jane Paule Rachel, Mme. *La Perse, la Chaldée et la Susiane*. Paris: Librairie Hachette, 1887.

Figuera, Don Garcia de Silva y. *L'Ambassade de Don Garcias de Silva y Figueroa en Perse*. Translated by De Wicqfort. Paris: Lovis Billaine, 1667.

Flandin, Eugene and Pascal Coste. *Voyages en Perse*. Paris: Gide et J. Baudry, 1851–1854.

Gul-Badan, Begam. *The History of Humāyūn (Humāyūn-Nāma), by Gul-Badan Begam*. Translated with introduction and notes by Annette S. Beveridge. New Delhi: Oriental Books Reprint Corporation, 1983.

Haravi, Qasem b. Yusof Abu Nasri. *Ershad al-zira'a*. Edited by Mohammad Moshiri. Tehran: Daneshgah-e Tehran, 1346/1967.

Herbert, Thomas. *Travels in Persia 1627–1629*. Abridged edn. Edited by W. Foster. London: G. Routledge and Sons, Ltd, 1928.

Jaberi Ansari, Mirza Mohammad Hasan. *Tarikh-e Esfahan va Ray*. Isfahan: Hossayn Emamzade, 1322/1943.

——. *Tarikh-e Esfahan*. New edition. Edited by Jamshid Mazaheri. Tehran: Mash'al, 1378/1999.

Jahangusha-ye khaqan. Edited by Allah Dotta Maztar. Islamabad: Center for Persian Studies of Iran and Pakistan, 1984.

Jonabadi, Mirza Beg ibn Hasan. *Rauzat al-safaviyye*. Edited by Gholamreza Majd Tabatabai. Tehran: Bonyad-e Mauqufat-e Doktor Mahmud Afshar, 1999.

——. *Rauzat al-safaviyye*. British Library, London, MS Or. 3388.

Kaempfer, Engelbert. *Amoenitatum Exoticarum, politico-physico medicarum fasciculi, quibus continentur variae relations, observations et descriptions rerum Persicarum et ulterioris Asiae*. Lemgovnia: Typis & impensis Henrici Wilhelmi Meyeri, 1712.

——. *Am Hofe des persischen Großkönigs 1684–85*. Edited by Walther Hinz. Tübingen: H. Erdmann, 1977.

Kashefi, Va'ez. *Fotovvatname-ye soltani*. Edited by Mohammad Ja'far Mahjub. Tehran: Bonyad-e Farhang-e Iran, 1350/1971.

Khatunabadi, Abd al-Hossayn. *Vaqayi' al-sanin v-al-a'vam*. Edited by M. B. Behbudi. Tehran: Ketabforushi-ye Eslamiyye, 1352/1973.

Khuzani Esfahani, Fazli. *Afzal al-tavarikh*. Cambridge University, Christ College, Ms. Dd. 5.6.

Khwajegi Esfahani, Mohammad Ma'sum ibn. *Kholasat al-siyyar*. Edited by Iraj Afshar. Tehran: Entesharat-e Elmi, 1368/1989.

Khwand Amir, Ghiyas al-Din b. Humam al-Din Mohammad. *Habib al-Siyar*. Edited by J. Homa'i. 4 vols. Tehran: Khayyam Publishers, 1333/1954.

Krusinski, Father Judasz Tadeuz. *The History of the Late Revolutions of Persia*. Reprint edition. New York: Arno Press, 1973.

al-Mafarokhi al-Esfahani, Mofzil ibn Sa'd ibn al-Hossayn. *Mahasen Esfahan*. Edited by Sayyed Jalal al-Din al-Hossayni al-Tehrani. Tehran: Eqbal, n.d.

Mar'ashi Safavi, Mohammad Khalil. *Majma' al-tavarikh*. Edited by Abbas Eqbal. Tehran: Sherkat-i Sami Chap, 1328/1949.

Membré, Michele. *Mission to the Lord Sophy of Persia (1539–1542)*. Translated, introduced and notes by A. H. Morton. London: School of Oriental and African Studies, University of London, 1993.

Mirza Rafi'a. *Dastur al-muluk*. Edited by Mohammad Taqi Daneshpajuh. *Majalle-ye daneshkade-ye adabiyyat va olum-e ensani* 16, nos. 1–4. Tehran University.

Monajjem, Kamal ibn Jalal. *Zobdat al-tavarikh*. Royal Asiatic Society, MS Morley 43.

Monajjem, Molla Jalal al-Din. *Tarikh Abbasi ya ruzname-ye Molla Jalal*. Edited by Sayf-Allah Vahidniya. Tehran: Entesharat-e Vahid, 1366/1987.

Monshi, Eskandar Beg. *The History of Shah 'Abbas the Great*. Translated by Roger M. Savory. 3 vols. Boulder: Westview Press, 1978–1986; New York: Bibliotheca Persica, 1986.

——. *Tarikh-e alam ara-ye Abbasi*. Edited by Iraj Afshar. 2 vols. Tehran: Entesharat-e Amir Kabir, 1350/1971.

Monshi, Eskandar Beg and Mohammad Yusof Movarrekh. *Zayl-e tarikh-e alam ara-ye Abbasi*. Edited by Sohayli-Khwansari. Tehran: Eslamiyye, 1317/1938.

Movarrekh, Mohammad Yusof. *Khold-e Barin*. British Library, London, MS Or. 4132.

A Narrative of Italian Travels in Persia, in the Fifteenth and Sixteenth Centuries. Translated and edited by Charles Grey. Works issued by the Hakluyt Society 49 pt. 2. New York: B. Franklin, 1960.

Naser Khosraw. *Safarnama*. Translated by Wheeler M. Thackston Jr. Albany, NY: Bibliotheca Persica, 1986.

Natanzi, Mahmud b. Hedayat-Allah Afushte. *Noqavat al-Asar fi zekr al-akhyar*. Edited by Ehsan Eshraqi. 2 vols. Tehran: Bongah-e tarjome va nashr-e ketab, 1366/1987.

Nizam al-Mulk. *The Book of Government*. Translated by Hubert Darke. 3rd edn. Richmond, Surrey: Curzon Press, 2002. First published 1960 by Routledge and Paul.

Olearius, Adam. *Relation du Voyage*. Paris, 1666.

——. *The Voyages and Travels of the Ambassadors Sent by Frederick Duke of Holstein, to the Great Duke of Muscovy, and the King of Persia*. Translated by John Davis. 2nd, corrected edn. London: John Starkey and Thomas Basset, 1669.

Qomi, Qazi Ahmad Ibrahimi Husayni. *Calligraphers and Painters: A Treatise by Qadi Ahmad, son of Mir Munshi (circa A.H. 1015/1606)*. Translated and edited by Vladimir Minorsky. Freer Gallery of Art Occasional Papers, v. 3, no. 2. Washington, DC: Smithsonian Institution, 1959.

——. *Golestan-e Honar*. Edited by Ahmad Sohayli Khwansari. Tehran: Manuchehri Publications, n.d.

——. *Kholasat al-tavarikh*. Edited by Ehsan Eshraqi. 2 vols. Tehran: Mu'assese-ye Entesharat va Chap-e Daneshgah, 1359/1980.

Rostamname-ye tarikh-e Bizhan. British Library, London, MS Add. 7655.

Rumlu, Hasan Bek. *Ahsan al-tavarikh*. Edited by 'Abd al-Hosayn Nava'i. Tehran: Bongah-e Tarjome va Nashr-e Ketab, 1978.

Ruzbehan-e Khonji, Fazl-Allah ibn. *Mihmanname-ye Bokhara*. Edited by M. Sotude. Tehran: Bongah-e Tarjomeh va Nashr-e Ketab, 2535/1976.

Sa'eb-e Tabrizi. *Divan-e Sa'eb-e Tabrizi*. Edited by Mohammad Qahraman. Tehran: Entesharat-e Elmi va Farhangi, 1370/1991.

——. *Kolliyyat-e Sa'eb-e Tabrizi*. Edited by Amiri Firuzkuhi. Tehran: Khayyam, 1333/1954-5.

Shamlu, Vali Qoli. *Qesas al-khaqani*. Edited by Hasan Sadat Naseri. 2 vols. Tehran: Vezarat-e Ershad-e Eslami, 1371/1992.

——. *Qesas al-khaqani*, British Library, London, MS Add. 7656.

Shaykh Baha'i. *Jame'-e Abbasi*. Tehran: Farahani Publishers, n.d.

Shirazi, Khwaje Zayn al-Abedin Ali Abdi Beg Navidi. *Jannat al-asmar/Zinat al-awraq/Sahifat al-Ekhlas*, edited by Abolfazl H. O. Rahimof. Moscow: Academy of Sciences of the Soviet Socialist Azarbaijan, 1979.

Tadhkirat al-muluk: A Manual of Safavid Administration. Reprint edition. Translated and explained by V. Minorsky. London: Trustees of the E. G. Gibb Memorial, 1980.

Taher-e Vahid-e Qazvini, Mohammad. *Tarikh-e Vahid* or *Abbasname*. British Library, London. MS Or. 2940.

——. *Abbasname*. Edited by Ebrahim Dehqan. Arak: Davudi Publishers, 1329/1951.

——. *Tarikh-e jahan-ara-ye Abbasi*. Edited by Seyyed Saʿid Mir Mohammad Sadeq. Tehran: Pajuheshgah-e Olum-e Ensani va Motaleʿat-e Farhangi, 1383/2005.

Tahvildar, Mirza Hossayn Khan. *Joghrafiya-ye Esfahan*. Edited by Manuchehr Sotude. Tehran: Tehran University, Faculty of the Literature, 1342/1963.

Tavernier, Jean Baptiste. *The Six Voyages of John Baptista Tavernier*. English trans. London, 1678.

——. *Les Six Voyages en Turquie et en Perse*. 2 vols. Paris: G. Clouzier, 1981.

Tazkare-ye Nasrabadi. Edited by Vahid Dastgerdi. Tehran: Foruqi Bookshop, n.d.

Tehrani, Mohammad Shafiʿ. *Merʾat-e varedat*. Edited by Mansur Sefat-Gol. Tehran: Miras-e Maktub, 1383/2004.

Tusi, Nasir al-din Muhammad ibn Muhammad. *The Nasirean Ethics*. Trans. G. M. Wickens. London: George Allen and Unwin Ltd, 1964.

Yazdi, Sharaf al-Din Ali. *Zafarnama*. Edited by Mohammad Abbasi. Tehran: Amir Kabir, 1336/1957–8.

Secondary Sources

Abisaab, Rula Jurdi. *Converting Persia: Religion and Power in the Safavid Empire*. London: I. B. Tauris, 2004.

Adamson, John. *The Princely Courts of Europe: Rituals, Politics and Culture under the Ancien Regime 1500–1750*. London: Weidenfeld and Nicolson, 1999.

Afshar, Iraj. "Maktūb and Majmūʿa: Essential Sources for Safavid Research." In *Society and Culture in the Early Modern Middle East: Studies on Iran in the Safavid Period*, edited by Andrew J. Newman, 51–61. Leiden; Boston: Brill, 2003.

Alam, Muzaffar and Sanjay Subruhmanyam. *Indo-Persian Travels in the Age of Discoveries, 1400–1800*. Cambridge: Cambridge University Press, 2007.

Alemi, Mahvash. "Il giardino persiano: tipi e modelli." In *Il Giardino Islamico: architettura, natura, paesaggio*, edited by Attilio Petrucciolo, 39–62. Milano: Electra, 1994.

——. "The Royal Gardens of the Safavid Period: Types and Models." In *Gardens in the Time of the Great Muslim Empires: Theory and Design*, edited by A. Petruccioli, 72–96. Leiden; New York; Köln: Brill, 1997

Allen, Terry. *A Catalogue of the Toponyms and Monuments of Timurid Herat*. Cambridge, MA: Aga Khan Program for Islamic Architecture at Harvard University and the Massachusetts Institute of Technology, 1981.

——. *Timurid Herat*. Beihefte zum Tübinger Atlas des Vorderen Orients, Reihe B, Nr. 56. (Wiesbaden: Reichert, 1983).

Amanat, Abbas. *Resurrection and Renewal; the Making of the Babi Movement in Iran, 1844–1850*. Ithaca; London: Cornell University Press, 1989.

Amir Arjomand, Said. *The Shadow of God and the Hidden Imam: Religion, Political Order, and Societal Change in Shiʾite Iran from the Beginning to 1890*. Chicago: University of Chicago Press, 1984.

Amoretti, B. S. "Religion in the Timurid and Safavid Periods." In *The Cambridge History of Iran*. Vol. 6, *The Timurid and Safavid Periods*, edited by Peter Jackson, 629–34. Cambridge: Cambridge University Press, 1986.

Andrews, Peter A. *Felt Tents and Pavilions: The Nomadic Tradition and its Interaction with Princely Tentage*. London: Melisende, 1999.

Aruz, Joan with Ronald Wallenfels, eds. *Art of the First Cities: The Third Millennium B.C. from the Mediterranean to the Indus*. New York; New Haven; London: Metropolitan Museum of Art and Yale University Press, 2003.

Asch, Ronald and Adolf Birke, eds. *Princes, Patronage and the Nobility: The Court at the Beginning of the Modern Age c. 1450–1650*. Oxford: Oxford University Press, 1991.

Asher, Catherine B. "Sub-Imperial Palaces: Power and Authority in Mughal India." *Ars Orientalis* 23 (1993): 281–302.

——. *Architecture of Mughal India, The New Cambridge History of India* I: 4. Reprint edition, New Delhi: Cambridge University Press, 1995.

——. "Delhi Walled: Changing Boundaries." In *City Walls: The Urban Enceinte in Global Perspective*, edited by James D. Tracy, 247–81. Cambridge: Cambridge University Press, 2000.

Aubin, Jean. "Chroniques persanes et relations italiennes: Notes sur les sources narratives du regne de Šâh Ismâ'il Ier." *Studia Iranica* 24 (1995): 247–59.

Avery, Peter. "Nadir Shah and the Afsharid Legacy." In *The Cambridge History of Iran*. Vol. 7, *From Nadir Shah to the Islamic Republic*, edited by Peter J. Jackson and Laurence Lockhart, 3–62. Cambridge: Cambridge University Press, 1986.

al-Azmeh, Aziz. *Muslim Kingship: Power and the Sacred in Muslim, Christian and Pagan Polities*. London; New York: I. B. Tauris, 1997.

Babaie, Sussan. "Safavid Palaces in Isfahan: Continuity and Change (1599–1666)." PhD diss., New York University, 1994.

——. "Shah Abbas II, the Conquest of Qandahar, the Chihil Sutun, and its Wall Paintings." *Muqarnas* 11 (1994): 125–42.

——. "Paradise Contained: Nature and Culture in Persian Gardens." *The Studio Potter* 25, no. 2 (June 1997): 10–13.

——. "Epigraphy iv. Safavid and Later Inscriptions." In *Encyclopaedia Iranica*, edited by Ehsan Yarshater, Vol. 8, 498–504. London; Boston: Routledge and Kegan Paul, 1998.

——. "Masjed-e Shah" [Royal Mosque], in *Da'irat al-ma'aref-i bozorg-e Eslami* [The Great Islamic Encyclopaedia] IX, 1999, p. 198–201. Tehran: The Centre for the Great Islamic Encyclopaedia.

——. Review of *Half the World: The Social Architecture of Safavid Isfahan 1590–1722*, by Stephen Blake. *Iranian Studies* 33, no. 3–4 (2000): 478–82.

——. "The Sound of the Image/The Image of the Sound: Narrativity in Persian Art of the Seventeenth Century." In *Islamic Art and Literature*, edited by Oleg Grabar and Cynthia Robinson, 143–62. Princeton: Marcus Wiener, 2001.

——. "Building for the Shah: The Role of Mirza Muhammad Taqi (Saru Taqi) in Safavid Royal Patronage of Architecture." In *Safavid Art and Architecture*, edited by Sheila Canby, 20–26. London: British Museum, 2002.

——. "Building on the Past: The Shaping of Safavid Architecture, 1501–76." In *Hunt for Paradise: Court Arts of Safavid Iran, 1501–1576*, edited by Jon Thompson and Sheila Canby, 27–47. New York and Milan: Asia Society, Museo Poldi Pezzoli and Skira Editore, 2003.

——. "Launching from Isfahan." In Babaie, Babayan, Baghdiantz-McCabe, and Farhad, *Slaves of the Shah*, 80–113.

——. "Isfahan x. Monuments." In *Encyclopaedia Iranica*, edited by Ehsan Yarshater, Vol. 14, 6–39. London; Boston: Routledge and Kegan Paul, 2007.

——. "In the Eye of the Storm: Visualizing the Qajar Axis of Kingship." In *Pearls from water, rubies from stone*: Studies in Islamic Art in Honor of Priscilla Soucek, edited by Linda Komaroff and Jackeline Kerner. Special issue, *Artibus Asiae* (2007): pp. 35–54.

Babaie, Sussan, Kathryn Babayan, Ina Baghdiantz-McCabe, and Massumeh Farhad. *Slaves of the Shah: New Elites of Safavid Iran*. London; New York: I. B. Tauris, 2004.

Babashahi, Maryam. "Barresi-ye manabeʿ-e tarikhi dar mored-e bana-ye Talar-e Taymuri (A Study of Historical Evidence about the Talar-e Taymuri)." *Asar* nos. 7, 8, 9 (Bahman 1361/January 1983): 187–231.

Babayan, Kathryn. "The Waning of the Qizilbâsh: The Spiritual and the Temporal in Seventeenth Century Iran." PhD diss., Princeton University, 1993.

——. "The Safavi Synthesis: From Qizilbash Islam to Imamite Shiʾism." *Iranian Studies* 27 (1994): 135–61.

——. "The ʿAqaʾid al-nisaʾ: A Glimpse at Safavid Women in Local Isfahani Culture." In *Women in the Medieval Islamic World: Power, Patronage, and Piety*, edited by G. R. G. Hambly, 349–81. Basingstoke: Macmillan, 1996.

——. *Mystics, Monarchs and Messiahs: Cultural Landscapes of Early Modern Iran*. Harvard Middle Eastern Monographs 35. Cambridge, MA: Harvard University Press, 2003.

——. "The Safavid Household Reconfigured: Concubines, Eunuchs and Military Slaves." In Babaie, Babayan, Baghdiantz-McCabe, and Farhad, *Slaves of the Shah*, 20–48.

Bacharach, Jere L. "Administrative Complexes, Palaces, and Citadels: Changes in the Loci of Medieval Muslim Rule." In *The Ottoman City and Its Parts: Urban Structure and Social Order*, edited by Irene A. Bierman, Rifaʾat A. Abou-El-Haj, and Donald Preziosi, 111–28. New Rochelle, NY: A. D. Caratzas, 1991.

Baghdiantz-McCabe, Ina. *The Shah's Silk for Europe's Silver: The European Trade of the Julfa Armenians in Safavid Iran and India (1530–1750)*. Atlanta: Scholars Press, 1999.

——. "Armenian Merchants and Slaves: Financing the Safavid Treasury." In Babaie, Babayan, Baghdiantz-McCabe, and Farhad, *Slaves of the Shah*, 49–79.

Banani, A. "Reflections on the Social and Economic Structure of Safavid Persia at Its Zenith." *Iranian Studies* 11 (1978): 83–116.

Batmanglij, Najmieh. *New Food of Life; Ancient Persian and Modern Iranian Cooking and Ceremonies*. Washington, DC: Mage Publishers, 1992.

Bausani, Alessandro. "Religion under the Mongols." In *The Cambridge History of Iran*, vol. 5 *The Saljuq and Monol Periods*, edited by J. A. Boyle, 538–49. Cambridge: Cambridge University Press, 1968.

Bazin, M. "Bāg ii., Garden, general overview." In *Encyclopaedia Iranica*, edited by Ehsan Yarshater, Vol 3, 393–5. London; Boston: Routledge and Kegan Paul, 1988.

Beach, Milo Cleveland. *The Imperial Image: Paintings for the Mughal Court*. Washington, DC: Freer Gallery of Art, Smithsonian Institution, 1981.

Beach, Milo and Ebba Koch, *King of the World; The Padshahnama, an imperial Mughal manuscript from the Royal Library, Windsor Castle*. London and Washington, DC: Azimuth Editions and Sackler Gallery, 1997.

Bergquist, Brigitta. "Sympotic Space: A Functional Aspect of Greek Dining-Rooms." In *Sympotica. A Symposium on the Symposion*, edited by Oswyn Murray, 37–65. Oxford: Clarendon Press; New York: Oxford University Press, 1994.

Berkey, Jonathan Porter. *The Formation of Islam: Religion and Society in the Near East, 600–1800*. Cambridge; New York: Cambridge University Press, 2003.

Blair, Sheila. *Islamic Inscriptions*. New York: New York University Press, 1998.

—— and Jonathan Bloom. *The Art and Architecture of Islam 1250–1800*. Yale University Press Pelican History of Art. New Haven; London: Yale University Press, 1994.

Blake, Stephen P. *Half the World: The Social Architecture of Safavid Isfahan 1590–1722*. Costa Mesa, CA: Mazda Publishers, 1999.

Bosworth, C. E. "Yaylak (t., originally yaylagh)," and "Kishlak." *Encyclopaedia of Islam* (Brill Online, 2007).

Boyle, J. A. "Dynastic and Political History of the Il-Khans." In *The Cambridge History of Iran*, Vol. 5, *The Saljuq and Mongol Periods*, edited by J. A. Boyle, 303–421. Cambridge: Cambridge University Press, 1968.

——, ed. *Cambridge History of Iran*. Vol. 5, *The Saljuq and Mongol Periods*. Cambridge: Cambridge University Press, 1968.

Brand, Michael and Glenn D. Lowry. *Akbar's India: Art from the Mughal City of Victory*. New York: Asia Society Galleries, 1985.

Brett, Michael. *The Rise of the Fatimids: the World of the Mediterranean and the Middle East in the Fourth Century of the Hijra, Tenth Century CE*. Leiden: Brill, 2001.

Briant, Pierre and Clarisse Herrenschmidt, eds. *Le Tribut dans l'empire perse*. Paris: Peeters, 1989.

Brancaforte, Elio. *Visions of Persia: Mapping the Travels of Adam Olearius*. Cambridge, MA; London: Harvard University Department of Comparative Literature, 2003.

Brown, Jonathan and J. H. Elliott. *A Palace for a King: the Buen Retiro and the Court of Philip IV*. New Haven: Yale University Press, 2003.

Burke, Peter. *The Historical Anthropology of Early Modern Italy*. Cambridge: Cambridge University Press, 1987.

Burton, John. *An Introduction to the Hadith*. Edinburgh: Edinburgh University Press. Reprint edition, 2001.

Calmard, Jean, ed. *Etudes Safavides*. Paris–Tehran: Institut Français de Recherche en Iran, 1993.

——. "Shi'i Rituals and Power II. The Consolidation of Safavid Shi'ism: Folklore and Popular Religion." In *Safavid Persia: The History and Politics of an Islamic Society*, edited by Charles Melville, 139–90. London: I. B. Tauris, 1996

Campbell, Mary B. *The Witness and the Other World: Exotic European Travel Writing, 400–1600*. Ithaca; London: Cornell University Press, 1988.

Canby, Sheila R. *The Golden Age of Persian Art: 1501–1722*. New York: Abrams, 2000.

——. "Safavid Painting." In *Hunt for Paradise: Court Arts of Safavid Iran, 1501–1576*, edited by Jon Thompson and Sheila Canby, 72–133. New York and Milan: Asia Society, Museo Poldi Pezzoli and Skira Editore, 2003.

Cannadine, David. "Divine Rites of Kings." In *Rituals of Royalty: Power and Ceremonial in Traditional Societies*, edited by David Cannadine and Simon Price, 1–19. New York; London: Cambridge University Press, 1987.

—— and Simon Price, eds. *Rituals of Royalty: Power and Ceremonial in Traditional Societies*. New York; London: Cambridge University Press, 1987.

Carboni, Stefano and Tomoko Masuya. *Persian Tiles*. New York: Metropolitan Museum of Art, 1993.

Chelkowski, Peter. "Popular Arts: Patronage and Piety." In *Royal Persian Paintings: The Qajar Epoch, 1785–1925*, edited by Layla S. Diba and Maryam Ekhtiar, 90–9. London: I. B. Tauris, in association with the Brooklyn Museum of Art, 1998.

Chesa, Fernando. "The Court of the Spanish Habsburgs 1500–1700." In *The Princely Courts of Europe: Rituals, Politics and Culture under the Ancien Regime 1500–1750*, edited by John Adamson, 43–65. London: Weidenfeld and Nicolson, 1999.

Cole, Richard G. "Sixteenth-Century Travel Books as a Source of European Attitudes toward Non-White and Non-Western Culture." In *Proceedings of the American Philosophical Society* 116, No. 1 (15 February 1972): 59–67.

De Certeau, Michel. *The Practice of Everyday Life*. Translated by Steven Rendall. Berkeley; Los Angeles: University of California Press, 1984.

Dehkhoda, Ali Akbar. *Loghatname*. The New Edition. Tehran: Tehran University Press, 1373/1994.

Dickson, Martin and Stuart Cary Welch, eds. *The Houghton Shahname*. 2 vols. Cambridge, MA: Harvard University Press, 1981.

Dodds, Jerrilyn, ed. *Al-Andalus: The Arts of Islamic Spain*. New York: Metropolitan Museum of Art, 1992.

Donohue, John Jay. *The Buwayhid Dynasty in Iraq: 334 H./945 to 403 H./1012*. Leiden: Brill, 2003.

Echraqi, Ehsan. "Description contemporaine des peintures murales disparues des palais de Šâh Tahmâsp à Qazvin." In *Art et société dans le monde Iranien*, edited by Chahryar Adle, 117–26. Paris : Editions Recherche sur le civilisation, 1982.

——. "Shahr-e Qazvin." In *Nazari ejmali be shahr-neshini va shahr-sazi dar Iran*, edited by M. Y. Kiyani, 320–36. Tehran: Ministry of Ershad-e Eslami Publications, 1365/1986.

——. "Le *Dar al-Saltana* de Qazvin, deuxième capitale des Safavides." In *Safavid Persia: The History and Politics of an Islamic Society*, edited by Charles Melville, 105–16. London: I. B. Tauris, 1996.

Elias, Norbert. *The Court Society*. Translated by Edmund Jephcott. Oxford: Blackwell, 1983.

Falsafi, Nasr-Allah. *Zendegani-ye Shah Abbas avval*. 4th reprint edn. 5 vols. Tehran: Entesharat-e Elmi, 1369/1990.

Farhad, Massumeh. *Safavid Single Page Paintings 1642–66*. PhD dissertation. Harvard University, Cambridge, MA, 1988.

——. " 'Searching for the New': Later Safavid Painting and the Suz u Gawdaz (Burning and Melting) by Nau'i Khabushani," *The Journal of the Walters Art Museum* 59 (2001): 115–29.

Farhat, May. "Islamic Piety and Dynastic Legitimacy: The Case of the Shrine of Ali al-Rida in Mashhad (10th–17th Century)." PhD diss., Harvard University, 2002.

Ferrante, Mario. "Dessins et observations préliminaires pour la restauration du palais de 'Ālī Qāpū." In *Travaux de Restauration de Monuments*

Historiques en Iran, edited by Giuseppe Zander, 133–206. Rome: IsMEO, 1968.

———. "Le pavillon des Hašt Bihišt, ou les Huit Paradis, a Ispahan: Relevés et problèmes s'y rattachant." In *Travaux de restauration de monuments historiques en Iran*, edited by Giuseppe Zander, 399–420. Rome: IsMEO, 1968.

———. "Quelques Précisions Graphiques au Sujet des Ponts Séfévides d'Isfahan." In *Travaux de Restauration de Monuments Historiques en Iran*, edited by Giuseppe Zander, 441–50. Rome: IsMEO, 1968.

Ferrier, Ronald W., trans. and ed. *A Journey to Persia: Jean Chardin's portrait of seventeenth-century empire.* London; New York: I. B. Tauris, 1996.

Flandrin, Jean-Louis and Massimo Montanari, eds. *Food; A Culinary History from Antiquity to the Present.* English edition by Albert Sonnenfeld; translated by Clarissa Botsford, et al. New York: Columbia University Press, 1999. Originally published as *Histoire de l'alimentation.* (Paris: Favard, 1996).

Flood, Finbarr Barry. *The Great Mosque of Damascus; Studies on the Making of an Umayyad Visual Culture.* Leiden; Boston: Brill, 2001.

Floor, Willem. *Ashraf Afghan dar takhtgah-e Esfahan: be revayat-e shahedan-e Holandi.* Translated by Abu al-Qasim Sirri. Tehran: Tus, 1367/1988.

———. "The Rise and Fall of Mirza Taqi, the Eunuch Grand Vizier (1043–55/1633–45)." *Studia Iranica* 26 (1997): 237–66.

———. *The Afghan Occupation of Safavid Persia, 1721–1729.* Paris: Association pour l'avancement des etudes iraniennes, 1998.

———. *A Fiscal History of Iran in the Safavid and Qajar Period, 1500–1925.* New York: Bibliotheca Persica Press, 1999.

———. *Safavid Government Institutions.* Costa Mesa, CA: Mazda Publishers, 2001.

———. "The Talar-i Tavila or Hall of Stables." *Muqarnas* 19 (2002): 149–63.

Fragner, Bert. "Social Reality and Culinary Fiction: the perspective of cookbooks from Iran and Central Asia." In *Culinary Cultures of the Middle East*, edited by Richard Tapper and Sami Zubaida, 63–71. London; New York: I. B. Tauris, 1994.

Galdieri, Eugenio. "Two building phases of the time of Šāh ʿAbbās I in the Maydān-i Šāh of Isfahan – Preliminary note." *East and West* 20 (1970): 60–9.

———. "L'acqua nell'antico aspetto di Isfahan attraverso le pitture parietali degli ultimi due secoli." In *Gururājamanjarikā: Studi in Onore di Giuseppe Tucci*, 1–15. Naples: Istituto Universitario Orientale, 1974.

———. *Esfahan, ʿAli Qapu: An architectural survey.* Restorations 5. Rome: IsMEO, 1979.

Gardner, Helen. *Gardner's Art Through the Ages.* 10th edn. Edited by Richard G. Tansey and Fred S. Kleiner. Fort Worth: Harcourt Brace College Publisher, 1996.

Garrison, M. B. and Margaret C. Root. *Seals on the Persepolis Fortification Tablets.* University of Chicago Oriental Institute Publications 117. Chicago: University of Chicago Oriental Institute Publications, 2001.

Gaube, Heinz. *Iranian Cities.* New York: New York University Press, 1978.

—— and Eugene Wirth. *Der Bazar von Isfahan.* Weisbaden: Ludwig Reichert Verlag, 1978.

Gell, Alfred. *Art and Agency: An Anthropological Theory.* Oxford: Clarendon Press, 1998.

Ghanoonparvar, M. R. "Culinary Arts in the Safavid Period." In *Iran and Iranian Studies. Essays in Honor of Iraj Afshar*, edited by Kambiz Eslami, 191–7. Princeton, New Jersey: Zagros Press, 1998.

Ghiyasvand, Mahbubeh Amir. "Bagh-e Saʻadatabad va kakhha-ye Safaviyan dar Qazvin." *Majalle-ye bastan-shenasi va tarikh* no. 1 (Fall/Winter 1367/1988): 28–41.

Gilanentz, Petros di Sarkis. *Soqut-e Esfahan*. Translated by Mohammad Mehryar. Isfahan: Omur-e Farhangi-e Shahrdari-e Esfahan: Entesharat-e Golha, 1992.

Gnoli, G. "*Farr*." In *Encyclopaedia Iranica*, edited by Ehsan Yarshater, Vol. 9, 312–19. London; Boston: Routledge and Kegan Paul, 1988.

Golombek, Lisa. "Anatomy of a Mosque: The Masjid-i Shah of Isfahan." In *Iranian Civilization and Culture*, edited by Charles J. Adams, 5–15. (Montreal: McGill University, Institute of Islamic Studies, 1973.

——. "Urban Patterns in pre-Safavid Isfahan." *Iranian Studies* 7, no. 3 (1974): 18–44.

——. "From Tamerlane to the Taj Mahal." In *Islamic Art and Architecture in Honor of Katharina Otto-Dorn*, edited by Abbas Daneshvari, 43–50. Malibu, CA: Undena Publications, 1981.

—— and Donald Wilber. *The Timurid Architecture of Iran and Turan*. Princeton NJ: Princeton University Press, 1988.

——. "Discourses of an Imaginary Arts Council in Fifteenth-Century Iran." In *Timurid Art and Culture; Iran and Central Asia in the Fifteenth Century*, edited by Lisa Golombek and Maria Subtelny, 1–17. Leiden: Brill, 1992.

—— and Maria Subtelny, eds. *Timurid Art and Culture: Iran and Central Asia in the Fifteenth Century*. Leiden; New York: Brill, 1992.

——. "The Gardens of Timur: New Perspectives." *Muqarnas* 12 (1995): 137–47.

Golriz, Mohammad Ali. *Minu dar ya bab al-jannat-e Qazvin*. Tehran: Entesharat-e daneshgah-e Tehran, 1337/1958.

Gordon, Stewart, ed. *Robes and Honor: the Medieval World of Investiture*. New York: Palgrave, 2001.

Grabar, Oleg. "The Visual Arts, 1050–1350." In *Cambridge History of Iran*. Vol. 5, *The Saljuq and Mongol Periods*, edited by J. A. Boyle, 626–48. Cambridge: Cambridge University Press, 1968.

——. *The Alhambra*. Cambridge, MA: Harvard University Press, 1978.

—— and Sheila Blair. *Epic Images and Contemporary History: The Illustrations of the Great Mongol Shahnama*. Chicago: University of Chicago Press, 1980.

——. "From Dome of Heaven to Pleasure Dome." *Journal of the Society of Architectural Historians* no. 49 (1990): 15–21.

——. *The Great Mosque of Isfahan*. New York: New York University Press, 1990.

——. "Umayyad Palaces Reconsidered." *Ars Orientalis* 23 (1993): 93–108.

Gray, Basil. "The Tradition of Wall Painting in Iran." In *Highlights of Persian Art*, edited by R. Ettinghausen and E. Yarshater, 312–29. Boulder, CO: Bibliotheca Persica, 1979.

Gülersoy, Celik. *Dolmabahce*. Istanbul: İstanbul Kitablığı, 1984.

Halm, Heinz. *The Empire of the Mahdi: the Rise of the Fatimids*. Translated by Michael Bonner. Leiden: Brill, 1996.

Haneda, Masashi. "The Character of the Urbanization of Isfahan in the Later Safavid Period." In *Safavid Persia: The History and Politics of an Islamic Society*, edited by Charles Melville, 369–88. London: I. B. Tauris, 1996.

——. "Maydan et Bagh. Reflexion à propos de l'urbanisme du Šah 'Abbas'." In *Documents et Archives Provenant de L'Asie Centrale: Actes du colloque franco-japonais, Kyoto* (Kyoto International Conference Hall et Univ. Ryukoku, 4–8 octobre 1988.), edited by Akira Haneda, 87–99. Kyoto: Association Franco-Japonaise des Études Orientales, 1990.

Hermann, G. "The Art of the Sasanians." In *The Arts of Persia*, edited by R. W. Ferrier, 61–79. New Haven and London: Yale University Press, 1989.

Hillenbrand, Robert. "Safavid Architecture." In *The Cambridge History of Iran*. Vol. 6, *The Timurid and Safavid Periods*, edited by Peter J. Jackson and Laurence Lockhart, 759–842. Cambridge: Cambridge University Press, 1986.

——. *Islamic Architecture: Form, Function and Meaning*. New York: Columbia University Press, 1994.

——, ed. *The Art of the Saljuqs in Iran and Anatolia*. Costa Mesa, CA: Mazda Publishers, 1994.

——. "The Iconography of the *Shāh-nāma-yi Shāhī*." In *Safavid Persia: The History and Politics of an Islamic Society*, edited by Charles Melville, 53–78. London; New York: I. B. Tauris, 1996.

——, ed. *Shahnama: The Visual Language of the Persian Book of Kings*. Edinburgh: Edinburgh University Press, 2004.

Holod, R., ed. *Studies on Isfahan*, special issue of *Iranian Studies* VII, nos. 1–2 (1974).

Honarfar, Lotf-Allah. *Ganjine-ye asar-e tarikhi-ye Esfahan*. Isfahan: Ketabforushi-e Saqafi, 1344/1965–1966.

——. "Bagh-e Hezar Jarib va Kuh-e Soffe, behesht-e Shah Abbas." *Honar va Mardom*, (Aban 1345/November 1966): 73–94.

Jackson, Peter, ed. *The Cambridge History of Iran*. Vol. 6, *The Timurid and Safavid Periods*. Cambridge: Cambridge University Press, 1986.

Jafarian, Rasul. *Maqalat-e tarikhi*. 3 vols. Qom: Ansarian Publishers, 1376/1997.

——. "Pishine-ye tashayyo' dar Esfahan (The Background of Shi'ism in Isfahan)." In Jafarian, *Maqalat-e tarikhi*, vol. 2, 305–36.

——. "Pishine-ye tashayyo' dar Kashan (The Background of Shi'ism in Kashan)." In Jafarian, *Maqalat-e tarikhi*, vol. 2, 341–67.

——. *Safaviyye dar 'arse-ye din, farhang va siyasat* (The Safavids in the arenas of Religion, Culture, and Politics). 3 vols. Qom: Pajuheshkade-ye Hauze va Daneshgah, 1379/2000.

——. "Namaz-e Jom'e dar daure-ye Safaviyye." In Jafarian, *Safaviyye dar 'arse-ye din, farhang va siyasat*, vol. 1, 251–334.

——. *Safaviyye az zohur ta zaval* (The Safavids from their Rise to their Fall). Tehran: Mo'assese-ye Danesh va Andishe-ye Mo'aser, 1381/2002.

Jarrard, Alice. *Architecture as Performance in Seventeenth-Century Europe: Court Ritual in Modena, Rome, and Paris*. Cambridge: Cambridge University Press, 2003.

Kamaly, Hossein. "Politics, Economy and Culture in Isfahan, 540–1040." PhD diss., Columbia University, 2004.

Kamps, Ivo and Jyotsna G. Singh, eds. *Travel Knowledge: European "Discoveries" in the Early Modern Period*. New York: Palgrave, 2001.

Kasravi, Ahmad. *Shaykh Safi va tabarash*. Tehran: Jar, 2536/1976.

Kaufmann, Thomas DaCosta. *Court, Cloister and City: The Art and Culture of Central Europe 1450–1800*. Chicago: University of Chicago Press, 1995.

Kennedy, Hugh. *When Baghdad Ruled the Muslim World: the Rise and Fall of Islam's Greatest Dynasty*. Cambridge, MA: Da Capo Press, 2005.

Kleiss, Wolfram. "Der safavidische Pavillon in Qazvin." *Archaeologische Mitteilungen aus Iran* 9 (1976): 253–61.

——. "Schlösser und Herrensitze auf dem Lande aus safavidischer und qadjarischer Zeit." *Archaeologische Mitteilungen aus Iran* 20 (1987): 346–68.

——. *Die Entwicklung von Palästen und Palastartigen Wohnbauten in Iran.* Vienna: Österreichischen Akademie der Wissenschaften, 1989.

——. "Schloss Aliabad bei Furk in Fars." *Archaeologische Mitteilungen aus Iran* 24 (1991): 261–8.

——. "Die safavidische Palastanlage von Tājābād." *Archaeologische Mitteilungen aus Iran* 27 (1994): 289–95.

Klingensmith, Samuel John. *The Utility of Splendor: Ceremony, Social Life, and Architecture at the Court of Bavaria, 1600–1800.* Chicago: University of Chicago Press, 1993.

Koch, Ebba. *Shah Jahan and Orpheus.* Graz: Akademische Druck-u. Verlagsanstalt, 1988.

——. *Mughal Architecture: An Outline of its History and Development (1526–1858).* Munich: Prestel, 1991.

——. "Diwan-i 'Amm and Chihil Sutun: The Audience Halls of Shah Jahan." *Muqarnas* 11 (1994): 143–65.

——. "Mughal Palace Gardens from Babur to Shah Jahan (1526–1648)." *Muqarnas* 14 (1997): 143–165.

——. "The Mughal Waterfront Garden." In *Gardens in the Time of the Great Muslim Empires: Theory and Design*, edited by Attilio Petruccioli, 140–60. Leiden; New York: Brill, 1997.

Kostof, Spiro. *The City Shaped: Urban Patterns and Meanings through History.* London: Thames and Hudson, 1991.

——. *The City Assembled: the Elements of Urban Form through History.* Boston, New York and London: Bullfinch, 1992.

La sociabilité à table: Commensalité et convivialité à travers les ages, Actes du colloque de Rouen (Rouen: University of Rouen Press, 1992).

Lambton, A. K. S. "Pishkash: Present or Tribute?" *Bulletin of the School of Oriental and African Studies* 57, no. 1 (1944): 144–58.

——. "Justice in the Medieval Persian Theory of Kingship." *Studia Islamica* 16 (1962): 91–119.

Landau, Amy. "*Farangi-Sazi* at Isfahan: The Court Painter Muhammad Zaman, The Armenians of New Julfa and Shah Sulayman (1666–1694)," PhD Diss., University of Oxford, 2007.

Lassner, J. "The Caliph's Personal Domain: The City Plan of Baghdad Re-Examined." In *The Islamic City*, edited by A. H. Hourani and S. M. Stern. Oxford: Cassirer; Philadelphia: University of Pennsylvania Press, 1970.

——. *The Topography of Baghdad in the Early Middle Ages.* Detroit: Wayne State University, 1970.

Lefebvre, Henri. *The Production of Space.* Translated by Donald Nicholson-Smith. Oxford: Blackwell. Reprint edition, 2000.

Lentz, Thomas W. and Glenn D. Lowry. *Timur and the Princely Vision: Persian Art and Culture in the Fifteenth Century.* Los Angeles: Los Angeles County Museum of Art, 1989.

Liu, Lydia. *Translingual Practice: Literature, National Culture, and Translated Modernity – China 1900–1937.* Stanford: Stanford University Press, 1995.

Lockhart, Laurence. "European Contacts with Persia, 1350–1736." In *The Cambridge History of Iran*. Vol. 6, *The Timurid and Safavid Periods*, edited by Peter Jackson, 373–411. Cambridge: Cambridge University Press, 1986.

Losensky, Paul. *Welcoming Fighani: Imitation and Poetic Individuality in the Safavid-Mughal Ghazal*. Costa Mesa, CA: Mazda Publishers, 1998.

——. "The Palace of Praise and the Melons of Time: Descriptive Patterns in ʿAbdi Bayk Sirazi's *Garden of Eden*." *Eurasian Studies* II, no. 1 (2003): 1–29.

Luschey, Heinz. "The Pul-i Khwājū in Isfahan: a Combination of Bridge, Dam and Water Art." *Iran* 23 (1985): 143–51.

Luschey-Schmeisser, Ingeborg. *The Pictorial Tile Cycle of Hašt Bihišt in Isfahān and its Iconographic Tradition*. Rome: IsMEO, 1978.

——. "Čehel Sotūn." In *Encyclopaedia Iranica*, edited by Ehsan Yarshater, 113. London; Boston: Routledge and Kegan Paul, 1988.

Maeda, Hirotake. "The Ghulams of Safavid Dynasty: The Case of Georgian Origin." *Toyo Gakuho* 81 (1999): 1–32.

Majzub, Mohammad Jaʿfar. *Aʾin-e javanmardi ya fotovvat*. New York: Bibliotheca Persica Press, 2000.

Manz, Beatrice Forbes. *The Rise and Rule of Tamerlane*. Cambridge: Cambridge University Press, 1989.

Mason, Peter. *Infelicities: Representations of the Exotic*. Baltimore; London: Johns Hopkins University Press, 1998.

Matthee, Rudolph P. "Politics and Trade in Late Safavid Iran: Commercial Crisis and Government Reaction under Shah Solayman (1666–1694)." PhD Diss., University of California, Los Angeles, 1991.

——. "Unwalled Cities and Restless Nomads: Firearms and Artillery in Safavid Iran." In *Safavid Persia: The History and Politics of an Islamic Society*, edited by Charles Melville, 389–416. London: I. B. Tauris, 1996.

——. *The Politics of Trade in Safavid Iran: Silk for Silver 1600–1730*. Cambridge: Cambridge University Press, 1999.

——. "Gift and Gift-Giving in the Safavid Period." In *Encyclopaedia Iranica*, edited by Ehsan Yarshater, Vol. 10, 609–14. London; Boston: Routledge and Kegan Paul, 2001.

——. *The Pursuit of Pleasure. Drugs and Stimulants in Iranian History, 1500–1900*. Washington, DC: Mage Publishers, 2005.

Mauss, Marcel. *The Gift*. New York and London: W. W. Norton, 1967.

Mazzaoui, M. "From Tabriz to Qazvin to Isfahan: Three Phases of Safavid History." *Zeitschrift der Deutschen Morgenlaendischen Gesellschaft* (1977): 514–22.

——. *Safavid Iran and Her Neighbors*. Salt Lake City: University of Utah Press, 2003.

McChesney, Robert. "Waqf and Public Policy: The Waqfs of Shah Abbas, 1011–1023/1602–1614." *Journal of Asian and African Studies* 15 (1981): 165–90.

——. "Four Sources on Shah Abbas's Building of Isfahan." *Muqarnas* 5 (1988): 103–34.

McClellan, Andrew. *Inventing the Louvre: Art, Politics, and the Origins of the Modern Museum in Eighteenth-century Paris*. New York: Cambridge University Press, 1994.

Melville, Charles. "From Qars to Qandahar: The Itineraries of Shah ʿAbbas I (995–1038/1587–1629)." In *Etudes Safavides*, edited by Jean Calmard, 195–224. Paris-Tehran: Institut Français de Recherche en Iran, 1993.

——. "Shah ʿAbbas and the Pilgrimage to Mashhad." In *Safavid Persia: The History and Politics of an Islamic Society*, edited by Charles Melville, 191–230. London: I. B. Tauris, 1996.

——, ed. *Safavid Persia: The History and Politics of an Islamic Society*. London: I. B. Tauris, 1996.

——. "New Light on the Reign of Shah ʿAbbas: Volume III of the *Afzal al Tawarikh*." In *Society and Culture in the Early Modern Middle East. Studies on Iran in the Safavid Period*, edited by Andrew J. Newman, 63–96. Leiden: Brill, 2003.

Milwright, Marcus. "So Despicable a Vessel: Representations of Tamerlane in Printed Books of the Sixteenth and Seventeenth Centuries." *Muqarnas* 23 (2006): 317–44.

Modarresi-Tabataba'i, Seyyed Husayn. *Torbat-e pakan: asar va banaha-ye qadim-e mahdudoh-ye kenuni-e dar al-muʾminin-e Qom.* 2 vols. Qom: Chapkhane-e Mehr, 1355/1976.

Mora, Paolo. "La restauration des peintures murales de Čihil Sutūn." In *Travaux de restauration de monuments historiques en Iran*, edited by Giuseppe Zander, 323–8. Rome: IsMEO, 1968.

Moreen, Vera Basch. *Iranian Jewry during the Afghan Invasion: The* Kitāb-i sar Guzasht-i Kāshān *of Bābāī b Farhād*. Stuttgart: Franz Steiner Verlag, 1990.

Morgan, David. *The Mongols.* Oxford; New York: Blackwell, 1986.

Morton, A. H. "The Ardabil Shrine in the Reign of Shah Tahmasp I." *Iran* 12 (1974): 31–64.

——. "The Ardabil Shrine in the Reign of Shah Tahmasp (Concluded)." *Iran* 13 (1975): 39–58.

——. "The *chūb-i tarīq* and *Qizilbāsh* Ritual in Safavid Persia." In *Etudes Safavides*, edited by J. Calmard, 225–45. Paris-Tehran: Institut Français de Recherche en Iran, 1993.

Mottahedeh, Roy P. *Loyalty and Leadership in an Early Islamic Society.* Princeton: Princeton University Press, 1980.

Mulryne, J. R. and Elizabeth Goldring, eds. *Court Festivals of the European Renaissance: Art, Politics and Performance.* Aldershot; Burlington, VT: Ashgate, 2002.

Murphey, Rhoads. "Review: Bigots or Informed Observors? A Periodization of Pre-Colonial English and European Writing on the Middle East." *Journal of the American Oriental Society* 110, No. 2 (April–June 1990): 291–303.

Nafisi, Saʿid. *Divan-e kamel-e Shaykh Baha'i.* Tehran: Nashr-e Chekame, 1361/1982.

Nasr, Vali. *The Shia Revival: How Conflicts within Islam Will Shape the Future.* New York; London: W. W. Norton, 2006.

Necipoğlu, Gülru. *Architecture, Ceremonial and Power: The Topkapı Palace in the Fifteenth and Sixteenth Centuries.* Cambridge, MA: MIT Press, 1991.

——. "Framing the Gaze in Ottoman, Safavid, and Mughal Palaces." *Ars Orientalis* 23 (1993): 303–42.

——. "An Outline of Shifting Paradigms in the Palatial Architecture of the Pre-Modern Islamic World." *Ars Orientalis* 23 (1993): 3–24.

——, ed. *Ars Orientalis* 23 (1993).

——. "The Suburban Landscape of Sixteenth-Century Istanbul as a Mirror of Classical Ottoman Garden Culture." In *Gardens in the Time of the Great Muslim Empires: Theory and Design*, edited by Attilio Petruccioli, 32–71. Leiden; New York: Brill, 1997.

Nelson, Robert S. "The Map of Art History." *The Art Bulletin* 79, no. 1 (March 1997): 28–40.

Newman, Andrew J., ed. *Society and Culture in the Early Modern Middle East. Studies on Iran in the Safavid Period*. Leiden: Brill, 2003.

——. *Safavid Iran: Rebirth of a Persian Empire*. London; New York: I. B. Tauris, 2006.

Northedge, Alastair. "An Interpretation of the Palace of the Caliph at Samarra." *Ars Orientalis* 23 (1993): 143–70.

O'Kane, Bernard. *Timurid Architecture in Khurasan*. Costa Mesa, CA: Mazda Publishers in association with Undena Publications, 1987.

——. "From Tents to Pavilions: Royal Mobility and Persian Palace Design." *Ars Orientalis* 23 (1993): 249–68.

——. "Monumentality in Mamluk and Mongol Art and Architecture." *Art History* 19, no. 4 (1996): 499–522.

Ovidio, Guaita. *Italian Villas*. New York: Abbeville Press, 2003.

Pomparato, Francesco Gianazzo di. *Famiglie e Palazzi: dalle Campagne Piemontesi a Torino Capitale Barocca*. Turin: Gribaudo Paravia, 1997.

Pope, Arthur U. "Isfahan Palaces." In *A Survey of Persian Art*, edited by A. Pope and P. Ackerman, vol. 2, 1192.

—— and Phyllis Ackerman, eds. *A Survey of Persian Art*. New edition. 14 vols. Tokyo; London: Oxford University Press, 1964–5.

Porter, Yves. "Les jardins d'Ashraf vus par Henry Viollet." In "Sites et monuments disparu d'apré les témoignes de voyageurs." *Res Orientales* 8 (1996): 117–38

—— and Arthur Thévenart. *Palaces and Gardens of Persia*. Paris: Flammarion, 2003.

Quinn, Sholeh. *Historical Writing during the Reign of Shah Abbas*. Salt Lake City: University of Utah Press, 2000.

Quiring-Zoche, Rosemarie. *Isfahan im 15. und 16. Jahrhundert: Ein Beitrag zur persischen Stadtgeschichte*. Freiberg: Schwarz, 1980.

Rabbat, Nasser O. *The Citadel of Cairo: A New Interpretation of Royal Mamluk Architecture*. Leiden; New York: Brill, 1995.

Redford, Scott. *Landscape and the State in Medieval Anatolia: Seljuk Gardens and Pavilions of Alanya, Turkey*. Oxford: Archaeopress, 2000.

Richard, Francis. *Raphaël du Mans, missionaire en Perse au XVIIe s*. 2 vols. Paris: Société d'Histoire de l'Orient–L'Harmattan, 1995.

Richards, John. *The Mughal Empire*. Cambridge and New York: Cambridge University Press, 1996.

Rizvi, Kishwar. "Transformations in Early Safavid Architecture: The Shrine of Shaykh Safi al-din Ishaq Ardabili in Iran (1501–1629)." PhD diss., Massachusetts Institute of Technology, 2000.

——. "'Its Mortar Mixed with the Sweetness of Life:' Architecture and Ceremonial at the Shrine of Safi al-Din Ishaq Ardabili during the Reign of Shah Tahmasb I." *The Muslim World* 90, no. 3/4 (Fall 2000): 323–51.

——. "The Imperial Setting: Shah 'Abbas at the Safavid Shrine of Shaykh Safi in Ardabil." In *Safavid Art and Architecture*, edited by Sheila Canby, 9–15. London: British Museum, 2002.

Rizvi, S. A. A. *Religious and Intellectual History of the Muslims in Akbar's Reign*. New Delhi: Munshiram Manoharlal Publishers, 1975.

Roemer, Hans R. "The Safavid Period." In *The Cambridge History of Iran*. Vol. 6, *The Timurid and Safavid Periods*, edited by Peter J. Jackson and Laurence Lockhart, 189–350. Cambridge: Cambridge University Press, 1986.

Rogers, J. M. "Samarra: A Study in Medieval Town-Planning." In *The Islamic City: A Colloquium*, edited by Albert Hourani and S. M. Stern, 119–55. Philadelphia: University of Pennsylvania Press, 1970.

Röhrborn, Klaus Michael. *Provinzen und Zentralgewalt Persiens im 16 und 17 Jahrhundert*. Studien zur Sprache, Geschichte und Kultur des Islamischen Orients, n.F., Bd. 2. Berlin: De Gruyter, 1966.

Root, Margaret C. *The King and Kingship in Achaemenid Art: Essays on the Creation of an Iconography of Empire*. Acta Iranica 19. Leiden: Brill, 1979.

Ruggles, D. Fairchild. *Gardens, Landscape, and Vision in the Palaces of Islamic Spain*. University Park, PA: Pennsylvania State University Press, 2000.

Rypka, Jan. *History of Iranian Literature*. Edited by Karl Jahn. Dordrecht, Holland: D. Reidel, 1968.

Sahlins, Marshall. "Food as Symbolic Code." In *Culture and Practical Reason*. Chicago: University of Chicago Press, 1976.

Sancisi-Weerdenburg, Heleen. "Gifts in the Persian Empire." In *Le Tribut dans l'empire perse*, edited by P. Briant and C. Herrenschmidt, 129–46. Paris: Peeters, 1989.

——. "Persian Food: Stereotypes and Political Identity." In *Food in Antiquity*, edited by John Wilkins, David Harvey and Mike Dobson, 286–302. Exeter: University of Exeter Press, 1995.

Sanders, Paula. *Ritual, Politics, and the City in Fatimid Cairo*. Saratoga Springs, NY: State University of New York Press, 1994.

Sarraf, Morteza, ed. *Rasa'el-e javanmardan*, with an introduction in French by Henry Corbin. Tehran and Paris: Department D'Iranologie de L'Institut Franco-Iranien de Recherche, 1973.

Savory, Roger. "The Safavid Administrative System." In *The Cambridge History of Iran*. Vol. 6, *The Timurid and Safavid Periods*, edited by Peter Jackson, 351–72. Cambridge: Cambridge University Press, 1986.

Scarce, Jennifer. "The royal palaces of the Qajar dynasty; a survey." In *Qajar Iran; Political, Social, and Cultural Change 1800–1925*. Reprint edn, edited by Clifford Edmund Bosworth and Carole Hillenbrand, 329–51. Costa Mesa, CA: Mazda Publishers, 1992.

Schwartz, Stuart B., ed. *Implicit Understandings: Observing, Reporting, and Reflecting on the Encounter between Europeans and Other Peoples in the Early Modern Era*. Cambridge: Cambridge University Press, 1994.

Sells, Michael. *Approaching the Qur'án: The Early Revelations*. Ashland, OR: White Cloud Press, 1999.

Shafaqi, Sirous. *Jughrafiya-ye tarikhi-ye Esfahan*. Isfahan: Isfahan University Press, 1381/2003.

Shirazi, Hossayn ibn Hasan Inju. *Farhang-e Jahangiri*. Mashhad: Daneshgah-e Mashhad, 1351/1972.

Simpson, Mariana Shreve. "The Making of Manuscripts and the Workings of the Kitab-khana in Safavid Iran." In *The Artist's Workshop, Studies in the History of Art*, edited by P. M. Lukehart, 105–21. Center for Advanced Study in the Visual Arts, Symposium Papers 22. Washington, DC: National Gallery of Art, 1993.

Simpson, Mariana Shreve with Massumeh Farhad. *Sultan Ibrahim Mirza's Haft Awrang: A Princely Manuscript from Sixteenth-century Iran*. Washington, DC: Freer Gallery of Art, Smithsonian Institution, 1997.

Sims, Eleanore. "Late Safavid Painting: The Chehel Sutun, The Armenian Houses, The Oil Paintings." In *Akten des VII. Internationalen Kongresses für Iranische Kunst und Archäologie*, 408–18. Berlin: D. Reimer, 1979.

Soruri, Mohammad Qasem. *Farhang-e majma' al-Fors*. Tehran: Elmi, 1338–41/1960–63.

Sotude, Manuchehr. *Az Astara ta Astarabad*. 7 vols. Tehran: Vezarat-e Farhang va Ershad-e Eslami, 1366/1987.

Soucek, Priscilla. "Persian Artists in Mughal India: Influences and Transformations." *Muqarnas* 4 (1987): 166–81.

——. "Ālī Qāpū." In *Encyclopaedia Iranica*, edited by Ehsan Yarshater, Vol. 1, 871–2. London; Boston: Routledge and Kegan Paul, 1988.

——. "Solomon's Throne/Solomon's Bath: Model or Metaphor." *Ars Orientalis* 23 (1993): 109–34.

Soudavar, Abolala. *Art of the Persian Courts*. New York: Rizzoli, 1992.

——. "Between the Safavids and the Mughals: Art and Artists in Transition." *Iran* 37 (1999): 49–66.

——. *The Aura of Kings: Legitimacy and Divine Sanction in Iranian Kingship*. Costa Mesa, CA: Mazda Publishers, 2003.

Stanfield-Johnson, Rosemary. "The Tabarra'iyan and the Early Safavids." *Iranian Studies* 37, no. 1 (March 2004): 47–71.

Stewart, Devin J. "The First Shaykh al-Islam of the Safavid Capital Qazvin." *Journal of the American Oriental Society* 116, no. 3 (1996): 387–405.

——. "Notes on the Migration of 'Amili Scholars to Safavid Iran." *Journal of Near Eastern Studies* 55, no. 1 (1996): 81–103.

Stokstad, Marilyn. *Art History*. New York: Abrams, 1995.

Stronach, David. "Čahārbāg." In *Encyclopaedia Iranica*, edited by Ehsan Yarshater, Vol. 4, 624–5. London; Boston: Routledge and Kegan Paul, 1988.

Strong, Roy. *Feast: A History of Grand Eating*. London: Jonathan Cape, 2002.

Subtelny, Maria. "Art and Politics in Early Sixteenth-Century Central Asia." *Central Asiatic Journal* 27, nos. 1–2 (1983): 121–48.

——. "Scenes from the Literary Life of Timurid Herat." In *Logos Islamikos: Studia Islamica in honorem Georgii Michaelis Wickens*, edited by Roger Savory and Dionisius A. Agius, 137–55. Toronto: Pontifical Institute of Medieval Studies, 1984.

——. "Making a Case for Agriculture: the *Irshād al-Zirā'a* and its Role in the Political Economy of Early Safavid Iran." In *Proceedings of the Second European Conference of Iranian Studies held in Bamberg, 30th September to 4th October 1991 by the Societas Iranologica Europaea*, edited by Bert G. Fragner, et al., 685–700. Rome; Istituto Italiano per il Medio ed Estremo Oriente, 1995.

——. "Agriculture and the Timurid Chahārbāgh: The Evidence from a Medieval Persian Agricultural Manual." In *Gardens in the Time of the Great Muslim Empires: Theory and Design*, edited by Attilio Petruccioli, 110–28. Leiden: Brill, 1997.

Szuppe, Maria. "Palais et Jardin: le complexe royal des premiers safavides à Qazvin, milieu XVIe-début XVIIe siècles." In "Sites et monuments disparus d'après les témoignages de voyageurs," edited by R. Gyselen, 143–77. *Res Orientales*, 8. Bures-sur-Yvette: Groupe pour l'Étude de la Civilisation du Moyen-Orient, 1996.

Tapper, Richard. "Blood, Wine and Water: social and symbolic aspects of drinks and drinking in the Islamic Middle East." In *Culinary Cultures of the Middle East*, edited by Sami Zubaida and Richard Tapper, 215–32. London and New York: I. B. Tauris, 1994.

Teply, Karl. *Die kaiserliche Grossbotschaft an Sultan Murad iv (1628): Die Freiherrn Hans Ludwig von Kuefsteins Fahrt zu Hohen Pforte*. Vienna: Verlag A. Schendl, 1976.

Thompson, Jon and Sheila Canby, eds. *Hunt for Paradise: Court Arts of Safavid Iran, 1501–1576*. New York and Milan: Asia Society, Museo Poldi Pezzoli and Skira Editore, 2003.

Tracy, James D., ed. *City Walls: The Urban Enceinte in Global Perspective*. Cambridge: Cambridge University Press, 2000.

Tucker, Ernest. *Nadir Shah's Quest for Legitimacy in Post-Safavid Iran*. Gainesville, FL: University Press of Florida, 2006.

Uluç, Lâle. "Selling to the Court: Late Sixteenth-Century Manuscript Production in Shiraz." *Muqarnas* 17 (2000): 73–96.

——. *Turkman Governors, Shiraz Artisans and Ottoman Collectors: Sixteenth-Century Shiraz Manuscripts*. Istanbul: İş Bankası yayınları, 2007.

Van Gelder, Geert Jan. *God's Banquet: Food in Classical Arabic Literature*. New York: Columbia University Press, 2000.

Varma, Pavan K. and Sondeep Shankar. *Mansions at Dusk: The Havelis of Old Delhi*. New Delhi: Spantech Publishers, 1992.

Walcher, Heidi. "Face of the Seven Spheres: Urban Morphology and Architecture in Nineteenth-Century Isfahan." *Iranian Studies* 33, no. 3 (2000): 327–47.

Wallace-Hadrill, Andrew. *Houses and Society in Pompeii and Herculaneum*. Princeton: Princeton University Press, 1994.

Weatherford, Jack. *Genghis Khan and the Making of the Modern World*. New York: Crown, 2004.

Welch, Anthony. *Shah Abbas and the Arts of Isfahan*. New York: Asia House Society, 1973.

Wilber, Donald Newton. "The Institute's Survey of Persian Architecture; Preliminary Report of the 8th Season of the Survey." *Bulletin of the American Institute for Iranian Art and Archaeology* 5, no. 2 (December 1937): 109–36.

——. "Aspects of the Safavid Ensemble." *Iranian Studies* 7, no. 3–4 (1974): 406–15.

——. *Persian Gardens and Garden Pavilions*. 2nd edn. Washington, DC: Dumbarton Oaks, 1979.

Wilkins, John, David Harvey and Mike Dobson, eds. *Food in Antiquity*. Exeter: University of Exeter Press, 1996.

Winter, Irene. " 'Seat of Kingship'/ 'A Wonder to Behold': The Palace as Construct in the Ancient Near East." *Ars Orientalis* 23 (1993): 27–55.

Woods, John. *The Aqquyunlu: Clan, Confederation, Empire*. Rev. and expanded edn. Salt Lake City: University of Utah Press, 1999.

Zoka', Yahya. *Tarikhche-ye sakhtemanha-ye arg-e saltanati-e Tehran va rah-nama-ye kakh-e Golestan*. Tehran: Entesharat-e Anjoman-e Asar-e Melli, 1349/1970.

Zumthor, Paul. "The Medieval Travel Narratives," *New Literary History* 25, no. 4, 25th Anniversary Issue (Part 2) (Autumn 1994): 809–24.

Illustration Acknowledgments

Figures 1.1 and 1.2; Maps, Babaie and Robert Haug.

Plate 1; Freer Gallery of Art, Smithsonian Institution, Washington, DC, Purchase, F1946.12.132.

Plate 2; Freer Gallery of Art, Smithsonian Institution, Washington, DC, Purchase, F1952.31.

Plate 24; Freer Gallery of Art, Smithsonian Institution, Washington, DC, Purchase, F1942.17–F1942.18.

Figure 5.13; Special Collection, Freer Gallery of Art and Arthur M. Sackler Gallery, Smithsonian Institution Libraries: Mme. Jane Paule Rachel Dieulafoy, *La Perse, la Chaldée et la Susiane* (Paris: Librairie Hachette, 1887), p. 247.

Figures 3.1, 3.2, 3.9, 4.1, 5.3 and 5.22; Special Collections Library, University of Michigan: Englebert Kaempfer's *Amoenitatum exoticarum politico-physico-medicarum* . . . (Lemgoviae: H. W. Meyeri, 1712). 3.1, Foldout between pp. 162 and 163; 3.2, detail of 3.1; 3.9, p. 170; 4.1, p. 179; 5.3, p. 35; 5.22, p. 217.

Figure 3.4; Cornelis de Bruyn. V*oyages au Levant, c'est-à-dire, dans les principaux endroits de l'Asie Mineure. 5 vols. Voyages de Corneille Le Bruyn par la Moscovie, en Perse, et aux Indes Orientals.* Volume 4, p. 97 (Paris: J. B. C. Bauche, le fils, 1725).

Figures 3.5, 5.5 and 5.6; Pascal Coste, *Monuments modernes de la Perse* (Paris: A. Morel, 1867). 3.5, Pl. XLVII; 5.5, Pl. XXXIII; 5.6, Pl. XXXV. Visual Resources Collections, Department of History of Art, University of Michigan.

Figure 6.12; slide from the Visual Resources Collections, Department of History of Art, University of Michigan

Figure 3.10 and 5.19 Jean Chardin, *Voyages du Chavalier Chardin, en Perse, et autres lieux de l'Orient.* Edited by L. Langlès. 10 vols., *Atlas* volume (Paris: Le Normant, 1811). 3.10, Pl. XXXVII; 5.19, Pl. XLV.

Figure 2.2; adapted from Maria Szuppe, "Palais et Jardin: le complexe royal des premiers safavides à Qazvin, milieu XVIe–début XVIIe siècles." In *Sites et monuments disparus d'après les témoignages de voyageurs*, edited by R. Gyselen, 143–77. Res Orientales, 8 (Bures-sur-Yvette: Groupe pour l'Étude de la Civilisation du Moyen-Orient, 1996), Figure 3.

Figure 3.6; adapted from Heinz Gaube and Eugene Wirth, *Der Bazar von Isfahan* (Weisbaden: Ludwig Reichert Verlag, 1978), Figure 15.

Figures 6.1 and 6.2; adapted from Gülru Necipoğlu, *Architecture, Ceremonial and Power: The Topkapi Palace in the Fifteenth and Sixteenth Centuries* (Cambridge, MA: MIT Press, 1991). 6.1, Plate 9; 6.2, Plate 10.

Figure 6.5; after Karl Teply, *Die kaiserliche Grossbotschaft an Sultan Murad iv (1628): Die Freiherrn Hans Ludwig von Kuefsteins Fahrt zu Hohen Pforte* (Vienna: Verlag A. Schendl, 1976), p. 121.

Figure 6.7; adapted from Ebba Koch, "Diwan-i 'Amm and Chihil Sutun: The Audience Halls of Shah Jahan," *Muqarnas* 11 (1994) p. 146.

Figure 6.8; adapted from Ebba Koch, *Mughal Architecture: An Outline of its History and Development (1526–1858)* (Munich: Prestel, 1991), Figure 127.

Figures 3.3 and 4.3; Plates 4, 5, 9 and 10; Dr Ataollah Omidvar, Tehran, Iran.

Figure 2.1; Babaie with John Comazzi.

Figure 2.3; Babaie with John Comazzi and Sam Zeller.

Figures 4.2 and 5.1; Babaie with John Comazzi.

Figures 3.7, 3.8, 5.2 and 5.4; Plate 11: Babaie with Sam Zeller.

All other photographs are by the author.

Index

Note: figure and plate numbers are indicated at the end of an entry using, respectively, bold and bold italics

Abbas I (Abbas the Great), Shah, 9, 12, 13, 46, 56, 58, 66, 71, 76, 79, 81, 83, 86, 87, 88, 89, 91, 95–6, 98, 99, 117, 118, 124, 125, 126, 127–8, 129, 132–3, 134, 142, 169–70, 172, 181, 194, 196, 207, 210, 211, 228, 230, 231, 244–5, 259
Abbas II, Shah, 71, 117, 118, 129, 135, 157, 166, 170, 172–4, 175, 182, 185, 186, 194, 197, 207–8, 211, 233, **5.17**
Abbasabad, Isfahan, 81, 84, 103, 207, 267; *see also* Hezar Jarib (Thousand Acres) Palace Gardens (also known as Abbasabad (Abode of Abbas)), Isfahan
Abbasabad, Mazandaran, 174–5, 176, **5.10**
Abbasi, Shaykh, 196–7
Abbasids, 4, 16, 17, 19, 20, 43, 249
Abbasname, 172–4; *see also* Taher-e Vahid, Mohammad
Abdi Beg-e Shirazi, 50–1, 53–5
    Dauhat al-azhar, 53
    Jannat-e 'adn (Garden of Eden), 50
    Rauzat al-safat, 53
Abisaab, 96–7
absolutism, 1–2, 20, 22, 225, 251, 257–8, 259, 271
    charismatic, 2, 12, 13, 225, 235, 238, 245, 259
    Perso-Shi'i, 2, 235, 238, 259
    sacred, 16–17
    Safavid, 5–6, 7, 8, 11, 12, 13, 22, 30, 39, 43, 58, 100, 128, 143
Abu Bakr, 4
Abu Eshaq, 94
Abu'l Fazl, 251, 252
Afghan invasion of Isfahan, 267–72

Agra, 32–3, 188
    Red Fort, 69, 100–1, 102, 116, 179–80, 195, 226, 252–3, 257, **6.7**, **6.9–11**
    Taj Mahal, 200
Ahl al-bayt, 4, 14, 94
Akbar, Emperor, 33, 69, 100, 251–2
    Din-e Elahi (Divine Creed), 251
Alhambra, Granada, 17
Ali, Imam, 2, 4, 13, 14, 56, 92, 132, 133, 229
Ali Qapu (Lofty Gate) Palace-Gateway, Isfahan, 15, 22, 23, 66, 68, 71, 79, 84, 85–6, 90, 97, 102, 115–16, 117, 118, 119, 120, 121, 123, 125, 126, 128, 130–4, 135, 136–7, 139, 141, 143–9, 162, 165, 182–6, 191, 194–5, 205, 206, 213, 236, 237–8, 252, 269, **3.3**, **3.7**, **4.1–4**, **4.6–7**, **5.4**, **5.17**, **10–13**
    audience hall, 146–9, 183, **4.7**
    Music Room, 148, **13**
    stairwell, 184–5
    talar, 157, 182, 183–4, 237
    water tower, 184
Ali Qapu (Lofty Gate), Qazvin, 52, 53, 115, 146, **2.3–5**
Allah Verdi Khan Bridge (also known as Si-o se Pol or Thirty-three-span Bridge), Isfahan, 66, 81, 84, 85, 126, 166, 208, **3.5**, **3.7**
Alpan Beg, 125
Alp Arsalan, 74
Amasya, Treaty of, 47, 57
Amir Mahmud ibn Khwand Amir, 41
andarun (private) zones, 68, 80, 117, 126–7, 130, 132, 141–2, 199
Angiolello, 243
animals, exotic, 236, **5.22**

Apadana Palace, Persepolis, 181, 238
Aq Sara, Samarqand, 242
Aq Saray (White Palace), Kesh, 40–3
Aqqoyunlus, 2, 5, 20, 34–5, 44, 202,
    203, 240
Ardabil, 30
    Shrine of Shaykh Safi al-Din, 57–8
arts, courtly, 45, 47–50, 53, 55
Asb-e Shahi, Maydan (Royal
    Hippodrome), Qazvin, 51–3, **2.2–3**
Asb, Maydan, Isfahan, 84
Asef, Mohammad Hashem (Rostam
    al-Hokama)
    Rostam al-tavarikh, 166
Ashraf, Mazandaran, 87, 128, 169–72,
    174–7, 182, 206, 244, **5.4**, **5.7**
Ashraf, the Afghan, 270–1
Ashura, 233
audience halls, 179, **6.1**
    Ali Qapu, Isfahan, 146–9, 183, 246,
        249, 253, **4.7**, **6.2**, **6.7**, **6.10**
    Ayenekhane Palace, Isfahan, 168
    Chehel Sotun, Isfahan, 186, 191–4,
        196, 197, 234–5, **5.12**, **17–20**
authority, 2, 4–7, 12, 20, 239, 257–8,
    259, 271–2
    architectural representation, 55–7,
        78, 90, 113, 124, 126, 141, 148–9,
        157, 207, 210–11
    caliphal, 5, 17, 18, 20, 225
    imperial, 5, 7, 12, 17–18, 20, 22, 30,
        46, 52, 56–7, 82, 95, 102, 113, 133,
        149
    papal, 258
    political, 5, 8, 17
    Safavid, 6–7, 8, 11, 12, 13, 14, 30, 35,
        52, 53, 55–6, 58, 69, 82, 86, 88–9,
        95, 96, 98, 113, 117, 125, 128, 133,
        139, 160, 183, 186, 194, 199, 212,
        213, 225, 229, 230, 259, 271–2
    spiritual, 4–5, 12, 13, 34–5, 55, 58, 69,
        89, 95, 125, 229, 248, 249–51, 252
    sultanic, 248, 249–51
    temporal, 7, 12, 20, 69, 89, 96
    universal, 5
Ayenekhane (Hall of Mirrors) Palace,
    Isfahan, 22, 118, 157, 166–9, 176,
    184–5, 208, 211, 213, 226, 235,
    269, **3.7**, **5.2**, **5.5–6**
ayvan-e chubin, 179
Ayvan-e Kasra, Ctesiphon, 181
ayvans, 1, 17, 37, 50, 52, 94, 98, 116,
    135, 140, 144, 146, 168, 180–1, 183,
    186, 190, 191, 233–4, 235, **2.4**, **6.4**
    Mughal, 179, 181
Ayyubids, 17

Babi Dispensation, 160
Babur, Emperor, 33, 40, 178–9, 201,
    251
Baghdad, 4, 16, 17, 18, 19, 20, 43, 73,
    92, 93, 132, 133, 170
Bagh-e Bolbol (Garden of the
    Nightingale), Isfahan, 80,
    199–200, **5.18**
Bagh-e Fin Palace, Kashan, 170, 172,
    176, **5.4**, **5.8–9**
Bagh-e Khargah (Tent Garden), 142, 200
Bagh-e Maydan, Kuhak, 201
Bagh-e Naqsh-e Jahan, Isfahan, 76, 78,
    84, 123, 124, 125, 128, 140, 145
Bagh-e Nau (New Garden),
    Samarqand, 200
Bagh-e Sa'adatabad (Garden of
    Felicity), Qazvin, 50, 51–2, 53
Bagh-e Takht, Isfahan, 81
Bagh-e Toot (Mulberry Garden),
    Isfahan, 200
Baha'i, Shaykh, 56, 96, 98–9, 133,
    230–1
    Jame'-e Abbasi, 99, 230
balakhanes, 174
banquets *see* feasting
Barbaro, Josafa, 240
Begum, Gulbadan, 244
Behzad, 45
Berbers, 17–18
birun (public) zones, 68, 80, 113, 117,
    130, 132, 139, 141, 195, 199, 205,
    245
bridges, 66, 81, 84, 85, 126, 166, 208,
    269, **3.5**, **3.7**, **5.5**, **5.21**
Buyids, 4, 12, 18, 92

Cairo, 16, 17, 20, 69, 251
caliphal rule, 4–5, 12, 16–17, 18, 19,
    20, 73, 82, 92, 94, 181, 225, 249,
    251, 269
ceremonial palaces, 7, 11, 36, 39, 68,
    117, 118, 120, 141, 144, 148–9,
    160, 165–6, 182–97, 205
ceremonial spaces, 39, 116–17,
    179–82, 190–1, 202, 205
ceremony, 2, 6, 10–11, 12, 14, 15, 19,
    23, 35, 37, 39, 41, 43, 53, 68, 74,
    79, 116, 130, 136, 144, 160–2, 168,
    183, 199, 205, 211, 213, 233, **5.3**;
    see also feasting; gifts, exchange of
Chahar Bagh (Chahar Bagh
    Promenade), Isfahan, 66, 67, 68,
    74, 79–85, 102–3, 126, 128, 130,
    141–3, 166, 200, 205–7, 210, **3.2**,
    3.4–8, **4.1**, **4**

Chahar Bagh-e Khwaju, Isfahan,
    208–9, **5.21**
chahar bagh (four-quadrant) gardens,
    31, 37, 53, 55, 67, 74, 103, 146,
    176, 200, **2.1, 5.7–9**
Chahar Hauz Gate (Dar-e Chahar
    Hauz or Four-Ponds Gate),
    Isfahan, 139, 140, 141
Chahar Hauz, Isfahan, 68
Chahar Hauz Maydan, Isfahan, 139,
    141, 269
Chahar Soffe, 126, 127, 140
Chardin, Jean, 9, 36, 74, 76, 78, 80–2,
    121–2, 127, 135, 136, 138, 139,
    142, 143, 160, 162, 163, 164, 186,
    194, 198, 202, 204, 224, 226, 232,
    233, 234, 235, 236, 237, 238
    Le Couronnement De Soleïmaan,
    199
    Voyages, **3.10, 5.19**
Chehel Sotun (Forty Columns) Palace,
    Isfahan, 1–2, 10, 15, 22, 23, 68,
    116, 118, 123, 141, 157, 162, 166,
    186–97, 226, 228, 233, 234, 235,
    236, **3.7, 4.1, 4.5, 5.2, 5.12–17,
    14–20**
    audience hall, 186, 191–4, 196, 197,
    234–5, **5.12, 17–20**
    talar, 186–91, **5.13–15, 16**
    throne ayvan, 186, 191, 234, 235
Chehel Sotun (Forty Columns) Palace,
    Qazvin, 53–5, 146, 176, 201, 202,
    2.2, 2.6, 5.4, 3
Cheshme Emarat (Spring Palace),
    Ashraf, 170–1, 176, **5.4, 5.7**
Chil Sutun, Samarqand, 201
citadel-palaces, 17, 19, 42, 69, 74
Clavijo, Ruy Gonzalez de, 41, 178,
    200, 241–3
Constantinople *see* Istanbul
    (Constantinople)
Coste, Pascal, 76, 167, **5.5–6**
Cotton, Sir Dodmore, 174, 244
Council Chamber, Topkapı Palace,
    Istanbul, 246, 248, **6.3, 6.5**

Daftarkhane (Royal Chancellery),
    Isfahan, 68, 119, 139–41, 269, **4.1,
    4.5**
dancing, 10, 47, 93, 226
*Dar danestan-e carevansara-ha-ye
    Esfahan* (On Knowing the
    Caravanserais of Isfahan), 139
Dar-e Khargah (Tent Gate), 142; *see
    also* Bagh-e Khargah (Tent
    Garden)

Dar-e Shahi *see* Daulat Gate (Gate of
    Felicity or Royal Gate), Isfahan
darshan, 252
Daryache (Lake) Garden, Isfahan,
    208
Dauhat al-azhar, 53
Daulat Gate (Gate of Felicity or
    Royal Gate), Isfahan, 78–9, 80, 85,
    142, 246, 248, 249, **3.6, 4.1, 6.2–4,
    6.6**
Daulatkhane (Royal Precinct), Isfahan,
    67–9, 80, 81, 102, 113–15, 119–43,
    195, 199–200, 269, 271, **3.7**
Daulatkhane (Royal Precinct), Qazvin,
    47, 50, 51, 243
Daulatkhane (Royal Precinct), Tabriz,
    31, 35, 36–7, 39, 240, **2.1**
decoration
    external, 204–5
    interior, 36, 53–5, 147–8, 168–9,
    170–1, 191–3, 196–7, 204, **2.5**
Dehkhoda, 178
Delhi
    Red Fort, 69, 116, 179–80, 195, 226,
    257, **6.8, 6.12–13**
    Tomb of Homayun, 200
Della Valle, Pietro, 121, 142–3, 144,
    170–1, 174, 177, 244, 245
Dervish Qasem, 44
Din-e Elahi (Divine Creed), 251
dining 245–6, 248; *see also* feasting
Divan-e Ayene (Hall of Mirrors),
    Isfahan, 127
Diwan-i Amm, Agra, 116, 180–1, 188,
    195, 197, **6.7, 6.10–11**
Diwan-i Amm, Delhi, 116, 180, 188,
    195, 197, **6.8, 6.12–13**
Diwan-i Amm, Lahore, 116, 188, 195,
    197
Diwan-i Khass, Agra, 179
Diwan-i Khass, Delhi, 179
Diwan-i Khass, Fatehpur Sikri, 179,
    252
Dolmabahce, Istanbul, 246
domes, 200, 201

economy, Safavid, 169–70
Edict of Sincere Repentance, 47, 57
Emarat-e Daryache, Isfahan, 127
Emarat-e Ferdaus (Paradise Mansion),
    Isfahan, 127
entertainment, 127, 167, 174–5, 237
Eshratabad (Garden of Joy), Tabriz, 31,
    35, 36, **2.1**
eunuchs, 132, 135–6, 137, 142, 181,
    182, 211, 234

Fabritius, Ludwich, 231
Farahabad, Isfahan, 206–7, 209–11, 267, 268–9
Farahabad, Mazandaran, 87, 97, 128, 169–70, 171–2, 175–6, 182, 210, 244
Farhad Beg, 74, 124
farr (royal splendor, also *khvarnah*), 2, 3, 12, 115, 133, 252, 259
Fatehpur Sikri Palace, 252
Fatima, 4, 14
Fatima Ma'sume (sister of Imam Reza), 92
Fatimids, 4, 12, 16, 17
feasting, 1, 10–11, 12, 136, 138–9, 186, 193–4, 196, 197, 199, 224–8, 231, 232–3, 235, 236, 237, 238, 246, 252, 257–8, 259, **5.16–17**, *1*
  early Safavid, 243–5
  Mughal, 257
  Ottoman, 257
  Timurid, 239–43
  Turco-Mongol, 257
Figuera, Don Garcia, 144, 148, 244, 245
Fin, Kashan *see* Bagh-e Fin Palace, Kashan
Firdausi, 18
Flandin, Eugene, 76, 167
food, 136, 226, 229, 232–3, 242–3, 244, 245; *see also* dining; feasting
fotovvat, 229–30
Fotovvatname-ye soltani, 229, 230
Friday prayer, 56, 86–7, 94, 95–6, 97, 99; *see also* prayer

Galdieri, Eugenio, 85
gardens, 15, 16, 19, 21, 32–3, 41, 42, 43, 46, 102, 103, 121, 146, 166, 175, 176, 177, 179, 180, 201
  extra-urban, 206–7, 208–10
  Isfahan, 32, 66–7, 68–9, 73, 74, 76–8, 79–80, 81–2, 84, 86, 120, 122, 123, 124, 125, 126, 128, 134, 141, 142, 144, 145, 162, 167, 170, 176, 195, 199–200, 205, **3.2**, **3.4**, **5.1**, **5.15**
  Qazvin, 50, 52, 53, 55
  Tabriz, 31, 35, 37, 38, 39, 42–3, **2.1**
  see also chahar bagh (four-quadrant) gardens
Gaube, Heinz, 76
gender segregation, 16
generosity, 136, 230
  obligation of, 228–30
  politics of, 230–1

Genghis Khan, 5, 19, 239
Ghaznavids, 18, 19
gholams see slaves, *gholams*
Ghurids, 18
gifts, exchange of, 231, 236–9, 240–1, *2*
Gilan, 128, 169
Golestan Palace, Tehran, 158, 246
Golestan (Rose Garden), Isfahan, 200
Gommans, Jos, 129
governance, Safavid, 211–12
Great Mosque, Isfahan, 71, 83, 86, 94
Great Mosque, Qazvin, 53
guests, 1, 10, 79, 127, 132, 144, 146, 162, 194–5, 234–5
  proximity to the shah, 234–5, 237
  status, 234–6

Hadi, Imam (Ali al-Hadi), 92
Haft Dast (Seven Buildings), Isfahan, 208
Hajem Khan, 125
Halime Begi Agha (Alamshah Khatun), 34
halls, pillared
  Mughal, 179–80
  see also audience halls; *talars*
Hammam-e Shahi (Royal Bathhouse), Isfahan, 137
hammams, 74, 120, 137, 172
Hanafis, 92
Harem Gate, Isfahan, 68, 135–6, 137, 141, **3.9**, **4.1**
harems, 9, 16, 36, 37, 38, 43, 53, 68, 79, 80, 81, 89, 96, 117, 118, 120, 126, 127–8, 129, 132, 135, 136, 141–2, 146, 148, 182, 191, 199, 205, 207, 211, 271, **3.7–8**, **4.1**, **5.18**
Hasanabad Bridge, Isfahan *see* Khwaju Bridge, Isfahan
Hasanabad Gate, Isfahan, 76, 78, 79, 80, 81, **3.6**
Hasan Beg ("Sultan Assambei"), 2, 31, 34, 35, 36, 38, 39, 42, 44, 202, 240, 241, 243
Hasht Behesht, Agra, 32–3
hasht-behesht model, 32–3, 46, 53, 146, 149, 170, 171, 199, 200–1, 202, 205–6, 212–13, **2.1**, **5.4**, **5.7–8**, **5.18**
Hasht Behesht Palace, Isfahan, 32, 33, 80, 123, 198–200, 202–6, **3.7**, **4.1**, **5.4**, **5.18–20**, *21–3*
Hasht Behesht Palace, Tabriz, 15, 31–2, 35–40, 44–5, 202, 240, 243, **2.1**

Hauzkhane Palace, Isfahan, 140, 160, 183
Haydar, Shaykh (Junayd Safavi), 34, 35, 92
Herat, 21, 40, 45, 55, 176
Herbert, Thomas, 66, 121, 170, 175–6, 226, 233, 244
Hezar Jarib (Thousand Acres) Palace Gardens (also known as Abbasabad (Abode of Abbas), Isfahan, 15, 66, 85, 103, 128, 207, 209, **3.2**
Hindus, 6, 251
Homayun, Emperor, 193–4, 244, 251, **5.16**
    Tomb of, 200
horses, 162, 195, 236
hospitality, 225, 240–3
Hossayn Bayqara, Soltan, 229, 241
Hossayn, Imam, 92, 93, 124–5, 160, 233
Hossayniyye, 124–5
housing projects, 81, 103, 207
Hülegu, 20
humility, 7, 132–3
hunting, 46, 172–4

ibn Ali Suzani, Mohammad, 178
Ibn Battuta, 94
Ibn Esfandiyar, 177
Ibn Hawqal, 73
Ilkhanids, 19–20, 92, 93, 200
Imami (Twelver) Shi'ism, 4, 5, 6–7, 8, 11, 12–13, 14, 15, 30, 50, 55, 56, 58, 66, 69, 83, 86–7, 88, 90–6, 98, 99, 128, 132, 133, 135, 194, 225, 230, 231, 251, 259, 269
Imamzades, 92
imperial space, 99–102
Isma'il, Shah, 2–4, 13, 18, 30, 31, 33–4, 35, 36, 37, 39, 41, 44–5, 47, 50, 55, 57, 76–8, 88, 95, 124, 202, 228, 229, 230, 243, 269
Isma'ilis, 4–5
Istanbul (Constantinople), 6, 14, 15, 21, 43, 58, 69, 99–100, 101, 116, 130, 136, 195, 212, 226, 246, 257, **6.1–6**

Jabal 'Amil, 56, 88, 95
Ja'farabad, Qazvin, 50
Ja'far al-Sadeq, Imam, 5
Jafarian, Rasul, 92, 94
Jahangir, Emperor, 69, 252
Jahan Nama (Reflection of the World) Pavilion, Isfahan, 79, 80, 142–3, **3.8**, **4.1**

Jannat-e 'adn (Garden of Eden), Qazvin, 50
Jannat Sara (Paradisiacal Palace), Ardabil, 134
javanmardi, 228–30
jharoka, 116, 180, 255, 256
jharoka-ye darshan (throne of beholding), 252
Jovayni family, 93
Ju'i Bridge, Isfahan, 208, **3.7**
Junayd, Shaykh (Seyyed Siet Gunet), 226
justice, 11, 133–4, 135, 230

Kaempfer, Engelbert, 80, 122, 163–4, 198, 200, 226, 228, 231, 235, 236
    Amoenitatum, **3.1**, **3.9**, **5.3**
    "A Night Reception at the Talar-e Tavile", 235, **5.3**
    Planographia, 126, 127, 135, 137–8, 139, 142, 233, 234, **3.2**, **3.7–8**, **4.1**
Karbala, 91, 170, 233
karkhane, 21
Karre, Mohammad, 76–8
Kashan, 92, 170, 176, **5.4**, **5.8–9**
Kashefi, Va'ez-e, 229
Kerman, 124, 128, 267, 268
Kesh (later Shahrisabz), 40–3
ketabkhane, 45, 47–9
khanaqahs, 21
Kharraqan, 200
Khatunabadi, Amir Mohammad Baqer, 210
Khoy, 46
khvarnah see farr (royal splendor, also khvarnah)
Khwajegi Esfahani, 140, 160, 162, 167
Khwaju Bridge, Isfahan, 166, 208, 269, **3.7**, **5.5**, **5.21**
Khwaju, Chahar Bagh, Isfahan, 208–9, **5.21**
Khwand Amir, 41, 241
kingship, 5–8, 9–11, 12, 13, 16–17, 18–20, 21–2, 33, 39, 41, 230
    caliphal, 4–5, 12, 16–17, 18, 19, 20, 73, 82, 92, 94, 181, 225, 249, 251, 269
    Hapsburg, 258
    Hindu, 252
    Islamic, 187
    Mongol, 20
    Mughal, 6, 69, 148, 251, 252–3
    Muslim, 5, 19
    Ottoman, 6, 148, 248–51
    Persianate, 3, 4, 11, 18, 19, 20, 30, 46, 117, 252

Perso-Shi'i, 7, 11, 23, 30, 33, 69, 82, 98, 99, 115, 117, 125, 132–3, 135, 136–7, 149, 164, 177, 181, 230, 235, 258, 259
sacral, 34
Safavid, 1–2, 6–8, 9–11, 12, 13, 14, 15, 39–40, 52, 55, 56, 86, 69, 74, 83, 86, 98, 103, 116, 118, 132, 136, 137, 144, 182–3, 186, 194, 205–6, 213, 224–5, 228, 238, 258–9
Sunni, 6, 12, 82, 225
Turco-Mongol, 6, 33, 42, 43, 239
Twelver-Shi'i, 6, 7, 12, 55, 57–8, 103, 132–3, 138–9
kiosks, 178–9
Kitchen Alley (Kuche-ye Matbakh), Isfahan, 137, 138
Kitchen Gate (darb-e matbakh), Isfahan, 136, 137–8, 141
Koch, Ebba, 181
Kohne Maydan (Old Maydan), Isfahan, 71–3, 76, 82, 83, 3.6
Krusinski, Tadeusz, 197, 268
Kubilai Khan, 20

Lahore
Red Fort, 69, 116, 179–80, 195, 257
landscaping, 31, 43, 113, 120, 188, 200
legitimacy
Fatimid, 4–5
Ilkhanid, 20
Mongol, 20
Mughal, 69, 251–2
Muslim, 5
Ottoman, 249–51
Persianate, 3
Perso Shi'i, 22, 82, 117, 183, 186
Safavid, 2, 6, 11, 12, 18, 34, 44, 58, 69, 82, 86–7, 89, 90, 95, 97, 117, 118, 149, 186, 225, 228, 230–1, 251
sultanic, 249–51
Twelver Shi'i, 56, 57–8, 69, 87, 88, 230, 259
leisure, 37, 66–7, 79, 102–3, 143, 175, 207, 243, 244, 3.4
Lotf-Allah, Shaykh (Lotf-Allah al-Maysi), 56, 96–8, 99, 231
Shaykh Lotf-Allah Mosque, Isfahan, 66, 84, 85–6, 90, 97, 126, 185, 238, 3.3, 3.7, 6
Louis XIV, 199, 257

Madinat al-Salaam, 17
Madinat al-Zahra, 16, 17, 43

madrasas, 21, 42, 69, 73, 81, 83, 93, 94, 96, 118, 178, 206, 209–10
Madrese-ye Soltani (Royal Madrasa also known as Chahar Bagh Madrese; Madrese-ye Jadid-e Soltani; Madrese-ye Madar-e Shah), Isfahan, 81, 118, 209–10, 3.7, 4
Madrid, 14, 69, 99, 100, 101
Al-Mafarokhi
Mahasen-e Esfahan (The Advantages of Isfahan), 74
Mahmud, the Afghan, 267–71
Majlesi, Mohammad Baqer the Younger, 231
Malik Shah, 74, 230
Mamluks, 17, 20
mansions, 50, 55, 66, 73, 101–2, 124, 127, 166, 206, 210, 246, 271
Maraghe, 40
Mashhad, 58, 91, 127, 128, 129, 210
Masjed-e Jadid-e Abbasi (Royal Mosque/Imam Mosque), Isfahan, 66, 83, 84, 86–7, 90, 97–8, 238, 3.3, 3.7, 7–8
mausoleums, 42, 200
Maydan-e Asb-e Shahi (Royal Hippodrome), Qazvin, 51–3, 2.2–3
Maydan-e Asb, Isfahan, 84
Maydan-e Chahar Hauz, Isfahan, 139, 141, 269
Maydan-e Kohne (Old Maydan), Isfahan, 71–3, 76, 82, 83, 3.6
Maydan-e Naqsh-e Jahan (Image of the World Square), Isfahan, 39, 66, 68, 78, 84, 85, 86, 89–90, 96, 98, 113, 123, 125, 126, 139, 144, 183–4, 210, 237, 3.3, 3.6–7, 3.9, 4.1–2, 5, 9
Maydan-e Nau, Isfahan, 68
maydans, 37, 38–40, 45
Mazandaran, 87, 97, 128, 129, 169–82, 206, 210, 244, 5.4, 5.7
McChesney, Robert, 83, 85
Mehmankhane, 127
Mehmet Fatih, Sultan, 101
Mehregan Festival, 11, 190
Membré, Michele, 36, 37, 38–40
Mian Kale, Mazandaran, 172, 174
Mehmanname-ye Bokhara, 178
Mir Damad, 96
Mirza Hossayn Khan, 141
Mirza Mozaffar Torke, 166
Mohammad Khodabande (Öljeitu), Soltan, 94

Mohammad Khodabande, Soltan (Safavid Shah), 98, 99, 124
Mohammad, Prophet, 2, 4, 5, 7, 12, 14, 16, 17, 35, 56, 92, 93, 94, 124, 133, 139, 149, 181, 229, 251, 258, 259
Mohammad Shaybani, 178
Mohebb Ali Beg Lale, 86–7, 98
Monajjem, Molla Jalal al-Din, 84, 126
Mongol empire, 19–20
Mongol invasions, 17, 18, 19
Monshi, Eskandar Beg, 85, 91, 144, 171–2
Morshed Qoli Khan Ostajlu, 58
Mosque of Ali Shah, Tabriz, 37
mosques, 16, 21
  Isfahan, 66, 71, 72, 73, 74, 76, 83–4, 85–7, 90, 94, 95–7, 98, 99, 100, 102, 118, 126, 128, 132, 183, 185, 210, 238, 239, **3.3, 3.6–7**
  Qazvin, 52–3, 55–7
  Tabriz, 37, 38–9, 42, 43, 45, 55–7
Movarrekh, Mohammad Yusof
  Khold-e barin, 160
Mughals, 5, 6, 14, 21, 88, 102, 129, 179–81, 225, 251
  ceremonial public spaces, 116
  Indicization, 251
Al-Muhaqqiq al-Karaki, 56
murals, 31, 55, 81, 84, 170, 185, 191–4, 196–7, 228, 234, **2.5–6, 5.16**
Musa al-Kazim, Imam, 4
music, 1, 10, 90, 47, 171, 232, 243

Nader Qoli (Nader Shah), 270
Nadr Mohammad Khan, the Uzbek, 185
Najaf, 91, 132, 133, 170, 182
Namakdan (Salt Cellar), Isfahan, 208
naqqarekhane (kettledrum house), 90, **3.10**
Naqshbandiyye Sufi Order, 251
Naqsh-e Jahan Maydan (Image of the World Square), Isfahan, 39, 66, 68, 78, 84, 85, 86, 89–90, 96, 98, 113, 123, 125, 126, 139, 144, 183–4, 210, 237, **3.3, 3.6–7, 3.9, 4.1–2, 5, 9**
Naser Khosrau, 73–4
Natanzi, Mahmud ibn Hedayat-Allah Afushte, 124, 125
nature, 43, 176, 188–90
Nauruz (Persian New Year), 11, 160, 172, 190, 233
Necipoğlu, Gülru, 248, 252

New Julfa, Isfahan, 84, 267, 269, 270, 271
Nezam al-Din Abu Eshaq, Maulana, 94
Nezam al-Molk, Khwaje, 93
  Siasatname, 230
nomadism, 19, 21, 40, 41–2, 45, 55, 129, 178, 225
Noqtavi, 98
Nur-Allah, 229

Oets, Jan, 206
Olearius, Adam 9, 121, 134, 143, 144, 162–3, 164, 236–7
Öljeitu (Mohammad Khodabande (Öljeitu), Soltan), 94
Omar, 4, 94
Othman, 4
Ottomans, 5, 6, 14, 21, 47, 57, 58, 86, 87, 88, 101, 102, 194, 225, 245, 246, 270, 271

painting, 47, 205–6
palace terminology, 121–2
paradise, 14, 99, 186, 195, 200, 204, 205; see also Hasht Behesht (Eight Paradises) Palace, Isfahan; Hasht Behesht, Agra; Hasht Behesht Palace, Tabriz
Paris, 66, 69, 99, 101, 212
peripatetic existence, 6, 19, 30–58, 129, 183, 212
piety, 13, 47, 97, 128, 137, 229–30
pilgrimage, 58, 128, 129
pillared halls, Mughal, 179–80; see also talars
power, 141, 225–6, 239–40
prayer, 55–6, 98, 133, 134
  Friday prayer, 56, 86–7, 94, 95–6, 97, 99
processions, 6, 16, 116, 132, 162, 180, 195, 206, 226, 235–6, 243

Qajars, 158–60
Qal'e Tabarrok, Isfahan, 74, 268, **3.6**
Qaraqoyunlus, 44
Qaysariyye (Royal Bazaar), Isfahan, 66, 84, 90, 97–8, 144, 145, **3.7, 3.10**
Qazi Ahmad Qomi, 35, 50
Qazvin, 2, 9, 14, 30, 33, 39, 45, 47–55, 57–8, 88–9, 91, 92, 94, 96, 98, 115, 116–17, 125, 129, 130, 146, 169, 176, 194, 201, 202, 212, 243, 244, 268, **2.2–3, 5.4**
qeshlaq, 41–2, 43

Qezelbash, 13, 33, 34, 47, 50, 57, 87, 88, 98, 134, 230, 231
Qom, 91, 92
Qostantaniyya (Constantinople), Treaty of, 58
Qur'an, 5, 94, 259

Rahimdad, Gwaliyor, India, 179
Rashidun Caliphs, 4
Rauzat al-safat, 53
Red Forts, Mughal, 68, 69, 100–1, 102, 115, 116, 121, 148, 179–80, 188, 195, 197, 226, 252–3, 257, **6.7–13**
religious law, 47, 99, 133, 230–1, 259
Reza, Imam, 92, 210
Shrine of, 96, 128, 210
Romano, Domenico 30–1, 35–6, 37, 38, 39, 46, 243
Rostam Khan, 160
Rostamname (*Tarikh-e Bijan*), 160

Sa'adatabad Palace (Abode of Felicity), Isfahan, 118, 166, 207, 208–9, 236, 271, **5.22**
Sadeq, Imam (Ja'far al-Sadiq), 92
Sa'eb-e Tabrizi, 186, 195–6
Safaviyye Sufi Order, 4, 13, 30, 34, 35, 228, 231
initiation, 228
Safi I, Shah, 71, 87, 117, 118, 129, 134, 160, 166, 167, 170, 182, 183, 197
Safi II, Shah *see* Solayman, Shah (Safi II)
Safiabad Palace, Farahabad, 170
Safi al-Din, Shaykh, 4, 34, 92, 228
Shrine of, 57–8
Samanids, 18
Samarqand, 21, 40–1, 42, 43, 55, 176, 200–1, 242
Samarra, 16, 17, 43
sanctity, 132–3
saqqānafār, 177, **5.11**
Saru Taqi, Mirza Mohammad, Grand Vizier, 157, 181–2, 184
Selim I, Sultan 251
Seljuqs 18, 19, 200, 230
Shafi'is, 92
Shah Jahan, Emperor, 101, 179, 180–1, 251, 252, **24**
Shahname (Book of Kings), 18, 45–6, 224
Shahrisabz (The Green City, formerly Kesh), 40–3
Shamlu, Vali Qoli, 157, 166, 182
shari'a, 47, 99, 133, 230–1, 259
Shaykh al-Islam, 13, 133, 211, 231

Shaykh Lotf-Allah Mosque, Isfahan, 66, 84, 85–6, 90, 97, 126, 185, 238, **3.3**, **3.7**, **6**; *see also* Lotf-Allah, Shaykh (Lotf-Allah al-Maysi)
Sher Mandal, Delhi, 33
Shi'ism, 4–5, 12, 13, 34, 87, 92, 229, 230
Twelver (Imami), 4, 5, 6–7, 8, 11, 12–13, 14, 15, 30, 50, 55, 56, 58, 66, 69, 83, 86–7, 88, 90–6, 98, 99, 128, 132, 133, 135, 194, 225, 230, 231, 251, 259, 269
Shiraz, 21, 40
Siasatname, 230
silk, 90, 128, 162, 169, 171, 226
slaves, 6, 57, 58, 87, 88, 231
*gholam*s, 14, 58, 86, 87, 89, 98, 118, 124, 134, 182, 211, 231
social conduct, 228–30
social order, 234–7
sodomy, 47, 181
Solayman, Shah (Safi II), 32, 80, 117, 118, 129, 135, 136, 160, 197, 198–9, 205–6, 211, 231
Solh-e Koll, 251
Soltan Hossayn, Shah, 196, 197, 206, 209, 210, 211, 212, 267, 268–9, 270
Soltaniyye, 40, 200
Soltan Mohammad, 45
space, use of, 190–1, 204–5, 235, 236
Stodart, Robert, 174
Sufism, 50, 88, 91, 134–5, 230–1
Sun-King construct, 252
Sunnis, 4, 5, 6, 92, 94, 251, 269, 270
Sunnism, 12, 20, 82, 88, 92, 225
symbolism, 55, 141
syncretism, 251, 252

Tabari, Emad al-Din
Manaqeb al-taherayn (Glorious Deeds of the Pure Ones), 93
Tohfat al-abrar, 93
Tabriz, 8–9, 14, 21, 30–1, 44, 45, 46, 47, 57, 58, 81, 87, 92, 176, 269
Taher-e Vahid, Mohammad, 174–5, 185
Tahmasb Mirza, 268
Tahmasb, Shah, 18, 33, 35, 36–7, 39, 45, 46, 47–9, 50, 55, 57–8, 88, 95, 134, 193, 230, 243, 244, 269, **5.16**
Edict of Sincere Repentance, 47, 57
Tazkere (*Memoirs*), 47
Tajiks, 33
Taj Mahal, Agra, 33, 146
Takht-e Solayman, 40

Talar-e Ashraf, Isfahan, 271
Talar-e Marmar (Marble Hall),
 Golestan Palace, Tehran, 158
Talar-e Tavile (Hall of Stables) Palace,
 Isfahan, 22, 116, 118, 157, 160–6,
 169, 176, 182, 184, 186, 233,
 236–7, **3.7**, **4.1**, **5.1–3**
 ayvans, 233–4
Talar-e Taymuri, Isfahan, 139–40,
 4.5
talars, 118, 129, 157–82, 183–97, 199,
 201, 205, 206, 211, 213, 225, 233,
 235, 236, 237, 244, 271, **4.6**, **5.1–2**,
 5.10, **5.13–15**, **5.22**
Tarikh-e Bijan (Rostamname), 160
Tarikh-e Tabarestan, 177
Tauhidkhane, Isfahan, 119, 134–5, **3.7**,
 4.1–2, **10**
Tavernier, Jean Baptiste, 120, 121,
 137, 162
Tazkerat al-moluk, 138
throne ayvans, 168, 180–1, 186, 190,
 191, 233–4, 235, **6.4**
thrones, 39–40, 163, 164, 180–1, 234,
 6.11, **6.13**
Timur, 21, 22, 40–1, 42, 239, 241–3
Timurids, 5, 20, 21, 22, 43–4, 228,
 241–3
Todar Mal, Fatehpur Sikri, 33
Topkapı Palace, Istanbul, 43, 101, 102,
 116, 121, 127, 136, 188, 226,
 246–9, 257, **6.2–6**
tribalism, 2, 4, 10, 12, 21, 33, 34, 42,
 138, 183, 206, 212, 224, 231, 235,
 239–40, 269, 271
Tughrul, 73
Turco-Mongol traditions, 41–2, 43, 55,
 58, 212

Twelver (Imami) Shi'ism, 4, 5, 6–7, 8,
 11, 12–13, 14, 15, 30, 50, 55, 56,
 58, 66, 69, 83, 86–7, 88, 90–6, 98,
 99, 128, 132, 133, 135, 194, 225,
 230, 231, 251, 259, 269

Umayyads, 4, 12, 16
Uzbeks, 45, 46, 58, 88, 95, 96, 128,
 170, 178,185, 192–4, 228, 244, **1.1**
Uzun Hasan, Soltan (Hasan Beg), 2,
 31, 34, 35, 36, 38, 39, 42, 44, 202,
 240, 241, 243

Vali Mohammad Khan, the Uzbek, 228
villa, 42, 102

walkways, 160–2
wall–gate debate, 78–80
walls, 68–9, 72, 73–4, 76, 78, 80–1, 82,
 3.6
water, 31, 32, 36, 50, 66, 74, 81, 163,
 167, 169, 170, 174, 176, 177, 184,
 204, **3.5**, **5.11**
 channels, 79, **3.4**, **5.7–9**
 lakes, 174–5, **5.10**
 pools, 37, 81, 126–7, 163, 167, 176,
 187, 188, 195, 200, 204, **2.6**, **3.4**,
 5.9
 qanat, 50
windows, 248, 252, **2.5**, **5.12**, **6.6**
wine, 47, 226–8, 232
Wirth, Eugen, 76

Yaqub, Soltan, 31, 34, 35, 39, 44, 241
yaylaq, 41–3, 212
Yuan dynasty, 20

Zuhhab, Treaty of, 194